Operating Systems and Shell Scripting
CIS 106 & 106L

Custom Edition for ECPI Colleges

Taken from:

Go! with Microsoft® Office: Windows XP Comprehensive
by Shelley Gaskin, Suzanne Weixel, John Preston, Sally Preston, and Robert L. Ferrett

Working With DOS 6
by Mark Allen and Jean Gonzalez

Go! Technology in Action, Third Edition
by Alan Evans, Kendall Martin, and Mary Anne Poatsy

Taken from:

Go! with Microsoft Office: Windows XP Comprehensive
by Shelley Gaskin, Suzanne Weixel, John Preston, Sally Preston, and Robert L. Ferrett
Copyright © 2006 by Pearson Education, Inc.
Published by Prentice Hall
Upper Saddle River, New Jersey 07458

Working With DOS 6
by Mark Allen and Jean Gonzalez
Copyright © 1995 by Prentice Hall, Inc.

Go! Technology in Action, Third Edition
by Alan Evans, Kendall Martin, and Mary Anne Poatsy
Copyright © 2007 by Pearson Education, Inc.
Published by Prentice Hall

This special edition published in cooperation with Pearson Custom Publishing.

Printed in the United States of America

10 9 8 7 6

ISBN 0-536-31771-2

2006200255

RG

Please visit our web site at *www.pearsoncustom.com*

PEARSON CUSTOM PUBLISHING
75 Arlington Street, Suite 300, Boston, MA 02116
A Pearson Education Company

Contents in Brief

Table of Contents

Instructor/Class Session Information, Course Grading, and College Policies

Instructor's Information	Class Session Information
Name:	Course ID:
Office:	Course Name:
Office Hours:	Meeting Dates:
Phone:	Meeting Times:
E-Mail:	Room Number:

Course Grading:

Final grades are determined by a weighted average of all work assigned in the course and is based on a combination of exams, papers/projects, writing assessments, and oral presentations. Your final letter grade in this course is based on the following:

Letter grades are determined as follows:

A   90–100% of the total percentage points possible
B   80–89% of the total percentage points possible
C   70–79% of the total percentage points possible
D   65–69% of the total percentage points possible
F   less than 65% of the total percentage points possible

Note: For specific grade breakdown, please refer to your course syllabi.

School Policies:

I. Late Assignments:
Assignments turned in late due to a documented excused absence will be graded as initially assigned. Late assignments due to unexcused absence will be assigned a grade of 0.

II. Retest/Make-up Exam:
A student who misses an original examination or scores below 65 on an examination may arrange with the instructor for a make-up/retest examination. All make-up/retest examinations must be taken within three days of the student's return to class or the awarding of a failing test grade. The maximum grade for any make-up/retest is 65 unless sufficient documentation is provided. Students will earn their full grade on make-ups for documented absences. Quizzes that are missed follow the same rules as above.

It is the student's responsibility to see the instructor of the course in order to schedule a retest/make-up examination. The appointment times for retest/make-ups are scheduled at the instructor's discretion.

III. Early Exam:

Students may elect to take an exam early due to a conflict. Arrangements should be made in advance with the instructor, and the student's grade will not be affected.

IV. Attendance:

Students are expected to attend all regularly scheduled class meetings. Students are encouraged to tell their instructor in advance or to call the administrative office if they will be absent.

Instructors may request a review board for students whose absences from class interfere with their ability to meet course objectives. Action may include being dropped from the course, probation, or suspension. If a pattern of excessive absences is noticed throughout the student's program, a review board may be held as well.

Whenever a student believes his/her attendance record is in error, a written request challenging the error may be submitted to the Academic Dean within three weeks of the end of the course.

V. Electronic Communication/Recording Devices:

To minimize classroom disruptions and protect the integrity of test-taking situations, activated electronic communication devices such as pagers, cellular telephones, and recording devices are not permitted in classrooms at the College unless you have the specific written permission of the instructor. The only exception to this policy will be for on-call emergency personnel (police, fire, EMS), who will be required to notify their instructor of their need for such devices at the beginning of the term and provide documentation verifying their occupation. However, on-call emergency personnel may not leave a testing situation; communicate by electronic means and return to complete an examination. In these cases, instructors should make arrangements for retesting. Use of personal laptop computers is acceptable during class.

VI. Students with Disabilities:

Students who have documented disabilities that require accommodations in compliance with the Americans with Disabilities Act should contact their campus Provost as well as the instructor of the course in order to insure that together we create an optimal environment for educational achievement.

VII. Honor Code:

The Honor System at college is based on individual integrity. This system assumes that every student will accept his or her role in the academic community with a feeling of self respect and duty.

The Honor Pledge States:
I pledge to support the Honor System of the college. I will refrain from any form of academic dishonesty or deception, such as cheating or plagiarism. I am aware that as a member of the academic community, it is my responsibility to turn in all suspected violators of the honor code. I understand that any failure on my part to support the Honor System will be turned over to a Judicial Review Board for determination. I will report to the Judicial Review Board hearing if summoned.

Since each student attending the college is required to sign the Honor Pledge; it follows that work submitted by a student must be his/her own work. Suspected violators of the Honor Code are to be referred to the Teacher, Associate Dean, or Dean of the college.

Plagiarism Policy

I. Purpose and Scope

The purpose of college's plagiarism policy is to promote awareness and adherence to copyright and intellectual property law. Refer to http://www.copyright.gov/laws/ for information on U.S. copyright law.

This policy applies to all students, faculty and staff of the college and all intellectual property including but not limited to all written and electronic publications, ideas and inventions, verbiage and phrasing. Refer to the college catalog for a description of intellectual property.

II. Definitions

A. The Writer

The Writer is defined as any student, faculty, or staff to whom this policy applies. However, plagiarism is not limited to writers, per the definition of plagiarism and the scope of this policy. Examples of plagiarism other than through writing include but are not limited to creators of software programs, hardware designs, schematics, multimedia, charts, graphs, tools and other inventions.

B. Plagiarism

Plagiarism is defined as n 1: a piece of writing that has been copied from someone else and is presented as being your own work 2: the act of plagiarizing; taking someone's words or ideas as if they were your own (www.dictionary.com, 2005).

III. Plagiarism can be intentional or unintentional.

A. Intentional Plagiarism

Plagiarism is intentional when one or more of the following conditions apply:

- the writer uses exact words from a source but neglects to include quotation marks;

- the writer paraphrases ideas from a source but neglects to cite the source using an acceptable documentation style such as MLA or APA;

- the writer copies someone else's work and presents it as his/her own;

- the writer purchases documents, ideas, and/or verbiage and presents it as his/her own;

- the writer fails to give credit to co-authors, team members, and/or editors of the writer's original work;

- the writer uses previously published work protected under copyright and presents the work as original and not copyrighted elsewhere;

- repeated violation of unintentional plagiarism rules is considered intentional plagiarism.

B. Unintentional Plagiarism

Plagiarism is unintentional when one or more of the following conditions apply:

- the writer demonstrates ignorance of copyright law and plagiarism policy;

- the writer fails to quote or paraphrase accurately but attributes the words and/or ideas to a source;

- the writer attempts to document the source but does so incorrectly;

- the writer attempts to give credit to an original source but does not use acceptable documentation methods;

- the writer uses ideas, text and/or verbiage without giving credit to the original source because the writer incorrectly believes the information is common knowledge;

- the writer inadvertently fails to give credit to co-authors, team members, and/or editors of the writer's original work;

- the writer inadvertently breaks copyright agreement of his/her own copyrighted work.

IV. Consequences of Violating Policies

Violation of the college's plagiarism policy, whether the plagiarism is intentional or unintentional, ***may result*** in disciplinary action up to and including suspension and expulsion from the college.

Disciplinary action ***may include*** initiation of a Judicial Review Board. For more information on college's general disciplinary actions, see the sections entitled, "Termination Policy" and "Academic, Judicial and Financial Review Boards" in the College catalog.

V. Resources and Prevention

The College offers several resources, which vary by campus, for students, faculty and staff who require information on plagiarism and documentation. These resources include:

- seminars and training on documentation methods;

- Writing Assistance Center, where available, handouts and workshops on avoidance of plagiarism;

- classroom instruction on documentation of sources;

- Librarians who are skilled in explaining the issues involved in copyright protection; and

- Library reference, books, e-books and the Online Library with searchable, full-text resources available from the Internet

Introduction
The Computer System

The computer system consists of both the hardware and software that are needed for performing computer activities. The computer hardware consists of the physical items shown in Figure 0.1.

- The system unit
- The keyboard
- The monitor
- The floppy disk drive(s)
- The hard disk drive
- The CD-ROM drive (optional)

The system may also have a mouse and a printer, as shown, and a modem for communications. It may be linked to several other computers, creating a network. Each of these parts performs a specific task in the operation of your computer system. These tasks can be grouped into four basic categories: processing, input, output, and storage.

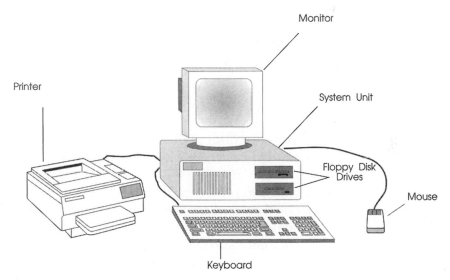

Figure 0.1
A computer system

Processing Components

Processing is the ability to change or manipulate data to produce information. This function is performed by the processing unit located within the system unit. The system unit shown in Figure 0.2 is the main component of your personal computer system. It includes a microprocessor chip (sometimes called the central processing unit or CPU) and memory, both of which are mounted on the motherboard.

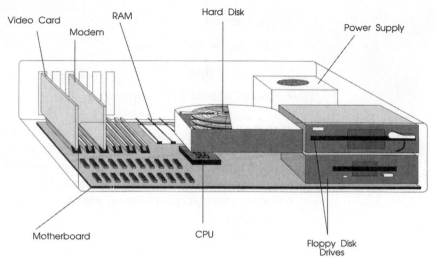

Figure 0.2
System unit showing motherboard

The CPU

The chip used in processing your work consists of hundreds of thousands of electronic devices. The CPU or microprocessor chip can be thought of as the "brains" of your computer. The type of microprocessor chip you have determines how much data your computer can process at one time and how fast you can process the work that you do with your computer. The 8088 microprocessor chip, made by Intel, was the most common chip found on the IBM PCs and compatibles during the 1980s. As the need for processing power increased, the 8088 chip became obsolete. It was replaced by the 80286 chip as the industry leader. The 80286 chip processes information over twice as fast as the 8088. Intel then introduced the 80386DX and SX, and then the 80486DX and SX processors. More recently, Intel has released the Pentium micro-processor. The Pentium chip is capable of processing up to four times as much data as the 80486DX chip running at 66 megahertz.

Megahertz (Mhz) is the unit for measuring how fast data and instructions are processed. A megahertz is one million cycles per second. The speed of the 8088 was 4.77 megahertz. The speed of the 80486, depending upon the model of the chip, is anywhere from 25 to 66 megahertz.

Primary Storage

Computer chips that provide the memory of the computer are also contained in the system unit. While the computer is running, memory chips hold the instructions that tell the computer what to do (that is, the programs) and the data on which the programs are working. The memory chips are the computer's primary storage. You will learn about the other type of storage, secondary storage, later in this introduction. Because memory can store information only while the computer is on, it is called short-term memory. The name given to this short-term type of memory is RAM, an acronym that stands for random access memory. It is called random access memory because you can write information to it and change any part of what you store without affecting the rest of what is stored. All RAM can be accessed randomly, rather than sequentially, meaning that the computer can locate what it is looking for quickly. When the computer is turned off, everything in RAM disappears.

Memory is measured in bytes. A byte is the amount of memory required to represent a single character. In order to perform various tasks on your computer, you must have a certain amount of available memory. Most personal computers have at least 640 kilobytes of memory. A kilobyte (abbreviated K) is equal to 1,024 bytes (approximately 1,000 bytes). A computer that has a storage capacity of 640K allows you to store approximately 640 thousand characters, which is the equivalent of about 200 pages of text. Although this sounds like a lot of memory, it does not nearly satisfy the requirements of today's higher-powered computer applications, such as programs that handle complex color computer drawings and video presentations. For this reason, memory is now often measured in megabytes. A megabyte (abbreviated MB) is equal to approximately one million bytes.

The computer you use must have enough memory and a chip fast enough to process the workload that you will be generating. For example, if you are using your computer to write papers, an 8088 chip and 640K of RAM may be sufficient, but if you are going to produce graphics, you will probably need at least an 80486 chip and 4 to 16 megabytes of RAM. If you are going to use Microsoft's Windows® program, you will want at least four megabytes of memory.

Another type of memory chip in the system unit is called a read-only memory (ROM) chip. The contents of a ROM chip can be read, but cannot be changed. This chip is used for special purposes such as providing the most basic instructions your personal computer needs to perform the startup operations (e.g., the self-test routines of the computer).

Input Devices

In order to process data into information, the computer must first obtain the data from somewhere. Data consist of words, numbers, characters, symbols, or commands that must be entered into the computer by means of a keyboard or some other input device such as a scanner, a disk drive, a modem, a mouse, or a touch-sensitive screen. The function of supplying the computer with data is called input.

The Keyboard

The keyboard is the most basic means of communicating with your computer. The computer converts every character you type into a code the machine can understand. A keyboard consists of three basic parts: the standard typewriter keyboard, function keys, and a numeric keypad. Figure 0.3 shows a standard typewriter keyboard enhanced with function keys and a numeric keypad.

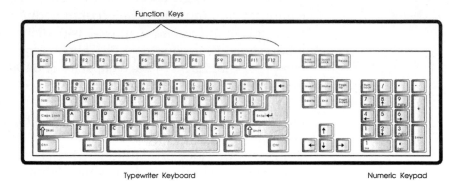

Figure 0.3
Enhanced keyboard

The alphanumeric keyboard is known as the QWERTY keyboard (named for the keys that appear from left to right across the top row of letters on this keyboard style). To this keyboard are added a number of special-purpose keys used to simplify many computer-related tasks. Some of the keys and what they are used for are shown in Figure 0.4.

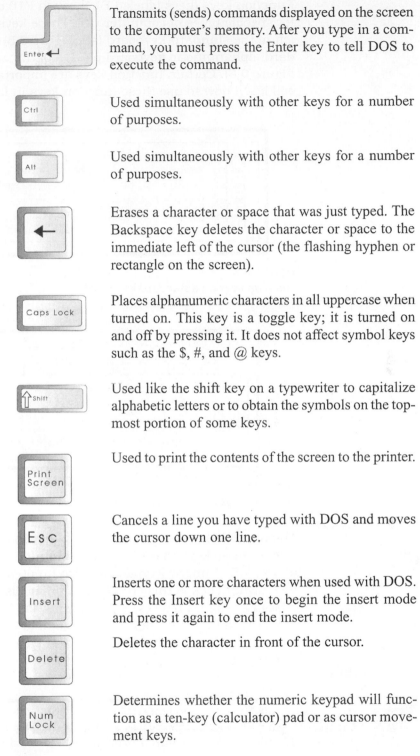

Transmits (sends) commands displayed on the screen to the computer's memory. After you type in a command, you must press the Enter key to tell DOS to execute the command.

Used simultaneously with other keys for a number of purposes.

Used simultaneously with other keys for a number of purposes.

Erases a character or space that was just typed. The Backspace key deletes the character or space to the immediate left of the cursor (the flashing hyphen or rectangle on the screen).

Places alphanumeric characters in all uppercase when turned on. This key is a toggle key; it is turned on and off by pressing it. It does not affect symbol keys such as the $, #, and @ keys.

Used like the shift key on a typewriter to capitalize alphabetic letters or to obtain the symbols on the top-most portion of some keys.

Used to print the contents of the screen to the printer.

Cancels a line you have typed with DOS and moves the cursor down one line.

Inserts one or more characters when used with DOS. Press the Insert key once to begin the insert mode and press it again to end the insert mode.

Deletes the character in front of the cursor.

Determines whether the numeric keypad will function as a ten-key (calculator) pad or as cursor movement keys.

Figure 0.4
Special purpose keys

Function keys (keys labeled F1 through F10 or F12) are keys designed for specific types of computer use. These keys are located on the extreme left of the standard keyboard (see Figure 0.5) or in a row above the standard alphanumeric keyboard portion of the enhanced keyboard (see Figure 0.6). Certain function keys are important when using DOS. You will learn how to use these function keys in later chapters.

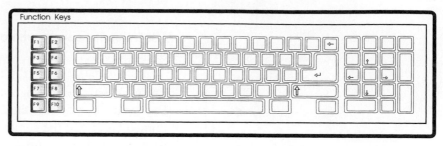

Figure 0.5
Function keys on a standard keyboard

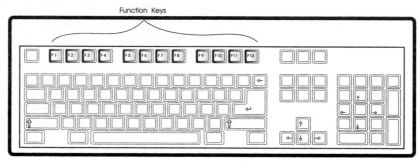

Figure 0.6
Function keys on an enhanced keyboard

The numeric keypad is located at the extreme right side of the keyboard. The numeric keypad can be used to input numbers when Num Lock is active. The numeric keypad can also function as cursor movement keys when Num Lock is turned off. The cursor (usually a flashing hyphen or small rectangle) on a screen represents the place in memory where action is occurring. Other important keys to note on this side of the keyboard are Ins, Del, Home, End, Page Up, and Page Down, which you will learn to use in later chapters. See Figure 0.7.

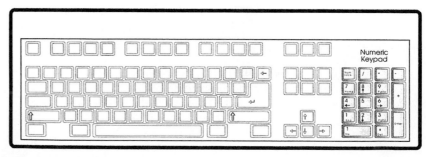

Figure 0.7
Enhanced keyboard with numeric keypad

The Mouse

Other input devices have been developed to provide alternatives to the keyboard. One of the most widely accepted tools is the mouse. A mouse is a pointing device originally designed for art design. It allows the computer user to point to a specific area on a monitor and either draw a line from one point to another, move a graphic from one place to another on the screen, highlight a section of text for deletion or modification, or perform other activities.

A mouse on a personal computer has one, two, or three buttons. On a two-button mouse, the left button usually responds the same way as the Return or Enter key. The right button represents the Esc key. To operate a mouse, you use a technique called clicking. Clicking obtained its name from the sound made when a button is pressed. Clicking occurs when you identify the portion of the screen you wish to make active and press the left button once. Double-clicking occurs when you wish to perform certain functions that require pressing the left button twice in rapid succession. (For left-handed people, the buttons may be reversed.)

Another technique used with a mouse is called dragging. For example, if you are using a graphics program to create art, you can draw a line by clicking and holding down the left mouse button and then dragging the mouse in any direction. Some people prefer using a mouse while others prefer using a keyboard for executing commands. A mouse can enhance but cannot totally replace a keyboard.

Other Input Devices

A number of other input devices exist, such as CD-ROM Drives, scanners, and digitizer pads. A CD-ROM Drive is similar to a disk drive, except that it allows you to use information stored on a compact disk. These drives are primarily used for multimedia presentations that use music and animation, pictorial libraries, encyclopedias, and other reference material.

A scanner is a device that is similar to a photocopier. Instead of producing a hard copy of what it scans, however, it converts what it reads into a form that can be directly used or manipulated by a computer. Scanners are made in various sizes and can scan in color or in shades of gray (called gray-scale scanning). They can scan either text or graphics, depending upon the type of scanner.

A digitizer pad is a device used primarily by artists and designers, but it is now entering the business world. A digitizer pad uses a pen-like device that, when placed on the pad, allows the user to draw graphics or write characters directly into the computer system. This device usually replaces a mouse.

Figure 0.8
(a) CRT monitors are big and bulky and look like television sets. (b) LCDs (flat-panel monitors) save precious desktop space and weigh considerably less than CRT monitors.

Output Devices

Once the data have been changed into information (data in usable form) within the processing unit, the information needs to be displayed, stored, and/or printed out from the work area inside the computer (RAM). The function of displaying, storing, or printing the finalized product is called output.

MONITORS

What are the different types of monitors? There are two basic types of monitors: CRTs and LCDs. If your monitor looks like a traditional television set, it has a picture tube device called a **cathode-ray tube (CRT)** like the one shown in Figure 0.8a. If your monitor is flat, such as those found in laptops, it's using **liquid crystal display (LCD)** technology (see Figure 0.8b), similar to that used in digital watches. LCD monitors (also called *flat-panel monitors*) are lighter and more energy efficient than CRT monitors, making them perfect for portable computers such as laptops. The sleek style of LCD monitors also makes them a favorite for users with small workspaces.

CRT Monitors

How does a CRT monitor work? A CRT screen is a grid made up of millions of **pixels,** or tiny dots (see Figure 0.9). Simply put, illuminated pixels are what create the images you see on your monitor. There are three pixel colors: red, blue, and green. The pixels are illuminated by an electron beam that passes back and forth across the back of the screen very quickly so that the pixels appear to glow continuously. The various combinations of red, blue, and green make up the components of color we see on our monitors. Figure 0.10 shows in more detail how a CRT monitor works.

Single CRT
Pixel

a

b

Single LCD
Pixel

Figure 0.9
A pixel, short for picture element, is one dot. CRT pixels (a) are round, whereas LCD pixels (b) are rectangular. There are three pixel colors: red, blue and green. Millions of pixels make up an image, and color is created by various shades and combinations of these pixels.

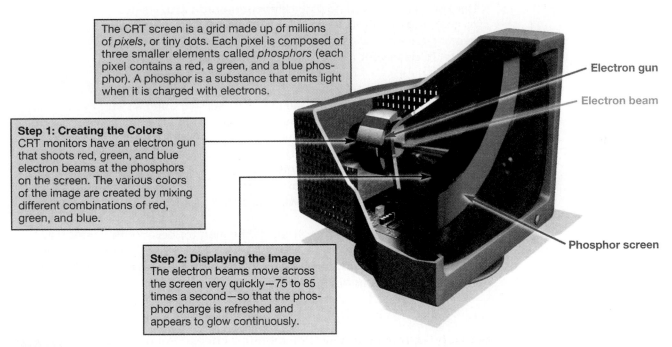

The CRT screen is a grid made up of millions of *pixels*, or tiny dots. Each pixel is composed of three smaller elements called *phosphors* (each pixel contains a red, a green, and a blue phosphor). A phosphor is a substance that emits light when it is charged with electrons.

Electron gun

Electron beam

Step 1: Creating the Colors
CRT monitors have an electron gun that shoots red, green, and blue electron beams at the phosphors on the screen. The various colors of the image are created by mixing different combinations of red, green, and blue.

Step 2: Displaying the Image
The electron beams move across the screen very quickly—75 to 85 times a second—so that the phosphor charge is refreshed and appears to glow continuously.

Phosphor screen

FIGURE 0.10
How a CRT monitor works.

What factors affect the quality of a CRT monitor? A couple of factors affect the quality of a CRT monitor. One is the monitor's refresh rate. **Refresh rate** (sometimes referred to as *vertical refresh rate*) is the number of times per second the electron beam scans the monitor and recharges the illumination of each pixel. Common monitors have refresh rates that range between 75 and 85 hertz (Hz). Although some monitors have higher refresh rates, they do not offer any significant benefits. Hertz is a unit of frequency indicating cycles per second, in this case meaning the electron beam scans the monitor 75 to 85 times each second. The faster the refresh rate, the less the screen will flicker, the clearer the image will be, and the less eyestrain you'll experience.

The clearness or sharpness of the image—its **resolution**—is controlled by the number of pixels displayed on the screen. The higher the resolution, the sharper and clearer the image. Monitor resolution is listed as a number of pixels. A high-end monitor may have a maximum resolution of 1,600 _ 1,200, meaning it contains 1,600 vertical columns with 1,200 pixels in each column. Note that you can adjust a monitor's resolution to either make the screen display larger (reducing the resolution) or to fit more on your screen (increasing the resolution).

Dot pitch is another factor that affects monitor quality. **Dot pitch** is the diagonal distance, measured in millimeters, between pixels of the same color on the screen. A smaller dot pitch means that there is less blank space between pixels, and thus a sharper, clearer image. A good CRT monitor has a dot pitch of 0.28 mm or less.

BITS AND BYTES — Cleaning Your Monitor

Have you ever noticed how quickly your monitor attracts dust? It's important to keep your monitor clean because dust buildup can act like insulation, keeping heat in and causing the electronic components to wear out much faster. To clean your monitor, follow these steps:

1. Shut off the monitor.
2. For a CRT monitor, wipe the monitor's surface using a sheet of fabric softener or a soft cloth dampened with window cleaner or water. Never spray anything directly onto the monitor. (Check your monitor's user manual to see if there are cleaning products you should avoid using.) For an LCD (flat-panel) monitor, use a 50/50 solution of isopropyl alcohol and water on a soft cloth and wipe the screen surface gently.
3. In addition to the screen, wipe away the dust from around the case.

Finally, don't place anything on top of the monitor because the items may block air from cooling it, and avoid placing magnets (including your speaker system's subwoofer) anywhere nears the monitor because they can interfere with the mechanisms inside the monitor.

So, if you're buying a new CRT monitor, choose the one with the highest refresh rate, the highest maximum resolution, and the smallest dot pitch.

LCD Monitors

How does an LCD monitor work? Like a CRT screen, an LCD screen is composed of a grid of pixels. However, instead of including a cathode-ray tube, LCD monitors are made of two sheets of material filled with a liquid crystal solution. A fluorescent panel at the back of the LCD monitor generates light waves. When electric current passes through the liquid crystal solution, the crystals move around, either blocking the fluorescent light or letting the light shine through. This blocking or passing of light by the crystals causes images to be formed on the screen.

Are all LCD monitors the same? You'll generally find two types of LCD monitors on the market: **passive-matrix displays** and **active-matrix displays.** Less expensive LCD monitors use passive-matrix displays, whereas more expensive monitors use active-matrix displays. Passive-matrix technology uses an electrical current passed through the liquid crystal solution to charge groups of pixels, either in a row or a column. This causes the screen to brighten with each pass of electrical current and subsequently fade. With active-matrix displays, each pixel is charged individually, as needed. The result is that an active-matrix display produces a clearer, brighter image with better viewing angles. As the price of active-matrix displays continues to drop, passive-matrix displays will soon become a thing of the past.

LCD vs. CRT

Are LCD monitors better than CRT monitors? LCD monitors have a number of advantages over CRT monitors, as shown in Figure 0.11. Certainly, size is an advantage, because LCD monitors take up far less space on a desktop than a CRT monitor. Additionally, LCD monitors weigh less, making them the obvious choice for mobile devices. LCD technology also causes less eyestrain than the refreshed pixel technology of a CRT.

Because of their different technologies, you can see more of an LCD screen than you can with the same size CRT monitor. For example, there are 17 inches of viewable area on a 17-inch LCD monitor but only 15 inches of viewable area on a 17-inch CRT monitor. LCDs are also more environmentally friendly, emitting less than half the electromagnetic radiation and using less power than their CRT counterparts.

One of the few disadvantages of LCD monitors is their limited viewing angle. Even with the most expensive models, you may have a hard time seeing the screen image clearly from an angle. Additionally, the resolution on a LCD screen is fixed and cannot be modified to the same degree as that of a CRT. CRT monitors also have better color accuracy than LCD monitors.

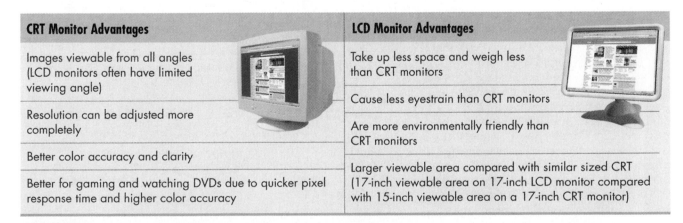

CRT Monitor Advantages	LCD Monitor Advantages
Images viewable from all angles (LCD monitors often have limited viewing angle)	Take up less space and weigh less than CRT monitors
Resolution can be adjusted more completely	Cause less eyestrain than CRT monitors
Better color accuracy and clarity	Are more environmentally friendly than CRT monitors
Better for gaming and watching DVDs due to quicker pixel response time and higher color accuracy	Larger viewable area compared with similar sized CRT (17-inch viewable area on 17-inch LCD monitor compared with 15-inch viewable area on a 17-inch CRT monitor)

FIGURE 0.11
CRT Monitors Versus LCD Monitors

Printers

A number of different printers have been developed for use with micro-computers. Three of the most popular printers used with personal computers are dot-matrix, inkjet, and laser printers. Dot-matrix printers print characters consisting of a series of dots using a hairbrush-like device that impacts the paper. Inkjet printers are printers that produce characters by spraying dots of ink that form the characters onto a page. Laser printers use a photocopying process similar to that of a copying machine. All three can produce graphics and characters of all sizes and shapes, but laser printers generally produce the best images and are the most expensive. Of the three, only dot-matrix printers can be used to print on forms with multiple copies. Ink-jet and laser printers are available in color or black and white.

Secondary Storage Devices

In an office, when you want to keep data or information permanently, you file it away. In a computer, when you wish to store data permanently, you need to transfer the data from primary storage (RAM) to a magnetic disk (the most common form of permanent storage) or another means of permanent storage such as magnetic tape or optical disk.

The main functions of secondary storage devices are storage and retrieval. When you finish your work, or a portion of your work, you can store it and later retrieve it for further use.

Computers may contain a number of different types of secondary storage devices. The most common are floppy disk drives and hard disk drives, both of which are usually located in the main system unit, as shown in Figure 0.12.

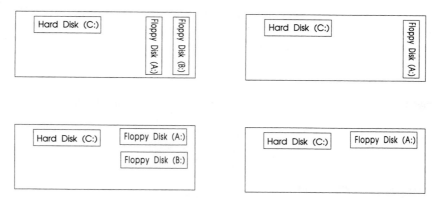

Figure 0.12
Floppy disk drive configurations

The disk drive allows data to be transferred to and from floppy or hard disks into RAM. The disk drive comprises a motor that spins the disk(s) and one or more read/write heads, which copy data to the disk from RAM or read data from the disk surface into RAM. The amount of data that can be stored on the disk depends on both the disk type and the disk drive technology.

Floppy Disk Drives

Disks used in floppy disk drives are either a thin, lightweight, flexible 5¼-inch disk encased in a flexible plastic envelope or a smaller 3½-inch disk encased in a hard plastic container to protect its recording surface. A 3½-inch disk is also called a microfloppy diskette (MFD). In this book, we use the terms disk and diskette interchangeably.

Floppy disk drives can be mounted either horizontally or vertically. A common configuration consists of two floppy drives: a 5¼-inch (360 K or 1.2 MB) and a 3½-inch (720 K or 1.44 MB).

Hard Disk Drives

Hard disk drives for most personal computers contain one or more rigid disks called platters. These disks are contained within an airtight unit and are normally permanently mounted within the computer. For this reason, they are also known as fixed disks.

Some newer types of permanent storage devices are optical drives and removable cartridge drives.

Modems

Modems are communication devices used when computers communicate with each other over phone lines. They are used to convert the information you want sent to another computer into signals that can be transmitted over phone lines. Modems can be found either inside the computer (internal) or as separate pieces of hardware (external). See Figure 0.13.

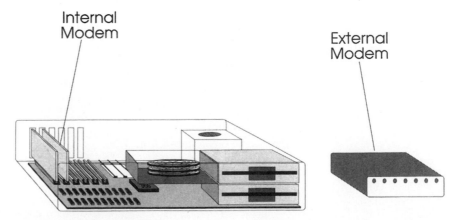

Internal Modem

External Modem

Figure 0.13
Internal and external modems

LANs

In many businesses, computers are linked together in order to make it possible for a number of users to access or share information. These computers form a local area network (LAN) (see Figure 0.14). Using DOS on a computer in a LAN environment is similar to using DOS on a single computer.

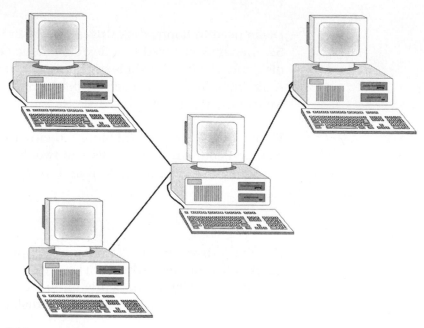

Figure 0.14
Four computers connected in a LAN

1 chapter**one**

Getting Started with Windows XP

In this chapter you will: complete this project **and** practice these skills.

Project 1A **Exploring the Basics of Windows XP**	**Objectives** • Start Windows XP • Start and Close a Program • Work with a Window • Use Commands in a Windows XP Program • Use Windows XP Help • End a Windows XP Session

Getting Started with Windows XP

Microsoft Windows XP is an operating system that coordinates the activities of your computer. It controls how your screen is displayed, how you open and close items, and the startup and shutdown procedures for your computer.

Before you can use your computer effectively, you need to have a basic familiarity with Windows XP.

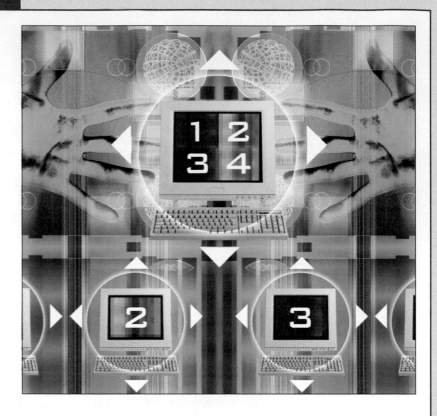

Introduction

Windows XP is the software that tells your computer how to be a computer. For example, Windows XP controls the display of text and graphics on your screen, the filing system that helps you locate your stored data, the printers and other hardware devices attached to your computer, and the manner in which other programs behave.

When you see the word *Windows* (with an uppercase *W*), it always refers to the software that controls your computer. The word *windows* (with a lowercase *w*), however, refers to a rectangular area on the screen that is used to display information or a program. The Windows operating system was named because of its use of windows.

Project 1A Working with Windows XP

In this project, you will examine features of Windows XP, identify the parts of the Windows XP desktop, start multiple programs, and practice using and switching among open windows. You will also use the Windows XP Help and Support Center, log off Windows XP, and shut down your computer.

Class Schedule

1A_Firstname_Lastname

In Activities 1.1 through 1.15, you will familiarize yourself with the Windows XP screen. You will open several programs and practice using menus, toolbar buttons, and dialog boxes. You will monitor your progress by comparing your screen with the figures in this textbook. While working through the project, you will use various screens and documents that look similar to those shown in Figure 1.1.

1A_Firstname_Lastname
December 14, 2005

Class Schedule

Figure 1.1
Project 1A—Working with Windows XP

Objective 1
Start Windows XP

The most important thing that Windows XP does for you is to manage your electronic *files*. A file is the basic unit of storage that enables a computer to distinguish one set of information from another. A file can consist of a software program or your own data. The Windows XP *operating system* starts automatically when you turn on your computer. An operating system is the software that manages the computer and the devices attached to your computer, such as printers and scanners. These items are known as *hardware*. *Software* is a group of instructions that tell the hardware which processes to run and how to display the results. The operating system also manages the electronic files stored on your disk drives and the *programs* on your computer. A program is a set of instructions to the computer. The Windows XP operating system was developed by Microsoft Corporation.

Windows XP uses text and visual elements, such as pictures, to help you communicate with your computer; this is referred to as the *graphical user interface*—GUI, which is pronounced *gooey*. By using a graphical user interface, you do not have to know complex computer programming commands. In Activities 1.1 and 1.2, you will start Windows XP, explore the screen elements, and practice using a *pointing device*. A pointing device is an input device that you use to interact with the computer.

Activity 1.1 Starting Windows XP and Identifying Parts of the Windows XP Desktop

In this activity, you will start the computer and identify the elements that display on your screen. You will use a pointing device called a *mouse* to point to objects on the screen and to activate *commands*—instructions from an individual to the computer program that cause an action to be carried out—and *features*—properties or characteristics of a program or computer.

1 If your computer is on, turn it off as follows: In the lower left corner of the screen, position the mouse pointer over the Start button **start**, and press and release the left mouse button one time. Then, position the pointer over *Turn Off Computer*, and press and release the left mouse button one time. Do the same thing at *Turn Off*, and then wait a few moments for the computer to complete the shutdown operation.

2 If you are working in a college computer lab, determine from your instructor or lab coordinator whether there is a log-on procedure that you must perform to start the Windows XP operating system or program.

To *log on* means to enter information that identifies you so that you can have access to a specific computer system or program. Additional information that may be required is a *user name*, which identifies you to the computer or program, and a *password*, which is a string of characters, such as a word or phrase, known only to you that verifies your identity to the computer. Typically, a password is a combination of text, numbers, punctuation, or other characters that cannot be guessed easily by unauthorized individuals.

3 Press the power switch to turn on your computer—and monitor, if necessary—and then, on your computer screen, watch as the Windows XP operating system software starts. If you need to log on, do so when prompted by Windows XP.

One or more introductory screens display briefly, and then the Windows XP *desktop* displays. The working area of the Windows XP screen is called a desktop because on it you can place electronic versions of items you have on your regular desk. The *background* is the color, pattern, or picture that displays on the desktop and on which elements such as icons are situated.

Alert!

Your Desktop May Look Different as You Work Through This Textbook

Individuals and organizations can change Windows XP to look and function in a manner suitable for them. For example, your background may include your college or company logo, or at home, your system may have a different background setting. As you work through the projects in this textbook, your screens will likely differ, and you might discover that some features, especially in a college lab, have been disabled.

4 Take a moment to study Figure 1.2 and the screen elements in the table in Figure 1.3 to become familiar with the parts of the Windows XP desktop.

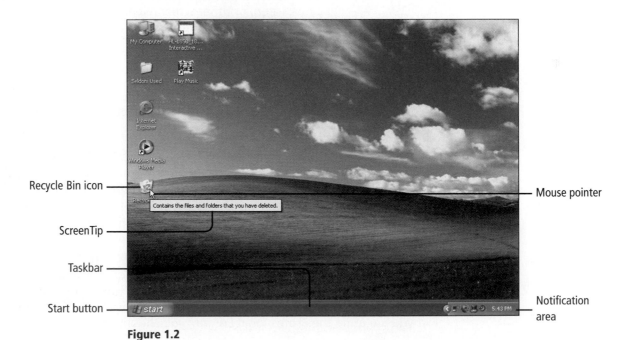

Recycle Bin icon

ScreenTip

Taskbar

Start button

Contains the files and folders that you have deleted.

Mouse pointer

Notification area

Figure 1.2

Windows XP Screen Elements

Screen Element	Description
Recycle Bin icon	The graphic icon for the Windows XP program that maintains a temporary storage place for files that you delete. An *icon* is a graphic representation of an object that you can select and open, such as a folder, a document, or a program. A document is a self-contained work that you create in a program and that you can save.
Start button	The button that displays the two-column Start menu. A *button* is a graphic representation of a command that, when clicked, performs the specified function or command. A *menu* is a list of commands.
Notification area	The area on the right side of the taskbar that contains the clock and system notifications.
Taskbar	The Windows XP toolbar, usually displayed across the bottom of the desktop screen, which contains the Start button, the notification area, and buttons and icons for programs. A *toolbar* is a row, column, or block of onscreen buttons or icons that, when chosen, start a command or function. The taskbar can be hidden to create more space on the screen.
Mouse pointer	The arrow or other shape that moves when you move the mouse pointing device.
ScreenTip	The note that displays when you point to an icon, button, or other screen element that provides information about that item.

Figure 1.3

More Knowledge — Windows Comes in Different Versions

Microsoft Corporation introduced the original version of Windows, called Windows 1.0, in 1983. The next version, introduced in 1987, was called Windows 2.0. After that came Windows 3.0, and then Windows 3.1, Windows NT, Windows 95, Windows 98, and so on. Windows XP, which is the operating system described in this textbook, was introduced in 2001. Older versions of Windows look significantly different from Windows XP.

Windows XP is available in two versions: *Windows XP Professional* for businesses and organizations and *Windows XP Home Edition* for individuals. The illustrations in this book are based on Windows XP Home Edition. However, these two versions are very similar in both appearance and functionality, so if you are using the Professional Edition, you should notice few differences.

Activity 1.2 Using a Pointing Device

The most common way to interact with Windows XP is by using your mouse. Moving the mouse moves the mouse pointer on the screen. Pressing the left mouse button selects or activates the button, icon, or command to which the mouse pointer is pointing. In this activity, you will practice using features of Windows XP, opening menus, and selecting commands.

1 On a flat surface such as a mouse pad, move your mouse to move the mouse pointer on the desktop. Move the mouse away from yourself to move the pointer toward the top of the desktop, and then move the mouse toward yourself to move the pointer toward the bottom of the desktop. Move the mouse to the left or right to move the pointer to the left or right. If you do not have enough space on the mouse pad, lift the mouse and reposition it.

2 On the desktop, without pressing and releasing either mouse button, move the mouse to position the mouse pointer over the **Recycle Bin** icon.

This action is called *pointing*. To point with the mouse, move the *mouse pointer* so that it is positioned over the element you want to select or activate. A mouse pointer is an arrow or other symbol whose location indicates the current position of the mouse on the screen. When you point to an element on the desktop, Windows XP displays a *ScreenTip*. Recall that a ScreenTip is the note that displays when you point to an icon or a toolbar button that provides information about the icon or button.

3 At the right end of the taskbar, in the **notification area**, point to the **clock** to display the ScreenTip—the current day and date—and then point to the **Start** button [start] to display the ScreenTip—*Click here to begin*.

Notice that the Start button becomes a lighter shade of green, indicating that it is the target of your next action.

Alert!

If Your Screen Does Not Display a Taskbar

The taskbar can be hidden to increase the amount of space available on the screen. If you are unable to see the taskbar, move your pointer to the bottom of the screen. The taskbar will display and remain displayed until you move the pointer away from the bottom of the screen.

4 On the desktop, verify whether the My Documents icon displays.

Be sure to avoid confusing the My Documents icon with the My Computer icon.

5 With the mouse pointer positioned over the **Start** button 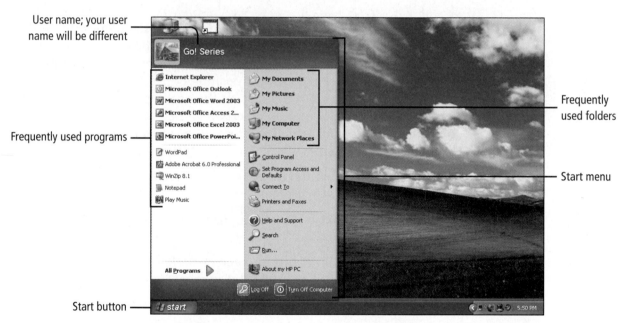, press and release the left mouse button to display the *Start menu* as shown in Figure 1.4.

To *click* means to press and release the left mouse button one time. Clicking activates the command or the action associated with a button or icon. The Start menu is the main menu for Windows XP. It provides access to almost everything you will want to do in Windows XP. Frequently used programs display in the left column, and frequently used folders, among other things, display in the right column.

A *folder* is the Windows XP electronic representation of the common paper manila file folder that you use to store real papers. A folder functions as a container for programs and files. The user name—a name that identifies an individual to the computer—displays at the top of the menu. Your Start menu will look similar but will display a different list of programs and folders, and your user name and the photo next to it will differ.

Figure 1.4

6 In the right column of the Start menu, point to **My Documents** to *highlight* it—the text color changes to white, and the area behind the text becomes dark blue—and then press the *right* mouse button one time. To highlight means to change the appearance of displayed characters for an item such as a command to indicate that it is the item to be acted on. Your text color and the area behind it may display with a different color depending on how Windows XP is set up on your computer.

This action is known as a *right-click*. In most instances, the action of right-clicking displays a *shortcut menu*, as shown in Figure 1.5. A shortcut menu is a menu that displays the most commonly used commands related to the item clicked. *My Documents* is a folder, created by Windows XP, in which you can store files and other folders that you create and use.

My Documents folder highlighted

Show on Desktop command

Shortcut menu

Figure 1.5

7 On the displayed shortcut menu, point to **Show on Desktop** to highlight it, and then click **Show on Desktop**.

Be sure to use the left mouse button to click the Show on Desktop command. In this textbook, whenever you see the word *click*, use the left mouse button. If the right button is required, you will be instructed to right-click. The icon that represents the My Documents folder is placed on the desktop; now you can have access to this folder from either the desktop or the Start menu.

Note — If Your *My Documents* Folder Was Already Displayed

If your My Documents folder icon was displayed, clicking the Show on Desktop command removed the icon from the desktop. To display the icon again, right-click the My Documents command, and then click Show on Desktop.

8 On the taskbar, click the **Start** button ![start] to close the Start menu. Alternatively, click anywhere on an empty area of the desktop to close the Start menu. Compare your screen with Figure 1.6.

My Documents folder icon
displayed on the desktop.

Figure 1.6

9 On the desktop, point to the **My Documents** icon, hold down the left mouse button, and then continue to hold down the mouse button and move the mouse to position the **My Documents** icon in the lower left corner of the desktop, slightly above the Start button. Release the left mouse button.

This action is called dragging. To **drag** means to point to an element, press and hold the left mouse button, move the mouse pointer to a different location, and then release the left mouse button. Dragging moves the element with the pointer and then drops it at the new location. The action is sometimes called **drag-and-drop**. If the icon pops back to its original location, the Auto Arrange feature is active. **Auto Arrange** sets Windows XP to automatically arrange items on the desktop in neat columns and rows.

10 On the desktop, point to the **My Documents** icon and then, without moving the mouse, press the left mouse button two times in rapid succession. This is called a **double-click**. Alternatively, point to the icon, right-click—recall that right-click means to click the right mouse button once—and then, from the displayed shortcut menu, click Open.

The My Documents window displays, as shown in Figure 1.7; yours may vary—for example, your window may not fill the entire screen. Instead of a list, you may see large file folder icons or small folder icons without any information other than the folder or file name.

A **window** is an area of the screen that displays information or a program, such as a letter or calculator. A window in Windows XP may display icons, folders, or programs. A window has the following characteristics: it can be opened and closed, resized, moved, minimized to a button on the taskbar, maximized to take up the entire screen, and can display at the same time as other windows. A **pane** is a separate area in a window.

Note — Keep the Mouse Still When You Double-Click

Double-clicking requires a steady hand and practice. It is important to keep the mouse very still; the two clicks do not have to be extremely fast. If you have difficulty double-clicking, right-click on the element, and then, from the displayed shortcut menu, click Open.

My Documents window; the arrangement of your window will vary. —

Close button —

— A pane within an open window

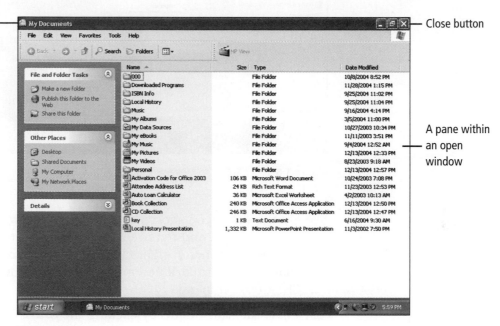

Figure 1.7

11 In the upper right corner of the **My Documents** window, point to the red **Close** button ☒ to display the ScreenTip *Close*, and then click the button.

Use the Close button to close any window.

12 On the taskbar, click the **Start** button 🏁 start , and then, in the right column of the Start menu, right-click **My Documents**. Notice on the shortcut menu that a check mark displays to the left of the Show on Desktop command, as shown in Figure 1.8.

The check mark indicates that the command is turned on—***active***. The Show on Desktop command is a ***toggle*** command, which means it has two settings: on and off.

Check mark indicates that the command is active.

Figure 1.8

13 On the displayed shortcut menu, click **Show on Desktop** to turn off the command and remove the My Documents icon from the desktop. On the Start menu, right-click **My Documents** again, and notice that the check mark no longer displays to the left of the Show on Desktop command.

14 Close the Start menu by clicking the **Start** button . Alternatively, you can close the Start menu by clicking an empty area of the desktop.

Objective 2
Start and Close a Program

You must have an operating system such as Windows XP to use other programs. Most individuals buy a computer to use sophisticated programs such as those included in Microsoft Office—Word, Excel, PowerPoint, Access, Outlook, and so on. Windows XP comes with a few small programs of its own that can be useful for simple tasks, such as creating and printing text files, drawing pictures, or performing mathematical calculations.

Regardless of whether you are using the programs that come with Windows XP or the more powerful programs for which you probably bought your computer, you can start more than one program at a time and then switch among them. The capability to open and work with multiple programs is known as *multitasking*.

Activity 1.3 Starting Programs

Windows XP includes simple programs that can be used to create business documents, design graphics, and perform calculations. These programs are easy to use for basic tasks. In this activity, you will start various programs.

1 On the taskbar, click the **Start** button 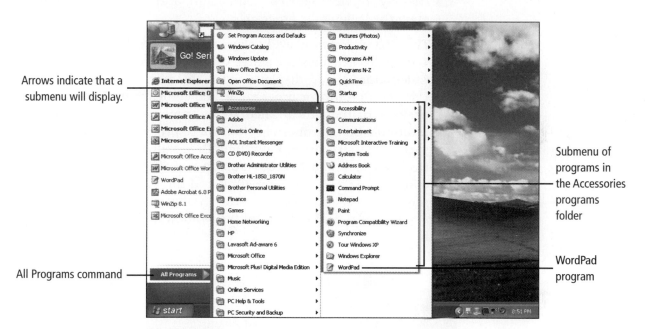 to display the Start menu, point to **All Programs** to display the list of programs installed on your computer, and then point to **Accessories** to display the menu of Accessories programs, as shown in Figure 1.9.

The **_All Programs_** menu lists all the programs available on your computer. The list on your computer will differ from the list in the figure, depending on the programs you have installed. Also, your All Programs menu may have been customized to display in a single column. A command with a small arrow to the right, such as the arrow to the right of *Accessories*, indicates that a submenu will display. A **_submenu_** is a secondary menu that displays when you select a command that includes an arrow on the right.

Arrows indicate that a submenu will display.

Submenu of programs in the Accessories programs folder

WordPad program

All Programs command

Figure 1.9

2 From the **Accessories** menu, click **WordPad** to start the WordPad program.

The WordPad window displays. **_WordPad_** is a simple word-processing program that comes with Windows XP. A **_word-processing program_**—or **_word processor_**—is a program used to create and manipulate text-based documents. A button representing the program displays on the taskbar.

3 With the WordPad window open, click the **Start** button 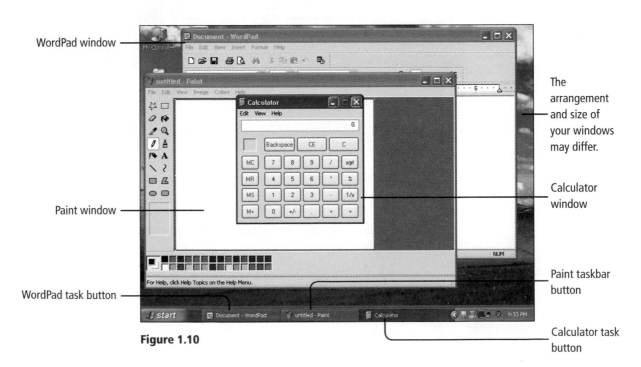, point to **All Programs**, and then point to **Accessories**. From the **Accessories** menu, click **Paint** to start the Paint program.

The Paint window displays and becomes the active window; it may cover the entire screen. The ***active window***—also called the ***current window***—is the window in which you are currently working. Both Paint and WordPad display buttons on the taskbar, indicating that both programs are open. The Paint program button, however, is a darker color, indicating that it is active.

Paint is a graphics program that comes with Windows XP. With a ***graphics program***, you can create and manipulate images.

4 Display the **Accessories** menu again, and then click **Calculator** to start the Calculator program.

The Calculator window displays on top of the Paint window. Calculator becomes the active window, and a button for the Calculator window displays on the taskbar, as shown in Figure 1.10. Use the ***Calculator*** program, which comes with Windows XP, to perform mathematical calculations, such as addition, subtraction, multiplication, or division. Now, three programs are in use at the same time—WordPad, Paint, and Calculator. Each has a window on the desktop and a ***taskbar button***—a button on the taskbar that displays the icon of the program and the name of the open file, if any. The size and position of the windows on your desktop may differ from the size and position of the windows in the figure, depending on how the windows displayed the last time they were opened.

Figure 1.10

More Knowledge — You Will Probably Want to Buy and Install More Programs

When you purchase a computer, it will likely include the Windows XP operating system, the Accessory programs that are included with Windows XP, and perhaps some other free programs provided by the company from which you purchased your computer. For the most part, these programs have limited usefulness and are fairly simple.

For serious computing—constructing complex documents, creating financial spreadsheets, creating presentations, setting up and maintaining a database, or creating brochures with desktop publishing—you may want to purchase programs such as Word, Excel, PowerPoint, Access, and Publisher, all of which are included in the program called *Microsoft Office*.

Other popular programs that can be used with the Windows XP operating system include Adobe Photoshop for editing photos, Macromedia's Studio MX for Web site development, and the many games and other personal software programs available. These programs, although not developed by Microsoft, rely on Windows XP to control the computer.

Activity 1.4 Arranging Windows and Switching Among Programs

Several windows can be open at the same time. Regardless of how many windows are open, only one can be active at a time. Windows XP provides different methods for arranging multiple windows on the desktop and switching among the windows. In this activity, you will practice arranging and switching among open windows.

1 On the taskbar, click the **untitled - Paint** button.

Clicking a taskbar button makes the window represented by that button active. The active window moves in front of other open windows; its *title bar*—the bar at the top of the window, in which the program name and program icon display—and taskbar button display darker than those in the other—*inactive*, or not currently in use—windows, as shown in Figure 1.11. Sometimes, Windows XP may not have enough space on the taskbar to display the entire taskbar button name. Instead, the first part of the name will display, and the last part of the name will display as an ellipsis (...). To view the full name of a taskbar button, point to the taskbar button to display the ScreenTip.

Inactive window title bar ———

Active window title bar ———

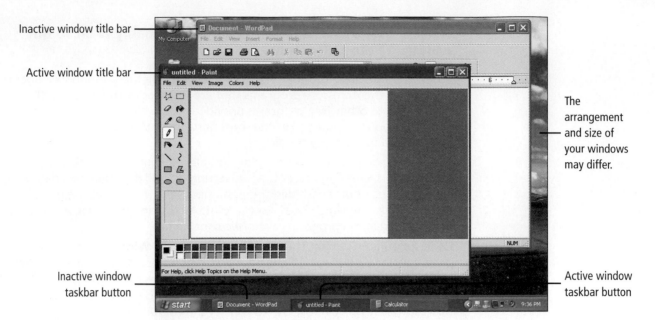

The
arrangement
and size of
your windows
may differ.

Inactive window
taskbar button ———

Active window
taskbar button

Figure 1.11

🔢 On the taskbar, click the **Document - WordPad** button to make
WordPad the active window.

🔢 On the taskbar, point to a blank area—so that no ScreenTip displays—
and then right-click to display a shortcut menu, as shown in
Figure 1.12.

When several windows are open, the blank area on the taskbar may
be limited. Move the mouse pointer just to the left of the notification
area. If no ScreenTip displays, it is a blank area.

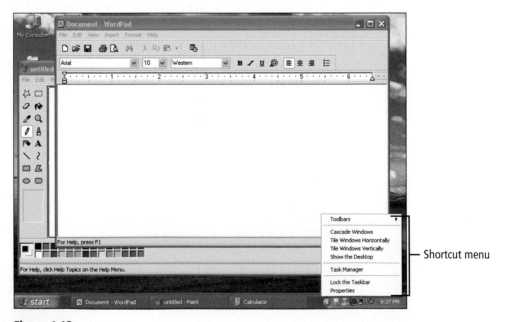

——— Shortcut menu

Figure 1.12

4 From the displayed shortcut menu, click **Tile Windows Vertically**.

Windows XP *tiles* the windows—arranges and sizes the windows so that all windows display in their entirety. None of the windows overlaps another, as shown in Figure 1.13. No window is active. The more windows that are open, the smaller each tiled window will be.

No window is active; none is a darker color

Three windows open

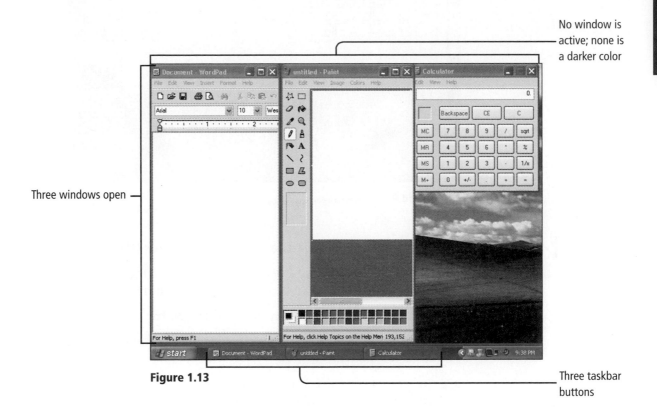

Figure 1.13

Three taskbar buttons

5 On the taskbar, right-click a blank area, and from the displayed shortcut menu, click **Cascade Windows**.

Windows XP *cascades* the open windows, as shown in Figure 1.14. Cascaded windows overlap one another so that each window's title bar is visible. You can see the top window in its entirety, but you can see only the title bars of the other open windows.

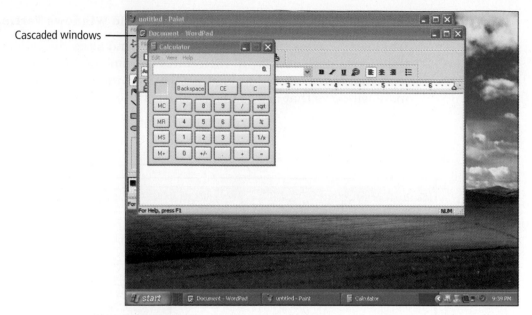

Cascaded windows

Figure 1.14

■6 On the desktop, click the title bar of the **WordPad** window.

The WordPad program becomes the active window, and on the taskbar, the WordPad button is active—a darker shade.

■7 On the desktop, click anywhere in the **Paint** window.

Paint becomes the active window. Clicking anywhere within a window makes it active.

■8 On your keyboard, hold down Alt and continue to hold it down while you press and release Tab, and then look at the screen.

A gray box displays icons representing the three open programs, and the active program is surrounded by a border. If you are unable to see the gray box, try again, and be sure to continue to hold down Alt. This is an alternative method of switching among open programs.

■9 Continue to hold down Alt and then press Tab several times to see how Windows XP cycles among the three open programs. Release Alt.

In this manner, you can press Tab until the program you want is selected—surrounded by a blue border—and then release both keys to make the selected program's window active.

More Knowledge — Tiling Horizontally

You can also tile windows horizontally from top to bottom. However, if more than three windows are open, a combination of horizontal and vertical tiling is used to fit all windows on the screen.

Activity 1.5 Closing Programs

When you finish working with a program, you close it. You can close a program in several ways. In this activity, you will close the programs that are open on the desktop.

1 Make the **WordPad** program active by clicking its taskbar button if necessary.

You can use the Close button, the File menu command, or the taskbar button to close a window. See Figure 1.15.

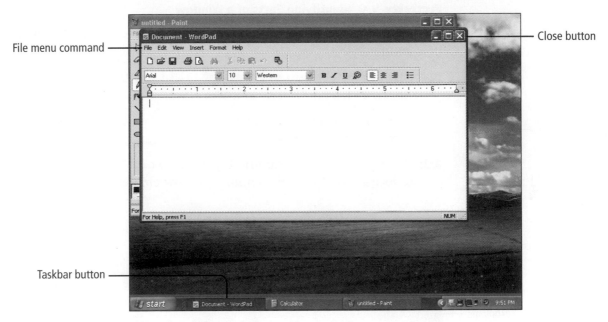

Figure 1.15

2 In the upper left corner of the WordPad window, click **File** to display the program's File menu, and then, at the bottom of the menu, click **Exit**. If prompted to save the current file, click **No**.

The WordPad program closes. For programs that include a File menu, this is one method of closing the program.

3 Right-click the **Calculator** taskbar button and then, on the displayed shortcut menu, click **Close**.

This method of closing a program can be used regardless of whether the program is active or inactive.

4 In the **Paint** window, at the right end of the title bar, click the red **Close** button ▨. If prompted to save the current file, click **No**.

You can always use the red Close button to close an open window that is active.

Objective 3
Work with a Window

Recall that windows share common characteristics that you can use to control the size and position of the window and select program commands: a window can be opened and closed, resized, moved, minimized to a button on the taskbar, maximized to take up the entire screen, and can display at the same time as other windows. In Activities 1.6 though 1.8, you will identify and work with the common parts of a window.

Activity 1.6 Identifying Parts of a Window

In this activity, you will start the WordPad program and identify the parts of a window.

1 Click the **Start** button ![start], point to **All Programs**, point to **Accessories**, and then click **WordPad**.

Recall that WordPad is a simple word-processing program that comes with Windows XP.

2 Take a moment to examine Figure 1.16 and the table in Figure 1.17 to locate and identify common window elements.

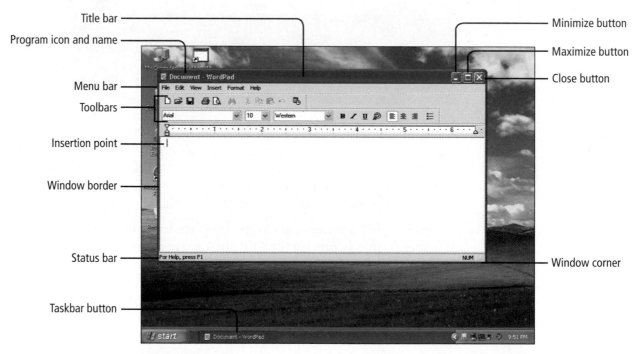

Figure 1.16

one

Common Window Elements

Element	Function
Title bar	The horizontal bar at the top of the window where the *program icon* (the icon used to identify the program) and the name of the program display.
Menu bar	The rectangular area displaying the names of menus that contain commands. Click a menu name to display the list of commands on a menu.
Toolbar	A row of buttons, each of which provides a one-click method to perform a common command.
Status bar	The area at the bottom of the window in which information about the contents of the window or about the current item displays.
Maximize / Restore Down button	The middle of three window control buttons on the right end of the title bar. The Maximize button is used to resize the window to fill the entire desktop. After a window is maximized, the Restore Down button displays in place of the Maximize button. Restore Down, which is sometimes called Restore, is used to return the window to its previous size and position.
Minimize button	The left of three window control buttons on the right end of the title bar, the Minimize button is used to reduce the window to a button on the taskbar. The window remains open but not visible; it is hidden.
Close button	The right of three window control buttons on the right end of the title bar, the Close button is used to close the window.
Taskbar button	A button on the taskbar represents each open window. Click a taskbar button to make that window active.
Title bar program icon and name	An icon representing the program displays at the left end of the title bar. The name of the current file and the program name display to the right of the program icon.
Window border	A line around the edge of a window that is not maximized is called the window border or *resize border*. You can drag the border to change the size of the window.
Insertion point	A blinking vertical bar on the screen that indicates the location at which inserted text will display.
Window corner	An area in the lower right corner of a window that can be used to resize a window vertically and horizontally at the same time.

Figure 1.17

Activity 1.7 Minimizing, Redisplaying, Maximizing, and Restoring a Window

Three window control buttons display at the right end of a window's title bar: Minimize, Maximize—or Restore Down, depending on the window's current size—and Close. Use these buttons to control the size and position of a window on the desktop. In this activity, you will practice using the window control buttons in the WordPad window.

1 In the **WordPad** window, click the **Minimize** button .

> *Minimizing* a window removes it from the desktop, but the window remains open. The window is reduced to a taskbar button, as shown in Figure 1.18. Minimizing a window that is using a program moves the window out of the way without closing the program. When you need the program again, the program need not go through its startup procedure, which can take a few moments if it is a large, complex program.

WordPad window reduced to a button on the taskbar

Figure 1.18

2 On the taskbar, click the **Document - WordPad** button to redisplay the WordPad window.

3 In the **WordPad** window, click the **Maximize** button. If your window is already maximized—that is, the Restore Down button displays instead of the Maximize button—proceed to step 4.

> *Maximizing* a window enlarges it to fill the desktop, giving you plenty of screen space to work in the program.

4 In the **WordPad** window, click the **Restore Down** button to restore the window to its previous size and position.

The Maximize button displays only in a window that has been restored down.

5 On the taskbar, right-click the **Document - WordPad** button.

Notice that the Maximize, Minimize, Restore, and Close commands also display on the taskbar button shortcut menu. Also notice that small icons display to the left of some commands on the shortcut menu, as a reminder that a button also exists for this command. If a command on any menu is *dimmed*—shown in a lighter color than other, active commands—the command is unavailable. Currently, the Restore command is dimmed because the window has already been restored down to its previous size. See Figure 1.19.

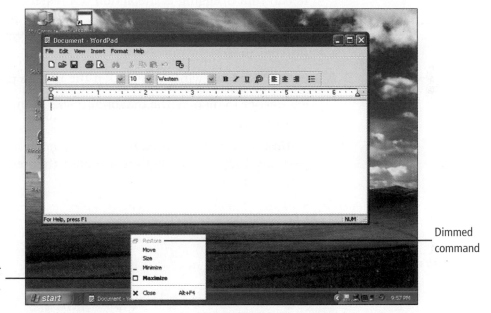

A button is also available for this command.

Dimmed command

Figure 1.19

6 From the displayed shortcut menu, click **Maximize** to maximize the window. Right-click the **Document - WordPad** taskbar button again, and then click **Restore**.

7 On the taskbar, right-click in a blank area to display the shortcut menu, and then click **Show the Desktop**.

Windows XP minimizes the WordPad window and displays the desktop.

8 On the taskbar, right-click a blank area to display the shortcut menu, and then click **Show Open Windows**.

Windows XP restores the open window to its previous size and position.

Activity 1.8 Resizing and Moving a Window

A window opens in the same size and location in which it was last used. You can move and resize a window that is not maximized. In this activity, you will practice moving and resizing the WordPad window.

1 In the **WordPad** window, be sure the window is *not* maximized. If necessary, click the Restore Down button 🗗 so that the window is not maximized.

You cannot resize or move a maximized window. When a window is not maximized, it has a window *border* that can be resized on all four sides. A border is a visible edge or frame around a window.

2 In the **WordPad** window, position the mouse pointer 🔙 over any blank part of the title bar, and then drag the title bar downward slightly—toward the bottom of the desktop.

Recall that dragging is the action of pressing and holding the left mouse button, moving the mouse, and then releasing the mouse button in order to move something on the screen. Dragging a window's title bar moves the entire window.

3 In the **WordPad** window, position the mouse pointer over the upper left corner to display the diagonal resize pointer 🔽, as shown in Figure 1.20.

A *diagonal resize pointer* is a two-headed arrow that indicates that you can drag diagonally to resize both the height and width of the window at the same time.

Diagonal resize pointer —

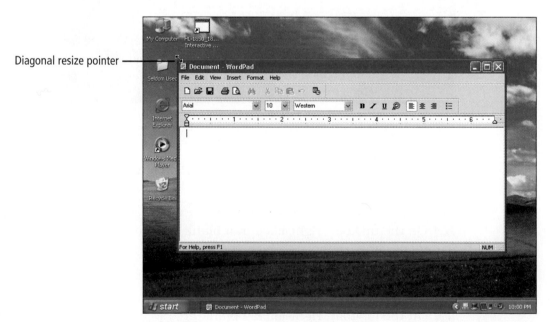

Figure 1.20

4 In the upper left corner of the **WordPad** window and with the diagonal resize pointer displayed, **drag** slightly down and to the right to make both the height and the width of the window smaller.

5 In the **WordPad** window, point to the left window border so that the *horizontal resize pointer* displays ↔, and then drag to the right slightly to make the window narrower.

Using the horizontal resize pointer, you can drag left or right to resize the width of the window.

6 In the **WordPad** window, point to the top window border so that the *vertical resize pointer* displays ↕, and then drag upward slightly to make the window taller.

Using the vertical resize pointer, you can drag up or down to resize the height of the window.

7 In the **WordPad** window, drag the title bar to the approximate center of the desktop, and then click the **Maximize** button ▢.

Notice that the window border does not display on the maximized window.

Objective 4
Use Commands in a Windows XP Program

Recall that a command is an instruction to a computer that causes an action to be carried out. A software program that works with the Windows XP operating system, referred to as a *Windows XP program*, uses similar commands. This includes programs such as Word and Excel, which were developed by Microsoft, and programs such as Adobe Photoshop and Macromedia Flash, which were developed by other companies.

This is one advantage of using a common operating system; you can transfer skills used in one program to another program. For example, the command to save a file is the same in Word, Excel, and most other programs that you use with Windows XP.

Activity 1.9 Using Toolbars to Activate Commands and Menus

In any program that works with Windows XP, commands are performed by clicking the name of a menu and then clicking the command name on the displayed menu. This involves at least two, and sometimes more, clicks. Commands that are used frequently are placed on a toolbar and represented by a small picture. A toolbar button is a one-click method to perform a command.

In this activity, you will use toolbar buttons in WordPad to activate commands related to *formatting*—changing the appearance of—text. You will then use a combination of computer keys and commands to capture an image of your computer screen and place it in a document.

1 In the maximized **WordPad** window, locate the toolbar as shown in Figure 1.21, and then point to the **New** button ⬚ to display the ScreenTip.

When you point to a toolbar button, its name displays in a ScreenTip, and information about the button displays in the Status bar, as shown in Figure 1.21.

New button on the toolbar

ScreenTip displays button name.

Ruler—set to measure in inches

Status bar displays information about the button.

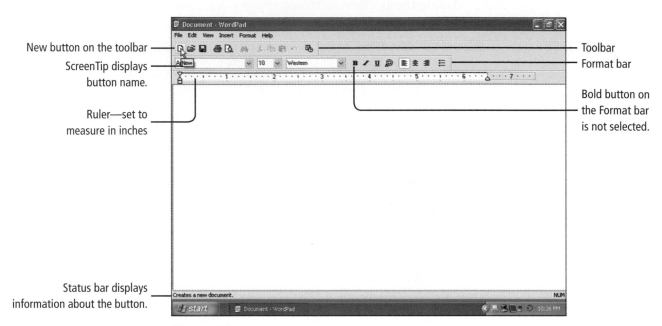

Toolbar

Format bar

Bold button on the Format bar is not selected.

Figure 1.21

2 On the Format bar, locate the **Bold** button **B** and notice that it is not selected, or highlighted.

The **Format bar** displays buttons for commands that you use to change the appearance of text. You use the **Bold** button to change text to bold, which is a style that makes the text display darker and heavier than the text that surrounds it.

3 Under the title bar, click **Format** to display the **Format menu**, and then, from the displayed menu, click the **Font** command. In the displayed **Font** dialog box, under **Font style**, click **Bold**, and then, at the right, click **OK**.

Notice that the Bold button on the Format bar is selected. Recall that a button that is selected displays a border and a white background color. This will set the text to be entered as bold.

4 Using the keyboard, type **Class Schedule** and then notice that the text you entered displays in bold. If you type a letter by mistake, immediately press ⌫ₖₛₚ to remove that letter.

5 On the toolbar, click the **Undo** button ↶.

The text is deleted, and the bold setting is turned off—the button on the Format bar is no longer selected. **Undo** is a command that reverses the previous action.

6 On the Format bar, click the **Bold** button **B** to select it, and then type **Class Schedule** again.

Although turning on the bold feature from the Format menu requires a number of clicks, you can turn on the bold feature with a single click by using a toolbar button. In any program that works with Microsoft Windows XP, a toolbar button represents a one-click method to perform a command that could otherwise be performed from a menu.

The Format bar displays buttons for commands that you use to format text. Compare your screen with Figure 1.22.

Text displays in bold ——

Bold button selected

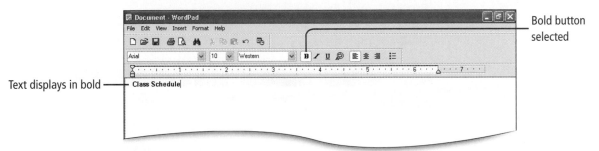

Figure 1.22

7 On the keyboard, press [Enter], and then, on the Format bar, click the **Bold** button **B**.

The insertion point moves down one line, and the bold feature is *deselected*, or turned off.

8 On the Format bar, click the **Font button arrow** [Arial] and then locate the scroll box on the right side of the displayed list, as shown in Figure 1.23.

Recall that a font is a set of characters with the same design and shape. The WordPad program includes an extensive list of fonts. You may have other fonts installed on your computer, which means your font list will differ from the one in the figure.

On a long list like this one, which is too long to display within the height of the desktop, you can *scroll*. To scroll means to move within the contents of a list or window by using a scroll bar. A *scroll bar* is a vertical or horizontal bar that displays at the side or bottom of a list or window and is used with a mouse to shift the content of that area. Drag the *scroll box*—the square box within the scroll bar—to shift the display of the list. Click the *scroll up arrow*—the arrow at the top of the scroll bar—to shift the display up, and click the *scroll down arrow*—the arrow at the top of the scroll bar—to shift the display down.

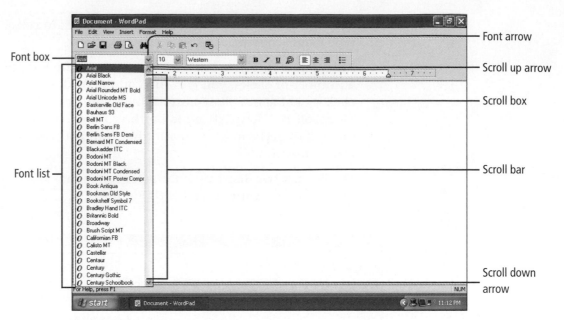

Font box

Font list

Font arrow

Scroll up arrow

Scroll box

Scroll bar

Scroll down arrow

Figure 1.23

9 In the Font list scroll bar, drag the scroll box down to the bottom to display the items at the bottom of the list, and then drag it back

to the top. Click the **scroll down arrow** ▼ repeatedly until the font name *Comic Sans MS* displays—the list is alphabetical. In the list, click **Comic Sans MS**.

Clicking a font name selects the font. The list closes, and the new font name displays in the Font box on the Format bar. If Comic Sans MS is not available on your system, select a different font, such as Times New Roman or Courier New.

More Knowledge — Moving Quickly in a List

When a list—such as the Font list—has many entries, you can move quickly down the list by typing the first letter of the desired list item. Typing the second letter will refine your search even further. For example, if you are looking for the Symbol font, typing **s** will take you to the first font that begins with that letter. If instead you type **sy** the first font name that begins with *sy* will be selected.

---

10 On the Format bar, click the **Font Size button arrow** [10 ▼], and then, on the displayed list, click **24**.

Font size is the height of an uppercase letter in a font set, measured in points. A *point* is 1/72 of an inch.

11 In the **WordPad** window, using your own first and last name, type **1A_Firstname_Lastname** and then press Enter. Compare your screen with Figure 1.24.

The text displays in 24-point Comic Sans MS, as shown in Figure 1.24.

Current font

Text displays in 24-point Comic Sans MS.

Current font size

Figure 1.24

🔢 On the toolbar, click the **Print** button 🖨 and then retrieve your printout from the printer. If you have been asked to submit this printout to your instructor, hold it until the end of this project.

WordPad prints the document using the default print settings. A **default** is the standard setting used by a program when you do not specify an alternative. In this case, WordPad uses the default printer to print a single copy of the document.

🔢 On the toolbar, click the **Undo** button ↺ two times to undo your typing. Notice that the font and font size revert to 10-point Arial, which is the default.

Activity 1.10 Using Menus and Dialog Boxes to Activate Commands

Commonly used commands are represented on toolbars so that they can be activated with a single click. Many commands, however, are activated from a menu of commands. Some menu commands result in the display of a **dialog box**, which is a special window that prompts you for additional information in order to complete a task. In this activity, you will practice using commands.

🔢 In the WordPad window, on the menu bar, click **File** to display the File menu, and then click **File** again to close the File menu. Alternatively, press [Esc] to hide a displayed menu, or click anywhere in the WordPad window. Click **Edit** to display the Edit menu.

On the Edit menu, notice that some commands are followed by a **shortcut key combination**, which is two or more keys that are pressed at the same time. You can use the key combination as an alternative method of selecting the command.

🔢 On the menu bar, move the mouse pointer to the right to point to **View,** and then click to display the View menu. Compare your screen with Figure 1.25.

Notice that the commands on the View menu display check marks. Recall that a check mark indicates that the item is selected, or active. Notice also that the Options command is followed by an **ellipsis** (...). An ellipsis to the right of a command on a menu indicates that when you click the command, a dialog box will display.

Check marks —

Ellipsis —

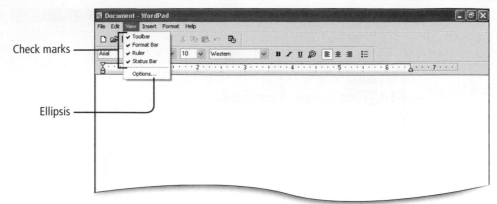

Figure 1.25

3 From the **View** menu, click **Options**.

The Options dialog box displays, with the Rich Text tab active, as shown in Figure 1.26. A **tab** is a page within a dialog box that displays a group of related commands and options. The active tab has a bold bar across its top and displays on top—or in front—of other tabs in the dialog box. Notice that the name of the dialog box displays in the dialog box title bar.

Active tab —

Dialog box title bar —
Inactive tabs —

Check boxes —

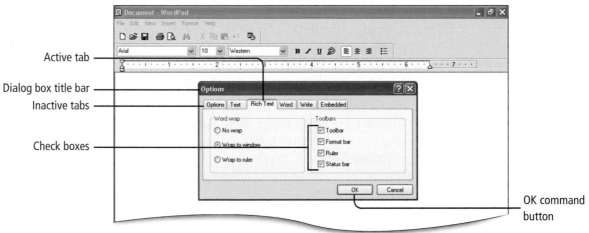

OK command button

Figure 1.26

4 In the **Options** dialog box, under **Toolbars**, click to clear the check marks from all four check boxes, and then click **OK**.

Clicking OK carries out the command. Alternatively, press Enter on your keyboard. Because you cleared the check boxes in the Options dialog box, the toolbars, ruler, and status bar no longer display in the WordPad window, as shown in Figure 1.27. A **check box** in a dialog box lets you click to select or deselect an option. A check mark in a check box indicates that the option is selected; no check mark indicates that the option is not selected.

More Knowledge — Cancel Changes to Dialog Box Settings

To close a dialog box without making any changes or entering any commands, click the Cancel button in the dialog box or press [Esc] on your keyboard.

5 On the menu bar, click **View**, and then click **Options** to display the **Options** dialog box with the **Rich Text Format tab** active. Under **Toolbars**, click to select all four check boxes.

6 In the **Options** dialog box, click the **Options tab**. Under **Measurement units**, click the **Centimeters** option button to select it, and then compare your screen with Figure 1.27.

An *option button* is a round button with which you select one of a group of mutually exclusive options—that is, if you select one, you are unable to select any of the others in the same group.

Toolbars not currently displayed

Selected option button

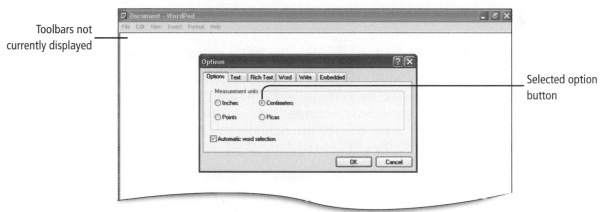

Figure 1.27

7 In the **Options** dialog box, click **OK**.

WordPad carries out the command. The toolbars, ruler, and status bar redisplay because you selected all the check boxes on the Rich Text Format tab. The unit of measurement on the ruler is changed from inches to centimeters because you selected the Centimeters option button on the Options tab.

8 In the **WordPad** window, using your own first and last name, type **1A_Firstname_Lastname** and then press [Enter].

9 From the menu bar, display the **View** menu, and then click **Options** to display the **Options** dialog box. Click the **Options tab**. Under **Measurement units**, click **Inches**, and then click **OK** to change the measurement units from centimeters back to inches.

10 From the menu bar, display the **Insert** menu, and then click **Date and Time** to display the **Date and Time** dialog box. In the **Available formats** list, verify that the mm/dd/yyyy date format is selected, and then click **OK**. The number of the month, day, and year of the current date will display in place of mm/dd/yyyy.

WordPad inserts the date in the selected format. A *list* offers a choice of items. If there are more items than can display within the box, a scroll bar displays so that you can scroll the list.

11 On the toolbar, click the **Undo** button 🔄 to reverse the date insertion, and then click the **Date/Time** button 🗒.

The Date and Time dialog box displays. Recall that a toolbar button is a one-click method of activating a commonly used command, but commands are also available from a menu.

12 In the **Date and Time** dialog box, in the **Available formats** list, click the date that displays the current month spelled out in letters, the date, and then the year, and then click **OK** to insert the date into the WordPad document.

13 On your keyboard, press Enter to move the insertion point in the WordPad window to the next line. On the toolbar, click the **Bold** button **B**, click the **Italic** button 🗾, and then click the **Center** button 🗒. Type **Class Schedule** and compare your screen with Figure 1.28. Your screen may differ because the date you insert will be the current date. *Italic* is a type style in which all characters slant toward the right.

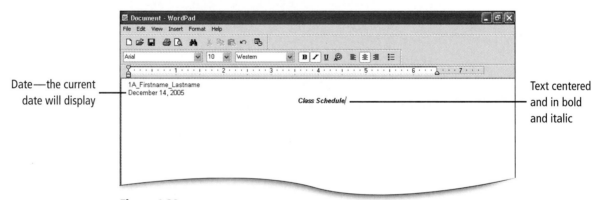

Date—the current date will display

Text centered and in bold and italic

Figure 1.28

More Knowledge — Aligning Text

The WordPad toolbar contains three text alignment buttons. The default is Align Left, which is the way most documents are typed. The Center button centers the text between the left and right edges of the document, and the Align Right button moves the text to the right edge of the text area, leaving the left edge uneven.

14 On the toolbar, click the **Print** button 🖨 to print the document.

15 From the **File** menu, click **Exit**.

Recall that you can close a program in a variety of ways—by clicking the Close button on the title bar, by right-clicking the taskbar button and clicking Close, or from the File menu by clicking Exit. Because you made changes to the document, WordPad displays a message asking whether you want to save the changes. When you **save**, you move the document from the computer's temporary memory and store the document as a file on a **disk drive** or other storage area. A disk drive is a hardware device that reads from and writes to devices that can store data.

16 In the **message box**, click **No** to close the WordPad program without saving the document.

Activity 1.11 Capturing an Image of a Screen

Occasionally a program may not work as expected, or you may have a problem using Windows XP. When this happens, use the **screen capture** feature built into Windows XP to record the problem you are having (or to record the error message) so that you can show it to someone at a help desk or send it to a customer support center. A screen capture is an image of the screen that can be printed or placed in a document. In this activity, you capture an image of the screen and place it in a WordPad document.

1 Click the **Start** button 🟢 start , point to **All Programs**, point to **Accessories**, and then click **WordPad**. Click the **Restore Down** button 🗗.

2 In the WordPad window, type **1A_Firstname_Lastname** using your own name. Press Enter two times.

Pressing Enter two times inserts a blank line.

3 On your keyboard, locate and press PrtScr.

The Print Screen key on your keyboard will probably be near the right side of the top row of keys. This key captures an image of the whole screen and places it in a temporary storage area called the **Clipboard**. Items in the Clipboard can be **pasted** in a document by using the Paste command.

4 From the WordPad menu, click **Edit**, and then click **Paste**.

The captured screen is pasted at the insertion point, as shown in Figure 1.29. The image is larger than the WordPad page and has a horizontal orientation, whereas the WordPad page has a vertical orientation.

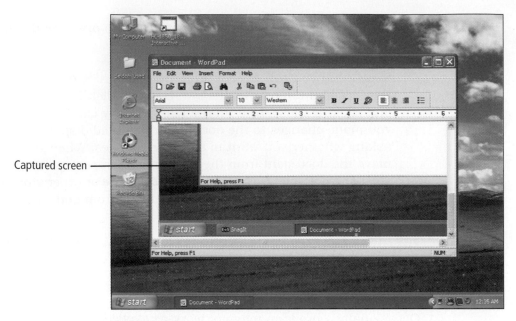

Captured screen

Figure 1.29

5 From the WordPad menu, click **File**, and then click **Page Setup**.

The Page Setup dialog box displays, as shown in Figure 1.30. Under Orientation, notice the Portrait and Landscape option buttons. In *portrait orientation*, the document will print with a vertical orientation in which the printed page is taller than it is wide; in *landscape orientation*, the document will print with a horizontal orientation in which the printed page is wider than it is tall.

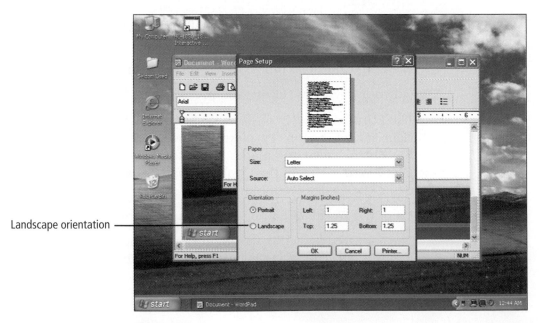

Landscape orientation

Figure 1.30

6 Under **Orientation**, click the **Landscape** option button, and then click **OK**.

The default margins change when you change the document orientation. The orientation is changed so that the page will be wider to accommodate the pasted image.

7 Move the pointer over the sizing handle—the small box—in the upper left corner of the image. If necessary, scroll so that you can view the upper left corner of the image you inserted.

When an image is selected, **sizing handles** are displayed in all four corners and in the middle of the side and top borders. Drag these small squares to resize the image in much the same way as you resize a window.

8 With the diagonal resize pointer ⬉, drag to the right and down about one inch. Use the ruler as a guide, as shown in Figure 1.31.

Recall that to drag an object, you need to point, click, and move the mouse pointer to the desired location.

One-inch mark

Diagonal resize pointer

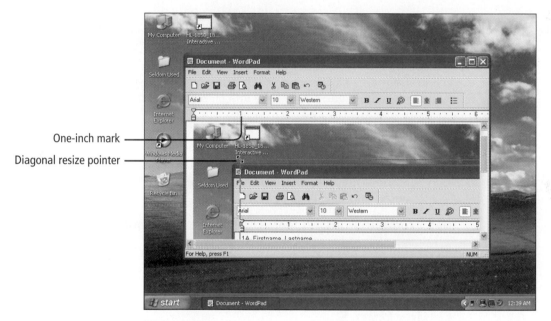

Figure 1.31

9 Release the mouse button. Click **File**, **Print Preview**.

The Print Preview window displays, as shown in Figure 1.32. Your screen may differ if Print Preview is set to display more than one page at a time.

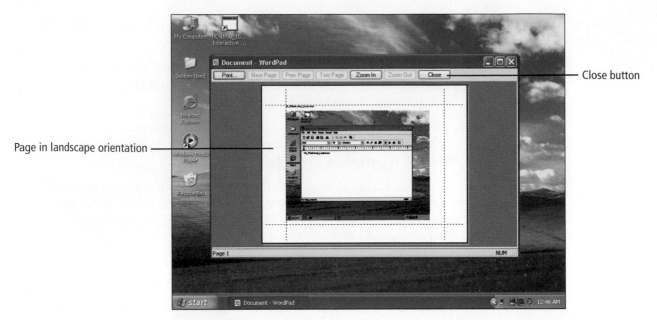

Page in landscape orientation

Close button

Figure 1.32

Alert!

What to Do If the Image Does Not Display in Print Preview

On some computers, if the image is larger than the page, the image will not display. If you cannot see your pasted image, close the Print Preview window and use the sizing handle to reduce the size of the image again. Repeat this procedure until you can see the image in the Print Preview window.

---

10 In the Print Preview title bar, click the red **Close** button ☒. Alternatively, you can click the large Close button in the Print Preview toolbar.

11 From the WordPad toolbar, click the **Print** button 🖨.

12 From the **File** menu, click **Exit**. When prompted to save your work, click **No**.

Objective 5
Use Windows XP Help

The Windows XP Help and Support Center provides information about how to use the features of Windows XP. It is organized into topics so that you can locate the information you need easily. You can use the alphabetical index of topics or search for the topic you need.

Activity 1.12 Starting the Help and Support Center and Using the Help Index

If you know the specific topic for which you need help, you can use the Help and Support Center's alphabetical index. In this activity, you will locate the Help pages that display information about maximizing and minimizing windows.

1 On the taskbar, click the **Start** button [start], and then click **Help and Support**. If necessary, click the Maximize button [□] to expand the window to fill the screen.

The Windows XP Help and Support Center home page displays. This page may vary, depending on the manufacturer of your computer and other system settings. The items on this page are *hyperlinks*—also called *links*—to other information. A hyperlink is text or a picture that you click to go to a different location—called the *link destination*—to display information, start a program, or access a command. When you point to a link, the *link select pointer*—a hand with a pointing finger—displays, and the link text is underlined.

2 In the **Help and Support Center**, on the toolbar, click the **Index** button [Index].

Windows XP displays the alphabetical index list in the left pane of the window. You can scroll through the list, or you can go directly to the topic.

3 In the **Type in the keyword to find** box, type **max** and then compare your screen with Figure 1.33.

As you type, Windows XP goes to the text that matches the characters. You do not have to complete the keyword *maximize* because *maximize, defined* is the first topic in the index that begins with the characters *max*.

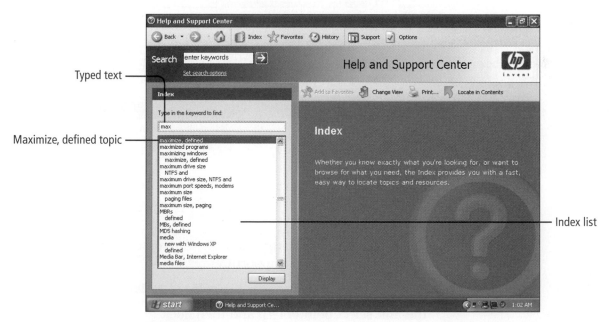

Figure 1.33

4 With *maximized, defined* selected in the left pane of the Help and Support Center, at the bottom of the pane, click **Display**.

The Help and Support Center glossary displays in the right pane, with the term *maximize* at the top. The **glossary** is an alphabetical list of terms and definitions. You can scroll through the glossary or click a letter at the top of the right pane to go to the first word that begins with that letter.

5 In the left pane, in the **Index**, scroll down to locate the topic **minimizing windows**. Under **minimizing windows**, click **overview**, and then click **Display**.

Because there are multiple pages for this topic, the Topics Found dialog box displays so that you can select the topic you want to view. See Figure 1.34.

Minimizing windows, overview topic

Two topics are found.

Display button

Figure 1.34

6 In the **Topics Found** dialog box, under **Title**, verify that *Minimize or maximize a window or restore it to its previous size* is selected, and then click **Display**.

The page of specific instructions for the topic displays in the right pane of the Help and Support Center.

7 At the bottom of the right pane, point to **Related Topics** to display the link select pointer [icon], and then click to display a menu of additional help topics that relate to the current topic. On the menu that displays, click **Resize an open window** to display the specific instructions for the task.

A Print button in the right pane enables you to print the current help topic if necessary.

Activity 1.13 Searching for a Help Topic

An alternative method of locating a Help topic is to use the Search box. The Search box displays in the upper pane of the Help and Support Center window, under the toolbar. In this activity, you search for information about what to do when you are finished using Windows XP.

1 In the **Help and Support Center**, in the **Search** box, click to place the insertion point, type **Log off** and then click the arrow to the right of the Search box to start searching. If text already displays in the Search box, click to the left of the first character, drag to the right to select the text, and then type over the selected text to replace it.

Selected text displays as light text on a dark background, indicating that it is the target for the next action. The Search arrow color varies, depending on how your Help and Support Center is configured, and the ScreenTip may display *Search* or *Start searching*.

In the left pane, Windows XP displays the **Search Results**—topics that relate to the **search text**—for the *Log off* text you typed in the Search box. The Search Results are organized into categories, including Suggested Topics and Full-text Search Matches, as shown in Figure 1.35. The **Suggested Topics** are tasks that are related to the search text; the **Full-text Search Matches** are pages that include the exact search text. Your system may also display the Microsoft Knowledge Base bar, which consists of articles stored on the Microsoft Web site. The number in parentheses next to the category name indicates the number of search result items in the category.

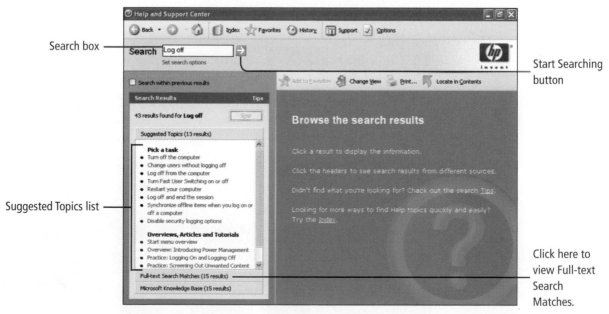

Search box

Start Searching button

Suggested Topics list

Click here to view Full-text Search Matches.

Figure 1.35

2 In the **Search Results** pane, click **Full-text Search Matches** to display the list of related items. In the list, scroll down, and then click the **Log off the computer** text.

In the right pane, the page that contains specific instructions for logging off from the computer displays. Notice that the words typed in the Search box are highlighted on the page.

3 In the **Help and Support Center** title bar, click the **Close** button .

Objective 6
End a Windows XP Session

When you finish your computer work, you should close any open files and programs. You can leave the computer turned on with the Windows XP operating system active if you or anyone else will be using the computer again. If you are finished using the computer, you can shut down Windows XP and turn off the computer.

Activity 1.14 Logging Off

To end your Windows XP session without turning off the computer, you must *log off*. Logging off closes any open programs and files but does not close the Windows XP operating system or turn off the computer. As long as the Windows XP operating system remains in use and the computer is turned on, others can log on without restarting the computer. Some systems require you to log off when you have completed your session at the computer. In this activity, you will log off and then log on again.

1 Before you log off or turn off the computer, be sure to close any open windows.

2 Click **Start** 🏁 **start**, and then at the bottom of the Start menu, click **Log Off**.

The desktop background fades to black and white, and Windows XP displays the Log Off Windows message box, as shown in Figure 1.36.

Figure 1.36

3 In the **Log Off Windows** message box, click **Log Off**.

Windows XP closes your session, but Windows XP remains active. The screen that displays depends on your computing environment. For example, you may see the Windows Welcome screen or a different logon screen.

4 On the screen, log on in the same manner as you did in Activity 1.1.

More Knowledge — Switching Users

To let another individual access his or her account for a brief period of time, use the Switch Users command. Your session remains active so that when the other user is finished, you can quickly switch back to continue your work. To switch users, click Start, and then click Log Off. In the Log Off Windows message box, click Switch Users. The other person can then log on by using the correct logon procedure for the computer. Use this only for brief periods because having multiple users can slow down the operation of Windows XP and your computer.

Activity 1.15 Turning Off the Computer

In this activity, you practice turning off the computer.

1 Click **Start** ![start], and then, from the **Start** menu, click **Turn Off Computer**.

Windows displays the Turn off computer message box, as shown in Figure 1.37. The colors on the desktop fade to black and white until you click a command. Three commands are available: Stand By, Turn Off, and Restart. In **standby mode**, the computer remains on, but the monitor and disk drives are not active. Standby is useful if you are leaving your computer for only a short time. Because standby mode uses less power than regular mode, it is used more often with notebook and laptop computers.

Figure 1.37

2 In the **Turn off computer** message box, click the **Restart** command.

Windows XP logs off, shuts down the computer, and then restarts. Restarting is useful when you want Windows XP to recognize new settings you have made in the hardware or software configuration of your computer.

3 On the screen, follow the procedure for logging on to your computer system.

4 Click **Start** 🏁 start , and then, from the **Start** menu, click **Turn Off Computer**.

5 In the **Turn off computer** message box, click **Turn Off**.

Windows XP logs off and then shuts down the computer.

6 If necessary, turn off your computer monitor.

On some systems, the monitor automatically turns off at the same time as the computer. On most systems, however, you must manually turn off the monitor.

7 Check your *Chapter Assignment Sheet* or your *Course Syllabus,* or consult your instructor, to determine whether you are to submit the printed pages that are the result of this project.

End You have completed Project 1A ━━━━━━━━━━━━━━━━━━━

Summary

In this chapter, you practiced how to start and exit Windows XP and how to log on to display the Windows desktop. You practiced using the mouse to click, double-click, right-click, and drag, and you identified the common elements of the Windows desktop, including desktop icons, the Start button, and the taskbar. You used the Start menu to start three Accessories programs—WordPad, Paint, and Calculator—and practiced maximizing, minimizing, redisplaying, and restoring windows. You arranged, resized, and moved windows and practiced switching among open windows. You activated commands from toolbars, menus, and dialog boxes, and you used the Paste command to place a captured image of your screen in a WordPad document. You used the Help and Support Center to find information about maximizing and minimizing windows, printing a Help page, and logging off the computer. Finally, you practiced logging off, restarting the computer, and shutting down Windows XP.

In This Chapter You Practiced How To

- Start Windows XP
- Start and Close a Program
- Work with a Window
- Use Commands in a Windows XP Program
- Use Windows XP Help
- End a Windows XP Session

Concepts Assessments

Matching   Match each term in the second column with its correct definition in the first column by writing the letter of the term on the blank line in front of the correct definition.

_____ **1.** The working area of the Windows XP screen.

_____ **2.** The Windows XP toolbar, usually displayed across the bottom of the desktop screen, which contains the Start button, the notification area, and buttons and icons for programs.

_____ **3.** A set of instructions to the computer.

_____ **4.** The basic unit of storage that enables a computer to distinguish one set of information from another and that can consist of a program or your own data.

_____ **5.** An arrow or other symbol whose location indicates the current position of the mouse on the screen.

_____ **6.** To press and release the left mouse button one time.

_____ **7.** A area of the screen that displays information or a program, such as a letter or calculator.

_____ **8.** A menu that displays the most commonly used commands related to the item clicked.

_____ **9.** The bar, which is blue by default, at the top of a window in which the program name and program icon display.

_____ **10.** To arrange and size all open windows so that they display without overlapping.

_____ **11.** The overlapping arrangement of multiple open windows on the desktop so that only the title bar of each window is visible.

_____ **12.** A two-headed arrow that displays when the mouse is correctly positioned for dragging a border to change the size of the current window.

_____ **13.** To move within the contents of a list or window by using the scroll bar.

_____ **14.** A standard setting used by a program when the person using the program does not specify an alternative.

_____ **15.** A special window that prompts you to enter information in order to complete a task.

A Cascade

B Click

C Default

D Desktop

E Dialog box

F File

G Mouse pointer

H Program

I Resize pointer

J Scroll

K Shortcut menu

L Taskbar

M Tile

N Title bar

O Window

Concepts Assessments (continued)

Fill in the Blank Write the correct answer in the space provided.

1. A graphic representation of an object that you can select and open, such as a drive, a folder, a document, or a program is a(n) _____.

2. System information, such as the time, can be displayed on the taskbar in the _____.

3. When you position your pointer on an onscreen element, the message that displays is a(n) _____.

4. A secondary menu that displays when you select a command that includes an arrow on the right side of the command name is called a(n) _____.

5. To return a window to its previous size and position, click the _____ button.

6. A page within a dialog box that displays a related group of commands and options is called a(n) _____.

7. A dialog box button that you use to select one out of a set of options is called a(n) _____.

8. The temporary storage area that stores the data most recently cut or copied so that it can be pasted into a new location is called the _____.

9. When you want to print a page that is wider than it is tall, you must choose _____ orientation.

10. When you want to print a page that is taller than it is wide, you must choose _____ orientation.

Project 1B — Supplies

Objectives: *Start Windows XP; Start and Close a Program; Work with a Window; and Use Commands in a Windows XP Program.*

In the following Skill Assessment, you will use Windows XP to start the WordPad program. You will size and position the WordPad window, use commands to format the text and insert the current date, and then print your document. Your document will look similar to Figure 1.38.

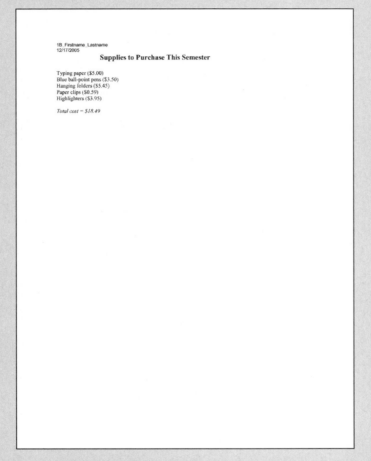

1B_Firstname_Lastname
12/17/2005
Supplies to Purchase This Semester

Typing paper ($5.00)
Blue ball-point pens ($3.50)
Hanging folders ($5.45)
Paper clips ($0.59)
Highlighters ($3.95)

Total cost = $18.49

Figure 1.38

1. Turn on your computer, and then log on by using the procedure required for your computer system. On the taskbar, click the **Start** button.

2. From the **Start** menu, point to **All Programs**, point to **Accessories**, and then, on the Accessories menu, click **WordPad**. Recall that WordPad is a simple word-processing program that comes with Windows XP.

(Project 1B–Supplies continues on the next page)

(Project 1B–Supplies continued)

3. In the WordPad window, take a moment to identify the common window elements, including the **title bar**, the **window control buttons**, the **menu bar**, and the **toolbars**.

4. Display the **Start** menu again, point to **All Programs**, point to **Accessories**, and then click **Calculator** to open the Calculator program. Recall that you can have more than one window open at a time but that only one window can be active. Notice that the Calculator title bar is darker than the WordPad title bar, indicating that the Calculator is active.

5. In the **Calculator** window, click the **Minimize** button to minimize the window to a button on the taskbar. A program that is minimized is still active and available but not occupying space on the desktop. On the taskbar, click the **Calculator** button to redisplay the Calculator window.

6. On the taskbar, click the **WordPad** button to make WordPad active. On the taskbar, right-click a blank area, and then, on the displayed shortcut menu, click **Tile Windows Vertically**. The two windows display side by side on your screen.

7. In the WordPad window, click the **Maximize** button to resize the WordPad window to fill the desktop.

8. In the WordPad window, type **1B_Firstname_Lastname** and then press ⏎Enter. Be sure to type your own name for *Firstname* and *Lastname*. The text displays in the default font, Arial, and at the default size, 10.

9. On the WordPad menu bar, click **Insert** and then, from the **Insert** menu, click **Date and Time**. Recall that clicking a menu command followed by an ellipsis displays a dialog box.

10. In the **Date and Time** dialog box, from the **Available formats** list, click the date that displays as the two-digit number of the month, the two-digit number of the day, and all four digits of the year, separated by slashes, and then click **OK**. Recall that clicking OK in a dialog box carries out the command.

11. On the keyboard, press ⏎Enter. Recall that each time you press ⏎Enter, WordPad begins a new line.

12. On the WordPad Format bar, click the **Bold** button, and then click the **Center** button. Recall that some buttons—such as Bold—are toggles that can be turned either on or off.

13. On the WordPad Format bar, click the **Font arrow**. On the Font list, scroll down and click **Times New Roman**. On the Format bar, click the **Font Size arrow**, and then, on the Font Size list, click **16**. Recall that a font is a set of characters with the same design and shape and that font size is measured in points, with each point equal to $\frac{1}{72}$ of an inch.

(Project 1B–Supplies continues on the next page)

(Project 1B–Supplies continued)

14. On the keyboard press Enter, type **Supplies to Purchase This Semester** and then press Enter two times.

15. On the Format bar, click the **Bold** button to turn off the feature, click the **Align Left** button which is the button to the left of the Center button, and then change the **Font Size** to **12**. Type the following list:

Typing paper ($5.00)
Blue ball-point pens ($3.50)
Hanging folders ($5.45)
Paper clips ($0.59)
Highlighters ($3.95)

16. Press Enter two times. On the Format bar, click the **Italic** button, type **Total cost =** and then press Spacebar.

17. On the taskbar, click the **Calculator** taskbar button to make the Calculator window active.

18. On the Calculator, click **5.00**, click the addition button, click **3.50**, click the addition button, click **5.45**, click the addition button, click **.59**, click the addition button, click **3.95**, and then click the equal sign button. Notice that in the box under the Calculator menu bar, the number *18.49* displays. This is the total cost of the supplies.

19. On the taskbar, click the **Document - WordPad button** to make the WordPad window active, and then type **$18.49**

20. Compare your screen with Figure 1.38. On the toolbar, click the **Print** button.

21. Close the WordPad window, and then, in the **message box**, click **No** to close the WordPad program without saving the document. Close the Calculator window.

 You have completed Project 1B _____

Project 1C — Capturing a Help Screen

Objectives: *Use Commands in a Windows XP Program; Use Windows XP Help; and End a Windows XP Session.*

In the following Skill Assessment, you will use Windows XP Help to look up information about WordPad, and you will capture and print a Help screen. You will end your Windows XP session. Your captured screen and WordPad document will look similar to Figure 1.39.

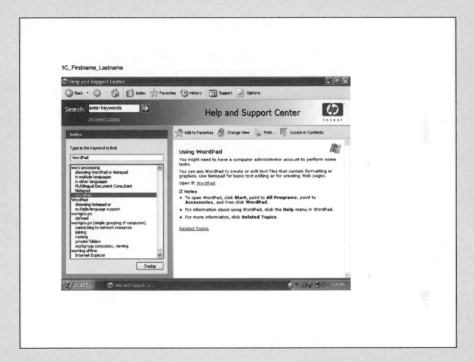

Figure 1.39

1. Display the **Start** menu, and then click **Help and Support** to display the Windows XP Help and Support Center. On the toolbar, click the **Index** button.

2. In the **Type in the keyword to find** box, type **Word** to scroll the index list to the entries that begin with the text *Word*.

3. In the **Index** list, under **word processing**, click the indented **WordPad** text, and then click **Display**. The Using WordPad page displays in the right pane.

4. On the keyboard, press PrtScr. Recall that this key captures an image of the whole screen and places it in a temporary storage area called the Clipboard.

(**Project 1C**–Capturing a Help Screen continues on the next page)

(Project 1C–Capturing a Help Screen continued)

5. Click the **Start** button , point to **All Programs**, point to **Accessories**, and then click **WordPad**. Click the **Maximize** button, if necessary.

6. In the WordPad window, type **1C_Firstname_Lastname** using your own name. Press Enter two times. From the WordPad menu, click **Edit**, and then click **Paste**.

7. From the WordPad menu bar, click **File**, and then click **Page Setup**. In the displayed **Page Setup** dialog box, under **Orientation**, click the **Landscape** option button, and then click **OK**.

8. In the upper left corner of the image, position the pointer over the sizing handle. When the pointer changes to a diagonal resize pointer, drag to the right and down about one inch. Release the mouse button.

9. Click **File**, **Print Preview**. Be sure the captured screen fits on the page, as shown in Figure 1.39. If not, close the preview window, and reduce the size of the image until it fits on one page.

10. In the Print Preview title bar, click the red **Close** button. Alternatively, you can click the large Close button in the Print Preview toolbar.

11. From the WordPad toolbar, click the **Print** button.

12. From the **File** menu, click **Exit**. When prompted to save your work, click **No**.

13. In the Help and Support Center window, click the **Close** button in the upper right corner of the window.

14. From the taskbar, click **Start** to display the **Start** menu. Click **Turn Off Computer** to display the **Turn off computer** message box. Click **Turn Off**. If necessary, turn off your computer monitor.

End You have completed Project 1C

Project 1D — My Documents

Objectives: *Start Windows XP; Start and Close a Program; Work with a Window; Use Commands in a Windows XP Program; Use Windows XP Help; and End a Windows XP Session.*

In the following Performance Assessment, you will log on to Windows XP and use the Windows XP Help and Support Center to find information about the My Documents folder. You will display the My Documents icon on the desktop and use it to display the My Documents window. You will start the WordPad program and arrange the windows on the desktop. You will use program commands in WordPad to type the names of the items in the My Documents window. You will print the WordPad file, close all open windows, and end your Windows XP session. Before printing, the desktop will look similar to Figure 1.40.

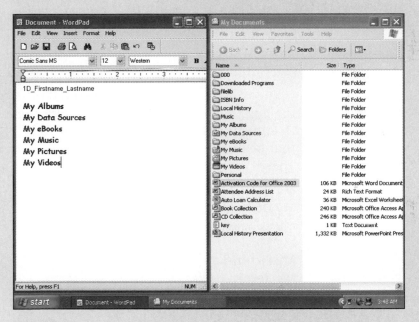

Figure 1.40

1. Turn on your computer. Log on to Windows XP by using the procedure required for your computer system.

2. Display the **Start** menu, and then display the **Help and Support Center** window. Display the **Index**, and then, in the **Type in the keyword to find** box, type **My Documents**

3. In the **Index** list, under **My Documents**, click **overview**, or a similar topic. In the displayed **Topics Found** dialog box, choose one of the two topics, and then click the **Display** button. Take a moment to review the results.

4. Use any appropriate method to close the **Help and Support Center**.

(Project 1D–My Documents continues on the next page)

(Project 1D–My Documents continued)

5. Display the **Start** menu, point to **My Documents**, and right-click. On the shortcut menu, check to see whether there is a check mark next to the command Show on Desktop. Recall that a check mark indicates that the item already displays. If there is no check mark, then on the shortcut menu, click **Show on Desktop**.

6. From the **Start** menu, point to **All Programs**, point to **Accessories**, and then click **WordPad**. Minimize the WordPad window.

7. On the desktop, double-click the **My Documents** icon to open the **My Documents** window. Notice the names of the items in the My Documents window.

8. On the taskbar, click the **Document-Wordpad** button to redisplay its window. On the taskbar, right-click a blank area, and then, from the shortcut menu, click **Tile Windows Vertically** to arrange the two open windows on the desktop.

9. In the WordPad window, type **1D_Firstname_Lastname** and then press Enter two times.

10. In the WordPad window, change the **Font** to **Comic Sans MS** and the **Font Size** to **12**. Examine the folder names in the My Documents window. In the WordPad window, type a list of the items that begin *My* in the list of folders in your **My Documents** folder. These may include (but are not limited to) the following:

    My Data Sources
    My Downloads
    My eBooks
    My Music
    My Pictures
    My Received Files
    My Videos

11. From the WordPad toolbar, click the **Print** button to print the file.

12. Use any appropriate method to close the WordPad and My Documents windows. Do not save the WordPad file.

13. Right-click the My Documents icon on your desktop. From the shortcut menu, click **Delete**. Click **Yes** when prompted to remove the icon from the desktop.

14. Click **Start**. Click **Turn Off Computer** to display the **Turn off computer** dialog box, and then click **Turn Off**. If necessary, turn off your computer monitor.

End You have completed Project 1D

Project 1E — Definitions

Objectives: *Start Windows XP; Start and Close a Program; Work with a Window; Use Commands in a Windows XP Program; Use Windows XP Help; and End a Windows XP Session.*

In this Mastery Assessment, you will log on to your computer and then start the Help and Support Center and WordPad. You will look up the definitions of two terms, type the information into a WordPad document, and then print the WordPad file. When you are finished, you will close all open windows and end your Windows XP session. Your completed WordPad document will look similar to Figure 1.41.

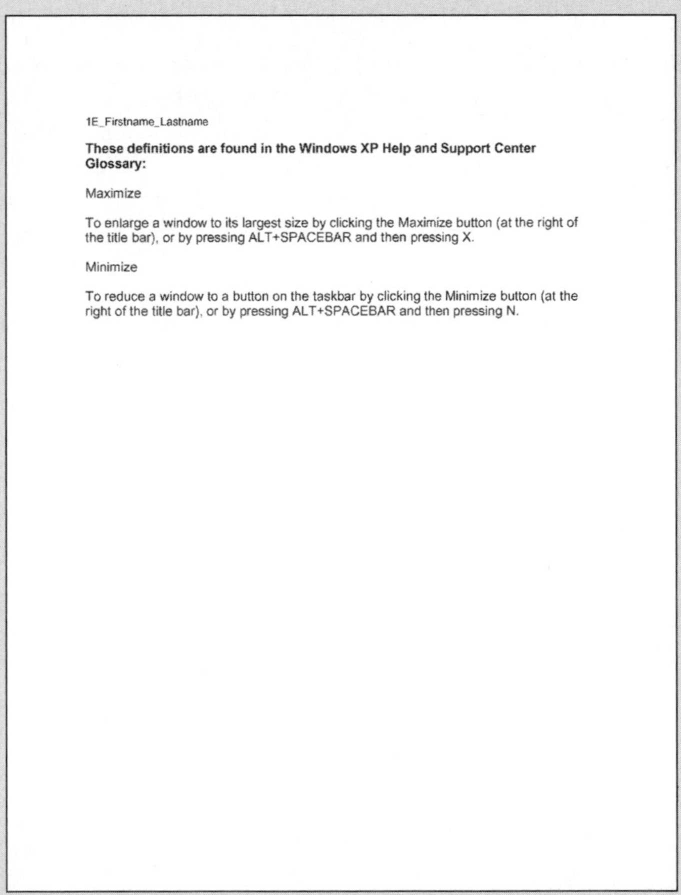

1E_Firstname_Lastname

These definitions are found in the Windows XP Help and Support Center Glossary:

Maximize

To enlarge a window to its largest size by clicking the Maximize button (at the right of the title bar), or by pressing ALT+SPACEBAR and then pressing X.

Minimize

To reduce a window to a button on the taskbar by clicking the Minimize button (at the right of the title bar), or by pressing ALT+SPACEBAR and then pressing N.

Figure 1.41

1. Start your computer and display the Windows XP desktop. From the **Start** menu, click **Help and Support**. Search for the term *maximize*, and then go to the Glossary entry where the term is defined.

2. Start **WordPad**. Recall that WordPad is located on the Accessories menu.

(Project 1E–Definitions continues on the next page)

Mastery Assessment (continued)

(Project 1E–Definitions continued)

3. In WordPad, type **1E_Firstname_Lastname** and then press Enter two times.

4. In WordPad, change the **Font** to **12-point Arial, Bold**.

5. Type **These definitions are found in the Windows XP Help and Support Center Glossary:** Press Enter two times. Turn off **Bold**.

6. Resize and position the two windows so that you can see both the definition for *maximize* and the WordPad window at the same time. It may be necessary to click Display again to view the Maximize definition. In the WordPad window, type **Maximize** and press Enter two times. Then type the definition from the Help and Support Center Glossary. Press Enter two times.

7. In the **Help and Support Center**, locate the definition for the term *minimize*. Notice that when you click in the Help and Support Center, the WordPad window is hidden. Make the WordPad window active, type the term **Minimize** and press Enter two times, and then type the definition from the Help and Support Center Glossary.

8. Close the Help and Support Center window and maximize the WordPad window. Compare your screen with Figure 1.41.

9. **Print** one copy of the **WordPad file**, and then close WordPad without saving the file. Log off and turn off Windows XP, and then turn off your computer monitor if necessary.

End You have completed Project 1E ──────────────────────

Problem-Solving Assessment

Project 1F — Word Processing

Objectives: *Start Windows XP; Start and Close a Program; Work with a Window; Use Commands in a Windows XP Program; Use Windows XP Help; and End a Windows XP Session.*

In this Problem-Solving Assessment, practice using Windows XP to start and close programs, to control windows, and to use commands. Use the Windows XP Help and Support Center to locate information about choosing a program for writing a document. After reading the Help information, type some key points or recommendations in a WordPad file, and then print the file.

 You have completed Project 1F

On the Internet

Learning More About Windows XP

Connect to the Internet, open a Web browser such as Internet Explorer, and then type **http://www.microsoft.com** to go to the Microsoft Corp. Web site. Under **Product Families**, click the **Windows** product family link to go to the Windows product page, and then, under **Products**, click the **Windows XP** link. From the Windows XP home page, explore some of the features available in Windows XP. See whether you can find out what features Windows XP offers that previous versions of Windows do not.

GO! with Help

Gathering System Information

You can use the Windows XP Help and Support program to list the components of your computer system.

1. Log on to **Windows XP**.

2. Open the **Start** menu, and then click **Help and Support**.

3. In the **Search** box, type **About My Computer** and then, under **Suggested Topics**, click **Get information about your computer**.

4. In the list of tasks on the right side of the screen, click **View general system information about this computer**.

5. If you want to print the information, click the **Print** button.

6. In the Help and Support window, click the **Close** button to close the window.

2 chaptertwo

Creating and Storing Files

In this chapter you will: complete this project **and** practice these skills.

Project 2A Creating and Organizing Files and Folders	Objectives
	• Create, Save, and Print a File
	• Create Shortcuts and Folders on the Windows XP Desktop
	• Work with My Computer
	• Set Folder Options

Creating and Storing Files

Much of the work you will do on a computer involves creating files. After you create a document, you need to save it before you turn off the computer. When the computer is turned off, any work you have completed is lost unless you have saved it to a storage device. When you save your work, it is saved as a file and is usually stored on the desktop or on a disk drive.

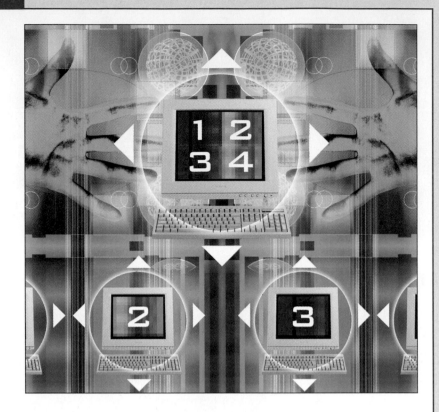

Managing Folders and Files with My Computer

To Windows XP, the storage devices that make up your computer system are like the filing cabinets you use to store paper folders and files. You tell Windows where to store the items and then where to find those items again when you need them.

For example, imagine you are searching for a new job. You could organize the filing system on your computer by creating one main folder, named *Job Search*, for storing all files related to job hunting. In the *Job Search* folder, you could create another folder to store copies of cover letters and another folder to store resumes.

2A

Project 2A Creating and Organizing Files and Folders

Computers store vast amounts of information. Even brand-new computers come with several folders and files already in place. In this project, you will use Windows XP to create and save files, and you will create folders in which to store the files.

MEMO TO: Mary Nelson

FROM: Firstname Lastname

DATE: November 24

SUBJECT: Student Orientation

Thank you for volunteering to help during Winter Orientation. High school seniors have a difficult decision to make in choosing a college. Your enthusiastic participation will be one of the key factors in helping these students decide to attend our school.

There will be a meeting of the Winter Orientation volunteers at 10 a.m. on Saturday morning, December 12. We will meet in the lobby of the Union.

Lunch will be provided at the Union. If you have any special dietary needs, please let me know.

In Activities 2.1 through 2.14, you will create two memos to students who have volunteered to help during the winter orientation for prospective students. You will create, save, edit, and print memos about the orientation, and you will create and name folders in which to store the files. You will also change the look of the screen that displays the files and folders. The completed memo files will look similar to Figure 2.1. You will save the memo files as *2A_Orientation_Firstname_Lastname* and *2A_Orientation2_Firstname_Lastname*.

MEMO TO: Bill McMahon

FROM: Firstname Lastname

DATE: November 24

SUBJECT: Student Orientation

Thank you for volunteering to help during Winter Orientation. High school seniors have a difficult decision to make in choosing a college. Your enthusiastic participation will be one of the key factors in helping these students decide to attend our school.

There will be a meeting of the Winter Orientation volunteers at 10 a.m. on Saturday morning, December 12. We will meet in the lobby of the Union.

Lunch will be provided at the Union. If you have any special dietary needs, please let me know.

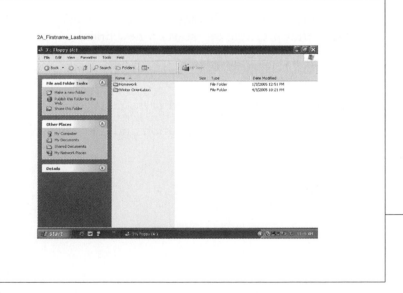

Figure 2.1
Project 2A—Orientation

Objective 1
Create, Save, and Print a File

Recall that a file is the unit of storage that enables a computer to distinguish one set of information from another, and which can consist of a program or your own data. After you use a program to create a file, you enter information in the file and then save the file so that you can use it again in the future. In Activities 2.1 through 2.5 you create, save, edit, open, preview, and print a memo.

Activity 2.1 Entering and Editing Text in a File

In this activity, you will use WordPad to create and edit a memo to a volunteer. Recall that WordPad is a simple word-processing program that comes with Windows XP.

1 Click the **Start** button **start**, point to **All Programs**, point to **Accessories**, and then click **WordPad**. If necessary, in the title bar, click the Maximize button.

The WordPad window opens and displays a new, blank *document*. A document is any self-contained piece of work created and saved using a program. Usually, a document is text based and is created in a word-processing program.

2 In the WordPad window, locate the insertion point.

Recall that the insertion point is a vertical blinking bar that indicates the location at which the text you type will be entered. In a new document, the insertion point always displays in the upper left corner of the document.

3 At the insertion point, type **MEMO TO: Bill McMahon** and then, on your keyboard, press (Enter) two times.

As you type, the characters display to the left of the insertion point. Recall that pressing (Enter) starts a new line.

4 Type **FROM: Firstname Lastname**—using your own name—and then press (Enter) two times.

5 Type **DATE: November 24** and press (Enter) two times.

6 Type **SUBJECT: Winter Orientation** and then press (Enter) two times.

7 Type the following paragraph:

Thank you for volunteering to help during Winter Orientation. High school seniors have a difficult decision to make in choosing a college. Your enthusiastic participation will be one of the key factors in helping these students decide to attend our school.

Notice that when a current line is full, the text automatically moves the next whole word to the start of the next line. By default, WordPad is set to move text to the next line when the current line reaches the right edge of the WordPad window. The line length of your text may differ, depending on the width of your monitor or the width of the WordPad window if the window is not maximized.

8 On your keyboard, press Enter two times, type the following paragraph, and then compare your screen with Figure 2.2.

There will be a meeting of the Winter Orientation volunteers at 10 a.m. on Saturday morning, December 12. We will meet in front of the Union.

Figure 2.2

9 On your keyboard, press ← fourteen times.

The insertion point moves to the right of the word *front*.

10 Press Bksp five times to remove the word *front*.

Pressing Bksp removes one character to the left of the insertion point.

11 Type **the lobby** and then press and hold → until the insertion point is at the end of the sentence.

This action is known as **editing**, which means to make a change to an existing document or file. When you press and hold an arrow key—or a key for a character—that key will repeat itself until you stop pressing the key.

More Knowledge — Moving the Insertion Point in a Document

You can move the insertion point to a different location within the text by pressing the arrow keys on your keyboard. The up and down arrow keys move the insertion point up and down one line, and the left and right arrow keys move the insertion point one character to the left or right. Alternatively, you can point to the new location and then click to move the insertion point.

---

12 Locate the paragraph that begins *Thank you*, point to the left of the uppercase *T* in the word *Thank*, and then drag down to the last character in the document—the period at the end of the last paragraph. Compare your screen with Figure 2.3.

Dragging selects the text. Recall that selecting an item indicates that the selected item is the target of the next action.

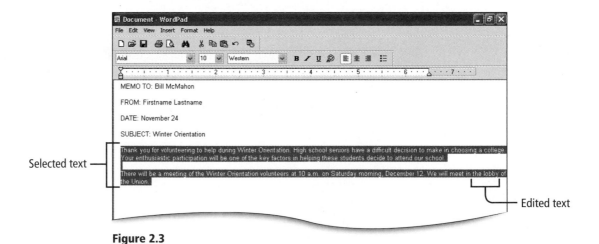

Selected text

Edited text

Figure 2.3

13 On the Format bar, click the **Font Size button arrow** 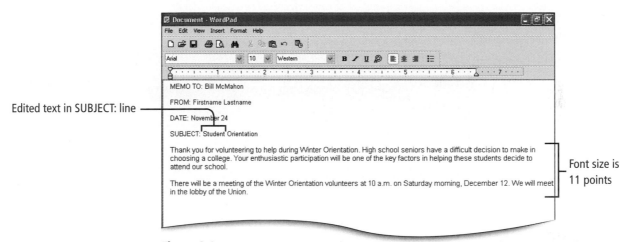, and then, on the displayed list, click **11**.

This changes the font size of the selected text to 11 points. Recall that font size is the height of an uppercase letter in a font set, measured in points. Also recall that a point is ½ of an inch.

14 In the WordPad document, click anywhere in the document window to cancel the selection. Alternatively, you can press any of the arrow keys to deselect the text.

15 On the *SUBJECT:* line, double-click to select the word **Winter**, type **Student** and then compare your screen with Figure 2.4.

Notice that *Student* replaces *Winter*. Double-clicking a word is a way to select an individual word.

Edited text in SUBJECT: line

Font size is 11 points

Figure 2.4

Alert!

If You Accidentally Delete Text

When you select text, any actions you take are reflected in the selected text. For example, you might want to select text and change the emphasis to bold, as you practiced earlier. If you forget to deselect the text, the next letter you type will replace the selected text. Also, pressing the Spacebar will replace the selected text with a single space. If this happens, recall that you can click the Undo button to reverse the last action.

16 Leave this document open for the next activity.

Activity 2.2 Saving a File on the Desktop

Most documents that you create will need to be stored for future reference or for editing. Windows XP has several storage locations that you can use. Saving a document to the desktop is useful for important or frequently edited files. The desktop is also a place where you can store a file that you know you will need to revise in the near future. In this activity, you will save your WordPad document on the desktop with the file name *2A_Orientation_Firstname_Lastname.*

1 On the WordPad toolbar, click the **Save** button ▣. Alternatively, from the File menu, click Save.

Because the file has not been saved yet, the Save As dialog box displays, as shown in Figure 2.5. In this dialog box, you enter both the file name and the location in which you want the file stored. The default file name is *Document.*

Default file name —

Default file name

Figure 2.5

2 If necessary, in the File name box, drag the word *Document* to select it.

Recall that when you type, you replace selected text.

3 In the **File name** box, over the selected text, substitute your name and type **2A_Orientation_Firstname_Lastname**

This will be the name of the file when you save it. Some computer programs cannot process file names with spaces, so the underscores between the words take the place of the spaces.

4 On the shortcut bar on the left side of the **Save As** dialog box, click the **Desktop** button. Compare your dialog box with Figure 2.6.

Clicking the Desktop button is a shortcut to saving a file to the desktop. When you store files in folders, you will need to use the Save in box at the top of the Save As dialog box or use the My Documents or My Computer buttons.

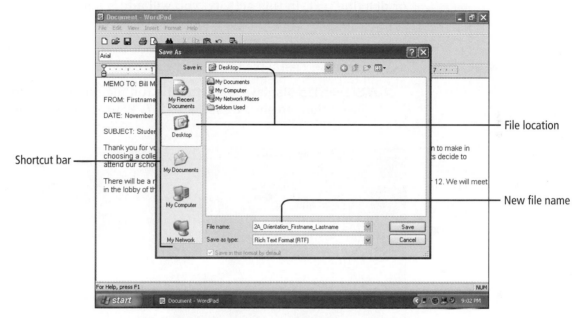

Figure 2.6

5 Near the bottom of the **Save As** dialog box, click the **Save** button.

The file is saved on your desktop.

6 In the WordPad title bar, click the **Close** button ☒. Close any other open windows.

Notice that the new icon displays on your desktop. Because space is restricted on the desktop, only the first few letters of your file name may display.

More Knowledge — Special Characters in File Names

A file name can have up to 255 characters, including spaces and periods, but a name cannot start with a space. Also, some programs and network devices cannot read names that are longer than eight characters or that contain spaces. A good practice is to use the underscore character in place of spaces in file names because it helps to separate words but does not cause errors that can occur when you use spaces. The following nine characters cannot be used in a file or folder name: \ / : * ? " < > |

Activity 2.3 Opening a File and Saving Changes

You can open a saved file at any time to make changes such as inserting or deleting text. In this activity, you will add a short paragraph to the *2A_Orientation_Firstname_Lastname* file.

1 On the desktop, locate and then point to the 2A_Orientation_Firstname_Lastname icon that you created in the preceding activity.

A ScreenTip displays, showing the full file name and other file information, as shown in Figure 2.7. Your icon may look different.

2A_Orientation_Firstname_Lastname icon

ScreenTip displays file information

The location of your icon may differ

Figure 2.7

2 Right-click the 2A_Orientation_Firstname_Lastname icon. From the shortcut menu, point to **Open With**, and then in the **Open With** dialog box, under **Programs**, click **WordPad**. Click **OK**.

The shortcut menu displays the programs installed on your computer that can open the WordPad file. Because WordPad saves in a universal word-processing format called **Rich Text Format (RTF)**, any word-processing programs installed on your computer—such as Microsoft Word or Corel WordPerfect®—will be displayed in the Open With list in addition to WordPad.

3 In WordPad, click to position the insertion point at the end of the last paragraph. Press Enter two times.

4 Type **Lunch will be provided at the Union. If you have any special dietary needs, please let me know.**

5 From the **View** menu, click **Options**.

This displays the Options dialog box, with the Rich Text tab active.

6 Under **Word wrap**, click to select the **Wrap to ruler** option button, and then click **OK**.

Word wrap is a feature that automatically breaks lines of text to the next line when the current line is full. By default, WordPad text is set to move text to the next line when the current line reaches the end of the WordPad window. Selecting **Wrap to ruler** changes the display to wrap the text when the current line reaches the page margins of the WordPad document, as indicated by the ruler. Compare your screen with Figure 2.8. The text in your document may wrap at a different place in each paragraph.

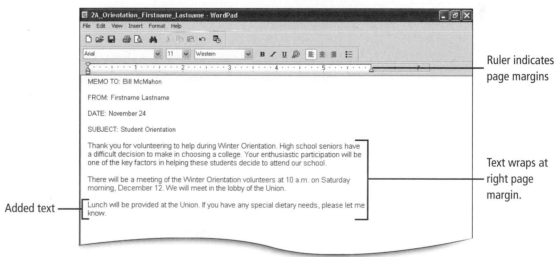

Figure 2.8

7 On the WordPad toolbar, click the **Save** button 🖫 to save your work.

Notice that this time, no dialog box displays when you click the Save button. The only time the Save As dialog box displays is when you are saving a document for the first time. When you save a file that has already been saved, the revised file replaces the original file.

Another Way

Saving a File

You can save a file by clicking Save from the File menu, although clicking the Save button requires fewer steps. You can also use the Ctrl + S keyboard shortcut to save the file without moving your hands from the keyboard. It is a good idea to get in the habit of saving your work every few minutes.

Activity 2.4 Saving a File Using a Different File Name

If you need to create two or three similar documents, it is often easiest to create and save one document and then make changes and save the file again using a different file name. In this activity, you will save a second version of your WordPad document as *2A_Orientation2_Firstname_Lastname.*

1 In the *MEMO TO: Bill McMahon* line, drag to select **Bill McMahon** and then type **Mary Nelson**

The new text replaces the selected text.

2 From the **File** menu, click **Save As**.

The Save As dialog box displays, with the current file name in File Name box.

3 In the **File name** box, click to position the insertion point at the end of *Orientation* but before the underscore, and then type **2** Be sure the Desktop button is selected on the shortcut bar. Compare your dialog box with the one shown in Figure 2.9.

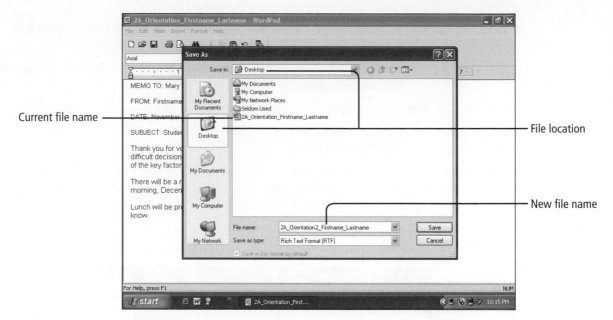

Current file name

File location

New file name

Figure 2.9

4 Near the bottom of the **Save As** dialog box, click the **Save** button.

The file is saved on your desktop.

5 Minimize your WordPad window and check to be sure that you have two memo files on the desktop. Leave the document open for the next activity.

Activity 2.5 Previewing and Printing a File

Before you print a file, you can ***preview*** it, which means you can see onscreen how the document will look when printed on paper. Earlier you practiced previewing a document to be sure a screen capture would fit. You can also enlarge your view of the page to look closely at the document and reduce the view so that you see the entire page. In this activity, you will practice previewing a document and printing from the Print Preview window.

1 On the taskbar, click the **WordPad** button to display the WordPad window.

2 On the WordPad toolbar, click the **Print Preview** button 🔍. Alternatively, from the File menu, click Print Preview.

The file displays onscreen as it will print. Notice that the entire page initially displays.

3 On the Print Preview toolbar, click the **Zoom In** button [Zoom In] two times to magnify the preview onscreen, and then compare your screen with Figure 2.10.

Clicking Zoom In one time magnifies the page, and clicking it a second time magnifies it further. Notice also that dashed lines indicate the page margins.

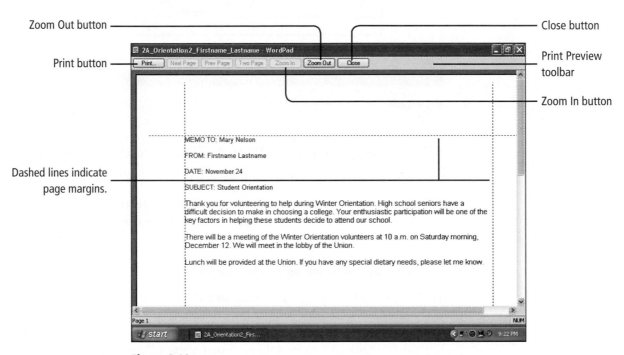

Zoom Out button

Print button

Close button

Print Preview toolbar

Zoom In button

Dashed lines indicate page margins.

Figure 2.10

More Knowledge — Zooming In and Out to Examine a Document

When you *zoom* a document, you change the size of the display on the screen without changing the size of the text in the document. *Zoom in* to increase— or *magnify*—the view of the document so that you can get a closer look at details. *Zoom out* to reduce the view of the document that so you can get an overall look at the entire page. Note that you cannot make changes to your document directly from the Print Preview window; you must close the Print Preview window and return to the document to make any changes.

4 On the Print Preview toolbar, click the **Zoom Out** button [Zoom Out] two times to return to the default display size.

5 On the Print Preview toolbar, click the **Close** button [Close].

6 On the WordPad toolbar, click the **Print** button [🖨].

The document is sent to the printer. If you have been asked to submit this printout to your instructor, hold it until the end of this project.

7 From the **File** menu, click **2 2A_Orientation_Firstname_Lastname**.

By default, WordPad keeps track of the last four documents that were edited using the program and places them in the File menu for quick access. When you open a second document in WordPad, the first document closes.

Alert!

If Your Document Does Not Display in the File Menu

If your work was interrupted after you last edited the 2A_Orientation_ Firstname_Lastname file and your file does not display in the File menu, return to the desktop and right-click the document icon. From the shortcut menu, click Open With, and then click WordPad.

8 From the **File** menu, click **Print**.

The Print dialog box displays. The options in the Print dialog box enable you to control which pages in a multipage document are printed, which printer you will use, and the number of copies you would like to have printed.

9 Under **Page Range**, click the **Pages** option button.

Notice that the default value in the Pages box is 1-65535, which ensures that all pages in a document—even a very long document— will print.

10 In the **Pages** box, over the selected default value, type **1** and then, in the **Number of copies spin box**, click the **up arrow** to increase the value to **2**. Compare your screen with Figure 2.11.

A *spin box* is a small box with upward-pointing and downward-pointing arrows that enable you to move—spin—through a set of values by clicking. Alternatively, you can type a value directly in the box.

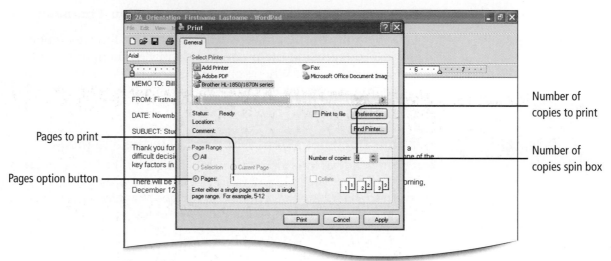

Pages to print

Pages option button

Number of copies to print

Number of copies spin box

Figure 2.11

11 In the **Print** dialog box, under **Select Printer**, click the name of the printer to which you will be printing, and then be sure that the printer has paper and that it is online.

Online means that a device—in this case, the printer—is connected correctly, turned on, and available for operation.

12 In the **Print** dialog box, click **Print**.

The Print dialog box closes, and two copies of the document are sent to the selected printer for printing. If you have been asked to submit these printouts to your instructor, hold them until the end of this project.

13 From the **View** menu, click **Options**. In the displayed **Options** dialog box, under **Word wrap**, click to select the **Wrap to window** option button, and then click **OK**.

This changes the word wrap setting back to the default.

14 In the WordPad window, click the **Close** button ☒.

Objective 2
Create Shortcuts and Folders on the Windows XP Desktop

You can also create new folders and **shortcuts** on the desktop. Recall that a shortcut is an icon on the desktop that you can double-click to immediately access a program, text or data file, or folders. Shortcuts are used to quickly access items that would otherwise require several mouse clicks. Create a shortcut when you do not want to—or cannot—store the actual item on the desktop. For example, if the actual program, file, or folder is located on another computer that is connected to your computer, or if it is a device such as a removable disk drive, you may be unable to move it to the desktop. In Activities 2.6 through 2.8, you will create a new folder on the desktop and place the *2A_Orientation_Firstname_Lastname* and the *2A_Orientation2_Firstname_Lastname* files that are already on the desktop into the new folder. You will also create a desktop shortcut to your removable disk drive.

Activity 2.6 Creating Folders on the Desktop

It takes only a few files to make a desktop appear cluttered to the point where files and programs are hard to find. This problem has two solutions. The first is to be careful to put only very important files on the desktop. The second is to create a folder in which you can store similar files.

1 On the desktop, right-click a blank area. From the displayed shortcut menu, point to **New**, and then click **Folder**. With the default *New Folder* name highlighted, type **Orientation** and then press Enter.

The new folder icon displays on the desktop, as shown in Figure 2.12. The folder icon on your screen may display in a different location from as the one shown, depending on where you clicked.

Folder icon

WordPad
document icons

Figure 2.12

2 On the desktop, drag the **2A_Orientation_Firstname_Lastname** file to the **Orientation** folder. When the Orientation folder changes to a darker color, release the mouse button.

Because you moved the file into the folder, the file icon no longer displays on the desktop. Recall that to drag means to point to an item you want to move, press and hold the left mouse button, drag the item to a new location, and then release the mouse button.

3 On the desktop, *right-drag*—drag an item using the right mouse button—the **2A_Orientation2_Firstname_Lastname** file to the **Orientation** folder.

When you release the mouse button after right-dragging an item, a shortcut menu displays.

4 From the shortcut menu, click **Copy Here**.

The file is copied to the folder, but the original copy remains on your desktop.

5 Double-click the **Orientation** folder.

A window opens, displaying the contents of the folder, and the folder name displays in the title bar, as shown in Figure 2.13. The contents could include files, folders, or shortcuts. Your view may differ.

Folder name ——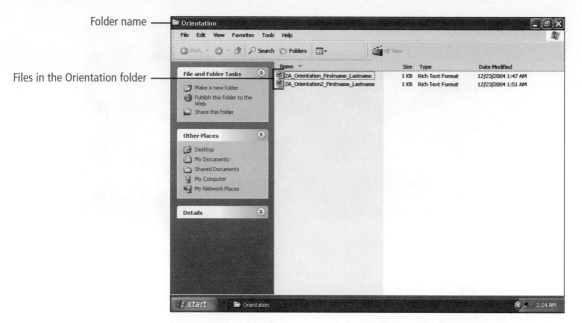

Files in the Orientation folder ——

Figure 2.13

▣6 Confirm that the **2A_Orientation_Firstname_Lastname** file and the **2A_Orientation2_Firstname_Lastname** file display.

▣7 In the Orientation window, click the **Close** button ☒.

Activity 2.7 Creating Shortcuts on the Desktop

You can also create shortcuts on the desktop. Recall that a shortcut is an icon on the desktop that you can double-click to immediately access a program, text or data files, or folders. In this activity, you will create a desktop shortcut to the Calculator and WordPad Accessory programs.

▣1 Click the **Start** button ![start], point to **All Programs**, point to **Accessories**, and then right-click **Calculator**.

▣2 From the shortcut menu, point to **Send To**, and then click **Desktop (create shortcut)**. On the desktop, click a blank area to close the Start menu.

A shortcut for the Calculator is placed on the desktop. The Calculator icon displays a small arrow, which indicates that it is a shortcut from the desktop to another location, as shown in Figure 2.14. When you saved WordPad documents to the desktop, they were not shortcuts and therefore did not display the arrow.

Shortcut icon

Figure 2.14

3 On the desktop, double-click the **Calculator** shortcut icon. Alternatively, you could right-click the icon and then, from the shortcut menu, click Open.

The Calculator opens.

4 On the Calculator, click **4**, click the times symbol (*), click **9**, and then click the equals symbol (=) to verify that the Calculator works. When you are finished, in the Calculator title bar, click the **Close** button ❎.

5 Click the **Start** button ❘ *start*, point to **All Programs**, point to **Accessories**, and then right-click **WordPad**.

6 From the shortcut menu, point to **Send To**, and then click **Desktop (create shortcut)**. On the desktop, click a blank area to close the Start menu.

A shortcut for WordPad is placed on the desktop. The WordPad icon displays a small arrow, which indicates that it is a shortcut.

7 On the desktop, right-click a blank area, and then, from the displayed shortcut menu, point to **Arrange Icons By**, and then point to **Auto Arrange**. Verify that there is a check mark next to the command name.

Auto Arrange aligns icons on the desktop or in a window into neat columns and rows, as if they were on a grid. When the Auto Arrange command is turned off—that is, there is no check mark next to the name—you can drag the shortcut icons to any position on the desktop.

8 If there is no check mark next to the **Auto Arrange** command, click **Auto Arrange** to turn on the feature so that the desktop icons neatly align. If a check mark displays next to the command name, click the desktop to close the menu.

Activity 2.8 Deleting Items from the Desktop

Desktop items can be moved or copied and can also be deleted when they are no longer necessary. In this activity, you will remove your WordPad file and the shortcuts to Calculator and WordPad.

1 On the desktop, locate and right-click the **2A_Orientation2_ Firstname_Lastname** icon.

A shortcut menu displays, as shown in Figure 2.15.

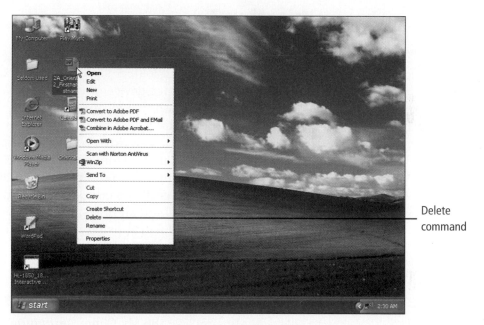

Figure 2.15

2 From the shortcut menu, click **Delete**.

The Confirm File Delete dialog box displays, asking whether you are sure you want to delete this item. Because this file is stored on the desktop, deleting it will remove it from storage and place it in the *Recycle Bin*—a temporary storage location for files that you delete.

3 In the **Confirm Delete** dialog box, click **Yes**.

The file is removed from the desktop and placed in the Recycle Bin.

4 On the desktop, locate and right-click the **Calculator** shortcut icon. From the shortcut menu, click **Delete**, and then click **Yes** to confirm the deletion. Alternatively, you could click to select the icon and then press Delete.

The shortcut is removed from the desktop and placed in the Recycle Bin. Deleting a shortcut icon does not remove the original program or file.

5 If you are working in a computer lab, repeat the procedure you used in step 4 to remove the WordPad shortcut.

Objective 3
Work with My Computer

To keep track of files and folders stored on your computer, you can display the contents of any storage device or folder in a window and then move from one window to another to locate the information you need. You can also create new folders on a disk drive in which you will store your files and folders. Recall that a disk drive is the hardware device that reads from and writes to devices that can store data. Data remains stored on a disk drive even when the computer's power is turned off. The *file system* on your computer is the overall structure in which files are named, stored, and organized in folders and on disks. In Activities 2.9 through 2.11, you will view the contents of a disk using the My Computer window. You will create two folders and then save your memo documents to one of the folders.

Activity 2.9 Using My Computer to View the Contents of a Disk

In this activity, you use the My Computer window to view the components of your computer and the contents of a disk to decide where to store the orientation information.

1 On the taskbar, click the **Start** button ![start], and then click **My Computer**. If necessary, maximize the My Computer window. Alternatively, you can double-click the My Computer icon on your desktop if your computer displays that icon.

In Windows XP, disk drives and files are managed by **Windows Explorer**—a file management program that comes with Windows XP and displays the hierarchical structure of files, folders, and drives on the computer. The My Computer icon provides you with easy access to this file management program. You use My Computer to manage your files and **navigate**—move—from one storage location to another. Navigating through your computer's folders and files is often referred to as **browsing**.

Your screen will differ depending on your computer configuration and the way drives, folders, and files are displayed in the **Contents pane**. The Contents pane is on the right side of the My Computer window. It displays files and folders stored on a storage device.

More Knowledge — Adding the My Computer Icon to the Desktop

If you do not see a My Computer icon on your desktop, you can create it. Click the Start button, move the pointer to My Computer, click the right mouse button, move the pointer to the Show on Desktop command, and then click the left mouse button.

---

2 From the **My Computer** menu bar, click **View**, and then point to **Toolbars**. In the displayed list of available toolbars, verify that a check mark displays next to *Standard Buttons*. If no check mark displays, click **Standard Buttons** to display the Standard Buttons toolbar; otherwise, click an empty area to close the View menu.

The **Standard Buttons toolbar** is the bar located directly under the menu. It displays important buttons that are shortcuts to menu commands. Recall that a check mark next to an item indicates that the item is selected and will display.

3 From the **My Computer** menu, click **View**, and then point to **Toolbars**. From the list of available toolbars, verify that no check mark displays next to **Address Bar**. If a check mark displays, click **Address Bar** to close the Address Bar toolbar; otherwise, click an empty area to close the View menu.

The **Address Bar** is a toolbar that you use to go directly to a specific storage location.

4 Take a moment to identify the elements of the My Computer window, as shown in Figure 2.16.

Notice that the window displays some of the same elements as windows for programs such as WordPad, including a title bar, menu bar, toolbar, and window control buttons. The window also displays a pane on the left side of the window and a Contents pane. The left pane displays links to common tasks related to the current window, links to other storage locations, and details about the currently selected item. Recall that the Contents pane is the area on the right side of a dialog box or window in which the current items display. *Local Disk (C:)*, or *drive C*, is a *hard disk drive*, which means that it is a storage device whose disk cannot be removed from the computer. Drive C: is often the primary storage device on a computer.

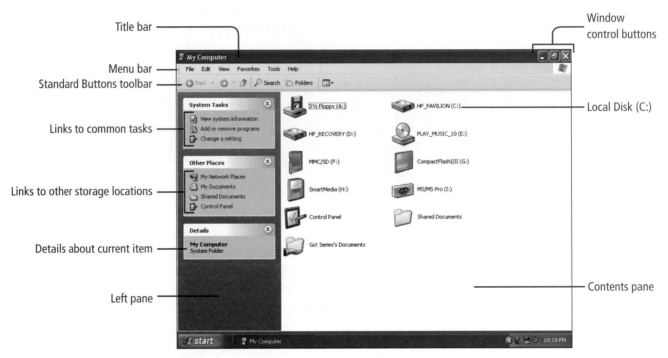

Figure 2.16

Alert! **If Disk Drives Do Not Display in the My Computer Window**

The My Computer opening window characteristics can be changed to display something other than what is shown in Figure 2.16, such as the contents of the My Documents folder. If you open My Computer and do not see a screen similar to the one shown, in the left pane, under Other Places, click My Computer.

5 In the **Contents pane**, click to select **Local Disk (C:)**. In the left pane, under **Details**, notice that specific information about the selected item displays. If necessary, to the right of Details, click the **Expand arrow** ⊗ to display details.

The details that display include the name of the drive, the type of drive, the amount of free space, and the total storage on the drive.

Alert! **Where Is Local Disk (C:)?**

Your drive C: may have a different name, such as HP_PAVILION (C:) or PRESARIO (C:). If so, look for the *C:* in the name next to one of the drive icons.

If you are working in a computer lab or on a network, Local Disk (C:) may not be available on your computer. If Local Disk (C:) is unavailable, use the network drive or removable device to which you have access, or select My Documents.

6 In the **Contents pane**, double-click the **Local Disk (C:)** icon. If a dialog box displays with the message that the files are hidden, click Yes to display the contents of the folder.

The folders and files stored on Local Disk (C:) display, and the drive name appears in the title bar, as shown in Figure 2.17. Your screen may differ, depending on the files and folders that are stored on your drive C. Recall that each folder can contain both files and additional folders, often referred to as *subfolders*.

Drive name ─────┐   Folders

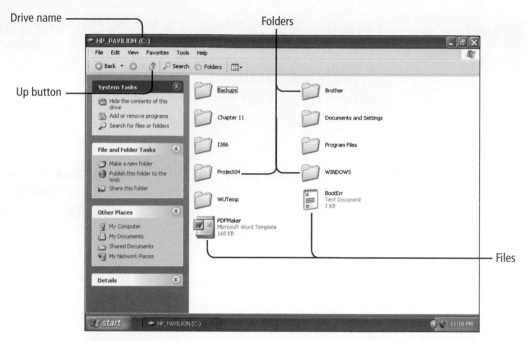

Figure 2.17

7 In the Standard Buttons toolbar, click the **Up** button ⬚.

The drives are displayed once again. The storage structure of your computer can be viewed as branching downward. For example, if you double-click a drive icon, you see the folders stored on that drive. Clicking on a folder displays more files and folders, and so on. Branching down one level at a time through the file structure is called ***drilling down***. Clicking the Up button moves you back up one level at a time.

Activity 2.10 Creating and Naming Folders

An effective way to organize data is to store files in separate, descriptively named folders. You will need a floppy disk to complete this exercise. If you do not have a floppy disk drive on your computer, use another removable storage device, the My Documents folder, or other storage location. In this activity, you will create two folders on drive A to store your files.

1 Place a floppy disk in drive A. In the My Computer **Contents pane**, double-click **3½ Floppy (A:)**.

The contents of the floppy disk display in the Contents pane. If you are using a new disk, nothing will display.

More Knowledge — What Is a Floppy Disk?

A floppy disk is a storage device made of a round piece of flexible plastic film enclosed in a rigid plastic shell; it is often referred to as a *floppy* or *3½-inch floppy*. The disk drive for a floppy disk is often called *drive A*. A floppy disk is a *removable device*, which means that it can be removed from the disk drive so that you can take it to a different location.

2 In the 3½ Floppy (A:) window—or the window for the location you are using to save files—locate the left pane, and then, under **File and Folder Tasks**, click **Make a new folder**.

A new folder displays in the Contents pane, as shown in Figure 2.18. When a new folder is created, it is given a default name—*New Folder*. You should immediately type a more descriptive name. An effective folder name should identify the types of files stored in the folder.

Disk drive name displays in the title bar

Click here to create a folder

File and Folder Tasks

New folder

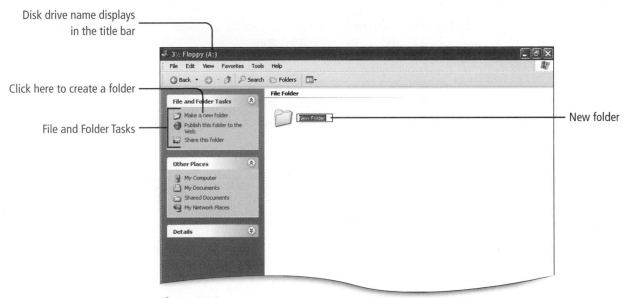

Figure 2.18

3 With the default name *New Folder* selected, type **Winter Orientation** and then press Enter. If you make a mistake, press Bksp until the mistake is removed, and then retype the folder name.

The new folder name is changed to *Winter Orientation*. You can now tell from the descriptive name that this folder contains information about the upcoming student orientation.

4 In the **Contents pane**, right-click a blank area, and then, from the displayed menu, point to **New**.

The New menu displays, listing the commands available for creating new items. If you click close to the right edge of the screen, the New menu will display to the left of the shortcut menu, as shown in Figure 2.19. The shortcut menu is an alternative way to create a new folder.

Figure 2.19

5 From the **New** menu, click **Folder** to create a new folder.

6 With the default name *New Folder* selected, type **Homework** and then press Enter.

Another Way — You can also create a folder using the menu. From the File menu, point to New, select Folder, type the folder name, and then press Enter.

7 In the 3½ Floppy (A:) title bar, click the **Close** button ⊠. If you are using a storage location other than a floppy disk, the name of your storage device will display in the title bar.

Activity 2.11 Saving a File to a Folder

In this activity, you will open the memo files you created in WordPad and save them to the Orientation folder you created.

1 Be sure your floppy disk is in the floppy disk drive. On the desktop, double-click the **Orientation folder**.

The two WordPad memo files you created display in a window.

2 Right-click the **2A_Orientation_Firstname_Lastname** file name. From the shortcut menu, click **Open With**, and then click **WordPad**.

The *2A_Orientation_Firstname_Lastname* file opens in WordPad. If an Open With dialog box, displays when you click WordPad, in the Open With dialog box, click WordPad, and then click OK.

3 From the **File** menu, click **Save As**.

4 In the displayed **Save As** dialog box, in the shortcut bar, click **My Computer**.

The available drives display in the Contents pane, as shown in Figure 2.20.

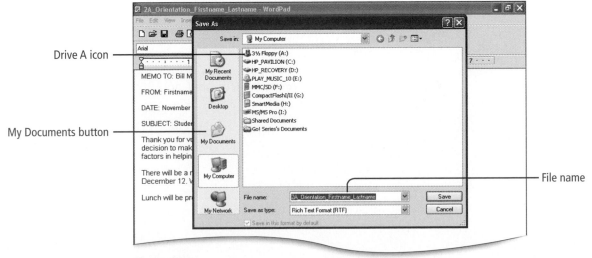

Drive A icon

My Documents button

File name

Figure 2.20

5 Click **3½ Floppy (A:)**, and then, near the bottom of the dialog box, click **Open**. Alternatively, double-click the drive A icon.

6 Double-click the **Winter Orientation** folder. Alternatively, double-click the Winter Orientation folder icon.

The Winter Orientation folder opens, and the folder name displays in the Save in box.

7 Near the bottom of the **Save As** dialog box, click the **Save** button.

In the WordPad title bar, click the **Close** button ☒.

The current file is saved in the *Winter Orientation* folder on drive A.

8 Repeat steps 2 through 7 to add the **2A_Orientation2_Firstname_Lastname** file to the Winter Orientation folder on drive A.

9 In the Orientation window title bar, click the **Close** button ☒.

10 On the taskbar, click the **Start** button 🔲 *start*, and then click **My Computer**. If necessary, maximize the My Computer window. Double-click **3½ Floppy (A:)**, and then double-click the **Winter Orientation** folder.

The Winter Orientation folder on drive A displays two files, as shown in Figure 2.21.

Folder name ———

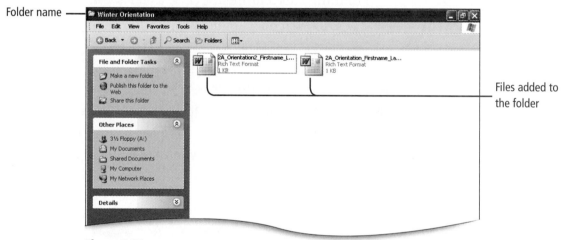

Files added to the folder

Figure 2.21

10 Leave the window open for the next activity.

Objective 4
Set Folder Options

Changing the way items display in a folder window makes it easier to locate files and folders. For example, you can display details about each item, sort the items alphabetically, or group the items by type. You can also customize the way folders display to suit your preferences. For example, you might set folders to display in a new window so that you can view multiple folders simultaneously, or you might set items to open on a single click instead of a double-click. In Activities 2.12 through 2.14, you will practice changing and restoring folder options.

Activity 2.12 Changing the Folder View

Windows XP has several options for displaying the contents of a folder. Most windows have five *views*, or ways in which icons display in the window. Depending on the view, you may be able to display more items in the window, display details about the items, such as the date the item was created, or preview picture files. In the following activity, you will change the view of the 3½ floppy (A:) window to explore which view you prefer to use for organizing files.

1 In the left pane of the 3½ Floppy (A:) window, under **Other Places**, click **My Documents**.

A list of files and folders displays in the My Documents window. The folders display at the top of the list, and any files display below the folders. Your list and view may differ.

2 On the Standard Buttons toolbar, click the **Views button arrow** .

A list of available views displays, as shown in Figure 2.22. A round, black bullet in the left column indicates the current view. Your view may be different.

Views button ───

Bullet indicates current view ───

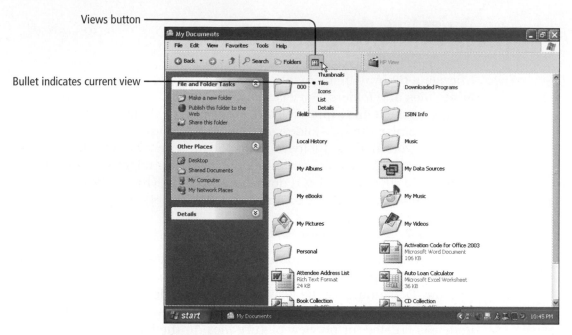

Figure 2.22

▣ On a piece of scrap paper, write down the current view of your screen so that you can restore the view when you finish this activity.

Click the **Views** button 📇▾ to hide the list.

▣ Take a moment to familiarize yourself with the view options, as described in the table in Figure 2.23.

Windows XP View Options

View	Description
Thumbnails	Displays icons of each file or folder stored in the folder, usually above the item's name. If the file is an image, a preview of the image displays instead of an icon. A ***thumbnail*** is a miniature image. Thumbnails view is useful for previewing picture files.
Tiles	The default view for most folders. Displays large icons representing each item stored in the folder next to the item's name.
Icons	Displays small icons representing each item stored in the folder, above the item's name. Because the icons are smaller than thumbnails or tiles, and because no additional information displays, you can display more items in the window.
List	All items stored in the folder are displayed in a list with a small icon to the left of the item's name. List view is an orderly view for displaying many items in the window.
Details	Displays a multicolumn list that includes information—such as the size, type, and date modified—about each item stored in the folder.

Figure 2.23

5 On the Standard Buttons toolbar, click the **Views button arrow** 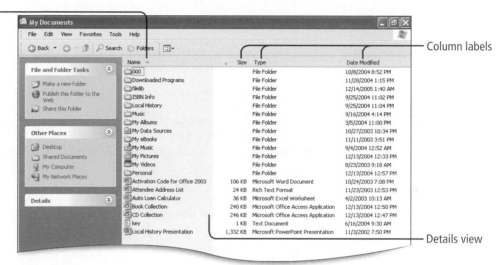,
and then click **Details**.

The contents of the folder display in Details view, as shown in
Figure 2.24. Notice that in Details view, an arrow displays next to
one column label, or column name, indicating the detail by which
the items are *sorted*, or arranged. In ascending order, folders are
sorted first, followed by files.

Arrow indicates that items are
sorted by name, alphabetically
in ascending order

Column labels

Details view

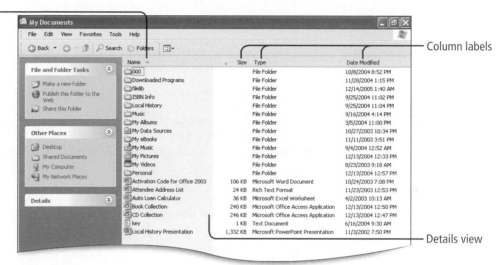

Figure 2.24

More Knowledge — Sorting the Contents of a Folder

Sorting can make it easier to locate an item in a folder that contains a lot of
items. For example, if you need a file that starts with the letter A, you can sort
the items alphabetically by name. An up arrow in Details view indicates that
the items are sorted in *ascending order*—alphabetically A to Z or numerically
0 to 9—and a down arrow indicates that they are sorted in *descending order*—
alphabetically Z to A or numerically 9 to 0. When you sort in descending order,
the folders display at the bottom of the list. Although you can sort items in
any view, the arrow displays only in Details view.

6 In the window, click the column label **Type** to sort the items by type, in ascending order, and then click it again to reverse the order to descending.

Type refers to the type of item—either folder or file—and to the *file type*. The file type is the structure of a file that defines the way it is stored on a disk and displayed on the screen.

7 On the Standard Buttons toolbar, click the **Views button arrow** 🔽, and then click **Tiles**.

The Tiles view displays.

8 On the Standard Buttons toolbar, click the **Views button arrow** 🔽, and then click **Details**.

The Details view displays again.

9 From the **View** menu, point to **Arrange Icons by**, and then click **Modified**.

The items are rearranged based on the *modification date*—the date they were last changed—from oldest to newest. In any view—including Details—the Arrange Icons by menu is an alternative method of selecting a sort order.

10 From the **View menu**, point to **Arrange Icons by**, and then click **Type**. From the **Arrange Icons by** menu, click **Show in Groups**.

Windows XP groups the items based on the current sort order—in this case, the type, as shown in Figure 2.25. You can group items in any view except List view.

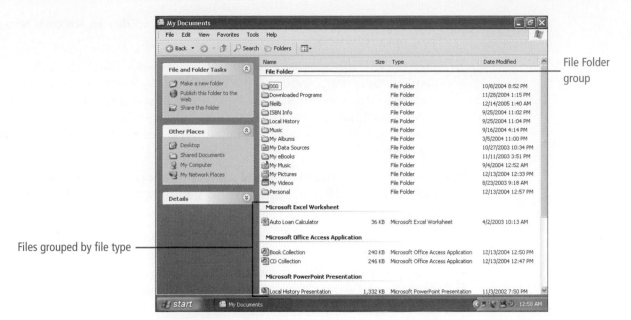

Files grouped by file type ——

File Folder group

Figure 2.25

11 From the **Arrange Icons By** menu, click **Show in Groups** to turn off the grouping. Restore the Contents pane to the same view that you wrote down in Step 2 of this activity. Leave the window open for the next activity.

Activity 2.13 Setting and Restoring General Folder Options

In this activity, you will explore more efficient ways to work with and organize folders.

1 From the **Tools** menu, click **Folder Options**.

The Folder Options dialog box displays with the General tab active.

2 In the **Folder Options** dialog box, under **Tasks**, click **Use Windows classic folders**.

This option sets Windows XP to hide the left pane in all folder windows and to instead display *Windows classic folders*, which look like the folders in versions of Windows prior to Windows XP. If you used Windows prior to using Windows XP, you may be more comfortable with this folder view.

3 Under **Browse folders**, click the **Open each folder in its own window** option button.

This option sets Windows XP so that each folder that you open displays in a new window. With this setting, you can see and access the contents of multiple folders—but the desktop can get crowded quickly with folders. With the default setting—*Open each folder in the same window*—each folder you open replaces the previous folder in the current window.

4 Under **Click items as follows**, click **Single-click to open an item (point to select)**. Compare your dialog box with Figure 2.26, and then click **OK**.

Notice that this option sets Windows XP so that you point to an item to select it and then single-click to open it. If you are accustomed to using a Web browser, you may find this method more familiar and easier to use. If you select to single-click items, you also have the option of underlining the names of items all the time or only when you point at them. The default is to always underline the names.

Figure 2.26

5 In the Standard Buttons toolbar, click the **Up** button [≡].

The Desktop window opens in a new window. Notice that the left pane is eliminated when you use the Windows classic folders option. Compare your screen with Figure 2.27.

Icon names are underlined.

Windows classic folders eliminates left pane in windows.

My Documents window

Desktop window

Taskbar buttons for both open windows

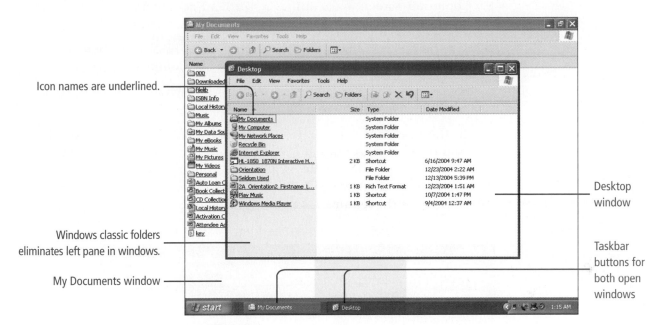

Figure 2.27

6 In the title bar of the Desktop window, click the **Close** button [X]. In the My Documents window, from the **Tools** menu, click **Folder Options**. In the displayed **Folder Options** dialog box, on the **General** tab, click **Restore Defaults**, and then click **OK**.

The folder options are reset to the default settings.

7 In the title bar of the My Documents window, click the **Close** button [X].

Activity 2.14 Applying the Current View to All Folders

By default, when you change the view in a folder window, only the current window is affected. You also have the option of applying the current view to all folders. In this activity, you will change the view in My Computer to Details view and then apply the view to all folders. You will capture the My Computer screen, paste it into a WordPad document, and then print the document. Finally, you will restore the original settings.

1 On the taskbar, click the **Start** button [start], and then click **My Computer**. If necessary, maximize the My Computer window.

By default, the My Computer window displays in Tiles view. Your window may display in a different view.

2 In the Standard Buttons toolbar, click the **Views button arrow** [icon], and then click **Details**. If necessary, on the window column labels, click **Name** to sort the items alphabetically by name. From the **View** menu, point to **Arrange Icons by**. If necessary, click **Show in Groups** to turn off the feature. Compare your screen with Figure 2.28.

Contents shown in Details view, alphabetically arranged by name in ascending order

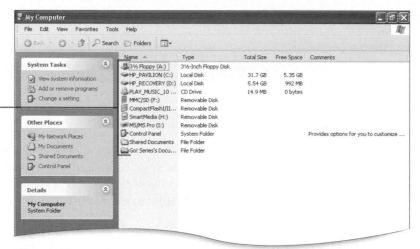

Figure 2.28

3 From the **Tools** menu, click **Folder Options**, and then click the **View tab**.

4 Under **Folder views**, click **Apply to All Folders**.

The Folder views dialog box displays, prompting you to confirm your decision to apply the current view to all folders.

5 In the **Folder views** dialog box, click **Yes**, and then, in the **Folder Options** dialog box, click **OK**.

6 In the My Computer window, in the **Contents pane**, double-click **3½ Floppy (A:)**—or the location you are using to display the window where your files are located—which now displays in the same view you applied to My Computer. Compare your screen with Figure 2.29.

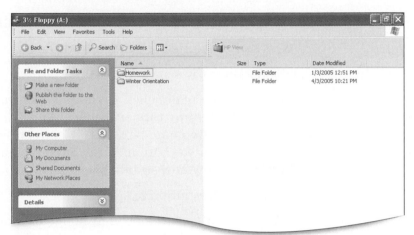

Figure 2.29

7 Locate and press [PrtScr] on your keyboard.

A copy of the screen is placed in the Clipboard. By capturing a copy of the screen, you can refer back to favorite settings or other changes you make to your computer.

8 Click the **Start** button [start], point to **All Programs**, point to **Accessories**, and then click **WordPad**. If necessary, click the Maximize button [□].

9 From the WordPad menu, click **File**, and then click **Page Setup**. In the **Page Setup** dialog box, under **Orientation**, click the **Landscape** option button, and then click **OK**.

10 In the WordPad window, type **2A_Firstname_Lastname** using your own name. Press [Enter] two times. From the WordPad menu, click **Edit**, and then click **Paste**.

The captured screen image is pasted into your document.

11 Move the pointer over the sizing handle in the lower right corner of the image. If necessary, scroll so that you can see the sizing handle.

When the pointer changes to the diagonal resize pointer ⬉, drag to the left and up about 1 inch. Release the mouse button.

12 From the **File** menu, click **Print Preview**. Be sure the captured screen fits on the page. If not, close the preview window and reduce the size of the image until it fits on one page.

13 On the Print Preview title bar, click the red **Close** button ✕. On the WordPad toolbar, click the **Print** button 🖨.

The document is sent to the default printer.

14 From the **File** menu, click **Save As**. Verify that the **Save in** box displays **3½ Floppy (A:)**, or the location where you are saving your files. In the **File name** box, type **2A_Screen_Firstname_Lastname** and then, near the bottom of the **Save As** dialog box, click the **Save** button. In the WordPad title bar,

click the **Close** button ✕.

The document is saved on your floppy disk or the location where you are saving your work.

Alert!

If Your Document Is Too Big for the Floppy Disk

You may see a message that states your disk is full. This means that the file is too big to fit in the remaining space on your floppy disk. The size of this document depends mostly on the size of the captured screen. If the file is too big for your floppy disk, save the file to another storage device.

15 From the **Tools** menu, click **Folder Options**, and then in the displayed **Folder Options** dialog box, click the **View tab**. Under **Folder views**, click **Reset All Folders**, and then in the **Folder views** dialog box, click **Yes**. In the **Folder Options** dialog box, click **OK**.

16 In the 3½ Floppy (A:) window, in the left pane, click **My Computer** to display the My Computer window.

The default view options are restored.

17 In the title bar, click the **Close** button ✕ to close the My Computer window. Check your *Chapter Assignment Sheet* or your *Course Syllabus*, or consult your instuctor, to determine whether you are to submit the printed pages that are the result of this project.

End You have completed Project 2A

Summary

In this chapter, you practiced how to use the filing system on your computer to organize files and folders. You used WordPad to create, save, edit, and print memos for orientation week, and you created and named folders to store the memo files. You practiced previewing a document before printing it by using the Print Preview command, including zooming in and out of the previewed document. Next, on the desktop, you created folders and shortcuts to files and programs. You also practiced deleting items from the desktop. To keep track of files and folders stored on your computer, you practiced working with and navigating My Computer. You used My Computer to view the storage components of your computer system and viewed the contents of a removable disk. You also changed and sorted the views of files and folders. Finally, you restored the default folder options.

In This Chapter You Practiced How To

- Create, Save, and Print a File
- Create Shortcuts and Folders on the Windows XP Desktop
- Work with My Computer
- Set Folder Options

Matching

Match each term in the second column with its correct definition in the first column by writing the letter of the term on the blank line in front of the correct definition.

____ **1.** Any self-contained piece of work that you create in a program and save.

____ **2.** The area in the My Computer window that displays the current files and folders.

____ **3.** To change text in an existing document.

____ **4.** The hardware device that reads from and writes to devices that can store data.

____ **5.** The structure of a file that defines the way it is stored on disk and displayed onscreen.

____ **6.** The feature that automatically breaks lines of text to the next line when the current line is full.

____ **7.** The overall structure in which files are named, stored, and organized in folders and on disks.

____ **8.** An item with upward- and downward-pointing arrows that enable you to move through a set of values by clicking.

____ **9.** The view that displays a multicolumn list including information about each item stored in the folder.

____ **10.** The sort order when items are arranged alphabetically from A to Z.

____ **11.** To create an exact replica of an item such as a file or folder in a new location.

____ **12.** A view in My Computer that displays a miniature image of a picture file.

____ **13.** A command used to reposition the icons on the desktop.

____ **14.** The sort order when items are arranged alphabetically from Z to A.

____ **15.** To move about in My Computer to manage your files and folders.

A Ascending order

B Auto Arrange

C Contents pane

D Copy

E Descending order

F Details

G Disk drive

H Document

I Edit

J File system

K File type

L Navigate

M Spin box

N Thumbnails

O Word wrap

Fill in the Blank Write the correct answer in the space provided.

1. Characters that you type display to the left of the
   _____.

2. To quickly select a single word, _____ the word.

3. To save a copy of an existing file with a new name, display the File
   menu, and then click _____.

4. By default, WordPad saves files in the file type called
   _____.

5. A file name can include up to _____ characters,
   including spaces.

6. To magnify the onscreen display without changing the size of data in
   a file, click the _____ button.

7. The Windows XP program used to manage files and folders is called
   _____.

8. Before you print a file, click the _____ button to see
   what it will look like on paper.

9. In versions of Windows prior to Windows XP, Windows classic folders
   display without the _____.

10. To sort similar items in a window, use the _____
    command.

Skill Assessments

Project 2B — First Week

Objectives: *Create, Save, and Print a File and Create Shortcuts and Folders on the Windows XP Desktop.*

In the following Skill Assessment, you will create a list of volunteers who will work the first week of student orientation. You will use WordPad to create the document and then save the file to the desktop. You will create a folder on the desktop and then save the document to the folder. You will save the document with the name *2B_First_Week_Firstname_Lastname.* You will capture an image of the desktop, paste it into a WordPad document, and save the document as *2B_Screen_Firstname_Lastname.* When completed, your desktop and file will look similar to Figure 2.30.

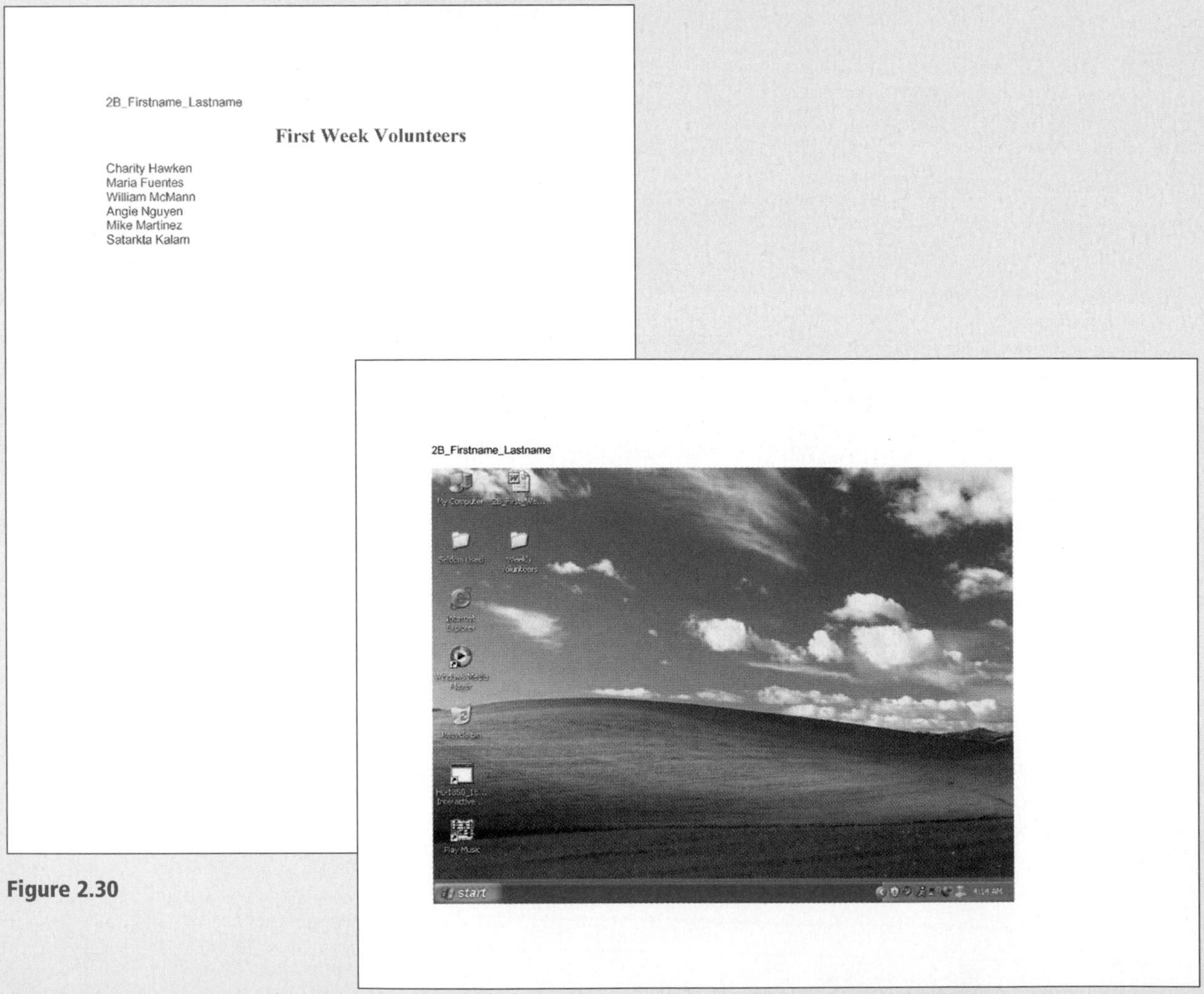
2B_Firstname_Lastname
First Week Volunteers
Charity Hawken
Maria Fuentes
William McMann
Angie Nguyen
Mike Martinez
Satarkta Kalam
2B_Firstname_Lastname
start

Figure 2.30

(**Project 2B**–First Week continues on the next page)

(Project 2B–First Week continued)

1. If necessary, turn on your computer and **log on** to Windows XP in the manner required for the system at which you are working.

2. Click the **Start** button, point to **All Programs**, point to **Accessories**, and then click **WordPad**.

3. In the WordPad document, type **2B_Firstname_Lastname** and then press ⏎Enter two times.

4. Type **First Week Volunteers** and then press ⏎Enter two times.

5. Type the following names, pressing ⏎Enter after each item to start a new line:

    Charity Hawken
    Maria Fuentes
    William McMann
    Angie Nguyen
    Mike Martinez
    Ben Ham

    Recall that if you make a mistake while typing, you can press Bksp until the mistake is removed and then continue typing.

6. In WordPad, from the **File** menu, click **Save**. In the **Save As** dialog box, in the shortcut bar, click to select **Desktop**. In the **File name** box, double-click to select *Document* if it is not already selected, type **2B_First_Week_Firstname_Lastname** and then click **Save**.

7. In the WordPad document, drag to select *First Week Volunteers*. On the Format bar, click the **Center** button, and then click the **Bold** button. Click the **Font arrow**, scroll down the font list, and then click **Times New Roman**. Click the **Font Size arrow**, and then, from the displayed list, click **16**.

8. At the end of the last line—*Ben Ham*—click to position the insertion point, and then press Bksp seven times. Type **Satarkta Kalam**.

9. On the WordPad title bar, click the **Minimize** button. In an empty area of the desktop, right-click, point to **New** on the shortcut menu, and then click **Folder**. Over the default folder name, type **Weekly Volunteers**, and then press ⏎Enter. If the folder name is not in edit mode, right-click the folder name, and then click Rename from the shortcut menu.

10. On the taskbar, click the **2B_First_Week_Firstname_Lastname - WordPad** button. In WordPad, from the **File** menu, click **Save As**. In the **Save As** dialog box, in the shortcut bar, click **Desktop**. In the **Contents pane**, click the **Weekly Volunteers** icon, and then click **Open**. Near the bottom of the **Save As** dialog box, click the **Save** button.

(Project 2B–First Week continues on the next page)

(Project 2B–First Week continued)

11. On the WordPad toolbar, click the **Print** button. On the WordPad title bar, click the **Close** button. With the desktop displayed, press PrtScr.

12. Click the **Start** button, point to **All Programs**, point to **Accessories**, and then click **WordPad**. If necessary, click the Maximize button.

13. From the WordPad menu, click **File**, and then click **Page Setup**. In the **Page Setup** dialog box, under **Orientation**, click the **Landscape** option button, and then click **OK**.

14. In the WordPad window, type **2B_Firstname_Lastname** using your own name. Press Enter two times. From the WordPad menu, click **Edit**, and then click **Paste**.

15. In the lower right corner of the image, move the pointer over the sizing handle. When the pointer changes to a diagonal resize pointer, drag to the left and up about 1 inch. Release the mouse button.

16. On the WordPad toolbar, click the **Print Preview** button. If the captured screen does not fit on the page with the *2B_Firstname_ Lastname* text, close the preview window and reduce the size of the image until it fits.

17. In the Print Preview window, click the **Zoom In** button two times to magnify the document. On the Print Preview toolbar, click the **Close** button. From the WordPad toolbar, click the **Print** button. Examine your printed document. Be sure your name and the screen image are on one page, and then, in the WordPad title bar, click the **Close** button.

18. In the **WordPad** dialog box, click **Yes** to save your document. In the **Save As** dialog box, click the **Save in arrow**, and then select your *Weekly Volunteers* folder, if necessary. In the **File name** box, type **2B_Screen_Firstname_Lastname**

19. Near the bottom of the **Save As** dialog box, click the **Save** button.

20. When you have completed the assignment to your satisfaction, right-click the *2B_First_Week_Firstname_Lastname* document, and then click **Delete** from the shortcut menu. Click **Yes** to confirm the file deletion.

21. Right-click the *Weekly Volunteers* folder, and then click **Delete** from the shortcut menu. Click **Yes** to confirm the folder and file deletion.

End You have completed Project 2B ——————————————

Project 2C — Second Week

Objectives: *Create, Save, and Print a File, Work with My Computer, and Set Folder Options.*

In the following Skill Assessment, you will create a list of volunteers who will work during the second week of student orientation. You will use WordPad to create the document and then use My Computer to save the document to a floppy disk or other storage location of your choice. You will create a folder on the floppy disk, save the document to the folder, and change the way My Computer displays files and folders. You will save the document with the name *2C_Second_Week_Firstname_Lastname*. Next, you will capture an image of the My Computer window, paste a copy of it into a WordPad document, and save the document as *2C_Screen_Firstname_Lastname*. When completed, your document and My Computer screen will look similar to Figure 2.31. Before beginning this project, you will need a floppy disk or other disk, depending on the storage device you are using.

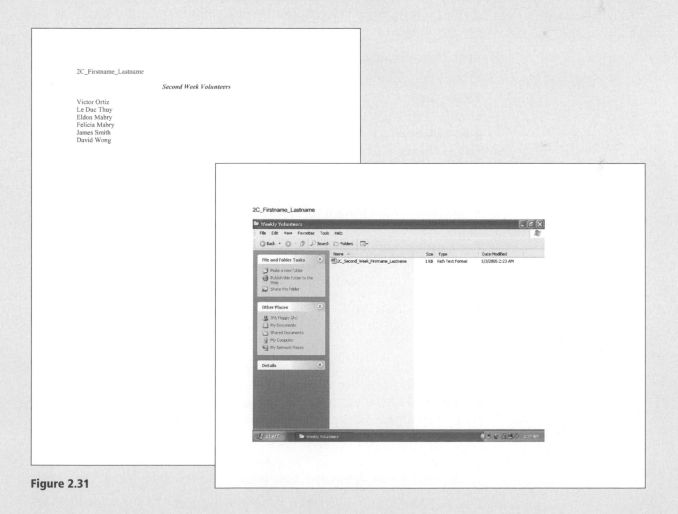

Figure 2.31

(Project 2C–Second Week continues on the next page)

(Project 2C–Second Week continued)

1. If necessary, turn on your computer and log on to Windows XP in the manner required for the system at which you are working. Place an empty floppy disk in drive A, or prepare the alternative storage device you are using. On the taskbar, click the **Start** button, and then click **My Computer**. If necessary, maximize the My Computer window.

2. In the My Computer **Contents pane**, double-click **3½ Floppy (A:)**.

3. In the left pane of the 3½ Floppy (A:) window, under **File and Folder Tasks**, click **Make a new folder**. Type **Weekly Volunteers** as the folder name, press [Enter], and then, in the Contents pane, click an open area.

4. Click the **Start** button, point to **All Programs**, point to **Accessories**, and then click **WordPad**.

5. In the WordPad document, type **2C_Firstname_Lastname** and then press [Enter] two times. Type **Second Week Volunteers** and then press [Enter] two times.

6. Type the following names, pressing [Enter] after each item to start a new line:

   Victor Ortiz
   Le Duc Thuy
   Eldon Mabry
   Felicia Mabry
   James Smith
   David Wong

7. In the document, drag from the left of the first line of text to the right of the last line of text to select all the text in the document. Click the **Font arrow**, scroll down the font list, and then click **Times New Roman**. Click the **Font Size arrow**, and then click **12**. Click anywhere in the WordPad window to deselect the text.

8. Drag to select *Second Week Volunteers*. On the Format bar, click the **Center** button, click the **Bold** button, and then click the **Italic** button.

9. From the **File** menu, click **Save**. In the **Save As** dialog box, in the shortcut bar, click **My Computer**. In the **Contents pane**, click **3½ Floppy (A:)** or the name of the storage device you are using, and then click **Open**. In the **Contents pane**, click **Weekly Volunteers**, and then click **Open**.

10. In the **File name** box, click to select *Document*, type **2C_Second_Week_Firstname_Lastname** and then click **Save**.

11. On the WordPad toolbar, click the **Print** button. On the WordPad title bar, click the **Close** button.

(Project 2C–Second Week continues on the next page)

(Project 2C–Second Week continued)

12. In the **3½ Floppy (A:)** window, in the **Contents pane**, double-click the *Weekly Volunteers* folder icon. From the **View** menu, click the **Details** command to display file and folder details. With the *Weekly Volunteers* window displayed, press PrtScr.

13. Start WordPad and, if necessary, click the Maximize button. Recall that to start WordPad, you click the **Start** button, point to **All Programs**, point to **Accessories**, and then click **WordPad**.

14. From the WordPad menu, click **File**, and then click **Page Setup**. In the **Page Setup** dialog box, under **Orientation**, click the **Landscape** option button, and then click **OK**.

15. In the WordPad window, type **2C_Firstname_Lastname** using your own name. Press Enter two times. From the WordPad menu, click **Edit**, and then click **Paste**.

16. In the lower right corner of the image, move the pointer over the sizing handle. When the pointer changes to the diagonal resize pointer, drag to the left and up about 1 inch. Release the mouse button.

17. On the Standard Buttons toolbar, click the **Print Preview** button. If the captured screen does not fit on the page, close the preview window and reduce the size of the image until it fits.

18. On the Print Preview toolbar, click the **Close** button. In the WordPad toolbar, click the **Print** button. Examine your printed document. Be sure your name and the screen image are on one page, and then, in the WordPad title bar, click the **Close** button.

19. In the **WordPad** dialog box, click **Yes** to save your document. In the **Save As** dialog box, be sure the **Save in** box displays your *Weekly Volunteers* folder. In the **File name** box, type **2C_Screen_Firstname_Lastname**

20. Near the bottom of the **Save As** dialog box, click the **Save** button.

21. When you have completed the assignment to your satisfaction, in the Weekly Volunteers window, right-click the *2C_Second_Week_Firstname_Lastname* document, and then click **Delete** from the shortcut menu. Click **Yes** to confirm the file deletion.

22. On the Standard Buttons toolbar, click the Up button. Right-click the *Weekly Volunteers* folder, and then click **Delete** from the shortcut menu. Click **Yes** to confirm the folder and file deletion. Close the My Computer window, and submit your document as directed.

End You have completed Project 2C

Project 2D—Outline

Objectives: *Create, Save, and Print a File, Create Shortcuts and Folders on the Windows XP Desktop, Work with My Computer, and Set Folder Options.*

In the following Performance Assessment, you will create and save an outline of the topics to be covered in a student orientation volunteer training session. You will save the file on a floppy disk with the name *2D_Outline_Firstname_Lastname* and then create a shortcut to the file on the desktop. You will change the look of the My Computer window, save a screen print of the changes in a document, and then restore the original settings. Your documents will look similar to the ones in Figure 2.32. Before beginning this project, you will need a floppy disk or other disk, depending on the storage device you are using.

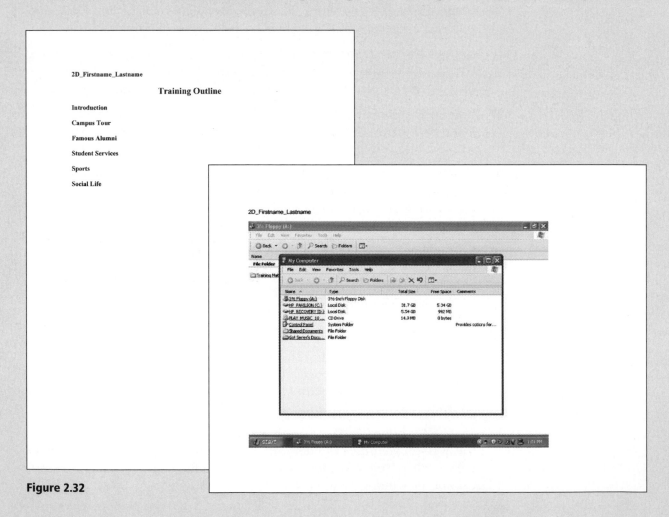

Figure 2.32

(Project 2D–Outline continues on the next page)

(Project 2D–Outline continued)

1. Start your computer if necessary. Place a floppy disk in drive A. Open **My Computer**, and then, in the **Contents pane**, navigate to drive A or the alternative storage device you are using for this exercise.

2. Under **File and Folder Tasks**, click **Make a new folder**. Name the folder **Training Materials**

3. From the **Tools** menu, click **Folder Options**. In the **Folder Options** dialog box, under **Tasks**, click the **Use Windows classic folders** option button.

4. Under **Browse folders**, click the **Open each folder in its own window** option button.

5. Under **Click items as follows**, click the **Single-click to open an item (point to select)** option button. At the bottom of the **Folder Options** dialog box, click **OK**.

6. On the Standard Buttons toolbar, click the **Up** button. Notice that My Computer opens in a new window. Press PrtScr.

7. Start WordPad. Type **2D_Firstname_Lastname** and then press Enter two times. Change the page orientation to landscape. Paste the captured screen in the document, resize as necessary, and then, in the location where you are saving your work, save the document as **2D_Screen_Firstname_Lastname**

8. **Print** the document, and then close WordPad.

9. Close the My Computer window. In the Drive A window, from the **Tools** menu, click **Folder Options**. Click to select the **General tab**, if necessary, click **Restore Defaults**, and then click **OK**.

10. Start WordPad. In the WordPad document, type **2D_Firstname_Lastname** and then press Enter two times. Type **Training Outline** and then press Enter two times. Enter the following text, pressing Enter two times after each entry:

    Introduction

    Campus Tour

    Famous Alumni

    Student Services

    Sports

    Social Life

11. Drag to select all of the text. Click the **Font arrow**, and then click **Times New Roman**. Click the **Font Size arrow**, and then click **12**. Select *Training Outline*. Change the **Font Size** to **16**, click the **Center** button, and then click the **Bold** button.

(Project 2D–Outline continues on the next page)

(Project 2D–Outline continued)

12. Save the document in the *Training Materials* folder as **2D_Outline_Firstname_Lastname** and then print the document.

13. Close WordPad. In the Drive A window, open the *Training Materials* folder.

14. Right-click the **2D_Outline_Firstname_Lastname** file. From the shortcut menu, point to **Send To**, and then click **Desktop (create shortcut)**.

15. Close the *Training Materials* window. On the desktop, right-click the shortcut icon that you created, and then open the document using WordPad.

16. Close WordPad, and delete the 2D_Outline_Firstname_Lastname shortcut from the desktop.

 End **You have completed Project 2D** ————————————————————

Project 2E — Staff

Objectives: *Create, Save, and Print a File, Create Shortcuts and Folders on the Windows XP Desktop, Work with My Computer, and Set Folder Options.*

You can create a new file directly on the Windows XP desktop. The file icon displays on the desktop so that you can double-click to open the file at any time. In this Mastery Assessment, you will write a letter that can be sent to potential student volunteers for the orientation program. You will save the letter as *2E_Invitation_Firstname_Lastname* and then print the letter. Your document and desktop will be similar to Figure 2.33.

Figure 2.33

1. On the desktop, right-click a blank area. From the shortcut menu, point to **New**, and then click **Text Document**. Windows XP creates a new text document on the desktop—represented by a text document icon—with the default file name—*New Text Document*—highlighted.

(Project 2E–Staff continues on the next page)

(Project 2E—Staff continued)

2. With the text *New Text Document* highlighted, type **2E_Invitation_Firstname_Lastname** and then press Enter.

3. On the desktop, double-click the **2E_Invitation_Firstname_Lastname** icon to open the file. In this case, the text file you created is associated with the ***Notepad*** program, which is a basic text editor program that comes with Windows XP. A ***text editor*** provides tools for entering and editing text but has limited formatting capabilities. Notepad works similarly to WordPad.

4. If necessary, maximize the Notepad window. From the Format menu, click Word Wrap to turn it on if necessary. On the first line of the memo, type **2E_Firstname_Lastname**

5. Press Enter two times. Type **MEMO TO:** and then press Enter two times. Type **FROM: Corey Finstad** and press Enter two times. Type **DATE: October 1** and press Enter two times. Type **SUBJECT: Orientation volunteers needed** and press Enter two times.

6. Type the following text:

   We are still looking for bright, energetic student volunteers to help out with the upcoming orientation program for potential students. We need people who can give guided tours of the campus. You should feel comfortable talking to small groups of people, and should have some familiarity with the campus. There will be a short training session the week of December 12.

7. From the **File** menu, click **Save**. Close the Notepad program.

8. On the desktop, double-click the **2E_Invitation_Firstname_Lastname** icon to be sure that the document opens in Notepad. Close Notepad.

9. On the desktop, right-click the **2E_Invitation_Firstname_Lastname** icon. From the shortcut menu, open the document with WordPad. Click **View**, **Options** and in the Options dialog box, under Text, click to select **Wrap to ruler**, if necessary, and then print the document. Close WordPad.

10. Capture the desktop screen. Open WordPad, type **2E_Firstname_Lastname** and then press Enter two times. Paste the captured screen in the document, resize the image until it fits on one page, and then print the document. Save the document as **2E_Screen_Firstname_Lastname** and then close WordPad.

11. From the desktop, remove any documents you created.

 End **You have completed Project 2E** ———————————————

Problem-Solving Assessment

Project 2F—Planning

Objectives: *Create, Save, and Print a File, Create Shortcuts and Folders on the Windows XP Desktop, Work with My Computer, and Set Folder Options.*

In this Problem-Solving Assessment, you will create a form to be filled out by potential volunteers. You will create a folder and a subfolder on a floppy disk—or other storage device—and practice using My Computer. To complete this exercise, do the following:

1. Create a WordPad document that has a list of items you would want to know about potential volunteers for a student orientation program. These could include phone number, days available, times available, previous experience in orientation programs, or other topics of your choice. The items should be aligned on the left side of the document and be followed by a colon (:).

2. Use My Computer to create a folder named **Orientation Program** on a floppy disk or other storage device. Open the *Orientation Program* folder, and create two subfolders, one called **Student Lists** and the other called **Volunteers**

3. Save your document as **2F_Volunteer_Information_Firstname_ Lastname** and place it in the *Volunteers* folder.

4. Create a desktop shortcut to the *Volunteers* folder.

5. Submit your document as directed. When you are finished, remove the shortcut from the desktop.

 End You have completed Project 2F ────────────────────

On the Internet

Searching for Information on Creating Files

Connect to the Internet, open a web browser, and then go to www.google.com. In the Google window, in the Search box, type **"creating folders"**—including the quotation marks. Click **Search**. Scroll through the list of sites. Click on the links to the sites that interest you. See whether you can find instructions on what special characters cannot be used in a folder name. When you are finished, close your web browser and Internet connection.

GO! with Help

Working with Windows XP Files and Folders

Almost every command in Windows XP can be accomplished by using either a keyboard or a mouse. To find out the keyboard shortcuts for common commands such as creating a new folder or copying a file, use the Windows XP Help and Support program.

1. From the Start menu, click Help and Support.

2. On the left side of the Help window, locate and click the **Windows basics** help topic.

3. Under **Windows basics**, click **Core Windows tasks**, and then click **Working with files and folders**.

4. Scan the list for topics covered in this chapter, and click on topics of interest.

5. Read through some of the help screens for interesting topics.

6. When you are finished, close the Help window.

3 chapter three

Working with the File Management Program

In this chapter you will: complete this project **and** practice these skills.

Project 3A Manage Files and Folders	Objectives
	- Copy and Move Files and Folders
	- Manage Folders Using Windows Explorer
	- Work with Explorer Bar Views
	- Compress Files
	- Work with Pictures
	- Share Files and Folders
	- Manage the Recycle Bin

Working with the File Management Program

In many offices, filing paper documents is a basic function. To ensure easy retrieval of forms, customer information, and other records, a filing system is established. Often paper records are placed in manila folders, which are labeled and filed in filing cabinets. These folders contain all the papers related to a specific topic. Windows XP includes a file management system that functions like an office filing cabinet.

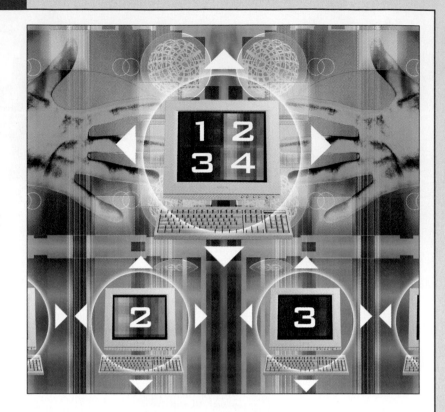

Introduction

Your computer provides a variety of storage locations. You can store files on the computer's hard drive, on a portable storage device such as a floppy disk, or on a network drive so that the files can be used by others.

Windows XP provides tools to help you organize all types of files and folders into the storage location most convenient for you. Working effectively with your computer requires an understanding of the various storage devices and locations so that you can organize your files in a manner that enables you to retrieve them easily.

Project 3A Managing Your Files

If you were to store all your files on your desktop, it would become cluttered quickly, which would make it difficult to locate and open the files you need. Floppy disks are an easy method for transporting files, but they cannot store large amounts of data. Most of your files should be saved to folders that are stored on your computer's hard disk or to a network drive.

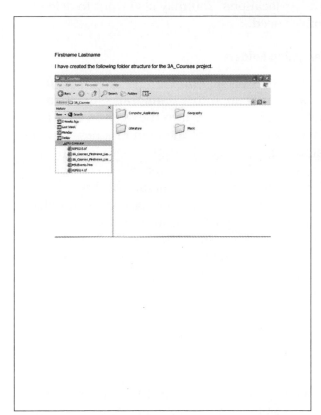

In Activities 3.1 through 3.13, you will create folders for college courses and practice moving them among various storage locations on your computer. To document your work, you will capture an image of the folder structure you have created and paste it into a WordPad file that is saved as *3A_Courses_Firstname_Lastname*. When completed, your document will look similar to the one shown in Figure 3.1. You will also practice working with picture files, sharing files, and using the Recycle Bin.

Figure 3.1
Project 3A—Managing Your Files

Objective 1
Copy and Move Files and Folders

A folder on your computer is similar to a manila folder that you might place in a filing cabinet. Folders help organize your files into logical groups. As you might move or make a copy of a folder in your filing cabinet, you can move or copy an electronic file or folder from one location to another. Moving or copying a file or folder is useful for keeping your data organized or for making it available in other locations. You may also want to delete files or folders that you no longer need.

Activity 3.1 Copying and Renaming Folders

Making a duplicate file or folder is a two-step process. First, you *copy* the file or folder, which places a duplicate into a temporary storage area, and then you *paste* the duplicate file or folder into the desired location. The resulting file or folder is an exact replica of the item in a new location. The original item remains stored in its original location. Duplicating a folder or file is useful when you want to make a *backup*—a copy stored away from your computer for safekeeping—or when you want to take the files away from your computer to use somewhere else. You can also duplicate a folder or file and then rename it to use for a different purpose. In this activity, you will create folders for courses for a college student. You will need a floppy disk to complete this activity. A new or empty floppy disk is preferred so that you will not run out of storage space while completing the activities.

1 On the Windows XP desktop, double-click the **My Computer** icon. Recall that if the My Computer icon does not display on your desktop, you can open it by clicking the Start button and then clicking My Computer on the Start menu.

The My Computer window displays. Recall that this is a view of the Windows Explorer program, which manages the files and programs stored on your computer.

2 Place a floppy disk in the floppy disk drive, which is typically drive A. In the My Computer **Contents pane**, double-click **3½ Floppy (A:)**. If the Address Bar is not displayed, on the menu, click View, point to Toolbars, and then click Address Bar.

The window title bar displays *3½ Floppy (A:)*, and the Contents pane displays the contents of any files or folders stored on the floppy disk. If you are using a new disk, nothing will display.

Alert!
My Computer Has No Floppy Disk Drive

If your computer does not have a floppy disk drive, use a different storage device, such as a USB drive, a writable CD drive, or a *network drive*—a storage location on another computer to which you are connected.

3 On the right side of the window, in an empty area of the Contents pane, **right-click**, and from the displayed shortcut menu, point to **New**, and then, on the submenu, click **Folder**.

A New Folder icon displays in the 3½ Floppy (A:) contents pane. *New Folder* is selected so that you can type a name for your folder.

4 Type **Geography** and then press Enter.

5 Right-click the Geography folder, and then, from the displayed shortcut menu, click **Copy**.

Windows XP creates and stores a copy of the *Geography* folder in the **Clipboard**, which is a temporary storage location for items that are copied or cut. The folder does not display on your screen but is stored in the computer's memory.

6 In an empty area of the Contents pane, right-click, and from the displayed shortcut menu, click **Paste**.

A copy of the Geography folder displays, with the name *Copy of Geography* as shown in Figure 3.2. The words *Copy of* are added to the folder name to differentiate the copied folder from the original because folders stored in the same location cannot have the same name.

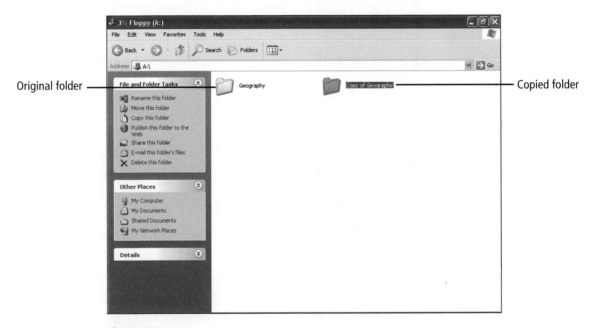

Original folder

Copied folder

Figure 3.2

7 In an empty area of the Contents pane, right-click, and then click **Paste** to create a second copy of the *Geography* folder—named *Copy (2) of Geography*. Right-click again and then click **Paste** to create a third copy of the folder—*Copy (3) of Geography*.

The copied item remains in the Clipboard until you copy another item, so you can repeatedly paste the item to create as many new copies as you want. This is a quick way to create several folders, which you can then rename as needed.

8 In the Contents pane, right-click the **Copy of Geography** folder, and from the displayed menu, click **Rename**. Type **Literature** and then press Enter.

9 In a similar manner, rename the folder *Copy (2) of Geography* to **Music** and *Copy (3) of Geography* to **Computer_Applications** Compare your screen with Figure 3.3. Your screen may differ, depending on the storage device you are using and on whether any files or folders are already stored on that device.

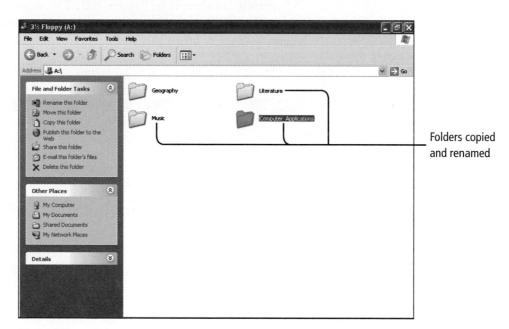

Figure 3.3

10 In an empty area of the Contents pane, right-click, point to **New**, and then click **Folder**. Type **3A_Courses** and then press Enter.

Windows XP creates a new folder named *3A_Courses*.

11 Point to the Geography folder, and then right-drag the **Geography** folder to the **3A_Courses** folder. From the displayed shortcut menu, click **Copy Here**.

Recall that to right-drag, you hold down the right mouse button, drag the item to the desired location, and then release the right mouse button. When you release the right mouse button, a shortcut menu displays. This shortcut menu gives you the option to copy or move the item or to create a shortcut. The default action—*Move Here*—displays in bold, which is the action that would have occurred if you had used the left mouse button to drag the folder. Dragging with the right mouse button enables you to choose between moving or copying the selected item.

12 Double-click the **3A_Courses** folder to open it and view its contents.

The Geography folder displays in the Contents pane. This is an alternative method of copying folders or files. The original folder is stored on drive A—or your current location—and a copy of the folder is stored in the 3A_Courses folder. You no longer need the original folder that is stored on drive A.

13 On the Standard Buttons toolbar, click the **Up** button ⬆. In the **3½ Floppy (A:)** window, click the **Geography** folder, and then in the left pane, under **File and Folder Tasks**, click **Delete this folder**. In the **Confirm Folder Delete** dialog box, click **Yes**.

When you delete a folder or file from a removable device, such as a floppy disk or a Zip disk, it is deleted permanently. The Recycle Bin stores only files deleted from drive C.

More Knowledge — Portable Storage Devices

The hard disk drive in a computer is normally built into the system case, which imposes limitations. If you want to make copies of your files that you can store in another location for security reasons, or if you want to move files between computers, portable storage devices are useful. Floppy disks are commonly used for this purpose, but they hold only 1.44 *megabytes* (MB). A megabyte is approximately one million bytes of data. A *byte* is a unit of data representing one character.

Many new computers are equipped with optical drives that can write data to CDs or DVDs, which have far more capacity than floppy disks. If your optical drive can write data to a CD, it may use a *CD-R* disc that may be written upon but not erased or a *CD-RW* disc that may be written upon, erased, and reused. A CD can hold 700 megabytes of data. Similarly, some optical drives can read and write data to *DVD* discs, which are available in both recordable and reusable formats. DVD technology is newer, and competing incompatible formats are available. A DVD can hold 8,750 megabytes.

Another option utilizes a *flash drive*—a type of permanent storage—that plugs into a *Universal Serial Bus (USB)* port, which is a small rectangular port found on the front of many computers. These devices have no moving parts. When you plug one into a USB port, Windows XP will assign a drive letter to it, and you can use it like a disk drive. Flash drive devices can hold 1,000 megabytes and easily fit in your pocket. They plug into most new computers, which makes them a good choice for transferring files.

Activity 3.2 Moving Files and Folders

When you *move* a file or folder, that file or folder—and all files or subfolders stored in that folder—is removed from its original location and is stored only in the new location. For example, you might want to move a folder to a network drive so that you can access it from a different computer or to a shared folder so that others can access it. The procedures for moving a file are the same as for moving a folder. In this activity, you will continue to organize folders for college courses by moving the Literature, Music, and Computer_Applications folders into the 3A_Courses folder.

1 In the 3½ Floppy (A:) window or the location you are using, right-drag the **Literature** folder to your **3A_Courses** folder, and then, from the displayed menu, click **Move Here**.

This moves the *Literature* folder into the *Courses* folder. Notice that the *Literature* folder no longer displays in the 3½ Floppy (A:) window.

2 Using the left mouse button, drag the **Music** folder to your **3A_Courses** folder.

When you release the left mouse button, the *Music* folder moves to the new location. Recall that dragging with the left mouse button is known simply as *drag*, compared to *right-drag*. When you drag an item, the shortcut menu does not display.

3 In the current location window, right-click the **Computer_Applications** folder, and then, from the displayed menu, click **Cut**. Right-click your **3A_Courses** folder, and then, from the displayed menu, click **Paste**.

When you *cut* an item, that item is removed from its original location and is stored on the Clipboard until you paste the item into a new location. The item remains on the Clipboard until you cut—or copy—another item. Using the Cut command is another method of moving a file or a folder.

4 In the current location window, double-click the **3A_Courses** folder, and then compare your screen with Figure 3.4. Notice that the 3A_Courses folder contains the four course folders.

Contents of your
3A_Courses folder

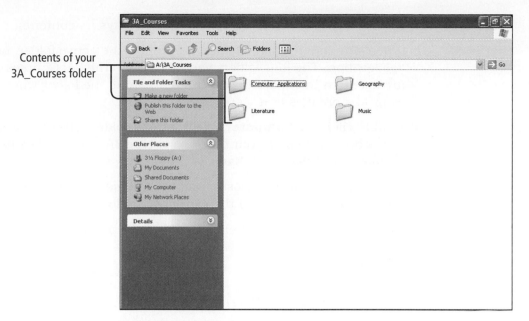

Figure 3.4

5 From the **View** menu, point to **Toolbars**, and then click **Address Bar** to hide the Address Bar. **Close** the 3A_Courses window.

Activity 3.3 Creating a File and Storing It in a Folder

To document the organizational structure of the files and folders that you are working with in this chapter, you will create a WordPad file and store it in the Computer_Applications folder.

1 Click **Start**, point to **All Programs**, point to **Accessories**, and then click **WordPad**.

2 In the displayed WordPad window, type your name, and press Enter two times.

3 On the new line, type the following:

I have created the following folder structure for the 3A_Courses project. and then press Enter twice.

4 On the toolbar, click the **Save** button . In the **Save As** dialog box, click the **Save in arrow** and then click **3½ Floppy (A:)**.

The Save As dialog box reads the floppy disk and displays the 3A_Courses folder.

5 Double-click the **3A_Courses** folder to displays its contents.

When you double-click a folder, it becomes the active folder, or storage location. The four folders you moved into the 3A_Courses folder are listed. In this manner you can navigate to the folder where you want to store files that you create.

6 Double-click the **Computer_Applications** folder. Click the **File name** box, and using your own name, type **3A_Courses_Firstname_Lastname** and then click **Save**.

The Save As dialog box closes, and *3A_Courses_Firstname_Lastname* displays in the title bar of the WordPad window.

7 On the WordPad title bar, click the **Close** button ⊠.

Objective 2
Manage Folders Using Windows Explorer

You have worked with the Contents pane of the My Computer window and used the commands displayed in the left pane to work with files and folders. The My Computer icon on your desktop provides easy access to the file management program, known as *Windows Explorer*, which is a feature of the Windows XP operating system. If you open the Windows Explorer program directly, it displays the file structure of your computer on the left side of the screen. Viewing the file structure on your computer helps you navigate the drives, locate files, and manage the overall organizational structure of drives, folders, and files. For example, you may want to view the hard disk drive or other storage devices or view the folder structure you have created for a project. This view also makes it easier to move folders from one storage area to another.

Activity 3.4 Navigating the Folders List

When you open Windows Explorer, it displays the *Folders list* on the left side of the window, which is a pane that displays the hierarchical structure of your computer. This structure is sometimes referred to as a *directory tree*. In this activity, you will use the Folders list to explore the overall organization of your computer.

1 From the **Start** menu, display the **All Programs** menu, and then display the **Accessories** menu. On the **Accessories** menu, click **Windows Explorer**. If necessary, display the Address Bar. Compare your screen with Figure 3.5.

The Folders list displays on the left with the My Documents folder selected. The Folders list displays the hierarchical organization of files and drives on your computer. The Desktop is listed at the top, and the My Documents folder branches off of the Desktop. Subfolders such as My Pictures branch off of My Documents. In this manner, folders and subfolders are considered branches of a tree. Your screen may differ from the one shown here, depending on the storage devices available on your system and the contents of your My Documents folder.

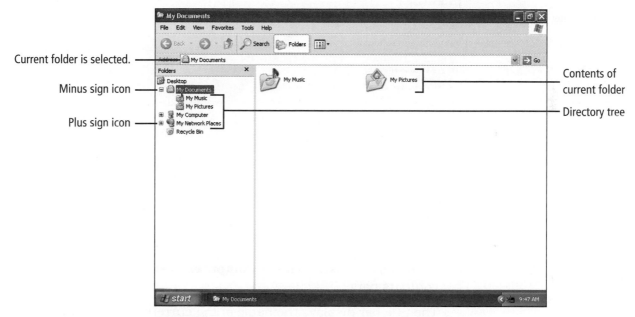

Current folder is selected.
Minus sign icon
Plus sign icon
Contents of current folder
Directory tree

Figure 3.5

2 In the Folders list, to the left of the My Documents folder icon, click the **minus sign** icon.

A minus sign icon to the left of any item in the Folders list indicates that you can click the minus sign icon to *collapse*—or hide—the contents of that folder. In this case, when you click the minus sign icon next to My Documents, the branches—or subfolders—associated with My Documents are hidden in the Folders list. This action is referred to as *collapsing*. My Documents is still the current folder, and its contents still display in the Contents pane.

3 In the Folders list, to the left of the My Computer folder icon, click the **plus sign** icon, and then compare your screen with Figure 3.6.

When you click the plus sign, the hidden branches off of My Computer *expand*—or display. Notice that My Documents is still the current folder. Your screen may differ from the one shown here, depending on the storage devices available on your system and the contents of your My Computer folder.

My Documents is collapsed.

My Computer is expanded.

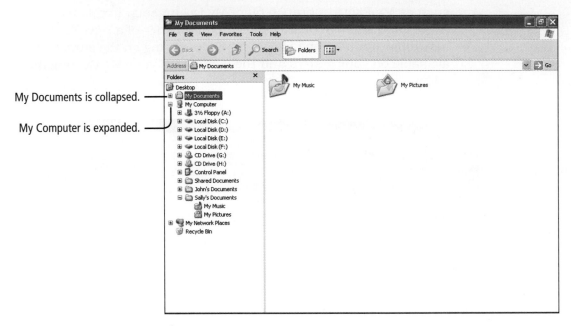

Figure 3.6

4 In the Folders list, click **My Computer** to show its contents in the contents pane.

The title bar displays the name of the current folder or window, in this case *My Computer*. The Contents pane displays the contents of My Computer, which includes the storage components of your computer system and a few select folders.

5 In the Folders list, under **My Computer**, to the left of 3½ Floppy (A:) or the storage location you are using click the **plus sign** to expand the contents. Then, to the left of your 3A_Courses folder, click the **plus sign**.

In the Folders list, you can now see the folder and subfolders stored on your floppy disk. My Computer still displays in the title bar of the window.

6 In the **My Computer** window, position the mouse pointer over the border between the Folders list and the Contents pane so that the horizontal resize pointer displays ⟷. Drag the border to the right or left to resize the panes just enough to display the names of all items in the Folders list, and then compare your screen with Figure 3.7. In this manner you can adjust the size of the left and right panes. Your screen may differ based on the view you are using.

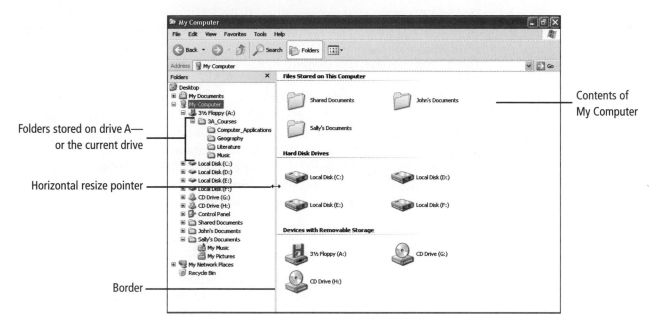

Figure 3.7

7 In the Folders list, under **My Computer**, click your **3A_Courses** folder to make it the current folder and display its contents.

The four subfolders that you moved into your 3A_Courses folder now display in the Contents pane.

8 In the Contents pane, double-click the **Computer_Applications** folder.

To open a folder and display its contents, you can click the folder one time in the Folders pane or double-click the folder when it displays in the Contents pane.

9 In the Contents pane, right-click the **3A_Courses_Firstname_ Lastname** file. From the shortcut menu, point to **Open with** and then click **WordPad**. If an Open With dialog box displays, click WordPad, and then click OK. Leave the file open for at least one minute to create a history of the file.

Windows XP starts WordPad and opens the file. Alternatively, you could double-click a file name, and the program that is associated with that type of file would open. If you had Microsoft Word installed on your computer, the file would probably open in Microsoft Word. Leaving the file open for a minute or longer creates a history record, which you will view later.

10 Close **WordPad**.

Activity 3.5 Moving Files and Folders Between Storage Devices

In the Folders list, each storage device on your computer is identified by a letter. Letters A and B are reserved for floppy disk drives. Many computers today no longer come with a floppy disk drive installed, but if one is installed, it is designated as drive A. The hard disk drive on your computer is identified by the letter C, but it may be *partitioned*—divided into separate sections—and therefore use more than one drive letter. If your computer has a CD drive or a DVD drive, those drives will generally be the next ones that are assigned drive letters. Your computer may also have other types of portable storage devices, such as a flash drive, that plug into a USB port. If your computer is connected to a network, additional drive letters will display.

To manage the resources of your computer, you will want to know the drive letter associated with each storage device and how to move files and folders among the various storage devices available to you. In this activity, you will create a new folder in My Documents and move the 3A_Courses folder and its contents from the floppy disk to the new folder. Then, you will copy the new folder and its contents back to the floppy disk. This method could be used to copy a folder from one floppy disk to another.

1 In the **Computer_Applications** window, on the Standard Buttons toolbar, click the **Folders** button [Folders].

The Folders list closes, and the left pane that you worked with in the My Computer view of Windows Explorer displays. Recall that My Computer is an icon that opens the Windows Explorer program to a particular window. You can switch between the My Computer view of Windows Explorer and the view that displays the Folders list by clicking the Folders button.

2 Click the **Folders** button [Folders] again. In the Folders list, click **My Documents** to make it current.

3 In the **Contents pane**, right-click a blank area, point to **New**, and then click **Folder**. Type **3A_Personal** and then press Enter.

The commands for managing files and folders are still available. You can create new folders, move, copy, rename, and delete files and folders.

4 In the Folders list, under **My Computer**, click **3½ Floppy (A:)** or the location you are using to make it current. In the **Contents pane**, click the **3A_Courses** folder.

5 From the menu bar, click **Edit**, and then click **Move to Folder**.

The Move Items dialog box displays, with the folders and files in the same organization as they have in the Folders list. Here you select the location where you want to move the selected folder. This is another method for moving files and folders.

Alert!

Move to Folder Option Not on Shortcut Menu

If you clicked the 3A_Courses folder in the Folders list instead of the Contents pane, the Move to Folder option will not display on the menu.

6 In the **Move Items** dialog box, scroll as needed, and to the left of *My Documents*, click the **plus sign**, if necessary, and then click **3A_Personal**. Compare your screen with Figure 3.8.

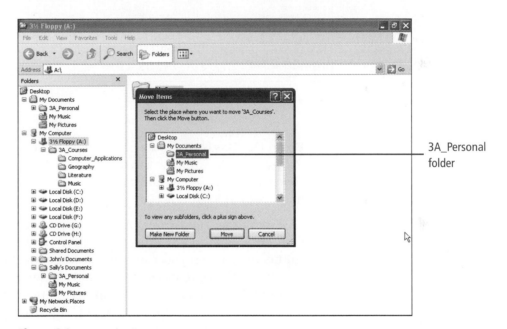

3A_Personal folder

Figure 3.8

7 In the **Move Items** dialog box, click **Move**.

A Moving dialog box may display briefly on your screen as the 3A_Courses folder and its contents move from drive A to the 3A_Personal folder in My Documents. You can also use the Copy to Folder command and the Copy Items dialog box to copy items to a new location.

8 In the Folders list, under **My Documents**, click the **3A_Personal** folder, and then to the left of the 3A_Courses folder, click the **plus sign** to expand the list of folders. Compare your screen with Figure 3.9.

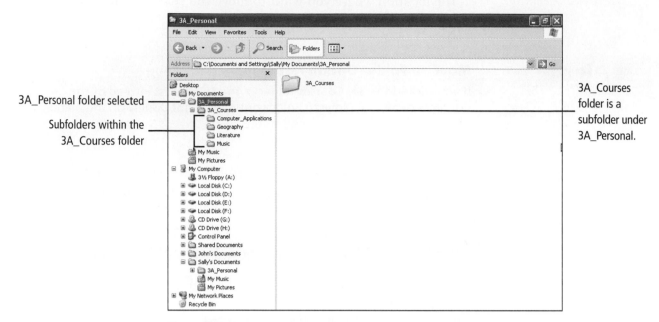

3A_Personal folder selected

Subfolders within the 3A_Courses folder

3A_Courses folder is a subfolder under 3A_Personal.

Figure 3.9

9 From the **Contents pane**, drag the **3A_Courses** folder to the **3½ Floppy (A:)** location or to your current location in the Folders list. Release the mouse button when the destination location is highlighted, as shown in Figure 3.10.

You can drag, right-drag, or cut, copy, and paste items from the Contents pane to any storage location in the Folders list. This is useful because when you can see a storage location in the Folders list, you do not have to navigate through folder windows to copy or move an item. When you drag an item between storage devices, the file or folder is copied. To move it instead, right-drag and then click Move Here from the shortcut menu.

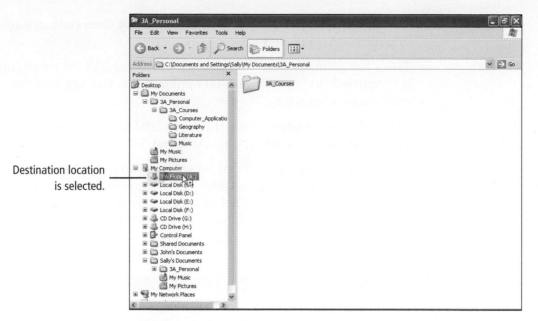

Destination location is selected.

Figure 3.10

Activity 3.6 Copying Groups of Files Using the Send To Command

If you select one or more files, you can use the Send To command to copy the files to another location. You can copy the files to the My Documents folder or to another location such as a floppy disk drive, CD drive, or other type of removable drive.

1 In the Folders list, use the techniques you have practiced to navigate to the location where the student files for this textbook are stored. Be sure the contents of the folder display in the Contents pane on the right side of the window.

Recall that in the Folders list you can click the folder to expand that location and see the folders and files that it contains. In the Contents pane, you can also double-click a drive or folder to display its contents.

2 On the Standard Buttons toolbar, click the **Views** button and then click **Details**.

3 In the Contents pane, click **3A_Picture1**, hold down Ctrl, and then click **3A_Picture3**.

Two nonadjacent picture files are selected. In Windows-based applications, use Ctrl to select nonadjacent items from a list.

4 Click an empty area of the Contents pane.

The two files are no longer selected.

5 In the Contents pane, click **3A_Picture1** and then hold down Shift and click **3A_Picture3**.

Three adjacent files are selected—3A_Picture1, 3A_Picture2, and 3A_Picture3. In Windows-based applications, use Shift to select adjacent items from a list.

6 Right-click anywhere on the three selected files, and then, from the displayed shortcut menu, point to **Send To**.

A submenu of commands displays. Here you can choose to send the files to the My Documents folder, the floppy disk drive, a CD drive, or another storage area. The list of items shown on your screen may differ from those shown in Figure 3.11, depending on your computer configuration.

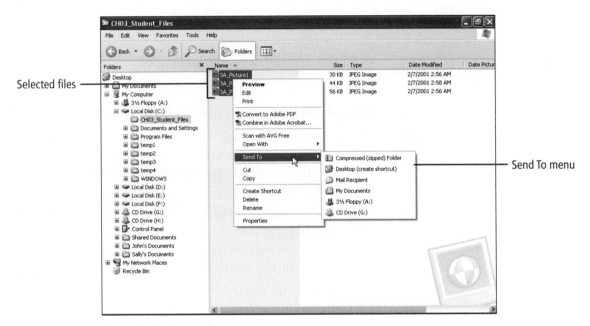

Figure 3.11

7 From the displayed submenu, click **3½ Floppy (A:)**.

When you use the Send To command, the files are copied to the new location rather than moved.

Alert! — Floppy Disk Drive Not Available

If your computer does not have a floppy disk drive and you are using an alternative location to store your files, the Send To option may not display the alternate location. You will need to use another method that you have practiced in this chapter to copy and paste the three files to the alternative storage device.

8 In the Folders list, click **3½ Floppy (A:)** to display the contents of the disk in drive A.

The picture files are displayed in the Contents pane.

9 In the Contents pane, right-click a blank area. From the displayed shortcut menu, point to **New**, and then click **Folder**. Type **3A_Pictures** and then press [Enter] to rename the folder.

10 Using one of the techniques you have practiced, move the picture files into the **3A_Pictures** folder you just created.

11 In the Folders list pane, scroll up as necessary so that the My Documents folder is visible. Be sure the minus sign displays next to the My Documents folder.

My Documents is visible in the Folders pane, but the contents of the floppy disk drive still show in the Contents pane.

12 In the Contents pane, drag the **3A_Pictures** folder to the **3A_Personal** folder under My Documents. When the 3A_Personal folder is selected, release the mouse button.

Because you dragged the folder from one storage device—drive A—to another—the My Documents folder on drive C—the folder and its files are copied.

Note — If the Folder You Want Is Not Visible

When you drag files and folders between storage devices, pause the mouse pointer over the destination folder, and the folder will expand to display any subfolders. In the previous step, if the My Documents folder is collapsed, while you are dragging the 3A_Pictures folder, pause the mouse pointer over the My Documents folder, wait for it to expand, and then move the pointer to the 3A Personal folder before releasing the mouse button.

Objective 3
Work with Explorer Bar Views

In addition to viewing folders, the left pane can display other features that help you locate and access your folders and files. For example, you can search for files, examine the history of recently used files, or add links to the Favorites folder.

Activity 3.7 Adding Items to Favorites

Favorites is a folder in which you store shortcuts—or links—to files or folders that you access frequently. In this activity, you will add the 3A_Courses folder, 3A_Pictures folder, and WordPad file to Favorites so that you can access them without having to navigate through menus and windows.

1 In the Folders list, under **My Documents**, click the **3A_Personal** folder, and then click the **3A_Courses** folder.

2 On the menu bar, click the **Favorites** menu, and then click **Add to Favorites**.

The Favorites menu lists links to the default Favorites locations. The Add Favorite dialog box displays, and in the Name box, the current folder name displays, as shown in Figure 3.12.

Current folder name displays in Name box.

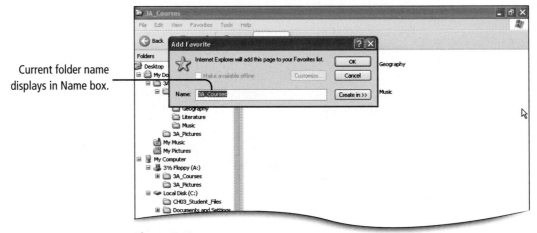

Figure 3.12

3 In the **Add Favorite** dialog box, click **OK** to add a link to the **3A_Courses** folder to Favorites.

4 From the **View** menu, point to **Explorer Bar**, and then click **Favorites** to display the Favorites pane.

The Folders list closes, and the Favorites pane displays on the left and lists the same links as the Favorites menu. Notice that the 3A_Courses folder now displays in the list.

5 In the Contents pane, double-click the **Computer_Applications** folder to display its contents.

6 From the Contents pane, right-drag the **3A_Courses_Firstname_ Lastname** WordPad file to a blank area in the **Favorites** pane. On the shortcut menu that displays when you release the mouse button, click **Copy Here**.

This adds a link to the text file to Favorites, as shown in Figure 3.13. To store a file in Favorites, you must copy the file from its current location into the Favorites pane.

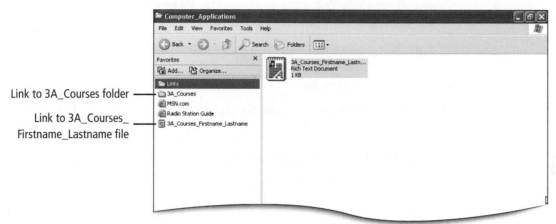

Link to 3A_Courses folder ──

Link to 3A_Courses_ Firstname_Lastname file ──

Figure 3.13

7 On the Standard Buttons toolbar, click the **Up** button 🔼 two times.

The contents of the 3A_Personal folder display on the right.

8 In the Contents pane, double-click the **3A_Pictures** folder to make it the current selection. At the top of the **Favorites** pane, click **Add** to display the **Add Favorite** dialog box. In the **Name** box, verify that 3A_Pictures displays, and then click **OK**.

A link to the current folder is added to Favorites. Notice that the folder is added to the list in the Favorites pane immediately. This is an alternative method for adding items to Favorites.

9 In the Favorites pane, right-click the **3A_Courses_Firstname_ Lastname** link. From the shortcut menu, point to **Open with**, and then click **WordPad** to open the file in WordPad. Leave the file open for at least one minute, and then close **WordPad**.

10 From the **View** menu, point to **Explorer Bar**, and then click **Favorites** to close the Favorites pane.

The left pane displays the command list you used in the My Computer view.

11 From the menu bar, click **Favorites** to display the **Favorites menu**, and then click **3A_Courses** to make that folder current.

You can use either the Favorites pane or the Favorites menu to access links stored in Favorites.

12 From the **Favorites** menu, right-click **3A_Courses**. On the displayed shortcut menu, click **Delete**. In the **Confirm File Delete** dialog box, click **Yes**.

After you delete the folder, the Favorites menu still displays.

13 From the **Favorites** menu, right-click **3A_Pictures**, click **Delete**, and then click **Yes**. Finally, from the **Favorites** menu, delete **3A_Courses_Firstname_Lastname**.

This deletes the links from the Favorites menu and returns the list to its previous state, but the file and folders remain stored in their original locations.

14 Click in a blank area of the Contents pane to close the Favorites menu.

Activity 3.8 Tracking Your File History

The *History pane* displays a list of files and locations you have accessed within the past two weeks, including folders and files stored on your computer, on a network, or on the World Wide Web. The *World Wide Web* is a vast network of computers connected to one another for the purpose of sharing information. In this activity, you use the History pane to open the WordPad file and document the file structure you have created.

1 In the 3A_Courses window, from the **View** menu, point to **Explorer Bar**, and then click **History**. In the History pane, click **View** and then click **By Date**.

The History pane displays links to items you have opened within the past few weeks, as shown in Figure 3.14. Items opened during the current week are grouped by day; items older than one week are grouped by week. The list on your screen reflects the activity on your computer, which will differ from the figure.

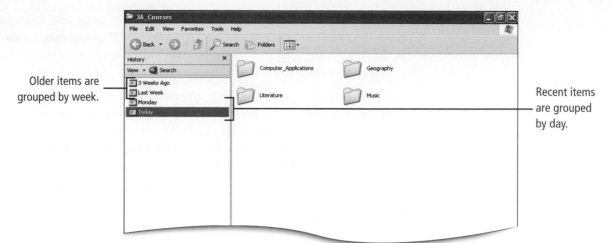

Older items are grouped by week.

Recent items are grouped by day.

Figure 3.14

2 In the **History** pane, click **Today**. Under **Today**, click **My Computer**.

The list expands to display links to the files stored on your computer that you have opened today. The links display in chronological order, with the file opened most recently at the bottom of the list, as shown in Figure 3.15. Your list may differ, depending on the files that you have opened today. Notice that some of the files—including 3A_Courses_ Firstname_Lastname—display more than once. This is because you opened the file from more than one location—the 3A_Courses folder and Favorites. History displays a link to each location. It is possible that you may see one, two, or three occurrences of the WordPad file. The file needs to be open long enough—approximately one minute—for the event to be recorded in the computer's history.

File was opened from two different locations today.

Figure 3.15

3 In the History pane, under **Today**, and then under **My Computer**, point to the first occurrence of **3A_Courses_Firstname_Lastname**. Read the ScreenTip that displays the specific storage location, or path, to the file.

The **path** is the route the computer takes through folders to find, sort, and retrieve files on a disk. Each location—drive, folder, and subfolder—is separated by a slash. By viewing the file path in the ScreenTip, you can identify where this link is stored. In this case, the link goes to the 3A_Courses folder.

4 In the History pane, point to the last occurrence of **3A_Courses_ Firstname_Lastname** to view its path in a ScreenTip.

This file was stored in the Favorites folder. Because you deleted the file from this location, if you clicked this link, Windows would not be able to locate the file.

5 Maximize the window, if necessary, and then press [PrtScr] to capture an image of this history and the folders you created.

6 Click the first occurrence of the **3A_Courses_Firstname_Lastname** file.

The file opens in Word or WordPad, depending on which program has been chosen as the default for this type of file on your computer.

7 Press [↓] four times to move the insertion point to the second empty line under the sentence. On the toolbar, click **Paste** [icon].

8 Drag a corner resize handle toward the center of the image to reduce its size so that the image will fit on one page. Drag the image to position it under the sentence, as shown in Figure 3.16.

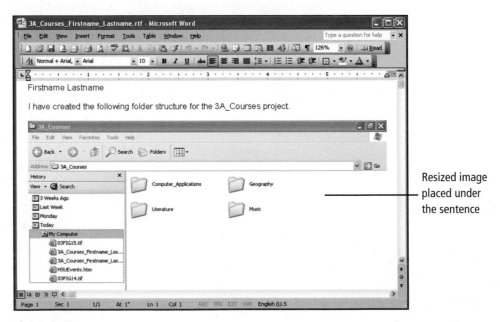

Resized image placed under the sentence

Figure 3.16

9 On the toolbar, click the **Print Preview** button 🔍. If necessary, close the Print Preview window and adjust the image again. Click the **Print** button 🖨.

10 On the menu bar, click **File**, and then click **Save As**. In the Save As dialog box, click the **Save in arrow**, and then click the **My Documents** folder. Double-click your **3A_Personal** folder. In this manner, continue to navigate to the **Computer_Applications** folder.

11 With the **Computer Applications** folder displayed in the **Save in** box, click **Save**. In the **Save As** message box, click **Yes** to *overwrite*—replace the saved file with the new version of the file—the 3A_Courses_Firstname_Lastname file. Close the document and close the program.

The file is saved to the hard disk drive because it is too large to save on your floppy disk.

Objective 4
Compress Files

Files that contain pictures and most *database files*—files that contain collections of related records, for the purpose of sorting, searching, and retrieving information—are often large and require a considerable amount of storage space. Usually this is not a problem for files that are stored on your hard disk drive or on a network drive. However, if you need to send a file as an attachment with e-mail or transport it using a floppy disk or some other portable storage device, you may first want to reduce the file size—which results in a *compressed file*. Windows XP has a program that examines the file and then creates a new file that records the frequency and position of letters and colors in the original file. If there is a lot of repetition of the same color in a picture or the same words and letters in a document, the resulting compressed file may require much less space. The compressed file may be stored or transmitted more efficiently, but compressed files must be uncompressed before they can be used.

Activity 3.9 Compressing Files by Using the Send To Command

1 On the Standard Buttons toolbar, click the **Folders** button 📁 Folders. In the Folders list, under the **My Documents** folder, navigate to the **3A_Courses** folder, and then display its contents in the Contents pane.

2 Double-click the **Computer_Applications** folder. On the Standard Buttons toolbar, click the **Views** button, and then click **Details**.

After adding the picture, the size of 3A_Courses_Firstname_Lastname file is approximately 2,900 kilobytes, or KB, sometimes written as 2.9 MB. *KB* is the abbreviation for *kilobyte*—approximately one thousand bytes of storage—and recall that MB stands for megabyte, approximately 1 million bytes. A floppy disk can hold up to 1,440 KB, which is same as 1.44 MB. Therefore, this file is too large in its current format to store on your floppy disk.

Alert!

Higher Screen Resolutions Result in Larger Screen Capture Files

If your screen is set to a higher resolution than was used to create the figures for this book, the size of the screen capture file will be larger than the size of the example in this activity. If you started with an empty floppy disk, you should have enough room for the compressed version, but you will need to verify that the compressed file size is less than 1,000 KB.

3 Right-click the **3A_Courses_Firstname_Lastname** file. On the displayed shortcut menu, point to **Send To**, and then click **Compressed (zipped) Folder**. If a message box displays prompting you to designate Compressed (zipped) Folders as the application for handling ZIP files, click **Yes**.

A zipped folder icon displays next to the file. The file size is reduced to approximately 100 KB. Windows XP includes a compression program, which is also referred to as a ZIP program.

4 Right-click the **3A_Courses_Firstname_Lastname** zipped folder, point to **Send To**, and then click **3½ Floppy (A:)**, or the storage location you are using for your files. If necessary, use another method to copy this file to your storage device.

The file is copied to your floppy disk.

5 In the Folders pane, click **3½ floppy (A:)**, and then compare your screen with Figure 3.17.

A list of the folders you created and the zipped file display.

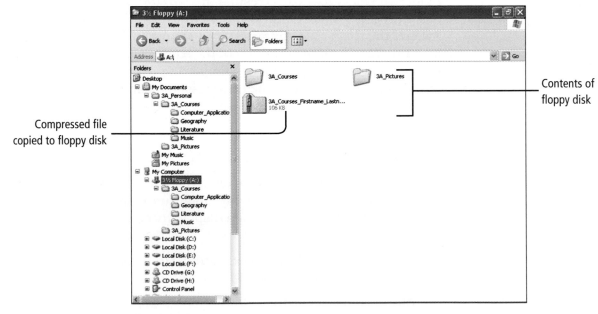

Compressed file copied to floppy disk

Contents of floppy disk

Figure 3.17

Objective 5
Work with Pictures

A *picture file* in Windows XP is a photograph or drawing that has been stored as an image in a graphics format. Windows XP provides unique views for displaying and previewing picture files. In Activities 3.10 and 3.11, you will preview some pictures files that display the geography of New Zealand.

Activity 3.10 Using Filmstrip View

Filmstrip view is available only in folders customized for storing pictures. In Filmstrip view, a preview of the selected picture displays in the Contents pane, with thumbnail-sized images of all pictures in the folder displayed in a row below. In this activity, you will view picture files in Filmstrip view.

1 In the Folders pane, under the **My Documents** folder, click the **3A_Pictures** folder. The folder opens in Filmstrip view, with the 3A_Picture1 file displayed. If the folder does not display in Filmstrip view, click the Views button, and then click Filmstrip.

Alert!

Filmstrip View Is Unavailable

Filmstrip view is available only in folders customized for storing pictures. If Filmstrip view is unavailable, Windows XP will not recognize the folder as storing pictures. To customize the folder for pictures, right-click the folder, click **Properties**, and then click the **Customize tab**. Under **What kind of folder do you want?**, click the **Use this folder type as a template arrow**, and then click **Photo Album (best for fewer files)**. In the **Properties** dialog box, click **OK**. *Properties* are characteristics that control the way an element, such as font size, button size, or color, displays on the screen. In this case, the element displays as a photo album.

2 In the Contents pane, click to select the thumbnail of **3A_Picture2**.

Directly under the preview image are controls for managing the images, as shown in Figure 3.18. The selected thumbnail displays with a selection box around it. Recall that a selection box is a rectangle that displays around an object to indicate that the object is selected. The preview changes to show the selected picture.

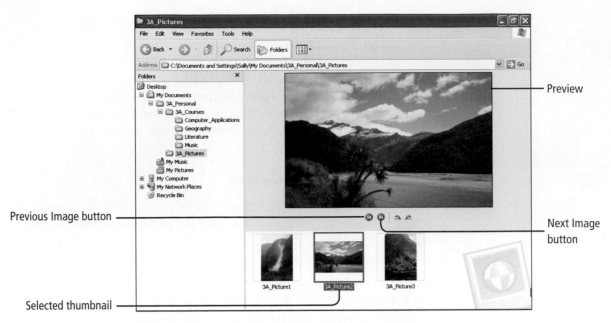

Previous Image button ——

Next Image button

Selected thumbnail ——

Preview

Figure 3.18

3 In the Contents pane, under the picture preview, click the **Previous Image** button ⬛ to scroll to the image to the left—3A_Picture1—and then click the **Next Image** button ⬛ two times to scroll to the image to the right—3A_Picture3.

The Previous image and Next image buttons let you scroll through the files stored in the folder. You can also use the arrow keys on your keyboard. Notice that 3A_Picture3 displays upside down. To display it correctly, you can rotate it *clockwise*—to the right—or *counter-clockwise*—to the left. To *rotate* an image means to turn the image around an axis at the image's center point.

4 In the **3A_Pictures** window, under the preview, click the **Rotate Clockwise** button ⬛ two times.

Each time you click a rotate button, the picture rotates 90 degrees, or one quarter turn. Now, the picture displays right-side up, as shown in Figure 3.19.

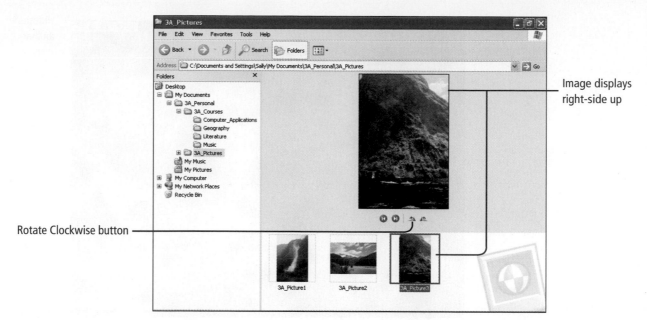

Image displays right-side up

Rotate Clockwise button

Figure 3.19

Activity 3.11 Using Slideshow View

Slideshow view is another view that is available only in folders that are customized for storing pictures. In Slideshow view, Windows XP uses **Windows Picture and Fax Viewer**, which is an image management program that comes with Windows XP, to scroll through full-sized images of all pictures in the folder in the order in which the pictures are currently arranged. In this activity, you will practice displaying the pictures in Slideshow view.

1 In the 3A_Pictures window, click the **Folders** button [Folders], and then under Picture Tasks, click **View as a slide show**.

The View as a slide show command is available only for folders that are customized to display photos or pictures. Windows XP starts the slideshow by displaying the selected picture at full size. If no picture is selected, the slideshow starts with the first picture in the folder. After approximately five seconds, the next picture displays, then the next picture, and then the next. After the last picture, the first picture displays again. You can control the slideshow using buttons on the Slideshow toolbar. For example, you can advance to the next picture, go back to the previous picture, pause, start, or stop the show.

2 On the desktop, move the mouse pointer. The Slideshow toolbar displays in the upper right corner of the screen, as shown in Figure 3.20.

Slideshow toolbar

Picture in Slideshow view

Figure 3.20

3 On the Slideshow toolbar, click the **Pause Slide Show** button 🔘.

When the slideshow is paused, the current image remains displayed indefinitely.

4 On the Slideshow toolbar, click the **Next Picture** button 🔘.

The slideshow advances to the next picture stored in the folder and then remains paused.

5 On the Slideshow toolbar, click the **Start Slide Show** button 🔘 to restart the slideshow from the first picture in the folder. On the

Slideshow toolbar, click the **Previous Picture** button 🔘 to display

the previous picture, and then click the **Next Picture** button 🔘 to display the next picture.

The pictures changes immediately, without waiting for the automatic progression.

6 On the Slideshow toolbar, click the **Close the window** button ❎ to close the slideshow and display the 3A_Pictures folder in Filmstrip view.

7 Close the **3A_Pictures** window.

Objective 6
Share Files and Folders

Windows XP enables you to create **user accounts**—which is a record of all information that identifies an individual to Windows XP, including the user name and any password required to gain access to the account. This provides a private My Documents folder on the computer for individual users to use in storing their files. Files and folders stored in your My Documents folder cannot be accessed by another person using a different account on the same computer unless the other person is logged in as the **administrator**. The administrator on a computer is the master user account that has the authority to add new users, install new programs, and make other types of changes. To make items available to others, you store them in a special folder to which all individuals have access. Sharing files and folders lets you collaborate with colleagues, even while you keep some items separate for your own use.

Activity 3.12 Sharing a Folder and Its Contents

To make a file or subfolder available to others, you store it in a shared folder. A **shared folder** is one that all users on a networked computer can access. It is also available to other users on the same computer. In this activity, you will copy the 3A_Pictures folder into a shared folder.

1 From the taskbar click the **Start** button ![start], and then click **My Computer**.

The default Shared Documents folder displays in the My Computer window, as shown in Figure 3.21. **Shared Documents** is the default shared folder that Windows XP creates during setup. If the folder is also shared over a network, an outstretched hand will display under the folder.

Shared Documents folder ——

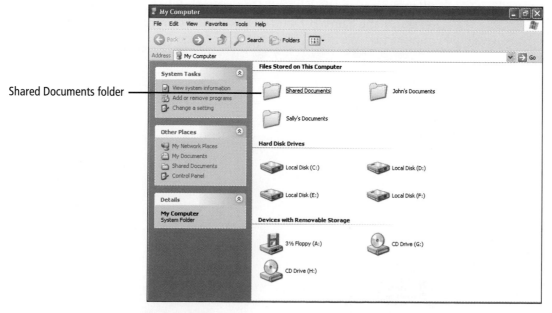

Figure 3.21

2 In the My Computer window, double-click the **Shared Documents** folder.

This folder is designated as a shared folder so that all individuals on the system can access all items stored within it. Windows XP creates subfolders in Shared Documents—including Shared Music and Shared Pictures—to help you organize different types of files. Any folder stored in Shared Documents is also shared.

3 On the Standard Buttons toolbar, click **Folders** 📁 Folders. In the Folders list, click the **My Documents** folder, and then click the **3A_Personal** folder.

The two subfolders—3A_Courses and 3A_Pictures—are displayed in the Contents pane.

4 If necessary, scroll the Folders list pane so that the Shared Documents folder is visible. From the Contents pane, right-drag the **3A_Pictures** folder to the **Shared Documents** folder. From the displayed shortcut menu, click **Copy Here**.

The original remains stored in your My Documents folder. Compare your screen with Figure 3.22. If the 3A_Pictures folder does not display under the Shared Documents folder, collapse and then expand the Shared Documents folder to refresh the view.

Original folder in 3A_Personal folder

Copy of 3A_Pictures in Shared Documents

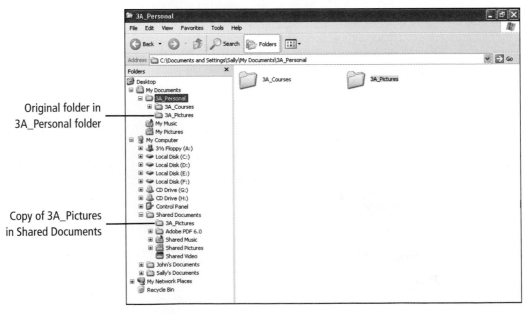

Figure 3.22

Objective 7
Manage the Recycle Bin

Items that you delete from your local drive are not really deleted. Their names are removed from the Folders list and placed in the Recycle Bin. Any time a file name displays in the Recycle Bin, you may re-establish that file's name at its original location. If you choose to delete the file name from the Recycle Bin, its name is removed, and its place on the hard disk is available for use to store other files. Because the file is not actually moved to the Recycle Bin, you cannot restore files that are deleted from other storage media, such as the floppy disk. You can delete individual items from the Recycle Bin, or you can *empty* the Recycle Bin, which means to remove its entire contents.

Activity 3.13 Deleting and Restoring Items and Emptying the Recycle Bin

When you *restore* a file or folder from the Recycle Bin, the file or folder names—including any file or subfolder names—return to their original locations. In this activity, you will practice deleting, restoring, and then emptying the Recycle Bin of its file names and folder names.

1 Under the **Shared Documents** folder, right-click the **3A_Pictures** folder, and then click **Delete**. In the **Confirm Folder Delete** dialog box, click **Yes**.

2 Minimize the window. On the desktop, double-click the **Recycle Bin** icon.

The Recycle Bin window opens.

3 From the **View** menu, click **Details** to change to Details view, and then click the **Date Deleted** column label two times.

The items are sorted in descending order by Date Deleted. The 3A_Pictures folder should display at the top of the list because it is the most recently deleted item. Compare your screen with Figure 3.23. The contents of the Recycle Bin depends on which items you have recently deleted, so your list may differ from the list in the figure. The items you deleted in this session—shortcuts and files—should display near the top of the list.

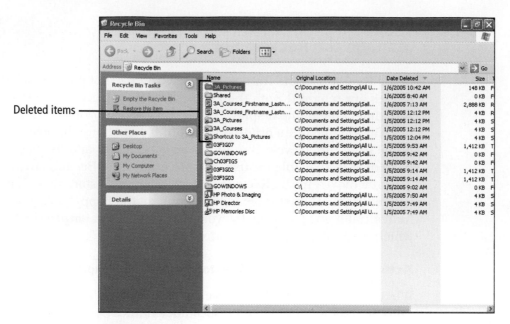

Deleted items

Figure 3.23

4 In the Recycle Bin window, click the **3A_Pictures** folder, and then, in the left pane, click **Restore this item**.

This action removes the item's name from the Recycle Bin and returns it to its original location—the Shared Documents folder.

5 From the taskbar, click the **3A_Personal** taskbar button to display the window. Notice that the 3A_Pictures folder is back in its previous location—the Shared Documents folder.

6 In the Shared Documents folder, right-click the **3A_Pictures** folder, click **Delete**, and then click **Yes**.

7 Make the **Recycle Bin** window active, and then click the **Date Deleted** column label two times to re-sort the list. In the Recycle Bin window, right-click the **3A_Pictures** folder, and then click **Delete**. In the **Confirm File Delete** dialog box, click **Yes** to permanently delete the folder and its contents.

8 In the **Recycle Bin** window, click the **Folders** button [Folders] to display the Folders list. In the Folders list, under **My Documents**, right-click **3A_Personal**, click **Delete**, and then click **Yes**.

9 In the Folders list, click **Recycle Bin** to make it current, and then click the **Folders** button to hide the Folders list.

The items you deleted should display in the list.

More Knowledge — Recovering Deleted Files after Emptying the Recycle Bin

Emptying the Recycle Bin does not delete the files. It removes the file name from the list of files and makes the file's space available for use. If the physical space on the disk has not yet been used to save another file, the original file may still be recovered. Programs designed to accomplish this task are available as freeware and may be downloaded from the Internet.

10 In the left pane, under **Recycle Bin Tasks**, click **Empty the Recycle Bin**. In the **Confirm Multiple File Delete** box, click **Yes** to permanently delete all items from the Recycle Bin.

11 In the **Recycle Bin** window, from the **Tools** menu, click **Folder Options**.

Recall that the Folder Options dialog box is used to control the way folder windows function and display.

12 Click the **View** tab, and then under **Folder views**, click **Reset All Folders**. Click **Yes**, and then click **OK**.

The next time they open, all folder windows will display in the default view.

13 Close the **Recycle Bin** and any remaining windows, and then log off Windows XP. If necessary, shut down your computer and turn off your monitor.

End You have completed Project 3A ――――――――――――――――――――――

Summary

In this chapter you practiced organizing files and folders. In Project 3A, you used the Copy and Move commands to create and organize folders for college courses. You used the WordPad program to document your folder organization. You added files and folders to Favorites so that you could access them from any folder window, and you used the History pane to locate a file you had opened previously. The Send To command was used to move files to a floppy disk and to compress files. You practiced using the Filmstrip and Slideshow views with a folder of pictures. Then you stored the files in a shared folder so that others could access them. Finally, you used the Recycle Bin to restore deleted items, and you emptied the Recycle Bin.

In This Chapter You Practiced How To

- Copy and Move Files and Folders
- Manage Folders Using Windows Explorer
- Work with Explorer Bar Views
- Compress Files
- Work with Pictures
- Share Files and Folders
- Manage the Recycle Bin

Concepts Assessments

Matching   Match each term in the second column with its correct definition in the first column by writing the letter of the term on the blank line in front of the correct definition.

____ **1.** The key used to select nonadjacent files.

____ **2.** A file format that reduces the storage space needed for a file.

____ **3.** A record of all information that defines an individual to Windows XP, including the user name and any password required to gain access to the account.

____ **4.** The key used to select adjacent files.

____ **5.** The left pane in the file management program that displays the hierarchical structure of your computer.

____ **6.** A rectangle that displays around an item onscreen to indicate that the item is selected.

____ **7.** A command that can be used to compress files or to copy files to another drive.

____ **8.** A folder where you can store shortcuts to files or folders that you access frequently.

____ **9.** An icon on your desktop that displays a view of the Windows XP file management program.

____ **10.** A copy of a file stored away from your computer for safekeeping.

____ **11.** The image management program that comes with Windows XP.

____ **12.** The route through the directories to find, sort, and retrieve files on a disk.

____ **13.** To turn an image around a center point.

____ **14.** A folder that all individuals with accounts on the same system can access.

____ **15.** To return a deleted item from the Recycle Bin to its original location.

A Backup

B Compressed

C Ctrl

D Favorites

E Folders

F My Computer

G Path

H Restore

I Rotate

J Selection box

K Send To

L Shared Documents

M Shift

N User account

O Windows Picture and Fax Viewer

Fill in the Blank Write the correct answer in the space provided.

1. When you drag an item between storage devices, the item is

   _____.

2. When you drag a file to a folder on the same storage device, the file is

   _____.

3. To change the pane displayed on the left, click View, and then point

   to _____ to display the available options.

4. To view items you have opened recently grouped by day, in the

   Explorer Bar display the _____ pane.

5. Filmstrip view is available only in folders that are customized for

   storing _____.

6. The view used to display full-sized images of all pictures in a folder is

   called _____ view.

7. The default shared folder that Windows XP creates during setup is

   called _____.

8. Onscreen, you can identify shared folders because the icon includes

   an outstretched _____.

9. The names of items that you delete from your local hard disk are

   added to the _____.

10. To permanently delete all items in the Recycle Bin,

    _____ the bin.

Project 3B — Student Organizations

Objectives: *Copy and Move Files and Folders; Manage Folders Using Windows Explorer; Work with Explorer Bar Views; Compress Files; Work with Pictures; Share Files and Folders; and Manage the Recycle Bin.*

In the following Skill Assessment, you will create and organize folders about student organizations at a typical community college. This will include pictures for the intercollegiate athletic program. You will use WordPad to document your folder organization and save it as *3B_Student_Organizations_Firstname_Lastname*. When completed, your document will look similar to Figure 3.24.

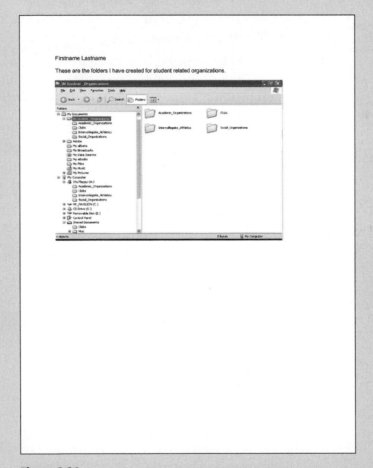

Figure 3.24

1. Place an empty floppy disk in drive A, or insert an empty disk into the storage device where you are saving your files. On the taskbar, click **Start**, and then click **My Computer**. Double-click **3½ Floppy (A:)** or the storage device you are using.

2. In the left pane, under **File and Folder Tasks**, click **Make a new folder**, type **Academic_Organizations** and then press [Enter].

(Project 3B–Student Organizations continues on the next page)

(Project 3B–Student Organizations continued)

3. Right-click the new **Academic_Organizations** folder, and from the displayed shortcut menu, click **Copy**.

4. In an open area of the Contents pane, right-click, and then click **Paste**. Repeat this process two more times to create copies 2 and 3.

5. Right-click the **Copy of Academic_Organizations** folder, click **Rename**, type Social_Organizations and then press Enter. Repeat this process to rename the other two folders you created to **Clubs** and **Intercollegiate_Athletics**

6. On the Standard Buttons toolbar, click the **Folders** button. In the Folders list, click the **My Documents** folder to make it active. In the Contents pane, right-click, point to **New**, and then click **Folder**. Type 3B_Student_Organizations and then press Enter.

7. Click **3½ Floppy (A:)** or the drive where you created the first four folders. From the Contents pane, right-drag the **Academic_Organizations** folder to the **3B_Student_Organizations** folder under My Documents. On the displayed shortcut menu, click **Copy Here**. This command is in bold on the shortcut menu; recall that when you drag between drives, *Copy Here* is the default command, which is the action that occurs if you drag rather than right-drag.

8. On the Standard Buttons toolbar, click **Views**, and then click **Details**. In the Contents pane, click **Clubs**, hold down Shift, and then click **Social_Organizations**—be sure the Clubs, Intercollegiate_Athletics, and Social_Organizations folders are selected. Drag the selected folders to the **3B_Student_Organizations** folder.

9. Click the **3B_Student_Organizations** folder to make it active. From the **3B_Student_Organizations** folder, right-drag the **Clubs** folder to the **Shared Documents** folder. From the displayed shortcut menu, click **Copy Here**. Expand the Shared Documents folder. Because you are dragging the folder to a different folder on the same device—the hard disk drive—you must right-drag to copy the file rather than move it.

10. In the Folders list, move the scrollbar as needed to display the list of the folders on the floppy disk drive, the My Documents folder, and the Shared Documents folder. Press PrtScr.

11. Start WordPad. Type your name and then press Enter two times. Type **These are the folders I have created for student related organizations.** and then press Enter twice. On the toolbar, click **Paste**. On the inserted image, drag a corner resizing handle toward the center of the image to reduce its size to fit on one page.

(Project 3B–Student Organizations continues on the next page)

(Project 3B–Student Organizations continued)

12. On the toolbar, click the **Save** button. Click the **Save in arrow** and navigate to the **3B_Student_Organizations** folder found under the My Documents folder. In the **File name** box, type **3B_Student_ Organizations_Firstname_Lastname** and then click **Save**. Print the WordPad document, and then close WordPad. Retrieve your printout from the printer.

13. In the Folders list, navigate to the location where the files for this chapter are stored. On the Standard Buttons toolbar, click the **Folders** button to display the left pane with the list of commands. Click **3B_Picture1**, hold down Ctrl, and then click **3B_Picture2**.

14. In the left pane, click **Copy the selected items**. In the displayed **Copy Items** dialog box, navigate to the **Shared Documents** folder, click the **Clubs** folder, and then click **Copy**. The pictures are now available in the shared folder.

15. On the Standard Buttons toolbar, click the **Folders** button. Under the **Shared Documents** folder, right-click the **Clubs** folder, point to **Send To**, and then click **3½ Floppy (A:)** or the storage location you are using. In the **Confirm Folder Replace** dialog box, click **Yes** to replace the Clubs folder that is already on the disk in drive A. If the storage location you are using does not display on the Send To list, use another method to copy the Clubs folder to your storage location.

16. Under **My Documents**, click the **3B_Student_Organizations** folder. In the Contents pane, right-click the **3B_Student_Organizations_ Firstname_Lastname** document, point to **Send To**, and then click **Compressed (zipped) Folder**. Use the **Send To** command to copy the compressed folder to the disk in drive A or to the location you are using to preserve a copy of your work. Now that you have copied your files to a portable storage device, they can be deleted from the My Documents and Shared Documents folders.

17. In the Folders list, under **My Documents**, right-click the **3B_Student_Organizations** folder, and then click **Delete**. In the **Confirm Folder Delete** dialog box, click **Yes**. Repeat this procedure to delete the **Clubs** folder found in the **Shared Documents** folder.

18. From the **View** menu, point to **Explorer Bar**, and then click **History**. In the History pane, click **Today**, and then click **My Computer**, and examine the file and folders that you have created in this exercise. Examine the path displayed in the ScreenTip for each file and folder, and determine whether any of these links are still valid. Close **Windows Explorer**.

19. On the desktop, double-click the **Recycle Bin** icon. Select the folders and files related to this exercise. Right-click the selected files, and then click **Delete**. In the **Confirm Multiple File Delete** dialog box, click **Yes**, and then close the Recycle Bin window.

End You have completed Project 3B

Project 3C—Human Resources

Objectives: *Copy and Move Files and Folders; Manage Folders Using Windows Explorer; Work with Explorer Bar Views; Compress Files; Work with Pictures; Share Files and Folders; and Manage the Recycle Bin.*

In the following Performance Assessment, you will create folders to organize files for the Human Resources department at a community college. You will create and print a WordPad document named *3C_Human_Resources_Firstname_Lastname*. When completed, your printed document will look similar to Figure 3.25.

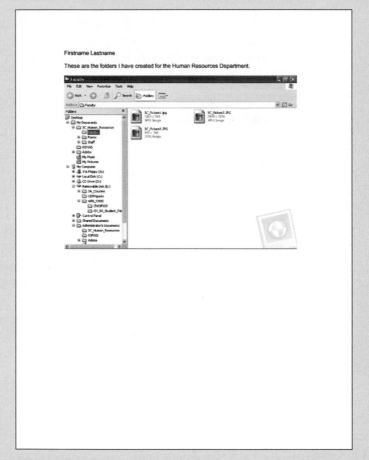

Figure 3.25

1. Open **My Computer**. In the left pane, under **Other Places**, click **My Documents**. In an open area in the Contents pane, right-click, point to **New**, and then click **Folder**. Type **3C_Human_Resources** and then press Enter.

2. Start WordPad. Type your name, press Enter two times, and then type **These are the folders I have created for the Human Resources Department**. Press Enter two times.

(Project 3C–Human Resources continues on the next page)

(Project 3C–Human Resources continued)

3. From the **File** menu, click **Save As**. Save the file in the **3C_Human_ Resources** folder with the file name **3C_Human_Resources_Firstname_ Lastname** and then minimize the WordPad window.

4. In the My Documents window, double-click to open the **3C_Human_ Resources** folder. From the **Favorites** menu, click **Add to Favorites**, and then, in the **Add Favorite** dialog box, click **OK**.

5. From the **3C_Human_Resources** window, click the **3C_Human_ Resources_Firstname_Lastname** file, and then, in the left pane, click **Copy this file**. In the **Copy Items** dialog box, click the **Shared Documents** folder, and then click **Copy**.

6. Click the **Folders** button to display the Folders list. Navigate to the location where the student files for this chapter are stored. Select the files **3C_Picture1**, **3C_Picture2**, and **3C_Picture3**. Right-click the three selected images, and click **Copy**. Navigate to the **3A_Human_Resources** folder, create a new folder named **Faculty**, and then make it the active folder. In the Contents pane, right-click, and then click **Paste**. The three pictures are copied to the Faculty folder.

7. Right-click the **Faculty** folder, and then click **Properties**. Click the **Customize tab**, and then change the **What kind of folder do you want?** list box to **Photo Album (best for fewer files)**. Click **OK**.

8. Close the **Folders list**. In the left pane, under **Picture Tasks**, click **View as a slide show** to display the pictures in the Windows Picture and Fax Viewer as a slideshow. Practice using the Slideshow toolbar to navigate among the pictures. Close the slideshow.

9. Click the **Up** button to move to the 3C_Human_Resources folder. Create a new folder named **Staff** and another named **Forms**

10. Display the **Folders list**, and then click the **Faculty** folder. Change the **View** to **Tiles**. Press PrtScr. On the taskbar, redisplay the WordPad window. Verify that the insertion point is on the last line in the document, and then, on the Standard Buttons toolbar, click **Paste**. Resize the image as needed to ensure that it will fit on one page.

11. On the Standard Buttons toolbar, click **Print Preview**. On the Print Preview toolbar, click **Print** and then, in the **Print** dialog box, click **Print**. Retrieve your printout, save your changes, and then close WordPad.

12. From the **View** menu, point to **Explorer Bar**, and then click **Favorites**. In the Favorites pane, click the **3C_Human_Resources** folder, and then double-click the **3C_Human_Resources_Firstname_Lastname** file to open the file. Because the Favorites pane contains a link, the file with the image of the folder structure displays. Close the file.

(Project 3C–Human Resources continues on the next page)

(Project 3C–Human Resources continued)

13. Display the **Folders list**, and then click the **Shared Documents** folder. Double-click the **3C_Human_Resources_Firstname_ Lastname** file to open it from this location. Because this file is a copy of the original file, it does not contain the image that was added. Close the file. Delete this file from the Shared Documents folder.

14. From the **View** menu, point to **Explorer Bar**, and then click **History**. Click **Today**, and then click **My Computer** to display the activity you have generated. Point to each 3C_Human_Resources file, and examine the path displayed by the ScreenTip to determine which file was opened from the Shared Documents folder. Right-click this file, and then click **Delete**. In the **Warning** box, click **Yes** to confirm that you want to delete the history.

15. Display the **Folders list**, and then click the **3C_Human_Resources** folder. Right-click the **3C_Human_Resources_Firstname_Lastname** file, point to **Send To**, and then click **Compressed (zipped) Folder**. Delete the original file.

16. Use the **Send To** command to copy the **3C_Human_Resources** folder to a blank disk in drive A or to the storage location you are using, to preserve a copy of your work.

17. Under My Documents, right-click the **3C_Human_Resources** folder, and then click **Delete**. From the **Favorites** menu, delete the link to the **3C_Human_Resources_Firstname_Lastname** file.

18. Display the **Recycle Bin**. Select the folders and files related to this exercise. Right-click the selected files, and then click **Delete**. In the **Confirm Multiple File Delete** dialog box, click **Yes**, and then close the Recycle Bin window.

 End You have completed Project 3C

Mastery Assessment

Project 3D — Departments

Objectives: *Copy and Move Files and Folders; Manage Folders Using Windows Explorer; Work with Explorer Bar Views; Compress Files; and Manage the Recycle Bin.*

In the following Mastery Assessment, you will create and organize folders for administrative departments in a typical community college. You will create and print a WordPad document named *3D_Departments_Firstname_ Lastname*. When completed, your document will look similar to Figure 3.26.

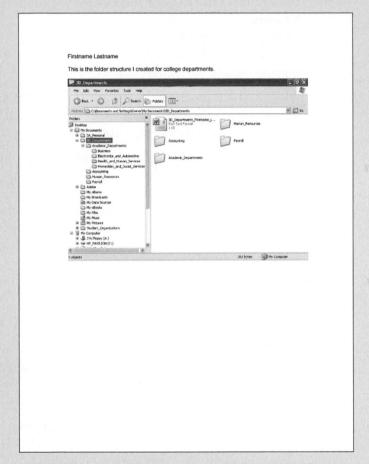

Figure 3.26

1. In the **My Documents** folder, create a new folder named **3D_Departments** and then make it the active folder.

2. From the **Favorites** menu, click **Add to Favorites**. Be sure **3D_Departments** displays in the **Add Favorite** dialog box, and then click **OK**.

3. Start **WordPad**. Type your name and press [Enter] two times. Type **This is the folder structure I created for college departments.** and then press [Enter] two times. **Save** the file in the **3D_Departments** folder using the name **3D_Departments_Firstname_Lastname** and then close WordPad.

(Project 3D–Departments continues on the next page)

(Project 3D–Departments continued)

4. In the **3D_Departments** folder, use the methods you have practiced to create folders with the following names:
   Human_Resources
   Accounting
   Payroll
   Academic_Departments

5. Make the **Academic_Departments** folder the current folder, and then create folders with the following names:
   Business
   Health_and_Human_Services
   Electronics_and_Automotive
   Humanities_and_Social_Sciences

6. Display the **Favorites** pane, and then make the **3D_Departments** folder the current folder. Expand the **Academic_Departments** folder to see the next layer of subfolders you created.

7. Display the **Folders list** pane, expand the folders you created, and compare your results with Figure 3.26. Press PrtScr. Open the **3D_Departments_Firstname_Lastname** file. Move the insertion point to the last line in this document, and then click **Paste**. Adjust the size of the inserted image as needed so that it will display on one page. Save the document, and then print the page if required by your instructor. Close WordPad.

8. Right-click the **3D_Departments_Firstname_Lastname** file, point to **Send To**, and then click **Compressed (zipped) folder**. Delete the original file.

9. Insert a blank disk in drive A or the storage location you are using. Right-click the **3D_Departments** folder, point to **Send To**, and then click **3½ Floppy (A:)** or the storage location you are using, to preserve a copy of your work.

10. Under My Documents, click the **3D_Departments** folder, press Delete, and then click **Yes** to confirm the deletion. You can also use the keyboard to delete files and folders.

11. Click the **Recycle Bin**, and then click the **Folders** button. In the Contents pane, right-click the **3D_Departments** folder you just deleted, and then click **Delete**. Repeat this procedure to delete the **3D_Departments_Firstname_Lastname** file from the Recycle Bin.

12. From the **Favorites** menu, delete the **3D_Departments** link.

End You have completed Project 3D

Project 3E — Concert

Objectives: *Copy and Move Files and Folders; Manage Folders Using Windows Explorer; Work with Explorer Bar Views; Compress Files; Work with Pictures; Share Files and Folders; and Manage the Recycle Bin.*

In this Problem-Solving Assessment, you will practice organizing files and folders to select a cover picture for a jazz concert program at a nearby community college. You will create a folder and a subfolder on a floppy disk—or other storage device—and practice using Windows Picture and Fax Viewer.

1. In the My Documents folder, create a folder named **Jazz_Concert** and within the Jazz_Concert folder, create a second folder named **Program**

2. Use pictures that you find on your own, or copy the files 3E_Picture1, 3E_Picture2, and 3E_Picture3 from the location where the student files for this textbook are stored. Store the files in the Program folder. View the pictures in the Program folder in Filmstrip view and in Slideshow view. Rotate the pictures as necessary. Select the picture you think will make the best program cover, display it in Slideshow view, and then capture it to the Clipboard.

3. Start WordPad, type your name, and then, on a new line, type a sentence to explain why you think the picture you have chosen will be the best one to use as a program cover. Paste the picture into the document. Save the WordPad file to the Program folder as **3E_Concert_Firstname_Lastname**

4. Preview and then print the document if required by your instructor, and then close WordPad. Compress the 3E_Concert_Lastname_Firstname file. Copy the Program folder to the Shared Documents folder so that it can be viewed by others. Move the Concert folder to a blank disk in drive A or to the storage location you are using.

5. Permanently delete the files and any links you have created. Practice all the skills covered in this chapter so that you are comfortable managing files and folders.

End You have completed Project 3E ────────────────────

On the Internet

Recovering Deleted Files

When you delete files and empty the Recycle Bin, Windows XP makes that space on your hard drive available for use. Until that area is overwritten by other files, it is possible to recover files that have been deleted. You can download software from the Internet that will help with this process.

Connect to the Internet, open a Web browser, and then go to **http://www.google.com**. In the Google window, in the Search box, type **restore recycle bin Windows XP** and then click **Search**. Explore some of the sites that are listed to see whether you can locate a program that you can download for free. If you are unable to locate a free program, go to **http://www.zdnet.com**. On the ZDNet site, click **Downloads**. In the **Search** box, type **restoration** and then click **Go**. If you have permission to download files to the computer you are using, in the **Search Results** list, click **Restoration 2.5**, and then click **Download Now**. Follow the instructions that are provided to load the program. Test the software by trying to restore some of the files you have deleted from the Recycle Bin throughout this chapter.

GO! with Help

Windows XP and Photos

Windows XP offers a variety of resources that can help you manage photos that you take.

1. From the **Start** menu, click **Help and Support**.

2. In the Pick a Help Topic section, click **Music, video, games, and photos**. In the displayed list, click **Photos and other digital images** to expand the list, and then click **Working with photos and graphics**.

3. Under Pick a task, explore the topics that are of interest to you.

4. In the left pane, under Photos and other digital images, click one of the other two subtopics listed under this topic.

5. If you want, click the **Print** button to print the information.

6. **Close** the Help and Support window.

Windows XP

4 chapterfour

Customize Windows XP

In this chapter you will: complete this project and practice these skills.

Project 4A Changing Display Settings

Objectives
- Change the Desktop
- Manage the Taskbar
- Customize the Start Menu

Project 4B Changing the Keyboard, Mouse, and User Account Settings

Objectives
- Customize the Keyboard
- Personalize the Mouse
- Modify Your User Account

Customize Windows XP

Businesses and organizations such as schools, city governments, and hospitals often create a desktop image that is representative of the organization. This image is placed on all computers so that the desktop projects a positive image of the organization. Windows XP provides tools that enable you to manage your computer environment to fit your needs and those of your organization.

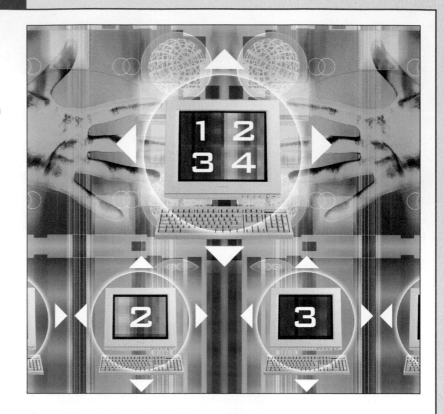

Introduction

Just as you can personalize your desk by adding staplers, pencil holders, and personal mementos, you can personalize Windows XP to suit your working style or your mood. For example, you can change the desktop background to a picture or a solid color, or you can move the taskbar to a different location on the desktop. You can also customize settings that control hardware devices, such as your mouse and keyboard.

Project 4A **Changing the Display**

In this project, you will change the look of desktop components to create a work environment that is visually appealing and enables you to work more efficiently.

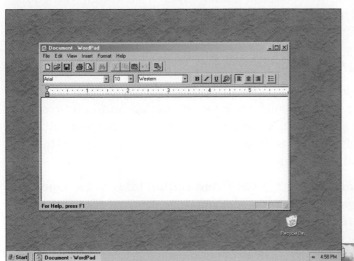

In Activities 4.1 through 4.11, you will standardize display and desktop settings that could be applied to all office computers in an organization. You will prepare three WordPad documents—complete with illustrations—with recommended display settings. You will save the documents as *4A_Display1_Firstname_Lastname*, *4A_Display2_Firstname_Lastname*, and *4A_Display3_Firstname_Lastname*. When completed, your documents will include images that look similar to those shown in Figure 4.1.

Figure 4.1
Project 4A—Changing the Display

Objective 1
Change the Desktop

You can customize the Windows XP environment by changing the appearance of the desktop. For example, you can change the color or picture that displays on the desktop. In Activities 4.1 through 4.4, you will apply display settings, capture the settings, and then paste them into a WordPad document.

Activity 4.1 Setting the Desktop Background

The Bliss picture displays as the background picture by default. You can change the picture or select a solid color for the background picture. In this activity, you will practice changing the picture and the color of the desktop, and you will capture an image of the settings and paste that image into a WordPad document.

1 Start **WordPad**, and then click the **Open** button 📂. In the **Open** dialog box, navigate to the location where the student files for this textbook are stored, and then open the file **wn04A_Display1**. In the document, replace the text *Firstname Lastname* with your own name and *Current Date* with the current date.

Alert!

If the Student Files Do Not Display

If you correctly navigate to the folder that contains your student files but no files are listed, it may be because the correct file type is not selected. The default file type for WordPad documents is rich text format (.rtf). In the Open dialog box, click the Files of type arrow, and then, from the displayed list, click All Documents (*.*). Any files that the selected folder contains will be displayed.

2 From the **File** menu, click **Save As**. In the displayed **Save As** dialog box, click the **Save in arrow**, and then click **Desktop**. In the **File name** box, using your own name, type **4A_Display1_Firstname_ Lastname** and then click **Save**. Minimize the WordPad window.

3 On the desktop, right-click a blank area, and then, from the displayed shortcut menu, click **Properties**. In the **Display Properties** dialog box, click the **Desktop tab** to display the Desktop display options, as shown in Figure 4.2.

To modify the desktop, you can change the background picture and color. The *background*—called *wallpaper* in earlier versions of Windows—is the color, texture, pattern, or picture displayed on the desktop. The Background list includes picture files that come with Windows XP but may also contain picture files that you have stored on your computer. The preview area displays the current selection so that you can see the image before you make a change.

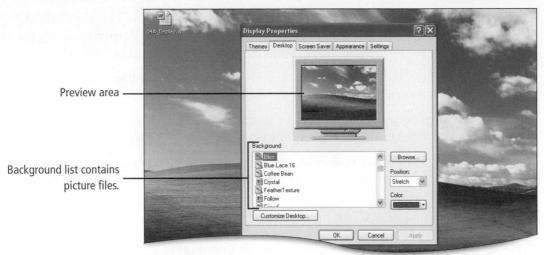

Preview area

Background list contains picture files.

Figure 4.2

4 On the **Desktop tab**, scroll to the top of the **Background** list and click **(None)**. The preview area displays the desktop as a solid color, without the Bliss picture. In the **Display Properties** dialog box, click **Apply**.

Windows XP immediately applies the new setting to the desktop but continues to display the dialog box so that you can select additional display properties.

5 On the **Desktop tab**, click the **Color arrow**.

The color palette displays, as shown in Figure 4.3. A *color palette* is a group of small squares of different colors. These small squares are called *swatches*.

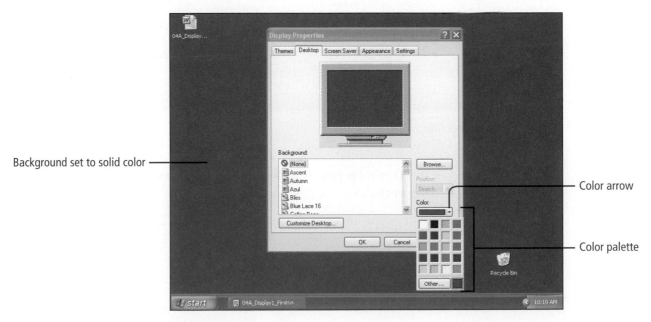

Background set to solid color

Color arrow

Color palette

Figure 4.3

6 On the color palette, click the first color in the last row—**light green**—and then, on the **Desktop tab**, click **Apply** to apply the color to the desktop and continue to display the dialog box.

7 On the **Desktop tab**, scroll the **Background** list, and then click **Santa Fe Stucco**.

The picture displays in the preview area. When you select a picture background, you must also select one of three positions:

- *Tile*—Displays multiple thumbnail-sized copies of the same image in columns and rows across the desktop. Tile is the default setting.

- *Center*—Displays a single image at its actual size, centered on the desktop.

- *Stretch*—Displays a single image, resized to fill the desktop.

8 On the **Desktop tab**, click the **Position arrow**, and then from the displayed list, click **Center** to preview the picture centered. Compare your screen with Figure 4.4.

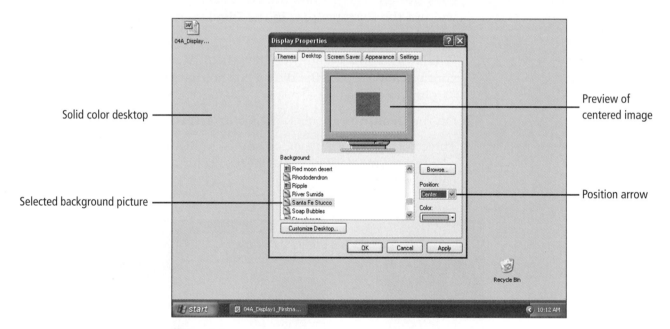

Figure 4.4

9 On the **Desktop tab**, click the **Position arrow**, and then click **Tile** to return to the default position.

10 On the keyboard, press and hold ⌈Alt⌉, press ⌈PrtScr⌉, and then release both keys.

Recall that ⌈PrtScr⌉ captures the entire image on the desktop. Pressing ⌈Alt⌉ at the same time as ⌈PrtScr⌉ modifies the command to capture only the current dialog box or window.

11 From the taskbar, display the WordPad document. After the period at the end of the last line—after the text *Display1*—click to place the insertion point, and then press ⌈Enter⌉ two times. On the toolbar, click the **Paste** button 🖼 to paste the image captured in the previous step.

12 On the toolbar, click the **Print Preview** button 🔍, and then compare your screen with Figure 4.5.

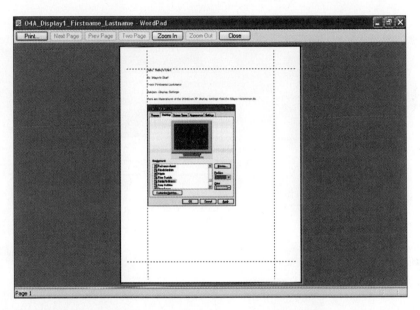

Figure 4.5

13 On the Print Preview toolbar, click **Close**. Save the changes to the file, and then minimize the WordPad.

14 In the **Display Properties** dialog box, click **OK**.

Windows XP displays the message *Please Wait* and then closes the dialog box and displays the new background.

Activity 4.2 Changing the Desktop Appearance

You can customize the desktop appearance to change the way screen elements—such as buttons and title bars—are shaped and sized. You can also change the size of text characters used on toolbar buttons and menus. In this activity, you will change the desktop appearance settings, capture an image of the dialog box, and paste it into the WordPad document.

1 On the desktop, right-click a blank area, and then click **Properties**. In the **Display Properties** dialog box, click the **Appearance tab**.

The Appearance options display, as shown in Figure 4.6. The default settings include the Windows XP style in the Default (blue) color scheme, with the Normal font size. The *style* is the way screen elements such as buttons and windows are shaped and sized. The *color scheme* is a set of coordinated colors applied to every window element.

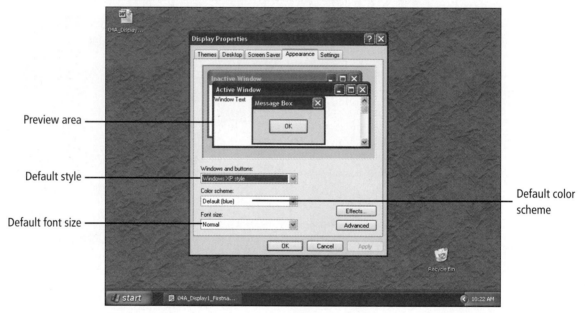

Preview area

Default style

Default font size

Default color scheme

Figure 4.6

2 On the **Appearance tab**, click the **Windows and buttons arrow** to display the list of available styles, and then click **Windows Classic style**.

The two style options are *Windows Classic style* and *Windows XP style*. The Windows Classic style, used in previous versions of Windows, has trim, straight-edged bars, borders, and buttons. The Windows XP style has larger bars and buttons, with rounded borders and bolder colors. After you select a style, you can select a color scheme and a font size. These settings override previously selected settings, including the background color.

3 On the **Appearance tab**, click the **Color scheme arrow** to display the list of available color schemes, and then click **Lilac**.

Windows Classic style has a lengthy list of color schemes. Windows XP style has only three color schemes.

4 On the **Appearance tab**, click the **Font size arrow**, and then click **Large**. Compare your screen with Figure 4.7.

The preview area displays the Lilac color scheme with a large font size, in the Windows Classic style. The number of available font sizes depends on the selected color scheme. Recall that the desktop does not change, because the settings take effect only after you click Apply or OK in the Display Properties dialog box.

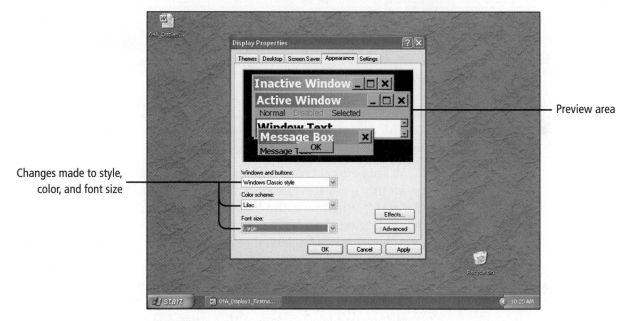

Figure 4.7

5 On the **Appearance tab**, display the list of color schemes, click **Desert**, and then click **Apply**.

A *Please Wait* message may display while Windows XP applies the new desktop appearance settings. The Desert theme also changes the font size back to Normal. The Display Properties dialog box continues to display, as shown in Figure 4.8.

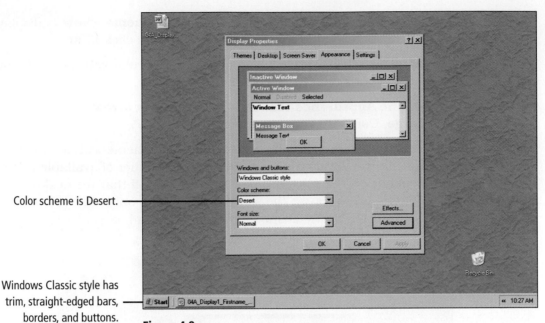

Color scheme is Desert. ————

Windows Classic style has
trim, straight-edged bars, ———
borders, and buttons.

Figure 4.8

6 On the **Appearance tab**, click **Advanced** to display the **Advanced Appearance** dialog box.

From this dialog box, you can customize each screen element independently from the others. For example, you can change the color of the active title bar or the font size used on icons. The options vary, depending on the selected screen element and the current style and color scheme. The selected screen element displays in the Item box.

7 In the **Advanced Appearance** dialog box, verify that **Desktop**—the screen element you want to change—displays in the **Item** box. Click the **Color 1 arrow**, click the fourth color in the third row—**teal**—and then compare your screen with Figure 4.9.

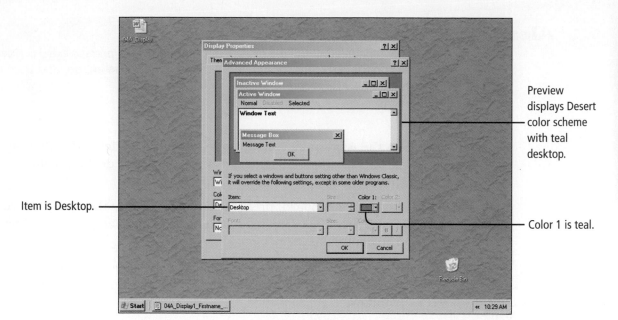

Item is Desktop.

Preview displays Desert color scheme with teal desktop.

Color 1 is teal.

Figure 4.9

8 On your keyboard, press [Alt] + [PrtScr] to capture an image of the **Advanced Appearance** dialog box, and then, from the taskbar, click to display the WordPad document. Press [Ctrl] + [End]—the keyboard shortcut to move the insertion point to the end of the document— press [Enter] two times, and then, on the toolbar, click the **Paste**

button 🔲 to paste the image into the document.

9 Press [Ctrl] + [End] and then press [Enter] two times. Using your own name, type **4A Display1 Firstname Lastname Save** the WordPad file, and then minimize the window.

When you print this document, the second image will print on a second page. You added the file name and your name after the second image to ensure that you will be able to find your work if you print it in a computer lab.

10 In the **Advanced Appearance** dialog box, click **OK**. The Display Properties dialog box displays with the new desktop color in the preview area.

11 On your keyboard, press ⌊Alt⌋ + ⌊PrtScr⌋. Display the **WordPad** document. Press ⌊Ctrl⌋ + ⌊End⌋, press ⌊Enter⌋ two times, and then **paste** the image into the document.

12 Press ⌊Ctrl⌋ + ⌊End⌋, press ⌊Enter⌋ two times, and then type **4A Display1 Firstname Lastname Save** the file, and then minimize the WordPad window.

13 In the **Display Properties** dialog box, click **OK**.

Windows XP applies the new desktop appearance settings, and the dialog box closes. The Desert color scheme and teal desktop color affect the display of windows and dialog boxes. The desktop background displays Santa Fe Stucco.

Activity 4.3 Using Desktop Themes

Windows XP comes with coordinated sets of icons, colors, and sounds that you can apply simultaneously. You can also save your current display settings as a set. In this activity, you will save the current settings and apply a different coordinated set.

1 From the **Start** menu, click **Control Panel**. If necessary, in the left pane, click Switch to Category View. In the Control Panel, click **Appearance and Themes**, and then under **or pick a Control Panel icon**, click **Display**.

The **Control Panel**—a folder that Windows XP creates during setup—provides access to commands for customizing your computer system hardware and software. This is an alternative method for opening the Display Properties dialog box. In the Display Properties dialog box, the Themes tab is active. In the Theme box, the name of the current *theme* displays, and in the Preview area, a preview displays. A theme is the term for a coordinated set of properties. A *desktop theme* includes a background color or picture and a collection of system sounds, icons, and colors.

2 On the **Themes tab**, click **Save As** to open the Save As dialog box, and then compare your screen with Figure 4.10.

By default, Windows XP stores a new theme file—with the name *My Favorite Theme*—in the My Documents folder. You can change the theme name in the Save As dialog box. Leave the storage location exactly as it is—otherwise, the new theme will not be available from the Theme list in the Display Properties dialog box.

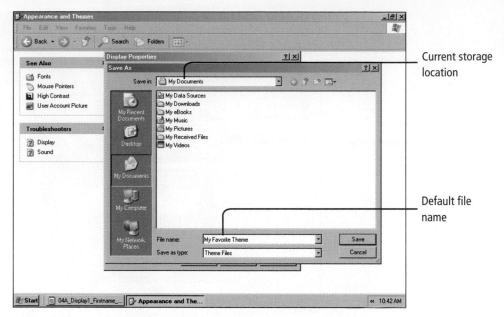

Current storage location

Default file name

Figure 4.10

3 In the **Save As** dialog box, with the default file name *My Favorite Theme* selected, type **Desert Theme** and then click **Save**.

Windows XP saves the new theme file. The Display Properties dialog box remains open, and in the Theme box, the name of the new theme displays.

4 On the **Themes tab**, click the **Theme arrow** to display the list of available themes, and then compare your screen with Figure 4.11.

The Themes list includes two built-in themes—Windows XP and Windows Classic. The new Desert Theme also displays. The More themes online option links to the Microsoft Plus home page, a commercial Web site from which you can purchase the program Microsoft Plus. If your computer has Microsoft Plus, you may be able to download additional themes without charge. Your Themes list may differ if additional customized themes have been created and saved on your computer. If changes have been made to any display properties settings, the Themes list will include a modified version of the current theme.

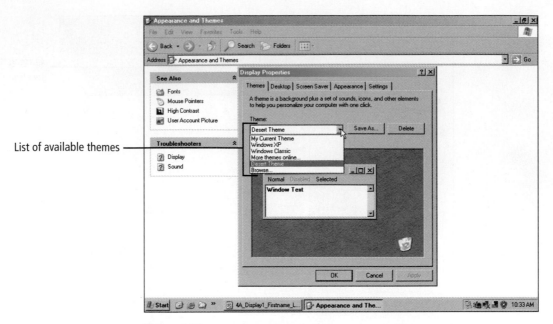

List of available themes ——

Figure 4.11

5 From the **Theme** list, click **Windows Classic**.

The preview changes to display the Windows Classic theme.

6 From the **Theme** list, click **Desert Theme**.

The preview changes to display the settings saved in the Desert Theme.

7 On the **Themes tab**, click **Delete**.

Windows XP deletes the Desert Theme. No delete confirmation dialog box displays.

8 Display the **Theme** list, and then, if necessary, click **Windows XP**. Click **OK** to apply the new settings and close the dialog box.

A *Please Wait* message displays while changes are made to your desktop. The Appearance and Themes Control Panel window still displays. When you select a theme, it overrides any previously set desktop properties, such as background or style.

9 In the **Appearance and Themes** Control Panel window, click the

Close button ✕.

The desktop displays the Windows XP theme.

Activity 4.4 Selecting a Screen Saver

A *screen saver* is a program that displays an animated image on the monitor when your computer is idle for a specified period of time and obscures the desktop and any open items. The animated image may be informational—for example, you could set the text *Back Soon* to scroll across the screen—or decorative—for example, dancing flowerpots. In this activity, you will select a screen image to display when the monitor is inactive, capture an image of the dialog box settings, and paste the image into the WordPad document. Finally, you will print the document.

1 Display the **Display Properties** dialog box, and then click the **Screen Saver tab**.

Recall that you can display the Display Properties dialog box by right-clicking the desktop and then clicking Properties or by using the Control Panel.

2 On the **Screen Saver tab**, click the **Screen saver arrow**, and then, from the displayed list of available screen savers, click **Starfield**.

The preview area displays the Starfield screen saver.

3 In the **Display Properties** dialog box, on the **Screen Saver tab**, in the **Wait** spin box, select the value displayed and then type **1** Alternatively, you can click the up or down arrows to change the setting. Compare your screen with Figure 4.12.

The value you enter in the Wait spin box is the amount of time in minutes that the system should remain idle—the keyboard is not touched and the mouse is not moved—before the screen saver displays.

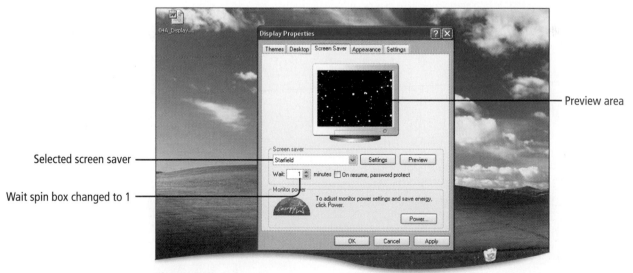

Preview area

Selected screen saver

Wait spin box changed to 1

Figure 4.12

4 On your keyboard, press ⟨Alt⟩ + ⟨PrtScr⟩. From the taskbar, click to display the **WordPad** document. Move the insertion point to the end of the document, press ⟨Enter⟩ two times, and then click **Paste**.

5 Press ⟨Ctrl⟩ + ⟨End⟩, press ⟨Enter⟩ two times, and then type **4A Display1 Firstname Lastname Save** the file, and then minimize the WordPad window.

6 In the **Display Properties** dialog box, click **OK**. Without touching your computer's keyboard or mouse, wait for one minute until the Starfield screen saver displays.

7 On the keyboard, press any key. Alternatively, move your mouse in any direction.

Either of these actions causes the screen saver to deactivate and the Windows XP desktop to display.

8 On the desktop, right-click any blank area, click **Properties**, and then, in the **Display Properties** dialog box, click the **Screen Saver tab**. On the **Screen Saver tab**, click the **Screen saver arrow**, and then, from the list of screen savers, click **Windows XP**.

9 In the **Wait** spin box, change the value to **15** and then click **OK** to apply the settings and close the dialog box.

10 From the taskbar, display the **WordPad** document. On the toolbar, click the **Print Preview** button ⟨🔍⟩.

The first page of the document displays in Print Preview. Only the typed text and the first image display on the first page. The other items display on their own pages.

11 On the Print Preview toolbar, if necessary, click **Two Page** to show two pages—pages 1 and 2—at the same time, as shown in Figure 4.13.

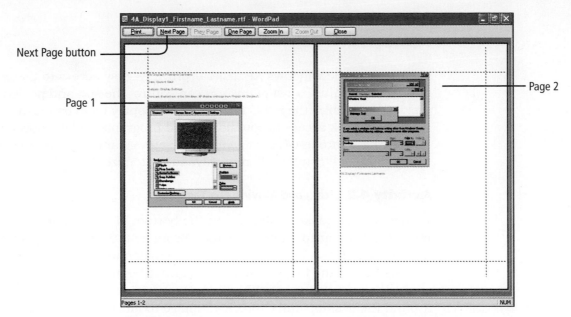

Next Page button ——

Page 1 ——

—— Page 2

Figure 4.13

☑ On the Print Preview toolbar, click **Next Page** to display pages 2 and 3, and then click **Next Page** again to display pages 3 and 4.

☑ On the Print Preview toolbar, click **One Page** to display only one page of the document at a time. Click **Print** to display the **Print** dialog box, and then click **Print** to print the document—all four pages—using the default settings.

☑ When the printing is complete, retrieve your printout from the printer, and then close the WordPad document and save all changes.

Objective 2
Manage the Taskbar

Customizing the Windows XP taskbar provides easy access to the programs and folders you use most often. You can control the size and position of the taskbar, customize the notification area, or display toolbars on the taskbar to provide quick access to commonly used programs and windows. In Activities 4.5 through 4.8, you will apply settings and capture images of the desktop to illustrate different ways to customize the taskbar.

Activity 4.5 Sizing and Moving the Taskbar

By default, the taskbar displays at the bottom of the desktop. You can move the taskbar to another location or make it wider to display more information. If you like the taskbar in a particular location, you can lock the position of the taskbar so that it cannot be moved. In this activity, you will create and save a WordPad document. You will move the taskbar around the desktop and capture an image to illustrate a different position.

1 Start **WordPad**, click the **Open** button ⌐. In the **Open** dialog box, navigate to the location where the student files for this textbook are stored, and then open the file *wn04A_Display2*. In the document, replace the text *Firstname Lastname* with your own name and *Current Date* with the current date.

2 From the **File** menu, click **Save As**. In the displayed **Save As** dialog box, click the **Save in arrow**, and then click **Desktop**. Click the **File name** box, type **4A_Display2_Firstname_Lastname** and then click **Save**. Minimize the WordPad window.

3 On the taskbar, right-click a blank area—an area that has no buttons and that is not in the notification area—to display the shortcut menu, and then point to the **Lock the Taskbar** command. If a check mark displays next to *Lock the Taskbar*, click Lock the Taskbar to turn it off. If no check mark displays, click a blank area of the desktop to close the shortcut menu.

A check mark to the left of the command means that the taskbar is *locked*, or fixed in its current position. You must turn off the Lock the Taskbar command in order to move the taskbar.

4 On the taskbar, point to a blank area, and then slowly drag the taskbar straight up toward the top of the desktop. Notice that when your mouse pointer reaches the middle of the screen, the taskbar moves to the top of the screen. If your taskbar moves to the left or right side of the desktop, you may have dragged left or right instead of up—continue dragging the taskbar straight up toward the top of the desktop to move the taskbar to the top of the screen.

This action is known as **docking**, which means to position a toolbar in a set location along any side of the desktop.

5 On the desktop, point to the lower edge of the taskbar to display the vertical resize pointer ⬍. When you the see the vertical resize pointer, drag down to increase the height of the taskbar, as shown in Figure 4.14.

Increasing the height or width of the taskbar provides more space to display information on the taskbar, including taskbar buttons and information in the notification area.

Wider taskbar across top of desktop

Time, day, and date in notification area

Vertical resize pointer over taskbar edge

Figure 4.14

6 Press PrtScr to capture an image of the desktop. On the taskbar at the top of the screen, click the **4A_Display2_Firstname_Lastname - WordPad** button. Insert a blank line after the last line of text, and then, on the toolbar, click the **Paste** button 📋.

chapter four

7 With the inserted image selected, use one of the sizing handles to reduce the size of the image so that it will fit on one page. On the toolbar, click the **Print Preview** button 🔍 and then verify that the image fits on the same page as the text. If it does not, repeat this procedure until you can see the image on the same page. **Close** the Print Preview window, **save** the file, and then minimize the WordPad window.

8 On the taskbar, right-click a blank area, and then click **Lock the Taskbar**. Try dragging the taskbar to the bottom of the desktop.

Notice that when the taskbar is locked, you cannot change its size or position.

9 On the taskbar, right-click a blank area, and then click **Lock the Taskbar** to unlock it. Drag the taskbar back to its default position at the bottom of the desktop, and then, on the taskbar, point to the top edge to display the vertical resize pointer ↕. Drag down to decrease the height of the taskbar to its original size.

Activity 4.6 Work with Taskbar Toolbars

You can display *taskbar toolbars*, which are Windows XP toolbars that display on the taskbar to provide one-click access to frequently used programs, folders, and features. You can also customize the toolbars to show a title or text labels to identify buttons or icons, and you can create shortcuts on a taskbar toolbar. In this activity, you will display and hide taskbar toolbars and customize how they display. You will also create a shortcut to floppy drive A on a toolbar. As you progress, you will capture images to illustrate the options and paste the images into the WordPad document.

1 On the taskbar, right-click a blank area, and then point to **Toolbars**.

The Toolbars submenu—as shown in Figure 4.15—displays the following taskbar toolbars. The items in your list may differ from the items shown in the figure.

- **Address**—Allows you to navigate to a particular folder, disk drive, or Web page.

- **Links**—Provides links to Web sites for many of the products installed on your computer.

- **Desktop**—Displays buttons representing the desktop items, such as the Recycle Bin and My Computer, and other items currently on your desktop.

- **Quick Launch**—Displays icons for commonly used Windows XP programs and features.

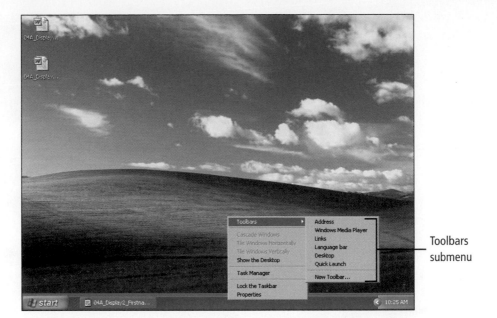

Toolbars
submenu

Figure 4.15

2 From the **Toolbars** submenu, if a checkmark does not display next to the text Quick Launch, click to select **Quick Launch**.

Windows XP displays the Quick Launch toolbar on the left side of the taskbar, next to the Start button. By default, this toolbar displays icons for **Internet Explorer**—a Web browser program that comes with Windows XP—and **Show Desktop**—an icon you click to display the desktop. Your Quick Launch toolbar may display other icons as well.

3 On the taskbar, right-click a blank area, point to **Toolbars**, and then click **Desktop**.

The Desktop toolbar displays on the taskbar, as shown in Figure 4.16. The toolbar handle—the dotted vertical line to the left of *Desktop*—is the beginning of the Desktop toolbar. This toolbar provides access to all items stored in the Desktop folder—even items not currently displayed on the desktop, such as Internet Explorer and **My Network Places**—a folder that contains links to folders on other computers to which you have access. The expand arrow in the upper right of the toolbar indicates hidden buttons.

Quick Launch toolbar

Expand arrow indicates hidden buttons

Desktop toolbar title

Toolbar handle

Figure 4.16

4 On the Desktop toolbar, click the **expand arrow** ⏩. On the displayed menu of Desktop toolbar buttons, point to **My Computer**, and then point to **Local Disk (C:)**.

Each menu item displays a new submenu. By using these menus, you can locate the specific item you want from the taskbar without navigating through multiple folder windows.

5 On the desktop, click anywhere outside the open menus to close them.

6 On the taskbar, drag the **Desktop toolbar handle**, as shown in Figure 4.16, to the left, to the edge of the WordPad taskbar button.

This increases the width of the Desktop toolbar and creates more space to display toolbar buttons.

7 Right-click *Desktop* to display a shortcut menu for the Desktop toolbar.

The shortcut menu that displays when you right-click a toolbar lists commands for that particular toolbar—in this case, the Desktop toolbar. You need to click a blank area on the toolbar—not a button. In this example, clicking the Desktop title is the same as clicking a blank area.

8 From the shortcut menu, point to **View**, and then click **Large Icons**.

The size of the icons on the Desktop toolbar—but not the Quick Launch toolbar—increases. Also, the height of the taskbar increases so that the larger icons have space to display.

9 On the Desktop toolbar, right-click a blank area, and then, from the shortcut menu, click **Show Title** to hide the toolbar title—*Desktop*. Display the **Desktop toolbar shortcut** menu again, and click **Show Text** to hide the names of the icons. Compare your screen with Figure 4.17.

When the title and text labels are hidden, the taskbar has more space to display additional icons. When all icons are displayed, the expand arrow is hidden.

Quick Launch toolbar

Wider taskbar

Expanded Desktop toolbar displays more icons.

Figure 4.17

10 On the right end of the Quick Launch toolbar, drag the toolbar handle to the right to create space for adding an icon.

11 From the Desktop toolbar, click the **My Computer** icon . From the My Computer window, right-drag the **3½ Floppy (A:)** icon to a blank area on the Quick Launch toolbar, and then release the right mouse button. Compare your screen with Figure 4.18. Alternatively, if you do not have a floppy disk drive, navigate to the storage device or folder you are using to save your files and drag that to the Quick Launch toolbar.

When you drag the icon onto the Quick Launch toolbar, a shortcut menu and an *I-beam* display. The I-beam indicates the location where an item can be inserted.

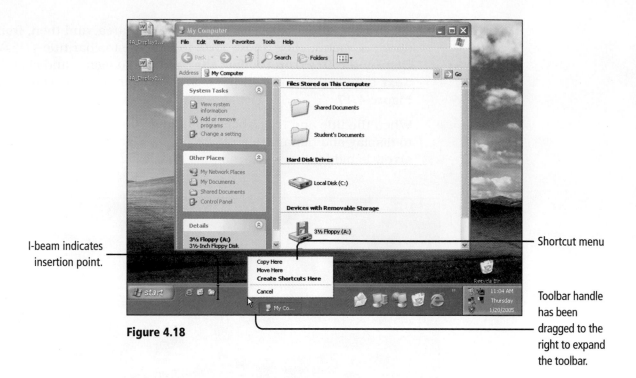

I-beam indicates
insertion point.

Shortcut menu

Toolbar handle
has been
dragged to the
right to expand
the toolbar.

Figure 4.18

12 On the shortcut menu, click **Create Shortcuts Here** to create the shortcut and display the drive icon on the Quick Launch toolbar. Close the My Computer window, and then compare your screen with Figure 4.19.

Shortcut to 3½
Floppy (A:) drive

Figure 4.19

13 Press PrtScr to capture an image of the desktop with the customized taskbar. From the taskbar, display the **WordPad** document, move the insertion point to the end of the document, press Enter two times, and then click the **Paste** button 🗐.

14 With the inserted image selected, drag one of the corner sizing handles to the center of the image so that the entire image will fit on one page—in this case, the second page. Recall that you can use Print Preview to view the page. If the image needs to be further reduced to fit, repeat this procedure until you can see the image on the second page. Press Ctrl + End, press Enter two times, and then type **4A Display2 Firstname Lastname Save** the file, and then minimize the WordPad window.

15 On the Quick Launch toolbar, right-click the icon of the shortcut to drive A, and then click **Delete**. In the **Confirm File Delete** dialog box, click **Yes**. Drag the Quick Launch toolbar handle to the left to remove the extra space.

You are deleting the shortcut to drive A, not the drive itself.

16 On the taskbar, right-click a blank area, point to **Toolbars**, and then click **Desktop** to hide the Desktop toolbar. If necessary, drag the top taskbar edge to return the taskbar to its default width.

More Knowledge — Create a Custom Taskbar Toolbar

You can create a custom toolbar from any existing folder so that you can access its contents directly from the taskbar. To create a custom toolbar, right-click a blank area of the taskbar, point to **Toolbars**, and then click **New Toolbar**. In the **New Toolbar** dialog box, click the folder you want to use as a toolbar—expand the folder list to locate the folder, if necessary—and then click **OK**. Alternatively, open the window where the folder is stored, and then drag the folder onto the taskbar. The folder name is the toolbar name, and all items stored in the folder display as toolbar icons.

Activity 4.7 Setting Taskbar Properties

Setting taskbar properties can control how the taskbar displays in relation to windows open on the desktop. Taskbar properties can also control whether the Quick Launch toolbar displays and whether similar windows display as a group—which happens when too many windows are open to display a button for each. The group properties cause all files that are opened by the same program to display together on one button, with an arrow that can be used to identify the particular file you want to display. In this activity, you practice setting taskbar properties.

1 On the taskbar, right-click a blank area, and then click **Properties**.

The Taskbar and Start Menu Properties dialog box displays with the Taskbar tab active. Recall that properties are the characteristics that control the way a screen element displays, such as font size, color, or button size.

2 On the **Taskbar tab**, click to select **Auto-hide the taskbar**, and then click **OK**.

The taskbar is no longer displayed. Windows XP applies the setting to hide the taskbar when it is not in use. To keep the taskbar visible at all times, you would click to clear Auto-hide the taskbar.

3 On the desktop, point to the bottom edge of the screen.

When the mouse pointer is over the area where the taskbar is docked, the taskbar displays.

4 On the taskbar, right-click a blank area, and then click **Properties**. In the **Taskbar and Start Menu Properties** dialog box, under **Taskbar appearance**, click to clear all check boxes, and then click **OK**.

The taskbar displays because you cleared the Auto-hide the taskbar check box. The Quick Launch toolbar is hidden because you also cleared the Show Quick Launch check box.

5 From the taskbar, display the WordPad window. Notice that the taskbar does not display. Point to the bottom edge of the desktop. Notice that the taskbar still does not display.

The WordPad window displays on top of the taskbar because you cleared the Keep the taskbar on top of other windows check box in the Taskbar and Start Menu Properties dialog box. Select this option to ensure that the taskbar always displays on top of open windows. To access the taskbar, you must close or minimize the open window.

6 Minimize the WordPad window. On the taskbar, right-click a blank area, and then click **Properties**. In the displayed dialog box, on the **Taskbar tab**, under **Taskbar appearance**, click to select the **Keep the taskbar on top of other windows**, **Group similar taskbar buttons**, and **Show Quick Launch** check boxes, and then click **OK**.

Activity 4.8 Customizing the Notification Area

Recall that the notification area at the right end of the taskbar displays the current time and *notification icons*, which are icons that represent currently running programs, hardware, or events, such as an incoming email message. In this activity, you will customize the notification area, and you will capture an image of the dialog box to paste into the WordPad document as an illustration.

1 On the taskbar, right-click a blank area, and then click **Properties**. In the displayed **Taskbar and Start Menu Properties** dialog box, under **Notification area**, click to clear the **Show the clock** and **Hide inactive icons** check boxes, and then click **Apply**.

This hides the clock and displays all inactive icons, as shown in Figure 4.20. The icons that display on your computer may differ from those shown here. Notice that under the Notification area in the dialog box is a preview of how the notification area in the taskbar will display.

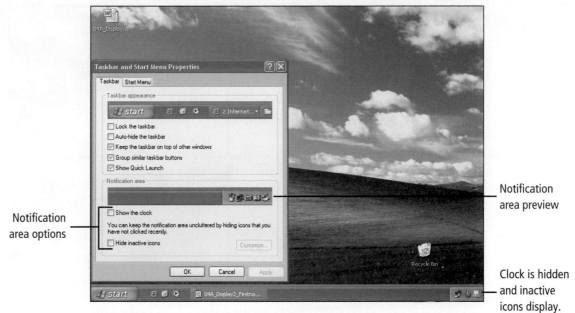

Notification area preview

Clock is hidden and inactive icons display.

Notification area options

Figure 4.20

2 Under **Notification area**, click to select the **Hide inactive icons** check box.

When the Hide inactive icons check box is selected, the Customize button becomes available so that you can select settings for individual icons.

3 On your keyboard, press Alt + PrtScr to capture an image of the dialog box. From the taskbar, display the **WordPad** document, move the insertion point to the end of the document, press Enter two times, and then click the **Paste** button .

4 Press Ctrl + End, press Enter two times, and then type **4A Display2 Firstname Lastname Save** the file, and minimize the WordPad window.

5 In the **Taskbar and Start Menu Properties** dialog box, under **Notification area**, click **Customize**.

The Customize Notifications dialog box displays a list of Current Items, which are items in use now, and Past Items, which are items that have been used previously. By default, all icons are set to be hidden when they are inactive. You can select to always hide or always show an icon—even when the icon is inactive.

6 In the **Customize Notifications** dialog box, in the list of **Current Items**, click to select the first item in the list.

An arrow displays at the right end of the selected line, as shown in Figure 4.21. The first item in your list may vary, depending on the programs and hardware you have installed. Click whichever item displays at the top of the Current Items list on your computer.

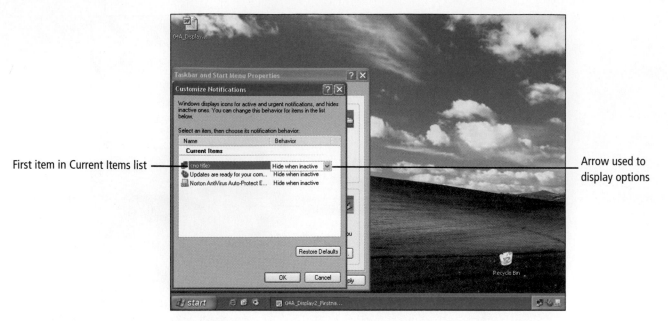

First item in Current Items list —————— (pointing to dialog box)

Arrow used to display options (pointing to dialog box)

Figure 4.21

7 On the selected item, click the arrow, and then, from the displayed menu, click **Always Show**.

This option sets the icon to display in the notification area even when it is inactive.

8 In the **Customize Notifications** dialog box, in the list of **Current Items**, click the second item in the list—yours will differ—click the down arrow, and then click **Always Hide**.

This icon will always be hidden when it is inactive, even if you set Windows XP to display all inactive icons.

9 In the **Customize Notifications** dialog box, in the **Current Items** list, set all remaining items to **Always Hide**.

10 Press [Alt] + [PrtScr] to capture an image of the dialog box. Display the WordPad document, move the insertion point to the end of the document, press [Enter] two times, and then click the **Paste** button.

11 Press [Ctrl] + [End], press [Enter] two times, and then type **4A Display2 Firstname Lastname**

12 From the toolbar, click the **Print Preview** button. Click **Two Page**, and then click **Next Page** to scroll through all pages in the document. On the Print Preview toolbar, click **One Page**, and then print the document with the default print settings. Retrieve your printout from the printer. Save your changes, and then close WordPad.

13 In the **Customize Notifications** dialog box, click **OK**, and then, in the **Taskbar and Start Menu Properties** dialog box, click **Apply**.

The first item in the list—the one you set to Always Show—displays in the notification area. Other active icons may display, but all inactive icons should be hidden.

14 On the taskbar, click the **Show hidden icons arrow** ◀. The notification area briefly expands to display all icons and then hides them again.

15 In the **Taskbar and Start Menu Properties** dialog box, click **Customize**. In the displayed **Customize Notifications** dialog box, click **Restore Defaults**, and then click **OK**.

16 In the **Taskbar and Start Menu Properties** dialog box, under **Taskbar appearance**, click to clear the **Show Quick Launch** check box. Under **Notification area**, click to select the **Show the clock** check box, and then click **OK**.

Objective 3
Customize the Start Menu

The Start menu provides access to all programs and is organized into two basic lists: on the left are frequently used programs, and on the right are links to useful Window XP folders and features. You can customize the Start menu to match your needs. For example, you can set items that you access frequently to always display, or you can change the size of the icons to increase the space available on the menu or to make the icons bigger and easier to read. In Activities 4.9 through 4.11, you will customize the Start menu and capture the settings so that you can paste them into a WordPad document.

Activity 4.9 Customizing the Left Side of the Start Menu

On the top left of the Start menu—above the separator line—is the pinned items list. A *pinned item* is a shortcut—a link to a program, command, or location—that always displays in the same place. A list of frequently used programs displays below the separator line. In this activity, you will change the size of icons on the Start menu, clear the frequently used programs list, and then change the number of programs to display. You will hide the pinned Internet and email programs, and you will add Paint to the pinned items list. As you progress, you will capture images of the settings and paste them into a WordPad file named *4A_Display3_Firstname_Lastname*.

1 Start **WordPad** and click the **Open** button 📂. In the **Open** dialog box, navigate to the location where the student files for this textbook are stored, and then open the file **wn04A_Display3**. In the document, replace the text *Firstname Lastname* with your own name and *Current Date* with the current date.

2 From the **File** menu, click **Save As**. In the displayed **Save As** dialog box, click the **Save in arrow** and select **Desktop**, and in the **File name** box, type **4A_Display3_Firstname_Lastname Save** your file and minimize the WordPad window.

3 On the taskbar, right-click the **Start** button 🔲 start, and then click **Properties**.

The Taskbar and Start Menu Properties dialog box displays, with the Start Menu tab active.

4 In the **Taskbar and Start Menu Properties** dialog box, be sure the **Start menu** option button is selected, and then click **Customize**.

The Customize Start Menu dialog box displays. Use this dialog box to change the size of the icons that display on the Start menu and to control the number of programs that display.

5 In the **Customize Start Menu** dialog box, under **Select an icon size for programs**, click to select the **Small icons** option button. Under **Programs**, click **Clear List** to clear the list of frequently used programs, and in the **Number of programs on Start menu** spin box, change the value to **2** so that up to two programs may display in the frequently used programs list.

6 Under **Show on Start menu**, click to clear the **Internet** and **E-mail** check boxes. Compare your screen with Figure 4.22.

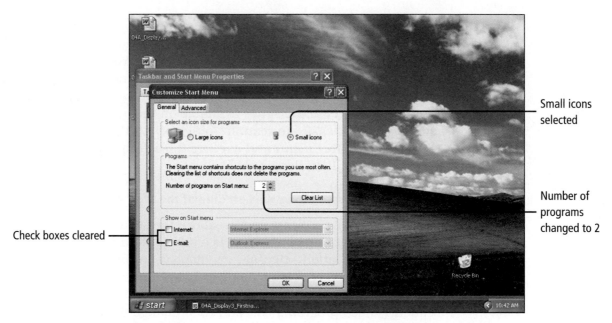

Figure 4.22

7 Press Alt + PrtScr to capture an image of the **Customize Start Menu** dialog box. Display the **WordPad** document, and at the end of the document, insert a blank line, and then click the **Paste** button. Save the document, and then minimize WordPad.

8 In the **Customize Start Menu** dialog box, click **OK**, and then, in the **Taskbar and Start Menu Properties** dialog box, click **Apply**.

The settings take effect, and the dialog box remains open.

9 From the taskbar, display the **Start** menu, and then compare your screen with Figure 4.23.

The left side of the menu is empty because you cleared the frequently used programs list and hid the links for Internet and E-mail.

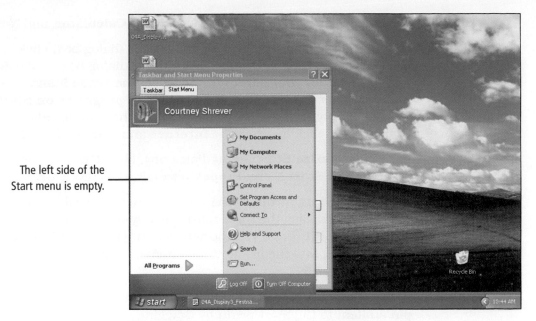

The left side of the Start menu is empty.

Figure 4.23

10 From the **Start** menu, point to **All Programs**, point to **Accessories**, and then click **Paint** to start the Paint accessory program. Display the **Start** menu, and then notice that the Paint program displays in the frequently used programs list. From the **Accessories** menu, start **Notepad**, and start the **Calculator**, and then display the **Start** menu.

Only two programs—Calculator and Notepad—display in the frequently used programs list, and the icons are small, as shown in Figure 4.24. Large icons, the default setting, are easier to read, but small icons take up less space, so more items can be displayed.

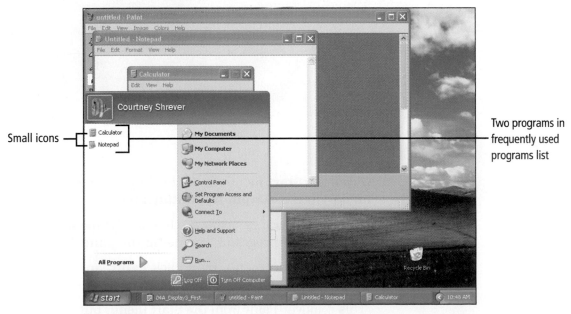

Small icons

Two programs in frequently used programs list

Figure 4.24

11 **Close** the **Start** menu, and then close **Paint**, **Calculator**, and **Notepad**.

12 In the **Taskbar and Start Menu Properties** dialog box, click **Customize**. In the **Customize Start Menu** dialog box, under **Select an icon size for programs**, click to select the **Large icons** option button. Under **Programs**, in the **Number of programs on Start menu** spin box, change the value to **6** and then, under **Show on Start menu**, click to select the **Internet** and **E-mail** check boxes.

13 In the **Customize Start Menu** dialog box, click **OK**, and then, in the **Taskbar and Start Menu Properties** dialog box, click **OK**.

14 Display the **Start** menu. In the list of frequently used programs—which now displays the three most recently opened programs—right-click **Paint**. From the shortcut menu, click **Pin to Start menu** to move Paint into the list of pinned items. Compare your screen with Figure 4.25.

A pinned item is always displayed on the Start menu. You can also pin an item to the Start menu by dragging it from its current location to the pinned items list.

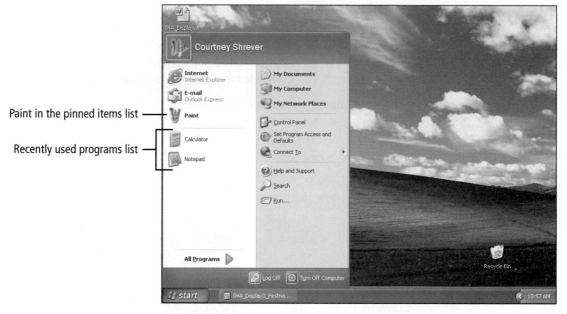

Paint in the pinned items list

Recently used programs list

Figure 4.25

15 From the **Start** menu, in the list of pinned items, right-click **Paint**, and then click **Unpin from Start menu**.

Paint now displays below the line on the menu in the list of frequently used programs and not in the pinned items list.

16 From the **Start** menu, right-click **Paint**, and then click **Remove from This List**.

This removes Paint from the Start menu, but the change is temporary. If you use Paint, it will be added to the list of frequently used programs.

17 Close the **Start** menu.

Activity 4.10 Setting Start Menu Item Preferences

On the Advanced tab of the Customize Start Menu dialog box, you can select the items you want to display on the right side of the Start menu. Some of the items have additional options. For example, you can specify whether you want My Documents to display as a shortcut link or as a menu. If My Documents is set as a link, clicking it opens the My Documents folder window; if it is set as a menu, using it opens a submenu. In this activity, you will display Favorites on the Start menu and then modify My Computer to display as a menu instead of as a link. Finally, you will capture an image of the dialog box and paste it into the WordPad document.

◾1 Right-click the **Start** button 🔳 start , and then click **Properties** to display the **Taskbar and Start Menu Properties** dialog box. With the **Start Menu tab** active, click **Customize,** and then click the **Advanced tab**.

◾2 In the **Start menu items** list, click to select the **Favorites menu** check box. Scroll down the list and then, under **My Computer**, click to select the **Display as a menu** option button. Compare your screen with Figure 4.26.

Favorites menu ⎯⎯⎯⎯⎯  My Computer options

Figure 4.26

◾3 Using the skills you have practiced in previous activities, capture an image of the dialog box, and then paste it at the end of the **WordPad** document, adding the file name and your name—**4A Display3 Firstname Lastname**—under the inserted image. **Save** your changes.

◾4 From the toolbar, click the **Print Preview** button 🔳 to display the document in Print Preview. Click **Two Page** to display both pages of the document at the same time. On the Print Preview toolbar, click **One Page**, and then print the document with the default print settings. When the printing is complete, retrieve your printout from the printer and close WordPad.

5 In the **Customize Start Menu** dialog box, click **OK**, and then, in the **Taskbar and Start Menu Properties** dialog box, click **Apply**.

6 Display the **Start** menu, point to **My Computer**, and then compare your screen with Figure 4.27.

The Favorites folder displays on the right side of the Start menu, and a submenu of the contents of My Computer displays instead of the My Computer window. The contents of your submenu may differ.

Favorites displays on Start menu

My Computer menu

Figure 4.27

7 From the **Start** menu, point to **Favorites** to display the **Favorites** menu. This is the same menu available from the menu bar in folder windows; it displays links to the same items as the Favorites menu and the Favorites pane.

8 Close the **Start** menu. From the **Taskbar and Start Menu Properties** dialog box, click **Customize** to open the **Customize Start Menu** dialog box, and then click the **Advanced tab**.

9 In the **Start menu items** list, click to the clear the **Favorites menu** check box and then, under **My Computer**, click to select the **Display as link** option button. In the **Customize Start Menu** dialog box, click **OK**, and then, in the **Taskbar and Start Menu Properties** dialog box, click **OK**.

Favorites is removed from the Start menu.

More Knowledge — Start Menu Settings

In the Customize Start Menu dialog box, on the Advanced tab, you can turn on or turn off the setting that displays submenus when you point to a Start menu item. You may find it more convenient to use a submenu to locate a file or activate a command rather than open a window and navigate to the file or action you need. You can also turn off the setting that highlights newly installed programs. Another useful Start menu setting is the Scroll programs check box—found in the Start menu items list. Select this option to display a scrollable All Programs menu in a single column. Clear it to display the default multicolumn All Programs menu. Finally, select the *List my most recently opened documents* check box to display a menu of the 15 files that you have used most recently.

Activity 4.11 Creating Shortcuts on the Start Menu

In this activity, you will move the three WordPad documents from the desktop to a new folder in My Documents, and you will create a shortcut to the folder on the Start menu. By doing this, the files are quickly accessible but not on the desktop.

1 From the taskbar, display the **Start** menu, and then click **My Documents**. Create a new folder named **4A_Display**. Double-click the new folder to open it, and then restore the window, if necessary, so that you can see the three files stored on the desktop. Compare your screen with Figure 4.28.

Three files on desktop ———

4A_Display window

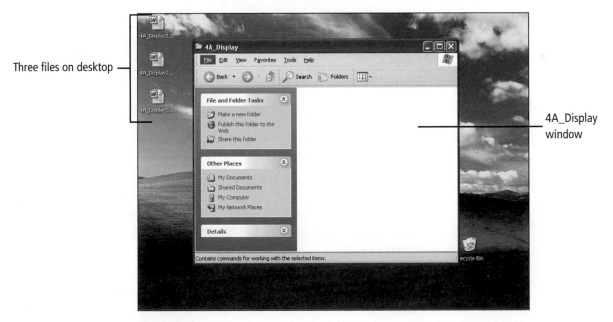

Figure 4.28

■2 On the desktop, click one of the three files, hold Ctrl, and then click each of the remaining files you have created. With all three files selected, right-drag the files from the desktop into the **4A_Display** folder, and then, from the shortcut menu, click **Move Here**.

■3 In the 4A_Display window, click the **Up** button ⬆, and then, from the My Documents window, drag the **4A_Display** folder to the **Start** button

start on the taskbar. Compare your screen with Figure 4.29.

When you drag the folder onto the Start button, a shortcut arrow displays, and then, after a brief moment, the Start menu displays. When you release the mouse button, the shortcut displays as a pinned item on the Start menu. The Start menu remains open.

Shortcut —

Figure 4.29

■4 On the **Start** menu, click the **4A_Display** icon to display the 4A_Display folder window. Close the window.

■5 On the taskbar, click the **Start** button *start*, and then, from the **Start** menu, in the pinned items area, right-click the **4A_Display** icon. From the shortcut menu, click **Remove from This List** to delete the shortcut from the **Start** menu, and then close the **Start** menu.

■6 In **My Documents**, move the 4A_Display folder to the location where you are storing the files for this project. Alternatively, right-click the **4A_Display** folder, and then click **Delete**. In the **Delete Confirmation** dialog box, click **Yes**. Close the My Documents window.

■7 Check your *Chapter Assignment Sheet* or your *Course Syllabus* or consult your instructor to determine whether you are to submit the pages that are the result of this project.

End You have completed Project 4A

Project 4B **Changing Input**

In this project, you will customize settings that control the way you interact with your computer, including settings for hardware devices such as your keyboard and mouse, and you will personalize your user account.

In Activities 4.12 through 4.18, you will practice modifying the keyboard, mouse, and user account. As you progress, you will create three WordPad documents that illustrate the changes to your dialog box settings. You will save the documents as *4B_Input1_Firstname_Lastname*, *4B_Input2_Firstname_Lastname*, and *4B_Input3_Firstname_Lastname* and print each of them. When completed, your documents will include images that look similar to those shown in Figure 4.30.

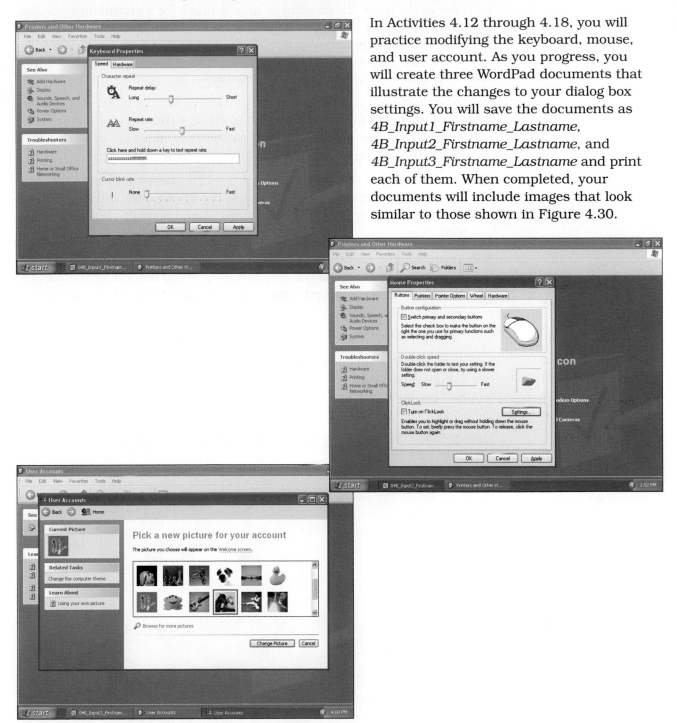

Figure 4.30
Project 4B—Changing Input

Objective 4
Customize the Keyboard

Although you cannot change the mechanical response of your particular keyboard or rearrange the keys, you can customize Windows XP to increase or decrease the amount of time it takes for a character to begin repeating when you press and hold down a key. You can also change the speed at which the insertion point blinks.

Activity 4.12 Setting the Keyboard Properties

In this activity, you will set keyboard properties to adjust the way the keyboard responds to a key press and to change the way the insertion point displays on the screen. You will capture an image of the dialog box displaying the settings, and paste it into a WordPad document.

1 Start **WordPad**. Click the **Open** button ![open icon], navigate to the student files for this textbook, and then open the file **wn04B_Input1**. In the document, replace the text *Firstname Lastname* with your own name and *Current Date* with the current date.

2 From the **File** menu, click **Save As**. In the displayed **Save As** dialog box, select **Desktop** as the location to save the file, name the file **4B_Input1_Firstname_Lastname** and then click **Save**. Minimize the WordPad window.

3 Click the **Start** menu, and then click **Control Panel**.

The Control Panel displays in *Category view*, as shown in Figure 4.31. In Category view, the Control Panel displays categories of related computer settings.

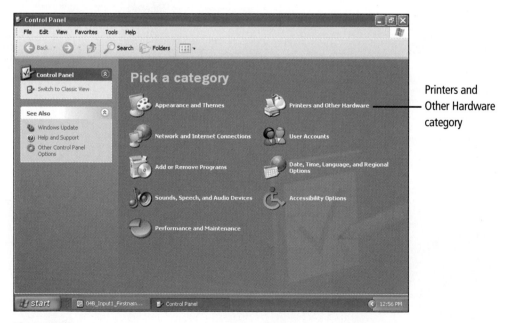

Printers and Other Hardware category

Figure 4.31

4 In the **Control Panel**, in the left pane, under the heading **Control Panel**, click **Switch to Classic View**.

Classic view is an alternative way to display the Control Panel. Instead of categories, icons display for different computer settings. This view was used in earlier versions of Windows.

5 In the left pane, under the heading **Control Panel**, click **Switch to Category View** to return to the default view. In the **Control Panel**, under **Pick a Category**, click **Printers and Other Hardware**, and then compare your screen with Figure 4.32.

When you click a category, the window for that category—in this case, **Printers and Other Hardware**—displays common tasks for changing the settings for the selected category. In the Printers and Other Hardware window, under the heading *Pick a task* is a list of common printer tasks; under the heading *or pick a Control Panel icon* are icons that represent general computer settings within the selected category. The left pane displays other actions related to the selected category, such as **Add Hardware**, which would enable you to add a new hardware device.

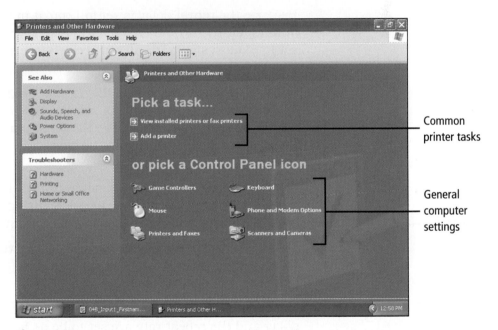

Common printer tasks

General computer settings

Figure 4.32

6 In the Printers and Other Hardware window, under **or pick a Control Panel icon**, click **Keyboard**. In the displayed **Keyboard Properties** dialog box, drag the **Repeat delay** slider as far to the left as it will go—next to the word *Long*—to set the maximum delay.

The **repeat delay** is the amount of time it takes for a character to begin to repeat when you press and hold down a key on your keyboard. Decrease the repeat delay to set the key to repeat faster, or increase the repeat delay if you want a longer time to elapse before the key you are holding down repeats. For example, you might want a longer delay if you are a slower typist because you may need more time to move your fingers off a key before that key repeats.

7 In the **Keyboard Properties** dialog box, drag the **Repeat rate** slider as far to the left as it will go—next to the word *Slow*.

The **repeat rate** affects the speed at which a character repeats after the repeat delay.

8 In the **Keyboard Properties** dialog box, click the **Click here and hold down a key to test repeat rate** box, and then, on your keyboard, press and hold ⑤ until ten characters display.

Because the repeat delay is set to *Long*, it may take half of one second or more for the second character to display. Because the repeat rate is set to *Slow*, a similar delay will occur between the display of each of the subsequent characters.

9 In the **Keyboard Properties** dialog box, drag the **Repeat delay** slider as far to the right as it will go—next to the word *Short*—to set the minimum delay, and then drag the **Repeat rate** slider as far to the right as it will go—next to the word *Fast*—to set the maximum repeat rate.

Setting the repeat rate to the maximum value can be helpful if you frequently use the Delete key to delete strings of characters because the faster rate deletes the characters more quickly.

10 Click the **Click here and hold down a key to test repeat rate** box, and then, on the keyboard, press and hold ⊤ until at least ten characters display.

It may be challenging to count the ten characters because both the delay and the repeat rate are set to be as fast as possible. It is okay if more than ten characters display.

11 Drag the **Repeat delay** slider to the mark that is second from the left, and then drag the **Repeat rate** slider halfway between **Slow** and **Fast**.

12 In the **Keyboard Properties** dialog box, drag the **Cursor blink rate** slider all the way to the right—to the word *Fast*—to set the blink rate as fast as possible.

The *cursor blink rate* is the speed at which the insertion point blinks. *Cursor* is another word for insertion point, which is the vertical bar that indicates where text will be inserted on the screen. Increase the cursor blink rate if you want the insertion point to flash quickly. Decrease the rate to set it to blink more slowly, or set it so that the insertion point never blinks but remains visible all the time. The sample cursor to the left of the slider enables you to preview the blink rate.

13 Drag the **Cursor blink rate** slider all the way to the left—to the word *None*. Compare your screen with Figure 4.33.

This turns off the blink completely, which may be helpful if you find the constant blinking to be a distraction.

Figure 4.33

14 Using the skills you have practiced in previous activities, capture an image of the **Keyboard Properties** dialog box, and then, in the WordPad document, after the last line of text, insert a blank line, and then paste the captured image into the document.

15 On the toolbar, click the **Print Preview** button. Preview the document, and then print it. When printing is complete, close WordPad, and save all changes.

16 Drag the **Cursor blink rate** slider halfway between *None* and *Fast*, and then, in the **Keyboard Properties** dialog box, click **OK** to apply the settings and close the dialog box.

The Printers and Other Hardware Home window continues to display.

17 Close the **Printers and Other Hardware** window. This closes the Printers and Other Hardware window and closes the Control Panel.

Objective 5
Personalize the Mouse

You can use different mouse devices with Windows XP. Your mouse may have one, two, three, or more buttons; a scroll wheel for scrolling through documents; or browse buttons for browsing Web sites. Regardless of what type of mouse device you use, you can customize mouse settings. Some of the settings depend on the type of mouse you have, but other settings are available for all mouse devices.

Activity 4.13 Customizing Mouse Buttons

You can change the functions of the buttons on your mouse, and you can also adjust the rate at which the mouse responds to a double-click. In this activity, you will switch the button configuration, and then you will adjust the speed of a double-click. You will capture an image of the dialog box and paste it into a WordPad document. The steps and figures in this activity assume that you are using a Microsoft Intellimouse or compatible device. If you are using a different type of mouse, the mouse properties may vary.

1 Start **WordPad**. Click the **Open** button 📂, navigate to the student files for this textbook, and then open the file **wn04B_Input2**. In the document, replace the text *Firstname Lastname* with your own name and *Current Date* with the current date.

2 From the **File** menu, click **Save As**. In the displayed **Save As** dialog box, select **Desktop** as the location to save the file, name the file **4B_Input2_Firstname_Lastname** and then click **Save**. Minimize the WordPad window.

3 From the **Start** menu, display the **Control Panel**. Under **Pick a category**, click **Printers and Other Hardware**. In the displayed **Printers and Other Hardware** window, under **or click a Control Panel icon**, click **Mouse**, and then click the **Buttons tab**.

4 On the **Buttons tab**, drag the **Double-click speed** slider to *Fast* to set it as fast as possible. If this setting is not on the Buttons tab, click the other tabs to locate the Double-click speed feature.

The ***double-click speed*** is the speed at which you must double-click in order for both clicks to register as a single double-click—instead of as two separate single clicks. Increase the speed of the double-click if you click quickly; decrease the speed if you click more slowly. Double-click speed may also be known as ***double-click timing***.

5 Under **Double-click speed**, locate the test area to the right, and then slowly double-click. Because the timing is set to Fast, the slow click does not register.

6 On the test area, double-click as quickly as possible.

When you click fast enough to register the double-click, the folder in the test area opens—or closes if it is already open.

7 On the **Buttons tab**, drag the **Double-click speed** slider halfway between *Slow* and *Fast*.

This selects a moderate double-click speed, which is a comfortable speed for many individuals.

8 On the **Buttons tab**, under **Button configuration**, click to select the **Switch primary and secondary buttons** check box.

This changes the configuration so that the right mouse button is the primary button and the left mouse button is the secondary button, and the change takes effect immediately. By default, the ***primary mouse button*** is the button on the left side of the mouse, and the ***secondary mouse button*** is the button on the right. Changing this configuration may be useful if you use your left hand to move the mouse. Recall that the options in the Mouse Properties dialog box may be different, depending on the type of mouse you have installed.

9 In the **Mouse Properties** dialog box, under **ClickLock**, click to select the **Turn on ClickLock** check box by using the right mouse button. Compare your screen with Figure 4.34.

Because you switched the configuration, you must use the right mouse button to click the check box. If you use the left mouse button, the Help pointer displays instead. ***ClickLock*** is a feature of some mouse devices that enables you to select and drag items without holding down the mouse button.

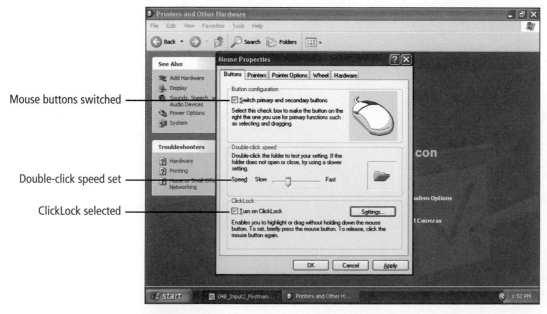

Mouse buttons switched ———

Double-click speed set ———

ClickLock selected ———

Figure 4.34

10 Capture an image of the **Mouse Properties** dialog box, and then, in the WordPad document, after the last line of text, insert a blank line, and then paste the captured image into the document. Save the changes and minimize the window.

Recall that you will need to use the right mouse button to perform the functions of opening the WordPad window, moving the insertion point, and clicking the Paste button.

11 In the **Mouse Properties** dialog box, click **Cancel** to close the dialog box without making any changes.

The previous settings for your mouse are returned, and the left mouse button is again the primary button.

Activity 4.14 Customizing a Pointer Scheme

You may have noticed that the mouse pointer changes shape depending on the current action. A *pointer scheme* is a set of coordinated pointer shapes that you can assign to different actions. The default Windows pointer scheme includes shapes such as an I-beam, an arrow, or a hand with a pointer finger. Windows XP comes with pointer schemes that you can use in place of the default scheme, and your mouse may have additional pointer schemes. In this activity, you select larger pointers, customize the pointers to stand out onscreen, and save a customized pointer scheme.

1 From the **Printers and Other Hardware** window, under **or pick a Control Panel icon**, click **Mouse**. In the **Mouse Properties** dialog box, click the **Pointers tab**.

On the Pointers tab, you can select a pointer scheme, customize individual pointers, and save a custom pointer scheme.

2 On the **Pointers tab**, click the **Scheme arrow** to display the list of available pointer schemes, and then click **Magnified (system scheme)**. Compare your screen with Figure 4.35.

Under the Customize area, the preview and the pointers change to display the selected scheme. This scheme uses larger pointers than the default scheme, so they may be easier to see on the screen.

Magnified scheme selected ————

Pointers in current scheme

Browse button

Figure 4.35

▣ In the **Mouse Properties** dialog box, on the **Pointers tab**, under **Customize**, verify that the **Normal Select** pointer is selected, and then click **Browse**.

The Browse dialog box displays the contents of the Cursors folder. All the files in the Cursors folder are available for use as pointer shapes.

▣ In the list of **available cursors**, click **Banana**, and then click **Open**.

The Banana shape replaces the arrow as the Normal Select pointer.

▣ In the **Mouse Properties** dialog box, under **Scheme**, click **Save As**. In the **Save Scheme** dialog box, replace the name *Magnified* with **Banana** and then click **OK**.

This saves the current settings as a custom pointer scheme named Banana. Compare your screen with Figure 4.36.

New scheme name

Example of selected pointer

Customized pointer

Figure 4.36

6 Capture an image of the **Mouse Properties** dialog box, and then display the WordPad document. At the end of the document, insert a blank line, and then paste the captured image into the document. Insert another blank line, and type **4B Input2** and your name. Save the changes and minimize the window.

7 In the **Mouse Properties** dialog box, click **Apply**, and then point to the taskbar. Notice that the Normal Select pointer is now an animated banana.

8 In the **Mouse Properties** dialog box, under **Scheme**, click **Delete**, and then, in the **Confirm Scheme Removal** dialog box, click **Yes**.

This deletes the Banana pointer scheme, but the scheme remains in effect.

9 In the **Mouse Properties** dialog box, click the **Scheme arrow** to display the list of pointer schemes, click **Windows Default (system scheme)**, and then click **Apply**. Leave the dialog box open for the next activity.

This applies the default pointer scheme without closing the Mouse Properties dialog box.

Activity 4.15 Setting Mouse Pointer Options

In this activity, you will adjust settings to control the way the mouse pointer moves and displays, and you will capture an image of the dialog box to paste in the WordPad document.

1 In the **Mouse Properties** dialog box, click the **Pointer Options tab**.

More Knowledge — Pointer Options

The options on the Pointer Options tab may vary, have different names, or be unavailable, depending on the mouse you have installed. For example, some Logitech mouse devices have a Motion tab instead of a Pointer Options tab, and the Snap To feature may be called Smart Move.

2 On the **Pointer Options tab**, under **Motion**, drag the **Select a pointer speed** slider to the word *Slow*.

This sets the ***pointer speed***—the rate at which the pointer moves across the screen—to slow, the minimum value. Clicking Apply is unnecessary because this setting takes effect immediately.

3 On your desk or mouse pad, move your mouse device.

With the pointer speed set to slow, the pointer responds slowly to the movement of the mouse device. You may find it necessary to pick up the mouse to reposition it on the surface of your desk in order to continue moving the pointer across the screen.

4 On the **Pointer Options tab**, if necessary, click to select the **Enhance Pointer Precision** check box.

This option provides more control over the pointer when you move the mouse small distances. The pointer responds to slower movements of the mouse device. Enhancing pointer precision may be particularly useful if you work with graphics or design programs.

5 On the **Pointer Options tab**, under **Snap To**, click to select the **Automatically move pointer to the default button in a dialog box** check box.

This enables the Snap To feature, which sets the pointer to ***snap-to***— or move to—the default button in a dialog box. The ***default button*** is the command button that is selected when a dialog box is initially displayed and the one that is in effect if you press Enter.

6 On the **Pointer Options tab**, under **Visibility**, click to select the **Display pointer trails** check box, and then drag the **pointer trails** slider all the way to the right, to the word *Long*. Compare your screen with Figure 4.37.

This option takes effect immediately. ***Pointer trails*** are images of the pointer that are repeated behind the pointer as it moves on the screen. Use the slider to adjust the length of the trail. Notice that the mouse trails follow the pointer as it moves across the desktop. Pointer trails may help you locate the current position of the pointer more easily.

Pointer speed set to slow ——

Snap To selected ——

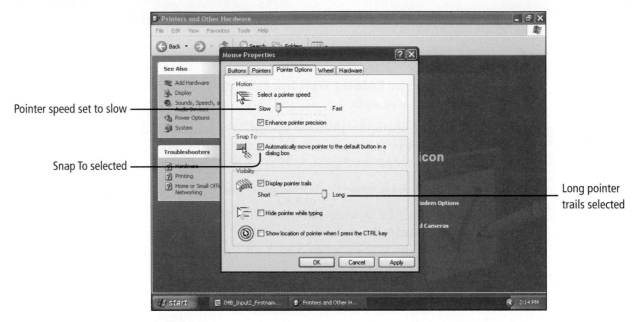

Long pointer trails selected

Figure 4.37

7 Capture an image of the **Mouse Properties** dialog box, and then display the WordPad document. Move the insertion point to the end of the document, insert a blank line, and then paste the captured image into the document. Insert another blank line, and type **4B Input2** and your name.

8 On the toolbar, click the **Print Preview** button [icon]. On the Print Preview toolbar, click **Two Page** to display pages 1 and 2 on the screen at the same time, and then click **Next Page** to display pages 2 and 3. Print the document with default print settings. When printing is complete, save your changes and close WordPad.

9 In the Mouse Properties dialog box, on the **Pointer Options tab**, drag the **Select a pointer speed** slider halfway between *Slow* and *Fast*. Click to clear the **Automatically move pointer to the default button in a dialog box** check box. Under **Visibility**, click to clear the **Display pointer trails** check box, and then click **OK**. In the

Printers and Other Hardware window, click the **Close** button [icon] to close the window and the Control Panel.

More Knowledge — Additional Mouse Properties

Other options may be available in the Mouse Properties dialog box, depending on the mouse device you have installed. Options on the Pointer Options tab may include the following:

- Hide pointer while typing. Enable this option if you do a lot of word processing and you do not want the pointer displayed while you type.

- Show location of pointer when I press the CTRL key. Enable this option if you have trouble locating the pointer on the screen. Every time you press Ctrl, animated circles emanate from the pointer location.

If you have a mouse with a scroll wheel, use the options on the Wheel tab to control how far a window scrolls when you spin the wheel one notch.

Objective 6
Modify Your User Account

Every person who uses Windows XP has a user account, which is a collection of information associated with an individual and includes a user name, an optional *password*, preferred desktop settings, and the contents of the My Documents folder. A password is a combination of upper- and lowercase letters, numbers, and symbols that you use to log onto the computer. This prevents others who may use the same computer from accessing your personal files. In the following activities, you customize a user account.

Activity 4.16 Changing Your Account Picture

Windows XP displays a picture next to the user name on the Windows XP Welcome screen and at the top of the Start menu. This picture is randomly assigned when the account is created. You can change the picture associated with your own account. In this activity, you will capture images of the desktop to illustrate how to change the account picture, and you will paste the images into a WordPad file.

1 Start **WordPad**. Click the **Open** button 📂, navigate to the student files for this textbook, and open the file **wn04B_Input3**. In the document, replace the text *Firstname Lastname* with your own name and *Current Date* with the current date.

2 From the **File** menu, click **Save As**. In the **Save As** dialog box that displays, select **Desktop** as the location to save the file. In the **File name** box, type **4B_Input3_Firstname_Lastname** and then click **Save**. Minimize the WordPad window.

3 From the **Start** menu, display the **Control Panel**, and then click **User Accounts**.

The displayed window may differ, depending on whether you have a *computer administrator account* or a *limited account*. Individuals with a limited account can control changes to their account only—for example, they can change their picture. From the User Accounts window, all settings affect the user's account. Individuals with an administrator account have full access to create, modify, or delete all user accounts on the computer. From the User Accounts window, you pick a task and then select the account that you want to modify. Some computers have a *guest account*, which is an account that anyone who does not have a user account on the computer can use. An individual using a guest account can change only the account picture. The steps in this activity assume you have a limited account.

4 In the **User Accounts** window, under **Pick a Task**, click **Change my picture**.

The User Accounts window displays the user pictures that come with Windows XP; the current picture displays in the left pane under Current Picture. The picture displayed on your computer may be different.

5 Under **Pick a new picture for your account**, scroll through the list of available pictures, and then click the picture of **horses**.

The Change Picture button becomes available. Compare your screen with Figure 4.38.

Figure 4.38

6 Capture an image of the **User Accounts** window, and then, in the WordPad document, after the last line of text, insert a blank line, and then paste the captured image into the document. Save the changes and minimize the window.

7 Under the **Pick a new picture for your account**, click **Change Picture**.

This changes the picture, and the main User Accounts window for your account displays. The new picture displays to the left of your user name.

8 In the **User Accounts** window, click the **Close** button ⊠. The Control Panel displays.

9 Display the **Start** menu, and then locate the picture of the horses, next to the account name. This picture will also display on the Welcome screen. Close the **Start** menu.

More Knowledge — .NET Passport

In your User Account window, you may have an option for creating a *.NET Passport*. A .NET Passport is a Microsoft service that enables you to register an email account name that is recognized by MSN—Microsoft Network—and other Web sites. When you access a site that recognizes your .NET Passport, you may bypass a sign-in procedure.

Activity 4.17 Creating an Account Password

In this activity, you will illustrate the procedure for creating a new password and then use it to log onto Windows XP. If you already have a password, skip this activity and go to Activity 4.18.

1 From the Control Panel, click **User Accounts**, and then, under **or pick a Control Panel icon**, click **User Accounts**.

The User Accounts window for your account displays with a list of the tasks you can perform on your account.

2 Under **What do you want to change about your account?**, click **Create a password**. In the **Type a new password** box, type **deputy** Be certain to use all lowercase letters.

As you type, black dots display instead of characters. This protects your privacy and keeps your password secure. Windows XP passwords are *case sensitive*, which means that you must always type the same combination of upper- and lowercase letters for the password to be recognized. For example, if your password is *abcde* but you type *ABCDE* when logging on, Windows XP will not recognize the password.

3 In the **Type the new password again to confirm** box, type **deputy**

You must type the same password two times—including identical capitalization—in order for the password to be recognized. If the two passwords do not match exactly, Windows XP prompts you to start again.

4 In the **Type a word or phrase to use as a password hint** box, type **job title** Compare your screen with Figure 4.39.

The password has been entered twice and the *password hint* once. A password hint is a word or phrase that can help you remember your password if you forget it. If you have difficulty remembering your password, you display the hint from the Welcome screen. Because the password hint can be displayed by anyone using your computer, it should be descriptive enough that you can remember the password but not so descriptive that unauthorized individuals can guess the password. The password hint is not case sensitive.

Password displays as dots instead of text.

Password hint

Figure 4.39

5 Capture an image of the current window, and then display the 4B_Input3 document. After the image, insert a blank line, and then paste the captured image into the document. Insert another blank line, and then type **4B Input3** and your name. Save the changes and close WordPad.

6 In the **User Accounts** window, click **Create Password**. If another window displays the question *Do you want to make your files and folders private?*, click No.

The password is set, and the User Accounts window displays the tasks for changing your account. The next time you log onto Windows XP, you will have to enter the password before you can access your account. Notice that, in the list of tasks, Change my password is listed instead of Create a password, and an option for removing the password is now available.

7 Close the **User Accounts** window, close the remaining **User Accounts** window—Control Panel—and then **log off**.

8 On the displayed **Welcome screen**, click your **user account name**.

A password box displays. You must type the password exactly as you typed it when you created it.

9 To the right of the **Type your password box**, click the **question mark** 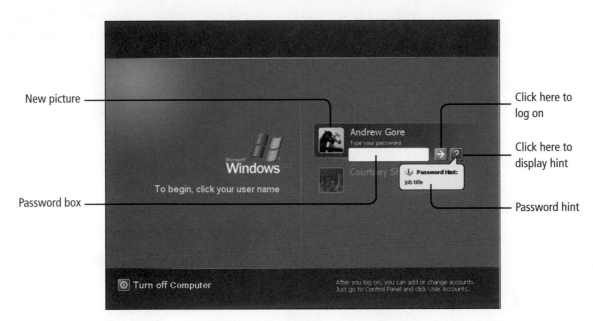 to display the password hint, as shown in Figure 4.40.

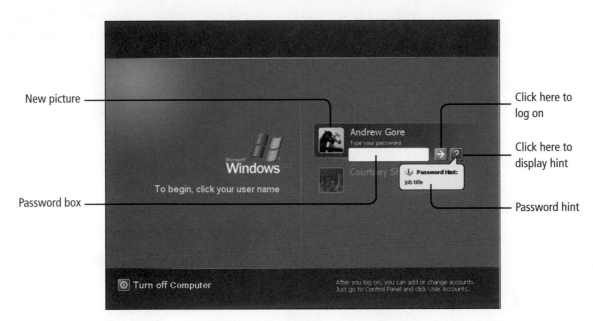

New picture

Password box

Click here to log on

Click here to display hint

Password hint

Figure 4.40

10 In the **password** box, type **deputy** and then press Enter to log on.

More Knowledge — Create a Password Reset Disk

A *password reset disk* stores information about your account so that you can recover your user account and personalized settings if you forget your password. The Forgotten Password Wizard—accessed from the command *Prevent a forgotten password* in the left pane of the User Accounts window—can prompt you through the steps for creating a password reset disk.

Activity 4.18 Changing and Removing an Account Password

You can change your existing password. You might want to do this when you suspect that an unauthorized individual has gained access to your account. You can also remove a password that you no longer need. In this activity, you will change and then remove your password. You will capture images of the procedures to paste into the WordPad document.

1 On the desktop, right-click the **4B_Input3_Firstname_Lastname** file icon, click **Open With**, and then click **WordPad**. Minimize the WordPad window.

Because Windows XP associates document files with Microsoft Word, the Open With command is used instead of double-clicking the file icon.

2 Display the **Control Panel** and then click **User Accounts**. Under **or pick a Control Panel icon**, click **User Accounts**. If you have a computer administrator account, click **your own account**.

3 In the second User Accounts window, under **What do you want to change about your account?**, click **Change my password**.

The Change your password window displays. It is similar to the Create a password window, except that you must first type your current password so that Windows can verify that you are the account owner and not an unauthorized individual.

4 In the **Type your current password** box, type **deputy** In the **Type the new password** box, type **deputy clerk** and then, in the **Type the new password again to confirm** box, type **deputy clerk** Compare your screen with Figure 4.41.

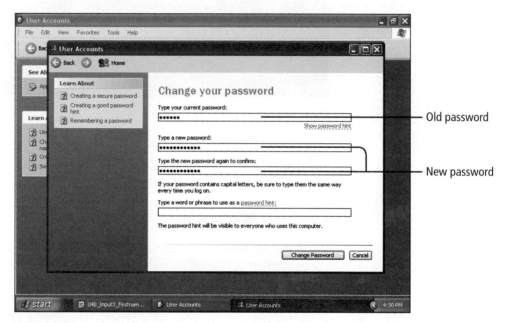

Figure 4.41

5 Capture an image of the current window, and then display the 4B_Input3 document. At the end of the document, insert a blank line, and then paste the captured image into the document. Add another blank line after the inserted image, and type **4B Input3** and your name. Save the changes and close WordPad.

6 In the **Change your password** window, click **Change Password** to create your password and display your User Accounts window. This time, you did not create a password hint. A password hint is optional. Close your **User Accounts** window, close the **Control Panel**, and then **log off**.

7 On the displayed **Welcome screen**, click your user **account name**. In the **Type your password** box, type **deputy clerk** and then press **Enter** to log onto your user account by using your new password.

8 From the desktop, open the **4B_Input3_Firstname_Lastname** file in WordPad, and then minimize the WordPad window.

9 Display the **Control Panel**, click **User Accounts**, and then click **User Accounts**. Under **What do you want to change about your account?**, click **Remove my password**.

The *Are you sure you want to remove your password?* window displays.

10 In the **To verify your identity, type your current password** box, type **deputy clerk** and then compare your screen with Figure 4.42.

Recall that you must type your existing password to change or remove a password so that Windows XP can verify that you are the account owner—not an unauthorized individual.

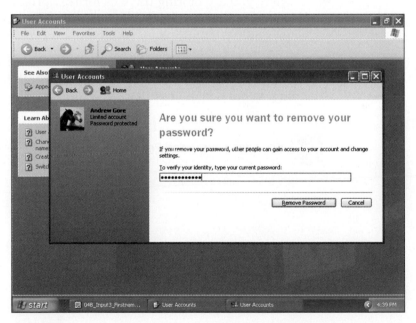

Figure 4.42

11 Capture an image of the current window, and then display the 4B_Input3 document. At the end of the document, insert a blank line, and then paste the captured image into the document. Add another blank line after the inserted image, and then type **4B Input3** and your name.

12 From the **File** menu, click **Page Setup**. In the displayed **Page Setup** dialog box, under **Orientation**, click to select the **Landscape** option, and then click **OK**. Preview all pages of the document, and ensure that each image displays on a page with your name and the file name. Adjust any images if necessary to fit on a page. Print the document and save the changes. Close WordPad.

13 In the User Accounts window, under **Are you sure you want to remove your password?** click **Remove Password**.

Your User Account window displays; you will no longer need to enter a password to log on.

14 Close the **User Accounts** window, and then close the **Control Panel** to display the desktop.

15 From the desktop, select the three WordPad files: **04B_Input1_Firstname_Lastname**, **04B_Input2_Firstname_Lastname**, and **04B_Input3_Firstname_Lastname**, and move the files to the location where you are storing the files for this project. Alternatively, delete the files from the desktop. If you have completed your session, log off Windows XP. Shut down your computer and monitor if necessary.

16 Check your *Chapter Assignment Sheet* or your *Course Syllabus*, or consult your instructor to determine whether you are to submit the pages that are the result of this project.

End **You have completed Project 4B** ————————————————————————

Summary

In this chapter you practiced personalizing the appearance of Windows XP and customizing Windows XP device settings. In Project 4A, you practiced modifying desktop components by using the Display Properties dialog box. You changed the desktop background and appearance, you applied a theme, and you created your own custom theme. You selected a screen saver and set the wait time for its activation. Also, you practiced managing the taskbar—including moving and resizing it—displaying toolbars, creating a shortcut on the Quick Launch toolbar, and customizing the notification area. You customized the Start menu by changing the icon size and by customizing the list of frequently used programs. You also selected Start menu settings and customized the items displayed on the Start menu. You practiced pinning, unpinning, and removing Start menu programs.

In Project 4B, you practiced customizing the keyboard, the mouse, and your user account. You changed the keyboard repeat rate and repeat delay, and you adjusted the cursor blink rate. You switched the mouse button configuration, changed the pointer scheme, and set mouse pointer options and pointer trails. Finally, you changed the user account picture, and you created, changed, and removed your password.

In This Chapter You Practiced How To

- Change the Desktop
- Manage the Taskbar
- Customize the Start Menu
- Customize the Keyboard
- Personalize the Mouse
- Modify Your User Account

Concepts Assessments

Matching   Match each term in the second column with its correct definition in the first column by writing the letter of the term on the blank line in front of the correct definition.

_____ **1.** Icons on the right end of the taskbar that represent currently running programs, hardware, or events, such as an incoming email message.

_____ **2.** A group of small squares of different colors.

_____ **3.** A set of coordinated colors applied to every window element.

_____ **4.** The style that displays trim, straight-edged bars, borders, and buttons.

_____ **5.** A set of coordinated pointer shapes that you can assign to different actions.

_____ **6.** A program that displays an animated image on the monitor when your computer is idle for a specified period of time.

_____ **7.** A symbol that resembles an uppercase letter *I* and indicates the location where an item can be inserted.

_____ **8.** Icons that represent programs, hardware, or events that are not currently running.

_____ **9.** The color, texture, pattern, or picture that displays on the desktop.

_____ **10.** A shortcut—a link to a program, command, or location—that always displays in the same place on the Start menu.

_____ **11.** The amount of time it takes for a character to begin to repeat when you press and hold down a key on your keyboard.

_____ **12.** The speed at which the insertion point blinks.

_____ **13.** A feature on some mouse devices that enables you to select and drag items without holding down the mouse button.

_____ **14.** The style that displays large bars and buttons, with rounded borders and bold colors.

_____ **15.** The rate at which the mouse pointer moves across the screen.

A Background

B ClickLock

C Color palette

D Color scheme

E Cursor blink rate

F I-beam

G Inactive icons

H Notification icons

I Pinned item

J Pointer scheme

K Pointer speed

L Repeat delay

M Screen saver

N Windows Classic style

O Windows XP style

Fill in the Blank Write the correct answer in the space provided.

1. To display a single image in its actual size as the desktop background, select the _____ position.

2. To display a single image, resized to fill the desktop as a background, select the _____ position.

3. To capture an image of the current window or dialog box, on your keyboard, hold down the _____ key and then press PrtScr.

4. The folder that provides access to commands for customizing your computer system hardware and software is called the _____.

5. When setting a screen saver, enter the amount of time in minutes that the system should remain idle before the screen saver displays in the _____ box.

6. A taskbar that is fixed in its current position is _____.

7. To change the speed at which a character repeats when you press a keyboard key, adjust the _____ rate.

8. To be sure the computer registers a double-click if you click slowly, decrease the _____.

9. To display images of the mouse pointer behind the pointer as it moves on the screen, display _____.

10. You can make changes only to your own user account if you have a _____ account.

Project 4C—Desktop

Objectives: *Change the Desktop; Manage the Taskbar; and Customize the Start Menu.*

In the following Skill Assessment, you will create a customized desktop that has a floral theme. You will capture an image of the desktop to paste in a WordPad document, which you will print. Your completed document will look similar to Figure 4.43. You will save your document as *4C_Desktop_Firstname_Lastname.*

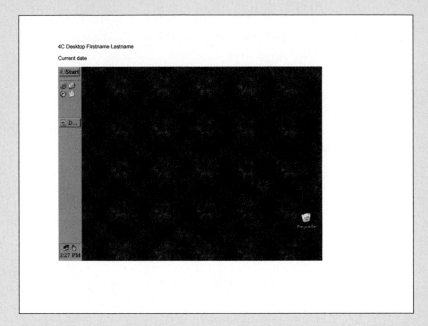

Figure 4.43

1. On the desktop, right-click a blank area, and then click **Properties** to open the **Display Properties** dialog box. Alternatively, you can use the Control Panel to open the **Display Properties** dialog box.

2. In the **Display Properties** dialog box, click the **Desktop tab**, and in the **Background** list, scroll, and then click **Rhododendron**. Recall that the background is a picture or color displayed on the desktop.

3. In the **Display Properties** dialog box, click the **Appearance tab**, click the **Windows and buttons arrow**, and then click **Windows Classic style**, which sets the style to display trim, straight-edged bars, borders, and buttons.

4. On the **Appearance tab**, click the **Color scheme arrow**, and then click **Rose**.

5. In the **Display Properties** dialog box, click the **Themes tab**, and then click **Save As**. In the **Save As** dialog box, in the **File name** box, replace *My Favorite Theme* with **Flowers** and then click **Save**.

(Project 4C–Desktop continues on the next page)

(Project 4C–Desktop continued)

6. In the **Display Properties** dialog box, click the **Screen Saver tab**, and then click the **Screen saver arrow**. On the **Screen saver** list, click **3D FlowerBox**, and then, in the **Wait** spin box, replace the value with **1** This sets the screen saver to display after the computer has been inactive for one minute.

7. In the **Display Properties** dialog box, click **OK** to apply the settings and close the dialog box.

8. On the taskbar, right-click a blank area, and then click **Properties**. In the displayed **Taskbar and Start Menu Properties** dialog box, on the **Taskbar tab**, under **Taskbar appearance**, click to select the **Show Quick Launch** check box. Under **Notification area**, click to clear the **Hide inactive icons** check box, and then click **OK**.

9. On the taskbar, point to a blank area, and then drag the taskbar to the left side of the desktop. If necessary, drag the Quick Launch toolbar handle to expand the toolbar to make space for a shortcut icon.

10. Open the **My Documents** folder. On the Standard Buttons toolbar, click the **Up** button to display the Desktop window, right-drag the **My Documents folder** icon to a blank area of the Quick Launch toolbar, and then, on the displayed shortcut menu, click **Create Shortcuts Here** to create a shortcut to My Documents on the Quick Launch toolbar. Close the Desktop window.

11. On the taskbar, right-click the **Start** button, and then click **Properties** to display the **Taskbar and Start Menu Properties** dialog box, with the **Start Menu tab** active. Click the **Customize** button to display the **Customize Start Menu** dialog box.

12. In the **Customize Start Menu** dialog box, click **Small icons**. Under **Programs**, click the **Clear List** button to clear the list of frequently used programs. Under **Show on Start menu**, click to clear the **Internet** and **E-mail** check boxes, and then click **OK**. In the **Taskbar and Start Menu Properties** dialog box, click **OK**. Recall that the Internet and E-mail items display in the Pinned Items list in the top left of the **Start** menu by default. Also, recall that the list of frequently used programs displays on the lower left side of the **Start** menu.

13. Start **WordPad**, and on the first line of the new document, type **4C Desktop Firstname Lastname** and then press Enter two times. Type the current date, press Enter two times, and then minimize the WordPad window.

14. Press PrtScr to capture an image of the desktop. From the taskbar, display the **WordPad** window, and on the toolbar, click the **Paste** button to paste the captured image into the document.

(Project 4C–Desktop continues on the next page)

(Project 4C–Desktop continued)

15. From the **File** menu, click **Page Setup**. Under **Orientation**, click **Landscape**, and then click **OK**. With the image selected, drag one of the corner sizing handles toward the center of the image to reduce the size of the image to fit within the printable area.

16. On the toolbar, click the **Print Preview** button. Verify that the image will print on one page, and then click the **Print** button. Click the **Save** button, and navigate to the location where you are saving projects for this chapter. In the **File name** box, type **4C_Desktop_Firstname_Lastname** and then click **Save**. Close WordPad.

17. On the desktop, right-click a blank area, and then click **Properties**. In the **Display Properties** dialog box, on the **Themes tab**, click **Delete** to delete the Flowers theme. If necessary, click the Theme arrow, and then click Windows XP. Windows XP does not display a delete confirmation box before deleting a theme.

18. Click the **Screen Saver tab**, and verify that the **Screen saver list** is set to **Windows XP**. On the **Screen Saver tab**, change the **Wait** spin box value from 1 to **15** and then click **OK**.

19. Point to a blank area on the taskbar, and drag the taskbar to the bottom of your screen.

20. On the Quick Launch toolbar, right-click the **Shortcut to My Documents** icon, click **Delete**, and then, in the **Confirm File Delete** dialog box, click **Yes**.

21. On the taskbar, right-click a blank area, and then click **Properties**. In the **Taskbar and Start Menu Properties** dialog box, on the **Taskbar tab**, under **Taskbar appearance**, click to clear the **Show Quick Launch** check box. Under **Notification area**, click to select the **Hide inactive icons** check box.

22. Click the **Start Menu tab**, and then click the **Customize** button to display the **Customize Start Menu** dialog box.

23. In the **Customize Start Menu** dialog box, click to select **Small Icons** if necessary. Under **Show on Start menu**, click to select the **Internet** and **E-mail** check boxes, and then click **OK**. In the **Taskbar and Start Menu Properties** dialog box, click **OK**. The taskbar and **Start** menu properties are returned to their original settings.

End **You have completed Project 4C**

Project 4D—Devices

Objectives: *Customize the Keyboard; Personalize the Mouse; and Modify Your User Account.*

In the following Skill Assessment, you will print a document to illustrate customized device and user account settings. Your completed document will look similar to Figure 4.44. You will save your document as *4D_Devices_Firstname_Lastname*.

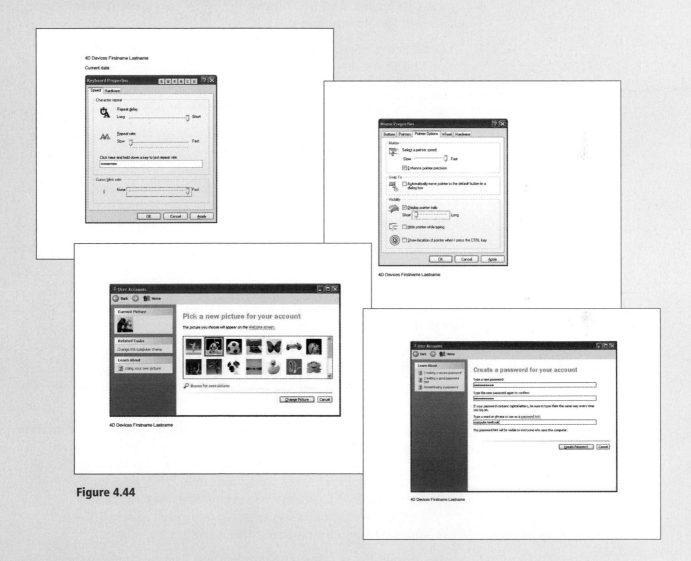

Figure 4.44

1. From the **Start** menu, click **Control Panel**. Recall that the Control Panel enables you use to customize the hardware and software on your computer. By default, it displays in Category View.

2. In the **Control Panel**, click **Printers and Other Hardware**, and then, under **or pick a Control Panel icon**, click **Keyboard** to display the **Keyboard Properties** dialog box.

(Project 4D–Devices continues on the next page**)**

(Project 4D–Devices continued)

3. Under **Repeat delay**, drag the slider all the way to the right—*Short*. Under **Repeat rate**, drag the slider all the way to the left—*Slow*. The repeat delay is the amount of time it takes for a character to begin to repeat when you press and hold down a key on your keyboard; the repeat rate is the speed at which a character repeats after the repeat delay.

4. In the **Click here and hold down a key to test repeat rate** box, click, and then press and hold down Ⓜ.

5. Under **Cursor blink rate**, drag the slider all the way to *Fast*. The cursor blink rate is the speed at which the insertion point flashes on the screen.

6. Press [Alt] + [PrtScr] to capture an image of the dialog box.

7. Start **WordPad**. On the first line, type **4D Devices Firstname Lastname** and then press [Enter] two times. Type the current date, press [Enter] two times, and then, on the toolbar, click the **Paste** button. Click the **Save** button and navigate to the location where you are saving projects for this chapter. In the **File name** box, type **4D_Devices_Firstname_ Lastname** and then click **Save**. Minimize the WordPad window.

8. In the **Keyboard Properties** dialog box, click **Cancel** to close the box without making any changes.

9. In the **Printers and Other Hardware** window, click **Mouse** to display the **Mouse Properties** dialog box, and then click the **Pointer Options tab**.

10. On the **Pointer Options tab**, drag the **Select a pointer speed** slider to the word *Fast*. Click to select the **Enhance pointer precision** and **Display pointer trails** check boxes. Drag the **pointer trails** slider to the left, to the word *Short*.

11. Hold down [Alt] and press [PrtScr]. From the taskbar, display the **WordPad** document, press [Ctrl] + [End] to move the insertion point to the end of the document, and then press [Enter] two times. On the toolbar, click the **Paste** button. Press [Ctrl] + [End], press [Enter] two times, and then type **4D Devices Firstname Lastname** You are adding your name after the second image to ensure that you can locate your printout in a lab. **Save** your changes and minimize the WordPad window.

12. In the **Mouse Properties** dialog box, click **Cancel** to close the dialog box without making any changes.

13. On the Standard Buttons toolbar, click the **Back** button to return to the Control Panel. Click **User Accounts**. If you have a limited user account, you can make changes only to your own account.

(Project 4D–Devices continues on the next page)

(Project 4D–Devices continued)

14. In the **User Accounts** window, under **Pick a Task**, click **Change my picture** to display the user pictures that come with Windows XP.

15. Under **Pick a new picture for your account**, click the **astronaut**, and then press ⎡Alt⎤ + ⎡PrtScr⎤ to capture an image of the current window. From the taskbar, display the **WordPad** document, move the insertion point to the end of the document, and then press ⎡Enter⎤ two times. Click the **Paste** button, Press ⎡Ctrl⎤ + ⎡End⎤, press ⎡Enter⎤ two times, and then type **4D Devices Firstname Lastname Save** your changes and minimize the WordPad window.

16. In the **User Accounts** window, click **Change Picture**. Under **Pick a task**, click **Create a password**. If you already have a password, click **Change my password**.

17. In the **Type a new password** box, type **GO! Series** In the **Type the new password again to confirm** box, type **GO! Series** In the **Type a word or phrase to use as a password hint** box, type **computer textbook**

18. Capture an image of the current window, display the WordPad document, move the insertion point to the end of the document and press ⎡Enter⎤ two times, and then **paste** the captured image into the document. Press ⎡Ctrl⎤ + ⎡End⎤, press ⎡Enter⎤ two times, and then type **4D Devices Firstname Lastname**

19. From the **File** menu, click **Page Setup**, and then, under **Orientation**, click the **Landscape** option. Click **OK**. From the toolbar, click the **Print Preview** button. Review the pages to ensure each screen capture is fully shown and that your name appears on each page. Click **Print** to print the document. **Save** your changes, and then close WordPad.

20. In the **User Accounts** window, click **Create Password**.

21. **Log off** Windows XP, and then log back on. The new picture should display on the Welcome screen. If necessary, click the **Password hint** button to display the hint. In the password box, type your new password, and then press ⎡Enter⎤.

22. From the **Start** menu, click **Control Panel**, and then click **User Accounts**. Under **or pick a Control Panel icon**, click **User Accounts**. Under **Pick a task**, click **Remove my password**.

23. In the **To verify your identity, type your current password** box, type **GO! Series** and then click **Remove Password**. Close all open windows.

End You have completed Project 4D

Performance Assessment

Project 4E—Office

Objectives: *Change the Desktop; Manage the Taskbar; Customize the Start Menu; Customize the Keyboard; Personalize the Mouse; and Modify Your User Account.*

In the following Performance Assessment, you will customize desktop and computer settings. You will capture images of the desktop and dialog boxes to illustrate a WordPad document, which you will print. Your desktop image will look similar to Figure 4.45. You will save your document as *4E_Office_Firstname_Lastname*.

Figure 4.45

1. From the desktop, right-click a blank area, and then click **Properties**. In the **Display Properties** dialog box, click the **Desktop tab**. Scroll the **Background** list, and then click **River Sumida**.

2. In the **Display Properties** dialog box, click the **Appearance tab**, click the **Windows and buttons arrow**, and then click **Windows Classic style**. Click the **Color scheme arrow**, and then click **Rainy Day**. The preview area displays the selected settings.

3. In the **Display Properties** dialog box, click the **Screen Saver tab**, and then click the **Screen saver arrow**. On the **Screen saver** list, click **Beziers**, and then, in the **Wait** spin box, type **5** Click the **Settings** button and drag the **Speed** slider to *Slow*. This changes the speed at which the screen saver image moves around the screen. Click **OK** two times.

(**Project 4E–Office continues on the next page**)

(Project 4E–Office continued)

4. On the taskbar, right-click a blank area, and then point to **Toolbars**. From the **Toolbars** submenu, click **Desktop** to display the Desktop toolbar on the taskbar.

5. On the Desktop toolbar, drag the **toolbar handle** to the left to expand the toolbar.

6. On the Desktop toolbar, right-click a blank area, and then click **Show Title**. Display the shortcut menu again, and then click **Show Text**. Recall that you can show or hide the toolbar title and the text labels for the buttons.

7. Right-click the **Start** menu, and then click **Properties**. In the displayed **Taskbar and Start Menu Properties** dialog box, on the **Start Menu tab**, click the **Customize** button.

8. In the **Customize Start Menu** dialog box, click to select **Large icons**, and then click the **Advanced tab**. In the **Start menu items** list, click to select the **Favorites menu** check box, and then click **OK**. In the **Taskbar and Start Menu Properties** dialog box, click **OK**. Recall that you can select to show or hide items on the right side of the **Start** menu and that for some items you can select whether to display the item as a menu or as a link.

9. Click **Start** to display the Start menu. Press [PrtScr] to capture an image of the desktop. Start **WordPad**, and then, on the first line of the new document, type **4E Office Firstname Lastname** and then press [Enter] two times. Type the current date, and then press [Enter] two times. On the toolbar, click **Paste**. Resize the image so that the entire image will fit on one page.

10. On the toolbar, click **Save**. In the displayed **Save As** dialog box, navigate to the folder where you are saving your projects for this chapter. In the **File name** box, type **4E_Office_Firstname_Lastname** and then click **Save**. Minimize the WordPad window.

11. From the **Start** menu, click **Control Panel**, click **Printers and Other Hardware**, and then, under **or pick a Control Panel icon**, click **Keyboard** to display the **Keyboard Properties** dialog box.

12. Under **Repeat delay**, drag the slider to *Long*. Under **Repeat rate**, drag the slider to *Slow*. Under **Cursor blink rate**, drag the slider so that it is halfway between *None* and *Fast*.

13. Capture an image of the current dialog box, and then display the WordPad document. Press [Ctrl] + [End] to move to the end of the document, press [Enter] two times, and then **paste** the image into the document. Press [Ctrl] + [End], press [Enter] two times, and then type **4E Office** and your name. Minimize the WordPad window.

(Project 4E–Office continues on the next page)

(Project 4E–Office continued)

14. In the **Keyboard Properties** dialog box, click **Cancel** to close the box without making any changes.

15. In the **Printers and Other Hardware** window, click **Mouse** to display the Mouse Properties dialog box, and then click the **Pointer Options tab**. Drag the **Select a pointer speed** slider to *Slow*. Click to select the **Enhance Pointer Precision** and **Display pointer trails** check boxes, and then drag the **pointer trails** slider to *Long*.

16. Capture an image of the current dialog box, and then display the WordPad document. Press Ctrl + End to move the insertion point to the end of the document, press Enter two times, and then **paste** the image into the document. Press Ctrl + End, press Enter two times, and type **4E Office** and your name. Minimize the WordPad window.

17. In the **Mouse Properties** dialog box, click **Cancel** to close the dialog box without making any changes.

18. In the **Printers and Other Hardware** window, click the **Back** button to return to the **Control Panel** window, and then click **User Accounts**. Under **Pick a Task**, click **Change my picture**.

19. Under **Pick a new picture for your account**, scroll, and then click the **snowflake**. Capture an image of the current window, and then display the WordPad document. Move the insertion point to the end of the document, press Enter two times, and then **paste** the image into the document. Press Ctrl + End, press Enter two times, and then type **4E Office** and your name. From the **File** menu, display the **Page Setup** dialog box, and change the orientation to **Landscape**. **Print** the document, **save** your changes, and then close WordPad.

20. Close all open windows. On the desktop, right-click a blank area, and then click **Properties**. In the **Display Properties** dialog box, on the **Themes tab**, click the **Theme arrow**, and then click **Windows XP**. Click the **Screen Saver tab**, and if necessary, change the **Screen saver** setting to **Windows XP**. Change the **Wait** box value to **15** Click **OK** to apply the settings and close the dialog box.

21. On the taskbar, right-click a blank area, point to **Toolbars**, and then click **Desktop** to hide the Desktop toolbar.

22. Right-click the **Start** menu, and then click **Properties**. In the displayed **Taskbar and Start Menu Properties** dialog box, be sure the **Start Menu tab** is active, and then click **Customize**. In the **Customize Start Menu** dialog box, click the **Advanced tab**. Click to clear the **Favorites menu** check box, and then click **OK** two times.

End You have completed Project 4E

Project 4F — Autumn

Objectives: *Change the Desktop; Manage the Taskbar; Customize the Start Menu; Customize the Keyboard; Personalize the Mouse; and Modify Your User Account.*

In the following Mastery Assessment, you will customize desktop and computer settings to display an autumn theme. You will capture images of the desktop and dialog boxes to illustrate the changes made and add them to a WordPad document, which you will print. The desktop image will look similar to Figure 4.46. You will save your document as *4F_Autumn_Firstname_Lastname*.

Figure 4.46

1. From the desktop, display the **Display Properties** dialog box, and then select the **Autumn** background picture. Be sure the image fills the screen. On the **Appearance tab**, be sure **Windows XP style** is selected, and then change the color scheme to **Olive Green**. Save the new theme with the name **Golden** Change the screen saver to **Mystify**, and then set it to start whenever the computer is idle for three minutes.

2. Display the **Taskbar and Start Menu Properties** dialog box, and then customize the taskbar to always display all **inactive icons** and to **hide the clock**.

(Project 4F–Autumn continues on the next page)

(Project 4F–Autumn continued)

3. Display the Address toolbar on the taskbar, without the toolbar title. Expand the width of the Address toolbar so that you can see the entire toolbar. Display the Quick Launch toolbar with **large icons**. On the Quick Launch toolbar, create a shortcut to **3½ Floppy (A:)**— or the location where you save files.

4. Display the **Customize Start Menu** dialog box, and then customize the **Start** menu to display **small icons**. Clear the **frequently used programs** list. Select to display **all available items** as **links** on the right side of the **Start** menu. If an item does not have the **Display as a link** option, do not display the item. If the item has a check box to display it or hide it, display the item.

5. Open and close **WordPad**, **Notepad**, **Calculator**, and **Paint**, and then pin the **Calculator** to the **Start** menu.

6. In a new WordPad document, on the first line, type **4F_Autumn_ Firstname_Lastname** and press Enter two times, and then type the current date. Minimize the WordPad window.

7. Set the keyboard repeat delay to **Long** and repeat rate to **Fast**. Set the **cursor blink rate** so that the insertion point does not flash. **Capture** an image of the **Keyboard Properties** dialog box, and then **paste** the image at the end of the WordPad document. Cancel the **Keyboard Properties** dialog box without making any changes.

8. **Switch the mouse button configuration** so that the right mouse button is primary. Increase the **double-click speed**. **Capture** an image of the **Mouse Properties** dialog box, and then cancel the **Mouse Properties** dialog box without making any changes. At the end of the WordPad document, add a blank line and then **paste** the image. Add another blank line and type the file name after the second image.

9. Customize your **user account** to change the picture to the **frog**. Display the **Start** menu and capture an image of the desktop.

10. At the end of the WordPad document, add a blank line, and then **paste** the desktop image. Resize the image so that all of it will display when printed. Add another blank line and type the file name. Change the page orientation to landscape, **print** all pages of the document, and then **save** the document as **4F_Autumn_ Firstname_Lastname**

11. Restore all **settings** to the defaults. Close any open windows and programs.

End **You have completed Project 4F**

Windows XP

chapter four

Problem-Solving Assessment

Project 4G — Customize Your Desktop

Objectives: *Change the Desktop; Manage the Taskbar; Customize the Start Menu; Customize the Keyboard; Personalize the Mouse; and Modify Your User Account.*

In this Problem-Solving Assessment, practice personalizing the appearance of Windows XP by customizing the desktop, the taskbar, and the Start menu, and by selecting folder options. Try different display properties until you find a combination that you like, and then save it as a theme— use your own name as the name of the theme file. Select a screen saver. Position the taskbar in the location that you prefer, and then adjust its width. Decide whether you need to display additional toolbars on the taskbar, and then set properties for each taskbar toolbar. Select the notification area icons that you want to display or hide. Customize the Start menu to show programs that you need, and set them to open the way you prefer. Create shortcuts to programs, folders, and files that you need on the Quick Launch toolbar or the Start menu. Adjust the keyboard properties to the settings that you prefer, and personalize the mouse by selecting or customizing a pointer scheme. Change your account picture. Finally, reset and restore all default settings. Practice all the skills covered in this chapter so that you are comfortable personalizing the appearance and customizing the settings of Windows XP.

End **You have completed Project 4G** ————————————————————

On the Internet

Backgrounds and Screen Savers

You can download background pictures and screen savers from many reputable Web sites, including Microsoft's Web site. Connect to the Internet, open a Web browser, and then, in the Address box of the Web browser, type **http://www.microsoft.com/windowsxp/downloads** to go to the main Microsoft downloads page. Scroll the window, and click the **Desktop Enhancements** link. Click any item, and then follow the instructions to download and install it. To locate free downloads of similar items on other Web sites, use the Google search engine to search for Windows XP desktop downloads.

GO! with Help

Use a Personal Picture as the Desktop Background

Use the Windows Help and Support Center to find out how to use one of your own pictures as the desktop background.

1. Display the **Start** menu, and then click **Help and Support**.

2. In the **Search** box, type **desktop picture** and then click the **Start searching** button.

3. On the left pane, under **Pick a task**, click **Use a picture as a desktop background**.

4. Follow the instructions that display in the right pane.

5. Close the Help and Support Center window.

5 chapterfive

Windows XP and the Internet

In this chapter you will: complete this project **and** practice these skills.

Project 5A Financial Aid	Objectives
	• Use Internet Explorer
	• Use Outlook Express
	• Add Active Desktop Items

Going Online with Windows XP

Many people buy a computer to use as a tool for getting on the Internet to find information, buy products at lower prices, locate hard-to-find items, and exchange e-mail. Windows XP contains integrated features that enable you to view and navigate the Internet and communicate with others.

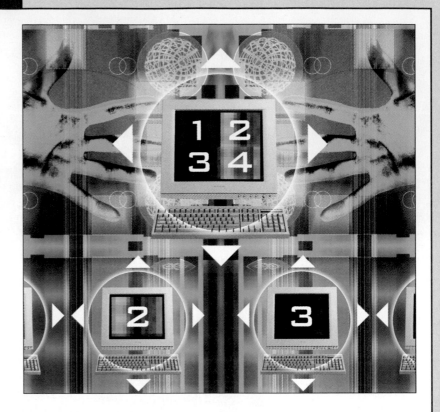

Windows XP and the Internet

The **Internet** has changed the way people communicate, shop, do business, and find information. The Internet is a global super **network**—linked computers that can exchange information—comprising many smaller networks. The **World Wide Web**, often referred to as the **Web**, is a subset of the Internet. The Web enables you to view the information posted on the Internet. It also enables you to send and receive electronic mail (**e-mail**)—messages or files transmitted over the Internet.

Internet Explorer and **Outlook Express** are programs that come with Windows XP. Internet Explorer is a Web browser, a program used to view Web pages and link to other Web pages. Outlook Express is an electronic mail management program that enables you to control and organize your Internet communications.

Project 5A **Information**

The Internet enables you to see information posted on other computers worldwide and is used to carry communications from one person to another. In this project, you will familiarize yourself with the Internet Explorer program and use it to navigate the Web. You will also use Outlook Express to manage your e-mail.

In Activities 5.1 through 5.12, you will start Internet Explorer, explore the Internet Explorer screen, and navigate the Web. You will find information about student financial aid from the Department of Education (ED) and save a Web page to your desktop. You will also start Outlook Express, set up your e-mail, and create, send, forward, and reply to a message. You will create a document about financial aid and create an e-mail message using several special e-mail features. Your completed document and e-mail messages will look similar to those shown in Figure 5.1. You will save your documents as *5A_Financial_Aid_Firstname_Lastname* and *5A_Information_Firstname_Lastname*.

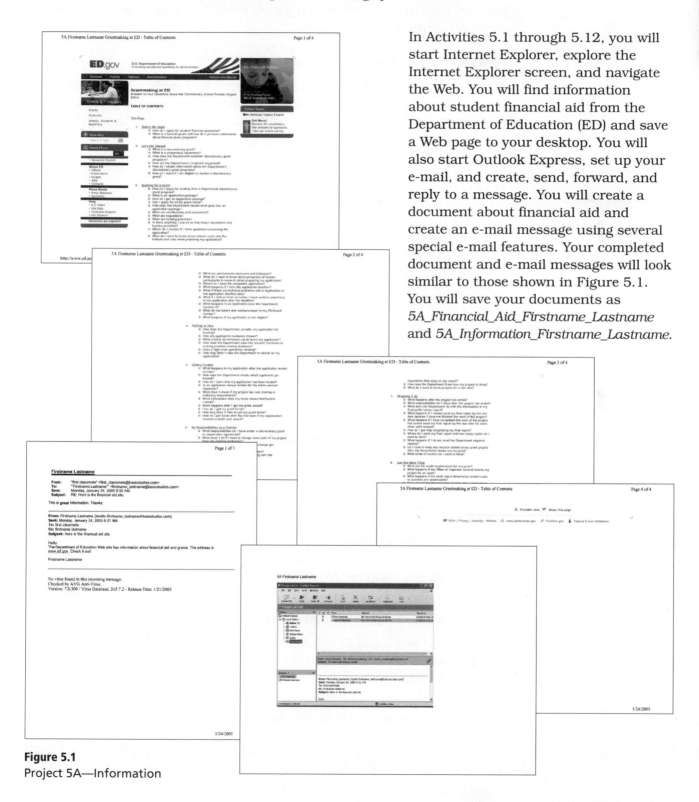

Figure 5.1
Project 5A—Information

Objective 1
Use Internet Explorer

The Web is part of the Internet and is made up of a network of linked documents—called **pages**—that are stored on computers called **servers**. There are tens of thousands of Web servers worldwide. Internet Explorer enables you to view information stored on Web servers. You can use Internet Explorer to display Web pages, print Web pages, or save Web pages on your computer.

Activity 5.1 Starting Internet Explorer

In this activity, you will start Internet Explorer and explore the Web site for the U.S. Department of Education. A **Web site** is a collection of related documents on the Web. Each of these documents is known as a **Web page**.

1 Verify that you have a connection to the Internet.

Alert!

Before Connecting to the Internet

Your computer must include a modem or other hardware that can connect you to a network that can access the Internet. Although businesses, schools, and other large organizations often have their own networks established and provide Internet connections to their students and employees, individuals need to go through a service provider for Internet service.

If you do not have an Internet connection, you must establish an account with an **Internet Service Provider (ISP)**. ISPs such as AT&T, AOL, and Earthlink set up large computers that act as servers, or **hosts**, to other computers called **clients**—computers that connect to servers or hosts—to connect via telephone, cable, and DSL lines.

2 Click the **Start** button ⟦ ⧸ start ⟧, point to **All Programs**, and then click **Internet Explorer**. If necessary, in the title bar, click the Maximize button ⟦⬚⟧.

Each time you start Internet Explorer when you are connected to the Internet, the **home page** that has been set up on your computer displays. Notice that the Internet Explorer window is similar to other Windows XP windows. It has a menu bar, a toolbar, a status bar, and an address bar. The name of your ISP—the company that provides Internet access and an e-mail account—may display on the title bar.

3 In the Internet Explorer **Address** box, type **http://www.ed.gov/**

The text you typed in the Address box is a called a **Uniform Resource Locator (URL)**, which specifies a location of a page on the World Wide Web.

4 Take a moment to identify the components that make up a URL, as described in the table in Figure 5.2.

Components of a URL

Part of Web Address	Description
http	The acronym for HyperText Transfer Protocol—the standard *protocol*, or method, used to transfer data between a Web server and a Web browser.
://	Three characters were identified by Internet creators to separate the protocol from the Web address.
www.ed.gov	The *domain name* identifies the owner of the Web address.

Figure 5.2

chapter five

5 Press [Enter] to display a page from the Department of Education (ED) Web site, as shown in Figure 5.3. Alternatively, in the Address bar, click the **Go** button [→ Go]. If the page does not display, check your connection to the Internet and be sure that you have signed in to your ISP using a logon name and a password, if necessary.

Because the content of this Web page changes frequently, your screen will look different. This first page that you see is the *start page*. Each Web site has a *home page*—a document intended to serve as the starting point for a Web site. However, the Web site can redirect you to an opening page that is not the home page.

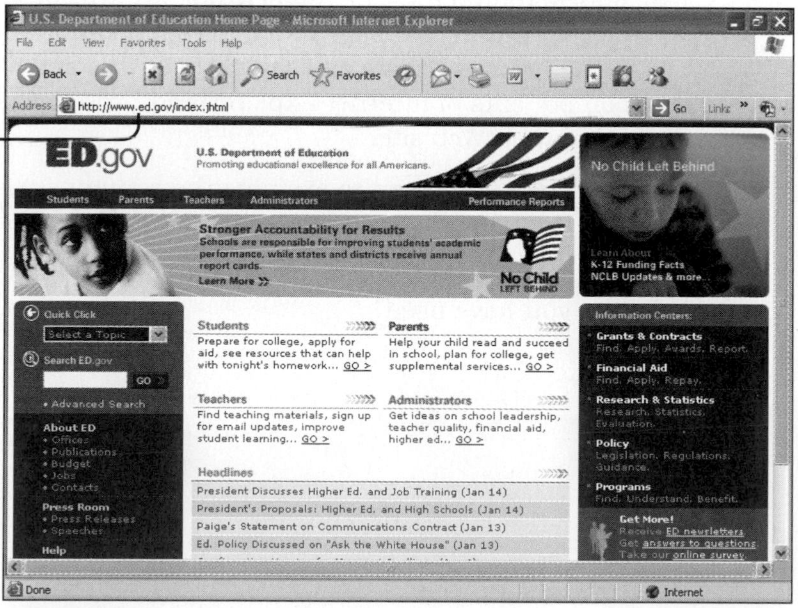

Address of the page being displayed

Figure 5.3

6 In the address bar, examine the URL.

Notice that more text displays to the right of the domain name. Web pages are special files that are stored in a folder and subfolder hierarchy in much the same way as files are stored on your computer. The location of the home page, called the *path*, is separated by forward slashes (/) to identify the folder and subfolders the browser needs to follow to open Web pages on the site. The last item in the list is the name of the page—in this case, *index.jhtml*. A *jhtml extension* means that a program using the Java programming language is running on the Web server.

7 Leave Internet Explorer and this Web page open for the next activity.

Activity 5.2 Browsing with Internet Explorer

After a Web page displays, use the *links* on the page to access related information. Links, or *hyperlinks*, are text or graphics that you click to display a different page or a different location on the same page. Clicking these links is known as *browsing*. In this activity, you will explore the components of Internet Explorer and browse the Department of Education Web site.

1 Take a moment to examine the components of the Internet Explorer browser, as described in the table shown in Figure 5.4.

Notice that the Internet Explorer window is similar to other windows you have used.

Internet Explorer Components

Component	Description
Title bar	Displays the name of the Web page and the standard Minimize, Maximize/Restore Down, and Close buttons
Menu bar	Displays the list of commands on a menu
Address bar	Displays the URL of the current Web page; also used to navigate to specific Web sites
Standard Buttons toolbar	Displays commonly used buttons, many of which are shortcuts for navigating the Web
Status bar	Displays messages and the URLs of links when you use the pointer to point to a link
Display area	Displays the current Web page

Figure 5.4

2 On the **ED** home page, locate the hyperlink list on the left side of the page.

Many Web sites use a pane on the left side of the window to display a menu of links to other locations on the same page, other pages in the Web site, or other Web sites. This Web site uses both a left and a right pane, both with menus of links, as shown in Figure 5.5. Notice also that the link pane contains a list of topics on the Web site, a Search box, and links to help topics.

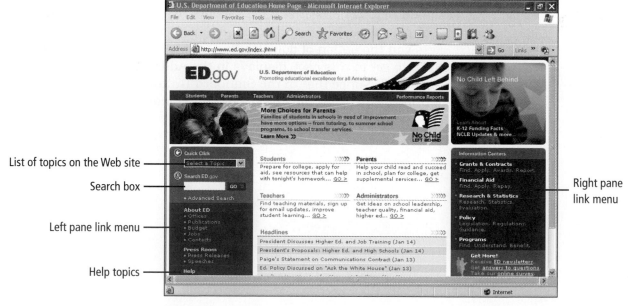

List of topics on the Web site

Search box

Left pane link menu

Help topics

Right pane link menu

Figure 5.5

3 In the right pane, under **Get More!**, click the **ED newsletters** link.

Another Web page, which is still part of the Department of Education Web site, displays a list of available newsletters. Notice that in the Standard Buttons toolbar, the Back button is active, as shown in Figure 5.6.

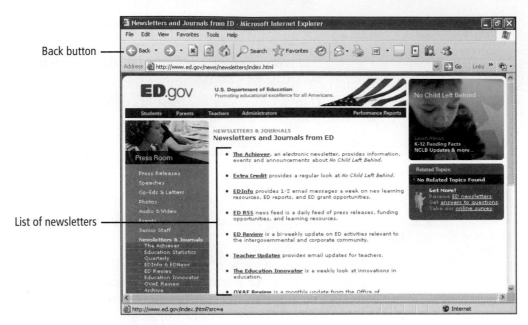

Figure 5.6

4 In the center of the Newsletters and Journals page, click **ED Review**.

The Ed Review newsletter page displays, containing links to the date of each past issue. Clicking these links opens the newsletter and also gives you the option of downloading that issue. The path you have taken to get to this page displays in the Address bar, as shown in Figure 5.7. Notice that in the Standard Buttons toolbar, the Back button is active and the Foward button is inactive.

Forward button

Back button

Home button

Path to the current Web page

Links to available newsletters

Figure 5.7

5 On the Standard Buttons toolbar, click the **Back** button.

Clicking Back displays the previously viewed Web page—the Newsletters page. The Forward button also becomes active when you click the Back button.

6 In the upper left corner of the Web page, point to the **ED.gov logo**. When the pointer changes to a hand pointer, click one time.

The logo is a link to the ED home page. Most Web pages contain a graphic or text link—or both—to the site home page. Clicking the ED.gov logo displays the ED home page.

7 On the Standard Buttons toolbar, click the **Back** button.

Recall that the Back button takes you to the previously displayed page. In this case, you were able to return to the Newsletters page without going through the intervening pages.

8 On the Standard Buttons toolbar, click the **Forward** button.

The home page displays once again.

9 On the Standard Buttons toolbar, click the **Home** button.

The same home page that opened when you started Internet Explorer—your default home page—displays.

10 On the Standard Buttons toolbar, click the **Back** button to return to the Department of Education home page. Leave Internet Explorer and the Department of Education Web page open for the next activity.

Activity 5.3 Using Favorites in Internet Explorer

Recall that Favorites is a folder in which you store shortcuts to folders and files that you access frequently. After you add an item to Favorites, the item displays on the Favorites menu and in the Favorites pane. In Internet Explorer, you use Favorites to store shortcuts to Web pages that you access frequently. In this activity, you add two Web sites to Favorites and practice using Favorites to go to the page.

1 Be sure the ED home page displays on your screen. From the Standard Buttons toolbar, click the **Favorites** button.

The Favorites pane opens on the left side of the Internet Explorer window. Your Favorites pane may be empty, or it may already contain shortcuts.

2 Near the top of the Favorites pane, click the **Add** button.

3 In the **Add Favorite** dialog box, in the **Name** box, drag to select the text, and then type **ED Home Page** Compare your dialog box with Figure 5.8.

Your Add Favorite dialog box may also display a list of folders below the Name box.

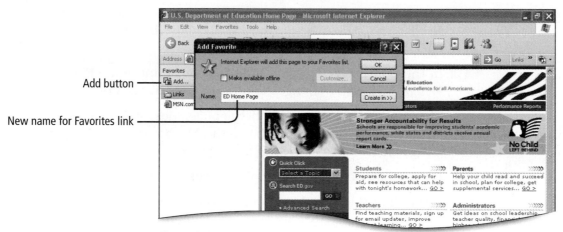

Add button —
New name for Favorites link —

Figure 5.8

4 In the **Add Favorite** dialog box, click **OK** to add the shortcut to your list of links.

5 Near the top of the **Favorites** pane, click the **Organize** button.

The Organize Favorites dialog box displays. You can use the Organize Favorites dialog box to create, rename, and delete folders or to move an existing Web site address to a different folder. Notice that the link to the ED home page displays in the list.

6 In the **Organize Favorites** dialog box, click **Create Folder**. Type the folder name **Financial Aid** and then press [Enter].

The new folder is created as a subfolder in Favorites, as shown in Figure 5.9.

New link

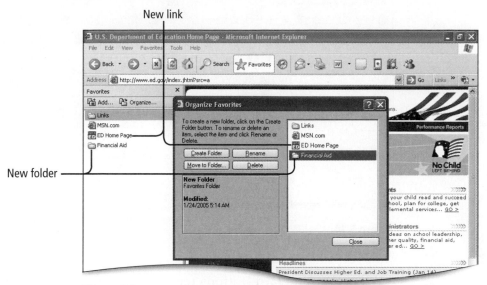

New folder

Figure 5.9

7 In the **Organize Favorites** dialog box, in the list of items, click **ED Home Page**, and then click **Move to Folder**.

More Knowledge — Organizing Favorites

If you have a small number of links in your Favorites pane, you can organize links in the Organize Favorites dialog box by dragging them up or down in the list. You can also drag a link to a folder, releasing the mouse button when the folder name is highlighted.

8 In the **Browse for Folder** dialog box, from the list of folders, click **Financial Aid**, and then click **OK**.

This moves the ED Home Page link to the Financial Aid folder. The Favorites pane can store links to many files, folders, and Web sites. You can create several folders to organize your links. Each folder can contain several—or even dozens of—links on related topics.

9 In the **Organize Favorites** dialog box, click **Close**. On the Standard Buttons toolbar, click the **Home** button [icon].

10 In the **Favorites** pane, click **Financial Aid** to display the link to the ED Home Page, and then click **ED Home Page** to display the ED home page, as shown in Figure 5.10.

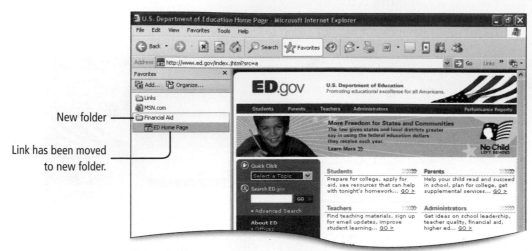

New folder

Link has been moved to new folder.

Figure 5.10

11 On the Standard Buttons toolbar, click the **Favorites** button.

The Favorites pane closes.

12 Leave Internet Explorer and the ED Web page open for the next activity.

Activity 5.4 Downloading Files from a Web Site

Some Web sites make documents available for you to **download**—save on your computer. Most Web documents that are available for download are in one of two formats—**Adobe Acrobat** or Microsoft Word. Adobe Acrobat files, often referred to as **PDF** (Portable Document Format) files—saved with the extension .*pdf*—are in a standard format that can be opened using a free program called **Adobe Reader**. Microsoft Word documents can be opened by Microsoft Word and several other word-processing programs. In this activity, you will download an Adobe Acrobat financial aid application from the ED Web site.

1 With the ED home page on your screen, in the right link pane, click **Financial Aid**.

The financial aid Overview page displays.

2 In the middle of the Web page, locate **Features**, and then, under **Apply for College Aid**, click **GO >**.

The FAFSA (Free Application for Federal Student Aid) page displays, as shown in Figure 5.11. The pages are revised regularly, so your page will differ. Notice in the Address bar that you have moved from the ED site to the FAFSA site.

Path indicates new Web site. ──

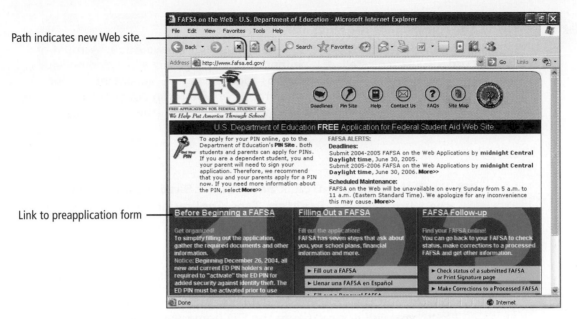

Figure 5.11

3 Locate and then click the **Before Beginning a FAFSA** link.

4 Under **Before Beginning a FAFSA Overview**, in the **Time Saving Suggestions** table, click **Pre-Application Worksheet**. Scroll down if necessary, and then click the **2005-2006 FAFSA on the Web Pre-Application Worksheet** link.

The years displayed in the link may vary. The FAFSA Pre-Application Worksheet opens in Adobe Reader, or Adobe Acrobat if you have the full version installed, as shown in Figure 5.12. Because Adobe Reader opens in the same Internet Explorer window as the previously viewed Web pages, the Back button is active.

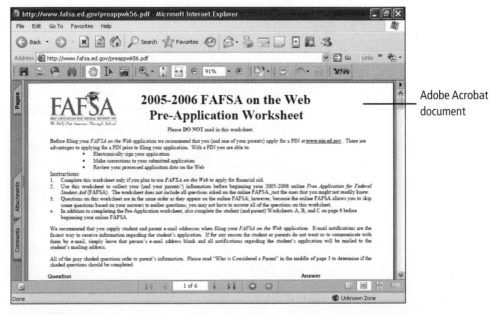

Adobe Acrobat document

Figure 5.12

5 From the **File** menu, click **Save**. In the **Save a Copy** dialog box, in the left pane, click **Desktop**. Type **Application** for the file name, and then click **Save**.

The document is saved to your desktop.

6 In the Standard Buttons toolbar, click the **Back** button [◀ Back ▾].

Notice that the FAFSA site displays, not the ED site. If you click the logo, you will not return to the ED home page.

7 In the Standard Buttons toolbar, click the **Back** button [◀ Back ▾] three times. When you reach the ED Web site, click the **ED.gov logo** in the upper left corner of the page to display the ED home page.

8 Leave Internet Explorer and the Web page open for the next activity.

Activity 5.5 Printing a Web Page

If you want to save a paper copy, you can print a Web page on your printer. In this activity, you navigate to the ED Grants Web page and then print the page.

1 With the ED home page on your screen, in the right pane, under **Information Centers**, click **Grants & Contracts**. Under **Features**, under **Grants at ED**, click **GO >**.

The Grantmaking at ED page displays, showing an outline of grant topics.

2 From the **File** menu, click **Print Preview**.

The Web page displays as it will appear when printed. By default, Internet Explorer inserts a *header* with the Web page address and page number and a *footer* with the Web page address and the date. The header is text that prints at the top of all pages, and the footer is text that prints at the bottom of all pages. Compare your screen with Figure 5.13. Notice that the right side of the Web page is cut off.

Page Setup button ———

Zoom arrow ———

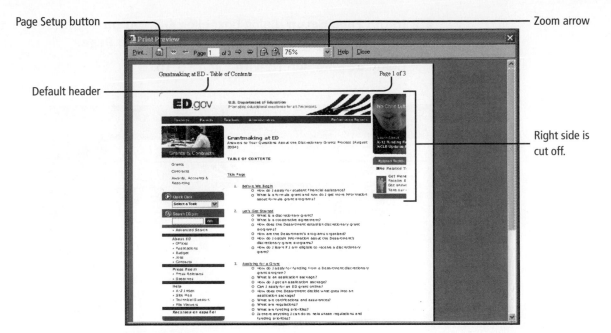

Default header ———

Right side is cut off. ———

Figure 5.13

3️⃣ On the **Print Preview** toolbar, click the **Page Setup** button 🖼️.

4️⃣ In the **Page Setup** dialog box that displays, under **Headers and Footers**, in the **Header** box, position the insertion point at the beginning of the existing text—a code that inserts the Web page name and the page number—type **5A Firstname Lastname** and then press ⎵Spacebar⎵.

The extra space is necessary to separate your name from the default header title.

5️⃣ Under **Orientation**, click to select the **Landscape** option, and then compare your **Page Setup** dialog box with Figure 5.14.

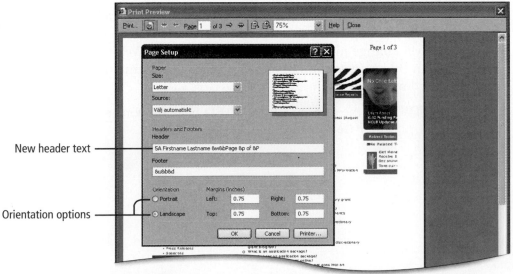

New header text ———

Orientation options ———

Figure 5.14

6 In the **Page Setup** dialog box, click **OK**. On the Print Preview toolbar, click the **Zoom arrow**, and then click **Whole Page**.

Compare your screen with Figure 5.15.

Header

Right edge of page now displays

Default footer

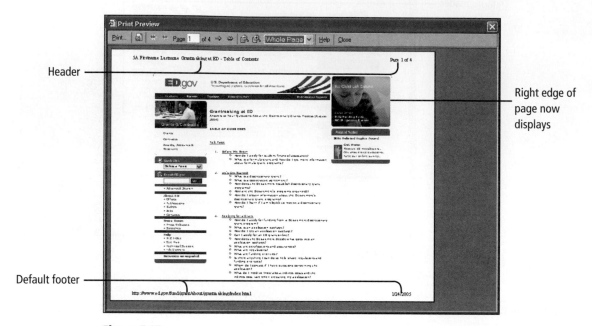

Figure 5.15

7 On the **Print Preview** toolbar, click **Print**. In the **Print** dialog box, under **Page Range**, click the **Current Page** option button, and then click **Print**.

The current page is printed. If you have been asked to submit this printout to your instructor, hold it until the end of this project.

8 Leave the Web page open for the next activity.

Activity 5.6 Saving a Web Page

If you want to show a Web page to someone who does not have an Internet connection, or if you want to be able to access a Web site that you know will change in the future, you can save the Web page to your computer. In this activity, you save a copy of the Grantmaking at ED page to your computer.

1 With the **Grantmaking at ED** page on your screen, in the right pane, under **Get More!**, click **ED newsletters**.

More Knowledge — Copyright Laws

Before you copy anything from a Web site, you need to find out who owns the copyright to the material. The Web has many copyright-free sites from which you can reproduce information and pictures. Federal government sites have a great deal of information that can be copied because the government is prohibited from copyrighting anything. However, be sure to look closely at the pictures on federal sites. Some pictures may have copyright notices indicating that the image is being used with permission from a copyright holder. Under some circumstances, you can use copyrighted materials for educational purposes.

2 From the **File** menu, click **Save As** to display the **Save Web Page** dialog box, as shown in Figure 5.16.

The Save Web Page dialog box is similar to the Save As dialog box you have used when saving your documents. You select where you want to store the file, specify the file type, and type a file name for the new file. Four file types are available:

- *Web Page, complete*—the default—saves all associated files needed to display the Web page, including graphics.

- *Web Archive*—saves a snapshot of the current Web page in a single file.

- *Web Page, HTML only*—saves the information on the Web page but does not save associated files, such as graphics. *HTML* is the acronym for *HyperText Markup Language*, the language used to create documents on the Web.

- *Text Only*—saves the information in plain text format.

Web page name

Default Web page type

Figure 5.16

3 In the **Save Web Page** dialog box, in the left pane, click **Desktop**.

4 Click the **Save as type arrow**, and then click **Web archive, single file (*.mht)**. In the **File name** box, type **5A_Financial_Aid_Firstname_Lastname** and then click **Save**.

Internet Explorer saves the file on the desktop in Web archive format.

5 In the Internet Explorer title bar, click the **Close** button ☒. Click the **Start** button ⊞ start , point to **All Programs**, and then click **Internet Explorer**. If necessary, in the title bar, click the Maximize button ▣.

6 From the **File** menu, click **Work Offline**.

When you select the Work Offline option, you can use Internet Explorer without an Internet connection.

7 From the **File** menu, click **Open**. In the **Open** dialog box, click **Browse**. If necessary, in the left pane, click Desktop. In the **Contents** pane, click **5A_Financial_Aid_Firstname_Lastname**. In the **Open** dialog box, click **OK**.

The Web page you saved opens in a new window without using an Internet connection.

8 In the right pane, under **Get More!**, use the pointer to point to the **online survey** link.

The pointer changes to a hand, indicating a link, but it also displays a small circle with a diagonal line, indicating that the link is not active, as shown in Figure 5.17.

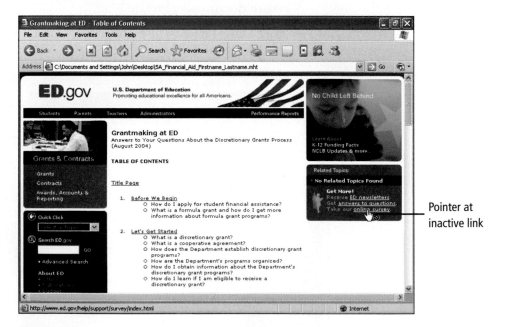

Pointer at inactive link

Figure 5.17

9 Click the **online survey** link.

A *Web page unavailable while offline* dialog box displays with the message that you are offline and gives you the option of connecting to the Internet, which will activate the links.

10 In the **Web page unavailable while offline** dialog box, click **Connect** to reactivate the Internet connection.

11 In the Internet Explorer title bar, click the **Close** button ☒. Repeat this action to close the other Internet Explorer window.

Objective 2
Use Outlook Express

Recall that Windows XP includes Outlook Express, a program that you can use to send and receive e-mail messages. You can also use this program to store *e-mail addresses*—strings of characters that identify the location where an e-mail message will be delivered—in an *address book*. You can also use Outlook Express to manage e-mail messages. E-mail is an electronic message or file transmitted over a network or the Internet.

In the following activities, you will create and send messages, receive and forward messages, and organize messages. To use Outlook Express to exchange e-mail, you must have an e-mail account with an Internet Service Provider, and the account must be set up for use with Outlook Express.

Activity 5.7 Starting Outlook Express

In Windows XP, Outlook Express is set up as the default e-mail program. Your system may have been customized to use a different program for e-mail. In this activity, you will start Outlook Express and examine the Outlook Express screen elements.

1 From the taskbar, display the **Start** menu, point to **All Programs**, and then click **Outlook Express** to open the program. If a dialog box displays and prompts you to use Outlook Express as the default e-mail program, *and* if you are using your own computer and would like to use Outlook Express as your e-mail program, click **Yes**; otherwise, click **No**. If necessary, maximize the Outlook Express window.

Alert!

If You Have Problems Opening Outlook Express

Many variables can affect the way Outlook Express opens. If you are using a network version of the program, you may be asked to log on. Alternatively, the Internet Connection Wizard may display, prompting you to set up Outlook Express, or you may see a dialog box prompting you to identify your network connection. Confirm that you have an active Internet connection. Follow the instructions to cancel any dialog boxes or wizards. Check with your lab director or network administrator if you are not sure how to respond to a dialog box.

2 Take a moment to familiarize yourself with the screen elements shown in Figure 5.18 and described in the table shown in Figure 5.19.

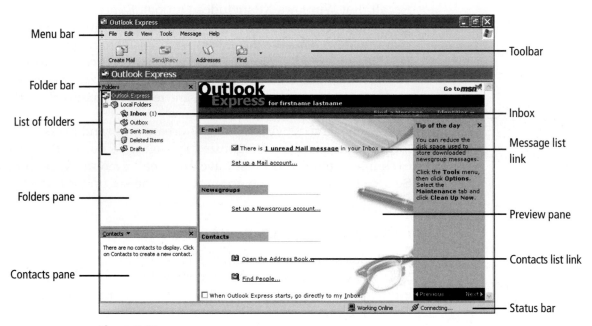

Figure 5.18

Outlook Express Screen Elements

Screen Element	Description
Folder list	Displays a hierarchical list of Outlook Express folders
Contacts	Displays items entered in your Address Book
Message list	Displays messages stored in the current folder
Preview pane	Displays either the content of the current message or tasks that are available
Inbox	The default mailbox in which incoming messages are stored
Menu bar	Displays the list of commands on a menu
Toolbar	Displays commonly used buttons for creating messages and navigating Outlook Express
Folder bar	Displays the name of the current folder
Folders pane	Displays a list of available folders
Contacts pane	Displays a list of people for whom you have saved e-mail addresses and other contact information
Status bar	Displays information about the current folder and whether your Internet connection is active

Figure 5.19

3 From the **View** menu, click **Layout**. If necessary, in the Window Layout Properties dialog box, under Basic, click to select the Contacts, Folder bar, Folder List, Status Bar, and Toolbar check boxes, and click to deselect the Outlook Bar and Views Bar check boxes.

The **Outlook bar** displays folder icons, which are also displayed in the Folders pane. The **Views bar** displays options for the way your e-mail messages are displayed. Compare your screen with Figure 5.20. When you are finished, click OK.

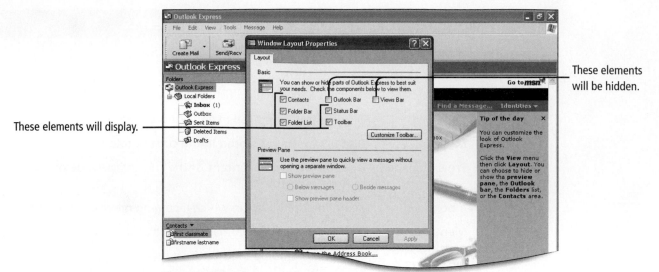

These elements will display.

These elements will be hidden.

Figure 5.20

4 Take a moment to familiarize yourself with the default Outlook Express folders, as described in the table in Figure 5.21.

The folders that display in your Folders pane will depend on how your system is set up; you may not see all these folders.

Outlook Express Folders

Folder	Description
Inbox	Stores messages that have been sent to you
Outbox	Stores messages that you want to send, called *outgoing messages*
Sent Items	Stores copies of messages that you have sent
Deleted Items	Stores messages that you have deleted; messages remain until you empty the Deleted Items folder
Drafts	Stores messages that you are in the process of writing
Local Folders	Contains folders that are stored on your computer and folders that are stored on your *mail server*—the computer that manages your e-mail account

Figure 5.21

5 Leave Outlook Express open for the next activity.

Activity 5.8 Setting Up an E-mail Account

To use Outlook Express, you must identify at least one e-mail account to use with the program. If you do not have an e-mail account associated with Outlook Express, or if you want to add another e-mail account, continue with this activity. If you already have an e-mail account associated with Outlook Express, skip this activity.

1 From the **Tools** menu, click **Accounts**.

The Internet Accounts dialog box displays, as shown in Figure 5.22, with the All tab selected by default.

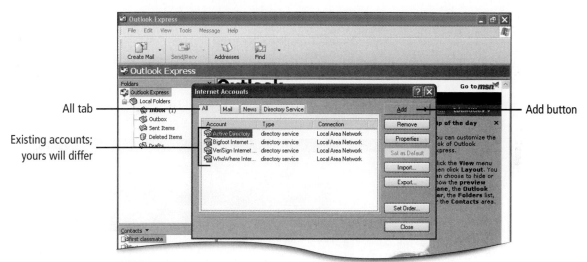

Figure 5.22

2 In the **Internet Accounts** dialog box, click the **Add** button, and then click **Mail**.

The first Internet Connection Wizard dialog box displays. A *wizard* is a feature of Windows XP that prompts you through the steps necessary to complete a task.

3 In the **Internet Connection Wizard** dialog box, under **Your Name**, in the **Display name** box, type your name, and then click **Next**.

The second Internet Connection Wizard dialog box displays, asking for your e-mail address.

4 Under **Internet E-mail Address**, in the **E-mail address** box, type the e-mail address you want to use, and then click **Next**.

The third Internet Connection Wizard dialog box displays, asking for details about your e-mail account.

More Knowledge — If You Need to Create a New E-mail Account

If you want to create a new e-mail account to use with Outlook Express, click the Start button, point to All Programs, and then click Internet Explorer. In the Address bar, type www.yahoo.com, and then follow the instructions to sign up for a new e-mail account. Write down your new e-mail address, close Internet Explorer, and use your new e-mail address in the Internet Connection Wizard dialog box. If you use a Yahoo! account, in the Internet Mail Logon dialog box, be sure to click the *Log on using Secure Password Authentication (SPA)* check box.

5 Under **E-mail Server Names**, enter the appropriate information. If necessary, check with your lab manager or mail service provider to get the correct information.

Compare your dialog box with Figure 5.23.

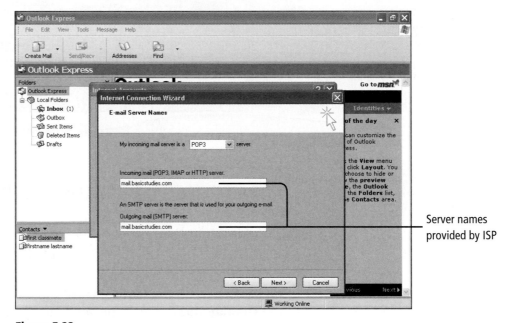

Server names provided by ISP

Figure 5.23

6 Near the bottom of the dialog box, click **Next**.

The fourth Internet Connection Wizard dialog box displays.

7 Under **Internet Mail Logon**, in the **Account name** box, type your e-mail address. In the **Password** box, type your e-mail password. If you are using Outlook Express in a lab, click to deselect the Remember password check box. If you are using a computer at home, choose whether you want the program to remember your password for you.

For security purposes, as you type the password, the letters change to large black dots, as shown in Figure 5.24.

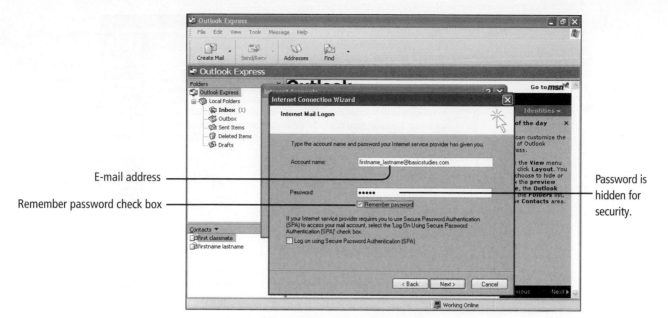

On the left side, labels point to the dialog box:
- E-mail address
- Remember password check box

On the right side, labels point to the dialog box:
- Password is hidden for security.

Figure 5.24

8 Near the bottom of the dialog box, click **Next**. In the final **Internet Connection Wizard** dialog box, which displays the text *Congratulations*, click **Finish**.

Your new account displays in the Internet Accounts dialog box.

9 In the **Internet Accounts** dialog box, click **Close**.

A dialog box may display, prompting you to download folders from the mail server that you just added.

10 If an Outlook Express dialog box displays, click Yes.

11 Leave Outlook Express open for the next activity.

Activity 5.9 Creating, Sending, Receiving, and Reading a Message

In this activity you create, send, and receive a message that provides the URL for the Department of Education Web site. You will send a message to a classmate or friend and receive another message from the same person. After you receive the message, you create and send a reply. You must be connected to the Internet and have an e-mail account to complete this activity. You will also need to obtain the e-mail address of a class-mate or friend who will send you an e-mail message.

1 On the Outlook Express toolbar, click the **Create Mail** button. In the New Message window that displays, click the Maximize button if necessary.

In the new message window, you will complete the message header information and type the message text. The screen elements of the New Message window are shown in Figure 5.25 and described in the table shown in Figure 5.26.

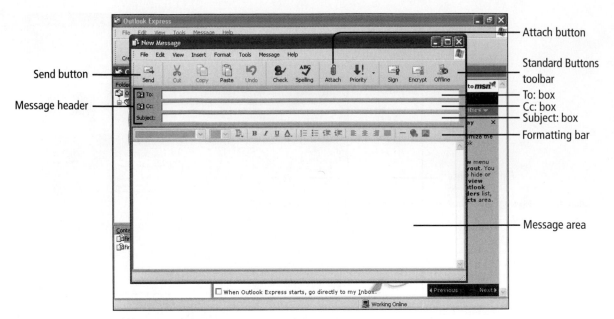

Send button

Message header

Attach button

Standard Buttons toolbar

To: box
Cc: box
Subject: box

Formatting bar

Message area

Figure 5.25

Components of the Outlook Express New Message Window

Component	Description
Message header	Information is entered in the To:, Cc:, and Subject: boxes at the top of the window.
Message area	The area of the window where the message is typed.
To: box	The e-mail address of the primary recipient of the message. You can include more than one e-mail address so that you can send the same message to more than one recipient.
Cc: box	The e-mail address of the recipient who will receive a *carbon copy*—also referred to as a *courtesy copy*—of the message. The primary recipient or recipients will be able to view the addresses of anyone copied on the message.
Subject: box	A brief synopsis of the contents of the message. A descriptive subject is important if you want the recipient to open the message.
Standard Buttons toolbar	Contains buttons used to create and manage the e-mail message.
Send button	Sends a copy of the message to each address entered in the To: and Cc: boxes.
Attach button	Attaches files to be sent with the message.
Formatting bar	Contains buttons to format the message text.

Figure 5.26

2 In the **To:** box, type the e-mail address of a classmate. In the **Cc:** box, type your own e-mail address. Ask a classmate to send you the same message.

By copying yourself on an e-mail message, you can remind yourself of an appointment or store important information that you want to keep. To type more than one e-mail address in the To: or Cc: box, separate the addresses with either a comma or a semicolon.

3 In the **Subject:** box, type **Here is the financial aid site**

4 In the message area, type the following, and then compare your screen with Figure 5.27:

Hello:
The Department of Education Web site has information about financial aid and grants. The address is www.ed.gov. Check it out!

Firstname Lastname

Notice that when you typed the URL, the text turned blue and was underlined. When you type a Web address, a link is created to the site.

Send button —

Active link to a Web address —

Your e-mail addresses will differ

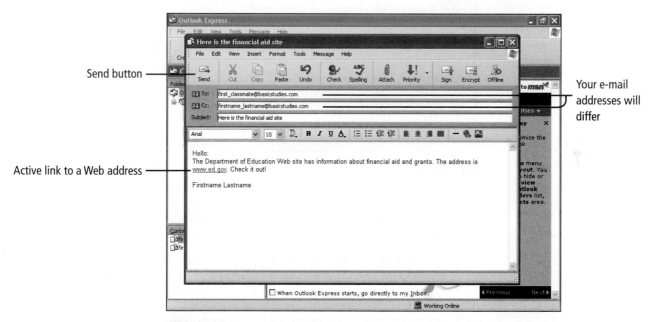

Figure 5.27

5 On the Standard Buttons toolbar, click the **Send** button.

The message is either temporarily stored in the Outbox or immediately sent to the recipients, depending on how your Outlook Express program is configured. If the message is stored in the Outbox, the Outbox text will be bold.

6 Click the **Send/Recv** button ![Send/Recv icon], and then click **Send and Receive All**. If you do not receive the expected messages, wait one minute and then click Send/Recv again.

Notice that the Inbox text is bold. You should have two messages: one from your classmate and one from yourself.

7 In the **Folders** pane, click the **Inbox**.

The contents of the Inbox are displayed in the Contents pane. The text of the active, or highlighted, message displays in the message preview pane below the Contents pane, as shown in Figure 5.28.

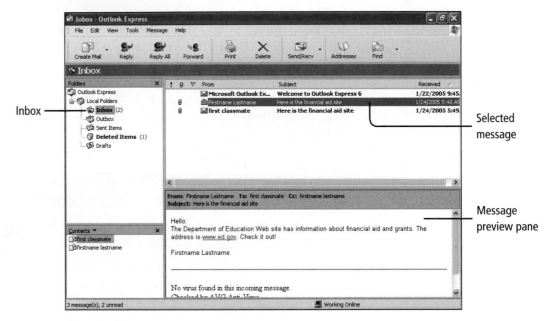

Figure 5.28

8 In the Contents pane, double-click the message sent by your classmate.

A message window opens, displaying the message, the e-mail address of the sender, the date and time the message was sent, and the message.

9 Leave the message open for the next activity.

Activity 5.10 Forwarding and Replying to a Message

When you receive a message, you have the option of replying to the message or forwarding the message to someone else. In this activity, you reply to a message, and you forward the message to another person.

1 On the Standard Buttons toolbar, click the **Reply** button ![Reply icon].

The Reply window displays. The original message displays at the bottom of the window, below the message area. The name of the window is *Re: Here is the financial aid site*. The text *Re:* is the e-mail abbreviation for Reply, as shown in Figure 5.29.

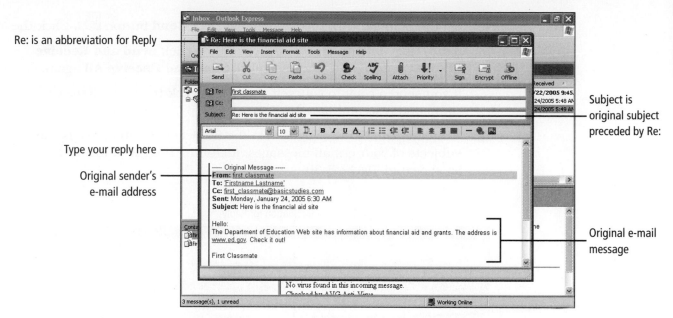

Re: is an abbreviation for Reply

Type your reply here

Original sender's e-mail address

Subject is original subject preceded by Re:

Original e-mail message

Figure 5.29

2 At the top of the message area, type **This is great information. Thanks.**

3 Highlight the word *great*. From the Formatting bar, click the **Bold** button **B**.

The word *great* displays with bold formatting. You can type and format your e-mail text in much the same way you type and format text using a program such as WordPad. Characters are inserted to the left of the insertion point. You can press Enter to start a new paragraph, and you can press Backspace or Delete to delete characters typed in error.

4 From the Standard Buttons toolbar, click the **Send** button. If the message is stored in the Outbox, click the Send/Recv button arrow, and then click Send and Receive All.

Typing a new message is similar to typing in WordPad.

5 In the Inbox, double-click the same message you replied to—the message from a classmate.

6 On the Standard Buttons toolbar, click the **Forward** button. In the **To:** box, type another classmate's e-mail address. In the **Cc:** box, type your own e-mail address.

Notice that in the title bar, the Subject line text is now preceded by *FW:* rather than *RE:*. In some e-mail programs, *FW:* is an abbreviation for Forward. Other programs use *FWD:* to indicate a forwarded message.

7 On the Standard Buttons toolbar, click the **Send** button . Click the **Send/Recv button arrow** , and then click **Send and Receive All**. Wait one minute, and then click **Send and Receive All** again.

If you send a copy to yourself, you must click the Send/Receive command a second time to receive the copy.

8 Examine your Inbox. Notice that the Subject column displays the subjects of your e-mail messages, including the *FW:* abbreviations, as shown in Figure 5.30.

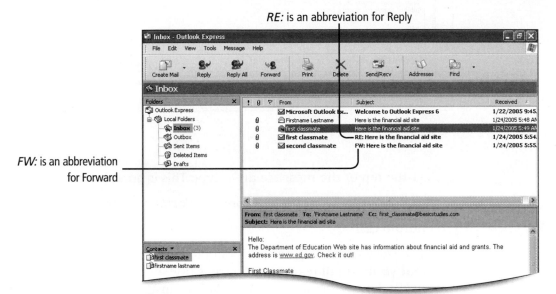

RE: is an abbreviation for Reply

FW: is an abbreviation for Forward

Figure 5.30

9 Leave Outlook Express open for the next activity.

Activity 5.11 Printing and Managing Messages

If you receive many messages, the list in your Inbox may become long and difficult to navigate. You can create folders for storing your messages and then move a message to a local folder so that you can keep your messages organized. You can also print a message to retain a paper copy, and you can delete a message you no longer need. In this activity, you will print a message. You will also create a new folder and move two messages to that folder.

1 In the **Folders** pane, be sure the **Inbox** is selected. In the message list, double-click the message with the *RE: Here is the financial aid site* subject.

2 On the Standard Buttons toolbar, click the **Print** button . Alternatively, from the File menu, click Print, select the pages to print and the number of copies, and then click Print to send the message to the default printer. If you have been asked to submit this printout to your instructor, hold it until the end of this project.

3 In the message title bar, click the **Close** button 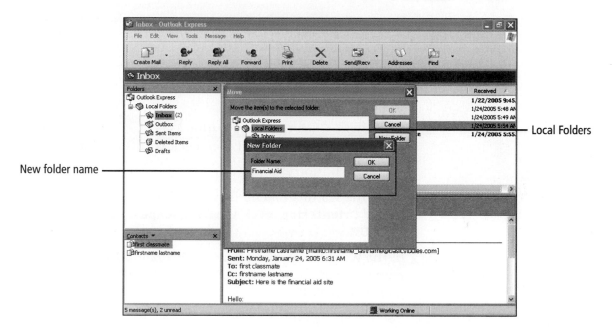.

4 In the message list, right-click the message with the *RE: Here is the financial aid site* subject, and then, from the shortcut menu, click **Move to Folder**.

5 In the displayed **Move** dialog box, click **Local Folders**, and then click **New Folder**. In the **Folder Name** box, type **Financial Aid**

Compare your screen with Figure 5.31.

New folder name ———

Local Folders

Figure 5.31

6 In the **New Folder** dialog box, click **OK**. In the **Move** dialog box, click **OK**.

Both dialog boxes close, and the selected message is moved to the new folder.

7 In the message list, right-click the message with the *FW: Here is the financial aid site* subject, and then from the shortcut menu, click **Move to Folder**.

The most recently used folder—Financial Aid—is selected by default.

8 In the **Move** dialog box, be sure the **Financial Aid** folder is selected, and then click **OK**.

A second message is moved to the new folder.

9 In the **Folders** pane, click the **Financial Aid** folder.

Notice that the two messages you moved display in the message list, as shown in Figure 5.32.

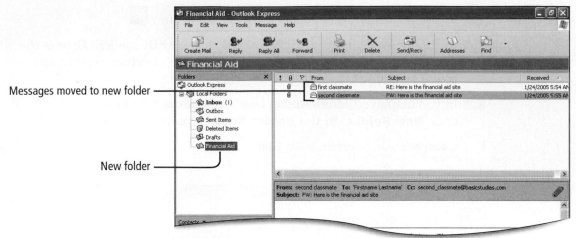

Messages moved to new folder

New folder

Figure 5.32

10 Press PrtScr. Click the **Start** button 🇭start, point to **All Programs**, point to **Accessories**, and then click **WordPad**. If necessary, click the Maximize button 🔲.

11 From the WordPad menu bar, click **File**, and then click **Page Setup**. Under **Orientation**, click the **Landscape** option button, and then click **OK**.

12 In the WordPad window, type **5A_Firstname_Lastname** using your own name. Press Enter two times. From the WordPad menu bar, click **Edit**, and then click **Paste**.

13 Use the sizing handle to resize the image so that it fits on one page. On the Standard Buttons toolbar, click **Print Preview** to confirm that the image fits on one page. If necessary, repeat this step until the image displays on one page.

14 On the toolbar, click the **Print** button 🖨. Retrieve your printout from the printer. If you have been asked to submit this printout to your instructor, hold it until the end of this project.

15 From the **File** menu, click **Save**. In the **Save As** dialog box, click **Desktop**.

16 In the **File name** box, type **5A_Information_Firstname_Lastname** and then click **Save**. Close WordPad.

17 In the Outlook Express title bar, click the **Close** button ✖.

five

Objective 3
Add Active Desktop Items

You can display Web content on the Windows XP desktop to help you stay up to date with changing information, such as breaking news, weather, sports scores, or stock quotes, found on the Internet. The item displays on the desktop but is automatically *synchronized*—updated—with the Web page that is the source of the information; when the data on the Web page updates, the data on the desktop updates.

Activity 5.12 Adding Web Content to Your Desktop

You can view Web content on your desktop without starting Internet Explorer. Create an *active desktop item*, which is an HTML item that displays on the desktop and is synchronized with a Web page, by adding *active content*, which is HTML content that updates *dynamically*—in real time—on the Web. To create an active desktop item, select it from the *Internet Explorer Desktop Gallery*, which is a Microsoft Web site that provides access to active desktop items. In this activity, you add a stock ticker and a weather map to the active desktop. You must be connected to the Internet to complete this activity.

1 On the desktop, right-click a blank area, and then, from the shortcut menu, click **Properties**.

Alert!

Internet Security

Before you create a continuous link to the Internet on your desktop, be sure you have up-to-date Internet security software installed and running on your computer, and update this software at least once a week.

If you are doing this activity in a computer lab or on a computer that is not your own, check with the lab manager or other person in charge of the computer to find out whether active desktop items are prohibited. Many labs disable this feature because of potential security problems and possible computer malfunctions.

2 In the **Display Properties** dialog box, click the **Desktop tab**, and then click **Customize Desktop**. In the **Desktop Items** dialog box, click the **Web tab**.

On the Web tab, you can create and manage active desktop items. Your home page is listed, but the empty check box indicates that it is not selected to display.

3 On the **Web tab**, click **New** to start the **New Desktop Item** wizard.

The New Desktop Item Wizard prompts you through the steps to identify the Web page or Web content that you want to display as an active item.

4 In the **New Desktop Item Wizard**, click **Visit Gallery**.

The Internet Explorer 4.0 Desktop Gallery Web page displays, as shown in Figure 5.33.

Web page URL in address bar ——

Click here to add Active Desktop item ——

Microsoft Investor Ticker item ——

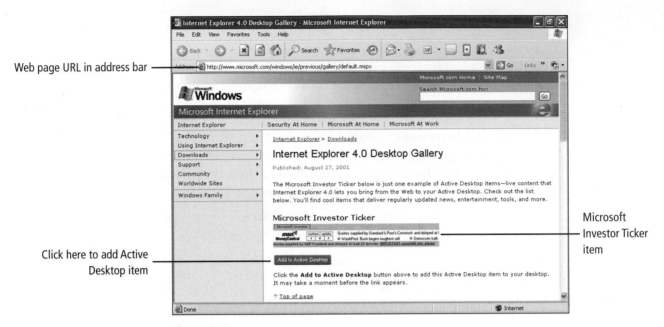

Figure 5.33

5 Under **Microsoft Investor Ticker**, click **Add to Active Desktop**. In the **Internet Explorer** message box, click **Yes**. In the **Add item to Active Desktop** box, click **OK**.

Internet Explorer and Windows XP synchronize the active content and then display the Internet Explorer window.

6 If Internet Explorer prompts you to download a program necessary to display active desktop items, verify in the message box that the program is certified by Microsoft, and then click OK.

7 Close the Internet Explorer window to display the desktop. If a yellow bar displays across the top of the stock ticker, click anywhere in the message, and then, from the shortcut menu, click **Install ActiveX Control**. In the **Windows Explorer - Security Warning** dialog box, click **Install**.

The active desktop item Microsoft Investor Ticker displays, as shown in Figure 5.34.

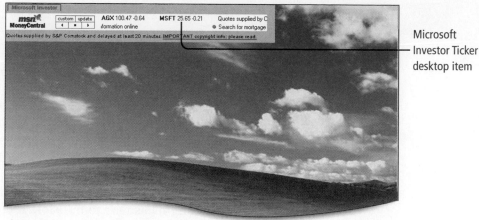

Microsoft Investor Ticker desktop item

Figure 5.34

8 Press PrtScr. Start **WordPad**, and, if necessary, maximize the window. From the WordPad menu bar, click **File**, click **Page Setup**, set the orientation to **Landscape**, and then click **OK**.

9 In the WordPad window, type **5A_Firstname_Lastname** and press Enter two times. From the WordPad menu bar, click **Edit**, and then click **Paste**.

10 Use the sizing handle to resize the image. On the Standard Buttons toolbar, click **Print Preview** to confirm that the picture fits on one

page. On the toolbar, click the **Print** button 🖨. If you have been asked to submit this printout to your instructor, hold it until the end of this project.

11 From the **File** menu, click **Save**. In the **Save As** dialog box, click **Desktop**. In the **File name** box, type **5A_Desktop_Firstname_Lastname** and then click **Save**. In the WordPad title bar, click the **Close**

button ⊠.

12 On the desktop, right-click a blank area, and then click **Properties**. In the **Display Properties** dialog box, click the **Desktop tab**, click **Customize Desktop**, and then click the **Web tab**.

13 In the **Web pages** list, click **Microsoft Investor Active Desktop Ticker**, and then click **Delete**. In the **Active Desktop Item confirm delete** dialog box, click **Yes**.

14 In the **Desktop Items** dialog box, click **OK**. In the **Display Properties** dialog box, click **OK**.

The item is removed from the desktop, and the active link to the Internet is closed.

15 Check your *Chapter Assignment Sheet* or your *Course Syllabus* or consult your instructor to determine whether you are to submit the printed pages that are the results of this project.

End You have completed Project 5A

Summary

In this chapter you practiced using Internet Explorer and Outlook Express, and you added and removed active desktop items. You used Internet Explorer to locate the Department of Education Web site. You browsed the Web site using the Internet Explorer toolbar's Back, Forward, and Home buttons, and you used links on the Web pages to move from one page to another and from one Web site to another. You also added a subfolder and a Web page to Favorites. Next, you used Outlook Express to create, send, receive, and forward e-mail messages. You practiced sending messages to multiple recipients. Finally, you used the Windows XP active desktop feature to add Web dynamic content to your desktop. You managed the active items to synchronize the data and to resize, close, and remove the active items.

In This Chapter You Practiced How To

- Use Internet Explorer
- Use Outlook Express
- Add Active Desktop Items

Concepts Assessments

Matching   Match each term in the second column with its correct definition in the first column by writing the letter of the term on the blank line in front of the correct definition.

_____ 1. The document intended to serve as the starting page of a Web site.

_____ 2. The text that specifies the location of a page on the World Wide Web.

_____ 3. The protocol used to transfer data between a Web server and a Web browser.

_____ 4. Linked documents on the Web.

_____ 5. A folder in which you store shortcuts to Web pages that you access frequently.

_____ 6. The file type that saves all of the associated files needed to display a Web page, including graphics.

_____ 7. The file type that saves a snapshot of the current Web page in a single file.

_____ 8. To update a desktop item to match current information on a Web site.

_____ 9. To save a document from the Web onto your computer.

_____ 10. A collection of related Web pages.

_____ 11. Messages or files transmitted over the Internet.

_____ 12. The Outlook Express folder in which messages that you receive are stored.

_____ 13. The string of characters that identifies the location where an e-mail message will be delivered.

_____ 14. An HTML item that displays on the desktop and is updated from a Web page.

_____ 15. HTML information that updates in real time on the Web.

A Active content

B Active desktop item

C Download

D E-mail

E E-mail address

F Favorites

G Home page

H HTTP

I Inbox

J Pages

K Synchronize

L Uniform Resource Locator (URL)

M Web archive

N Web site

O Web page, complete

Fill in the Blank Write the correct answer in the space provided.

1. The company that provides you with Internet access and an e-mail account is called a(n) _____.

2. The set of rules or standards that let computers connect to one another is called a(n) _____.

3. The mouse pointer resembles a hand with a pointing finger when it rests on a(n) _____.

4. To save the information on a Web page but not the associated files, such as graphics, use the file type called Web Page, _____ only.

5. HTML is the acronym for _____.

6. The folder in Outlook Express where copies of messages that you send are stored is named _____.

7. The computer that manages your e-mail account is called the _____.

8. When you delete an e-mail message in Outlook Express, the message is stored in the folder named _____.

9. To send an e-mail message, type the recipient's e-mail _____ in the To: box.

10. The Microsoft Web site that provides access to active desktop items is called the Internet Explorer Desktop _____.

Project 5B — Educational Testing

Objectives: *Use Internet Explorer and Use Outlook Express.*

A great deal of information about education is available online. In this Skills Assessment, you will use Internet Explorer to visit the Educational Testing Service (ETS) site and download registration materials for taking the Graduate Records Examination (GRE). You will use Outlook Express to send an e-mail message to a classmate that contains information about the site, and then you will print the e-mail message, which will look similar to Figure 5.35. You need to have an Internet connection to complete this activity.

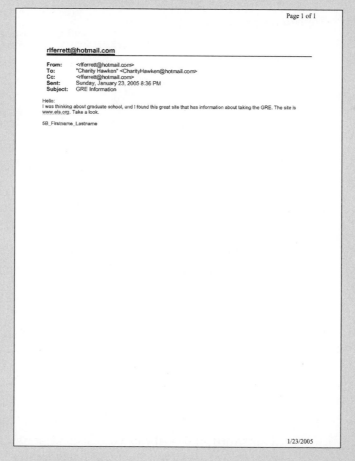

Figure 5.35

1. Click **Start**, point to **All Programs**, and then click **Internet Explorer**. If necessary, in the title bar, click the Maximize button.

2. In the Internet Explorer **Address** bar, type **www.ets.org** and then press [Enter] to connect to the Educational Testing Service home page.

3. Near the top of the window, on the ETS menu bar, click the **Download** tab.

(Project 5B – Educational Testing continues on the next page)

(Project 5B–Educational Testing continued)

4. Locate and click the **GRE** download link. On the **Download Library** page, under **Directory**, click **Registration Materials**.

5. In the **Registration Materials** list, click the top link. Either a Save As dialog box will display, prompting you to save the file, or the file will open in Adobe Reader. If the Save As dialog box displays, click Desktop, and then click Save. If the document opens in Adobe Reader, from the File menu, click Save. In the dialog box that displays, click **Desktop**, in the **File name** box, type **GRE_Information** and then click **Save**.

6. In the Internet Explorer title bar, click the **Close** button to close the PDF window. Click the **Close** button a second time to close the ETS window.

7. From the taskbar, click **Start**, point to **All Programs**, and then click **Outlook Express**. If you see the dialog box that prompts you to specify whether you want to use Outlook Express as the default e-mail program, click No.

8. On the Outlook Express toolbar, click the **Create Mail** button.

9. In the **To:** box, type the e-mail address of a classmate. In the **Cc:** box, type your own e-mail address. In the **Subject:** box, type **GRE Information**

10. In the message area, type the following:

    Hello:
    I was thinking about graduate school, and I found this great site that has information about taking the GRE. The site is www.ets.org. Take a look.

    5B_Firstname_Lastname

11. On the Standard Buttons toolbar, click the **Send** button.

12. In the **Folders** pane, click the **Inbox**. On the Standard Buttons toolbar, click the **Send/Recv** button. Double-click your message when it displays in your Inbox.

13. On the Standard Buttons toolbar, click the **Print** button. Retrieve your printout, and submit your message as directed.

14. Close the message, and then close Outlook Express.

 End **You have completed Project 5B**

Project 5C—Satellites

Objective: *Add Active Desktop Items.*

Microsoft provides several active content items at the Internet Explorer Desktop Gallery. Some of these are for entertainment value and keep you informed about favorite topics. In this Skills Assessment, you will add the J-Track: Satellite Tracking active content item to your desktop. You will capture the screen and place it in a WordPad document that you will name *5C_Satellites_Firstname_Lastname*. Your document will look similar to Figure 5.36.

Figure 5.36

1. On the desktop, right-click a blank area, and then from the shortcut menu, click **Properties**.

2. In the **Display Properties** dialog box, click the **Desktop tab**, and then click **Customize Desktop**. In the **Desktop Items** dialog box, click the **Web tab**.

3. On the **Web tab**, click **New** to start the **New Desktop Item** wizard.

4. In the **New Desktop Item Wizard**, click **Visit Gallery**.

5. Under **J-Track: Satellite Tracking**, click **Add to Active Desktop**. In the **Internet Explorer** message box, click **Yes** to confirm that you want to add a desktop item. In the **Add item to Active Desktop** box, click **OK**. Close the **Internet Explorer** window.

(Project 5C–Satellites continues on the next page)

(Project 5C–Satellites continued)

6. If Internet Explorer prompts you to download a program necessary to display active desktop items, verify in the message box that the program is certified by Microsoft, and then click OK. Follow instructions to install the ActiveX Control program.

7. After a few seconds, a dialog box displays, prompting you to specify whether you want to run the J-Track program offered by the National Aeronautics and Space Administration (NASA). Click **Run** to set up the desktop item.

8. Point to the top edge of the **J-Track desktop item** to display a **control bar**. On the **desktop item control bar**, drag a blank area to move the item to the lower right corner of the desktop.

9. Press PrtScr. Start **WordPad** and, if necessary, maximize the window. From the WordPad menu bar, click **File**, and then click **Page Setup**. Under **Orientation**, click the **Landscape** option button, and then click **OK**.

10. In the WordPad window, type **5C_Firstname_Lastname** using your own name. Press Enter two times. From the WordPad menu, click **Edit**, and then click **Paste**.

11. Use the sizing handle to resize the image. On the Standard Buttons toolbar, click **Print Preview** to confirm that the picture fits on one page. On the toolbar, click the **Print** button.

12. From the **File** menu, click **Save**. In the **Save As** dialog box, click **Desktop**. In the **File name** box, type **5C_Satellites_Firstname_Lastname** and then click **Save**. In the WordPad title bar, click the **Close** button.

13. On the desktop, right-click a blank area, and then click **Properties**. In the **Display Properties** dialog box, click the **Desktop tab**, click **Customize Desktop**, and then click the **Web tab**.

14. In the **Web pages** list, click **J-Track: Satellite Tracking**, and then click **Delete**. In the **Active Desktop Item confirm delete** dialog box, click **Yes**.

15. In the **Desktop Items** dialog box, click **OK**. In the **Display Properties** dialog box, click **OK**.

End You have completed Project 5C

Project 5D — References

Objectives: *Use Internet Explorer and Use Outlook Express.*

A number of sites on the Internet can be used as references while you are working on homework, doing research, or working at your job. Some of these sites are so useful that you will want quick access to them. In this Performance Assessment, you will use Internet Explorer to locate and use reference materials on the Web. You will add two of the sites to your Favorites folder and send an e-mail message that contains instructions on how to get to these sites. You will capture an image of your screen, paste it in a WordPad document, and save the document as *5D_References_Firstname_Lastname.* Your document and printed message will look similar to Figure 5.37.

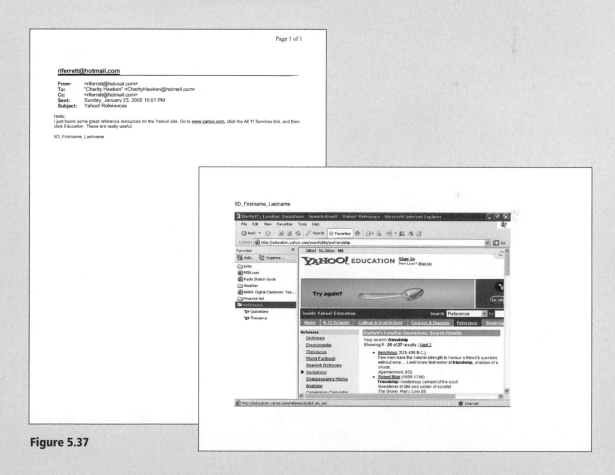

Figure 5.37

1. Start **Internet Explorer** and maximize the screen. In the Internet Explorer **Address** bar, type **http://www.yahoo.com** and press Enter.

2. In the Yahoo! list of services, locate and click **All Y! Services**. Scroll down the page. In the **E** section of the index, click **Education**.

(Project 5D–References continues on the next page)

(Project 5D–References continued)

3. In the **Resources** list, click **Thesaurus**. If the Favorites pane is not displayed on your screen, from the Standard Buttons toolbar, click the Favorites button.

4. Near the top of the **Favorites** pane, click **Organize**. In the **Organize Folders** dialog box, click **Create Folder**. Name the folder **References** and then click **Close**.

5. Near the top of the **Favorites** pane, click **Add**. In the **Add Favorite** dialog box, under **Create in**, click the **References** folder.

6. In the **Name** box, type **Thesaurus** and then click **OK** to add the Thesaurus page to your References folder.

7. To test the thesaurus, in the **Search Thesaurus** box, type **standard** and then click **Search**. Notice that two definitions display, along with a number of synonyms for each definition.

8. In the **Resources** list, click **Quotations**. Add a **Favorite** called **Quotations** to the **References** folder. Test the Quotations feature by typing **friendship** in the **Search** box.

9. In the **Favorites** pane, click the **References** folder to display the two new shortcuts you added. Press [PrtScr]. Close Internet Explorer.

10. Start WordPad. Change the document to **Landscape** orientation. Type **5D_Firstname_Lastname** and then press [Enter] two times. Paste the image of the screen in the document, and resize the image to fit on one page. Print the document, save the document as **5D_References_Firstname_ Lastname** and then close WordPad. Compare your screen with Figure 5.37.

11. Start **Outlook Express**. On the Outlook Express toolbar, click the **Create Mail** button.

12. In the **To:** box, type the e-mail address of a classmate. In the **Cc:** box, type your own e-mail address. In the **Subject:** box, type **Yahoo! References**

13. In the message area, type the following:

    Hello:
    I just found some great reference resources on the Yahoo! site. Go to www.yahoo.com, click the All Y! Services link, and then click Education. These are really useful.

    5D_Firstname_Lastname

14. Compare your message with Figure 5.37. Send the message. When you receive your message, open and print it. Submit both documents as directed.

15. Close the message, and then close Outlook Express.

 End You have completed Project 5D

Project 5E—Student Loans

Objectives: *Use Internet Explorer and Use Outlook Express.*

In Project 5A you visited the Department of Education Web site to locate information about financial aid available from the U.S. government. Financial aid is also available from each state. In this Mastery Assessment, you will use Internet Explorer to find your state's financial aid Web site. You will add this site to your Favorites list and then capture an image of the screen and paste it into a WordPad document that you will save as *5E_Student_Loans_Firstname_Lastname*. You will write and print an e-mail message. Your documents should look similar to Figure 5.38.

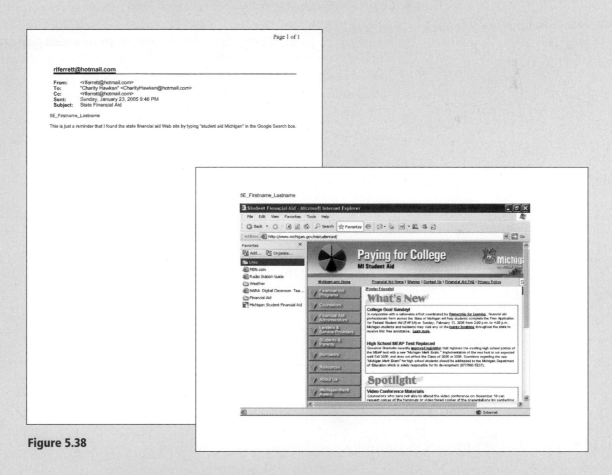

Figure 5.38

1. Start **Internet Explorer**. Go to the Google Web site at **www.google.com**

2. In the Search box, type **student aid** and the name of your state; for example, *student aid Michigan*. Press Enter.

3. Examine the links, and then click the link that looks like the official state Web site for your state. Open the **Favorites** pane, and then add this site to your Favorites list.

(Project 5E–Student Loans continues on the next page)

(Project 5E–Student Loans continued)

4. Explore the site to see what types of financial aid are available in your state.

5. Capture an image of your screen showing the Favorites folder and the new shortcut. Start **WordPad**. Change the document to **Landscape** orientation. Type **5E_Firstname_Lastname** and press Enter two times. Paste and resize the screen image to fit on one page. Print the document, and then save it as **5E_Student_Loans_Firstname_Lastname**

6. Compare your document with Figure 5.38. Close **WordPad**, and then close **Internet Explorer**.

7. Start **Outlook Express** and create a new message to send to yourself. Enter the subject text **State Financial Aid** On the first line of the message, type **5E_Firstname_Lastname** and then press Enter two times. Type the message text, substituting the name of your state: **This is just a reminder that I found the state financial aid Web site by typing "student aid Michigan" in the Google Search box.**

8. Send the message. When the message displays in your Inbox, open and print it. Close **Outlook Express**. Compare the printed message to Figure 5.38.

9. Submit the documents as directed.

 End You have completed Project 5E

Problem-Solving Assessment

Project 5F—Colleges

Objectives: *Use Internet Explorer and Use Outlook Express.*

In this Problem-Solving Assessment, you will practice using Internet Explorer to research colleges and universities and find a graduate school in which you might be interested in the future.

Start **Internet Explorer**, go to **www.yahoo.com**, and then click the **All Y! Services** link. Click the **Education** link, and then click **Find a College or Grad School**. Click the **School Search** link, and then click **Grad School**. Follow the instructions on the screen to explore the schools by the programs that interest you. Start **Outlook Express** and send an e-mail to yourself describing how you got to this site. When you are finished, delete all messages and empty the **Deleted Items** folder. Close all open programs.

 You have completed Project 5F ———————————————

Locating Online Classes

Many classes are available online. Some online classes are available from established colleges and universities; some are available from accredited online schools; and some are offered by special interest groups, but not for college credit.

To explore some of the available offerings, start Internet Explorer, go to www.google.com, and search for online classes. Click any of the links you find interesting. You can refine your search by adding another word to the search term; for example, search for **online classes genealogy** if you are interested in family history classes. Many of these classes are noncredit, and some are free. Or, for example, search for **online classes mba** to display links to for-credit masters of business administration classes, almost none of which are free. When you are finished, close Internet Explorer.

GO! with Help

Working Offline with Outlook Express

To reduce the time you spend connected to the Internet, you can configure Outlook Express to work offline. This enables you, for example, to write and respond to messages and delete messages, but the actions are not completed until you go online again.

1. Start **Outlook Express**.

2. On the **menu bar**, click **Help**, and then click **Contents and Index**.

3. In the left pane, click **Working Offline**, and then, under **Working Offline**, click **Reading e-mail messages offline**.

4. In the right pane, read the introduction to the subject. Click the **Set up Outlook Express to reduce online time** link.

5. Read the instructions, and then set your Outlook Express program to work offline if you so desire.

6. Close the **Help** window, and then close **Outlook Express**.

6 chaptersix

Searching for Information

In this chapter you will: complete this project **and** practice these skills.

Project 6A	Objectives
Search	• Search for Local Files
	• Search the Internet

Finding the Information You Need

The ability to locate information when you need it is an important computer skill. Windows XP provides the tools you need to locate files stored anywhere on your computer or anywhere on the Internet. By using Windows XP, you can search for files on your computer, even if you cannot remember the file name. You can use the same Windows XP search feature to search the Internet for information, or you can use Internet Explorer to access a program designed specifically for Internet searching.

Introduction

One of the main functions of a computer is to store files. Organizing your files in a logical manner is the first step in being able to retrieve files when you need them. However, you may forget where you stored a particular file, folder, or picture. Windows XP provides tools to help you locate files even if you no longer remember the file name. The Internet has billions of Web pages available to you. To locate information on the Internet, you also need to know how to use Internet search tools.

Project 6A Search

In this project, you practice using Windows XP to search for files related to recreational topics that are stored on your computer and to search the Internet for related information stored anywhere in the world.

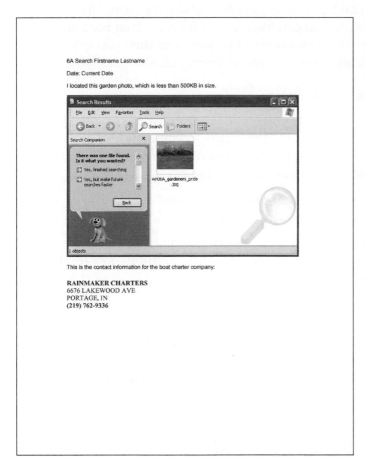

Figure 6.1
Project 6A—Search

In Activities 6.1 through 6.6, you will locate and organize gardening-related files that are stored on your computer. To make a record of your work, you will paste images into a WordPad document. You will save the WordPad file, which will look similar to Figure 6.1, as *6A_Search1_Firstname_Lastname*. You will also save search information in a file named *6A_Search2_Firstname_Lastname*. In Activities 6.7 through 6.11, you will use Internet search tools to locate information about national parks and about lodging and recreational activities in the area of a specific park. You will print three Web pages to document the search results.

Objective 1
Search for Local Files

You can use Windows XP to search for and locate files and folders stored anywhere on your computer—even if you are unable to remember the file name. A *search* is the process of seeking a particular file or specific data. Windows XP provides tools that help you define the item for which you are searching. You can search based on details such as file name, file type, modification date, or size. You can also search for a file that contains specific text. Locating files by searching can save you time you might otherwise spend navigating through many levels of folders and subfolders.

Activity 6.1 Searching by File Name

If you know the name of the file you want to locate, you can quickly search your computer to find it. In this activity, you copy the data files provided for this project into the My Documents folder. You then perform a basic search to locate a file using the file name.

1 From the **Start** menu, open **My Computer**, and then navigate to the location where the student files for this textbook

are stored. If necessary, click the **Views** button ![Views button], and then click **Details**. If necessary, click the column label **Name** to sort the files alphabetically by name.

2 In the list of files, locate and select the nine files that begin with *wn06A*. Recall that to select a group of adjacent files, you click the first file, press and hold (Shift), and then click the last file.

3 In the left pane, under **File and Folder Tasks**, click **Copy the selected items**. In the **Copy Items** dialog box, click **My Documents**, and then click **Copy**. Close the current window.

4 Click the **Start** button ![start button], and then, in the right column, click **Search**. Click the **Maximize** button ![maximize button] to maximize the Search Results window.

The Search Results window displays with the *Search Companion* in the left pane, as shown in Figure 6.2. The Search Companion is a feature of Windows XP that helps you locate files and information. You enter *search criteria*, which are terms or conditions that the item must meet in order for Windows XP to locate it. To start, Search Companion prompts you to select the type of item you want to find.

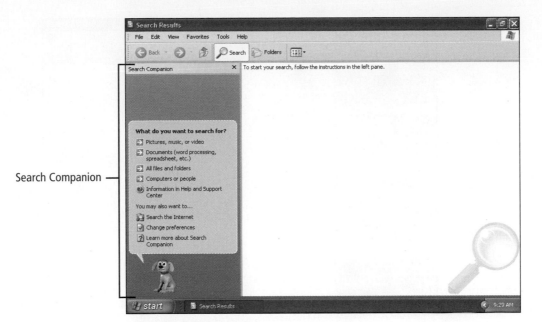

Search Companion

Figure 6.2

5 In the Search Companion, click **All files and folders**.

The Search Companion displays the options for searching for files and folders by file name.

6 In the **All or part of the file name** box, type **wn06A_rock_garden**

7 In the **Look in** box, click the **arrow**, and then click **My Documents**. If you copied the data files to a different location, click that location instead.

Limiting the search to a particular folder reduces the amount of time it takes to locate files. It takes much longer to search the entire C drive for a file than to search one folder. Whenever possible, try to limit the search to the folder where you think the file is located. Compare your screen with Figure 6.3. If you need to locate a subfolder, you can click *Browse* at the bottom of the Look in list to locate the subfolder you need.

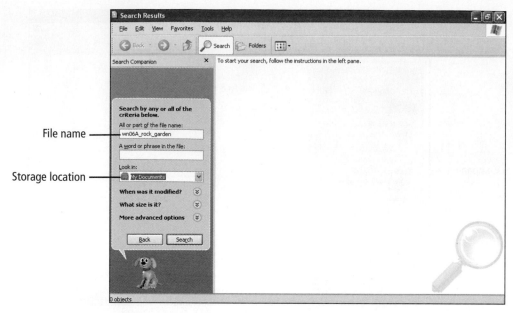

File name

Storage location

Figure 6.3

8 In the Search Companion, click **Search**.

The Search Companion searches through all the files and folders stored in My Documents to find the file or folder named wn06A_rock_garden. It displays the **search results**—items that match the specified search criteria—in the Search Results window, as shown in Figure 6.4.

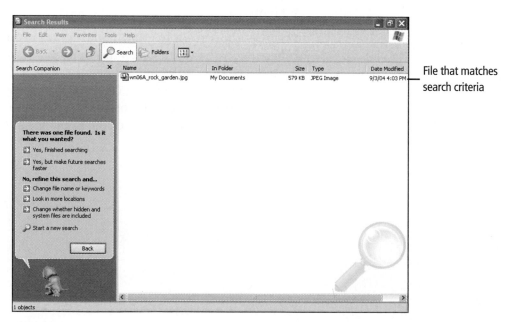

File that matches search criteria

Figure 6.4

9 In the Search Companion, click **Yes, finished searching**.

The Search Companion closes, but the Search Results window remains open.

10 In the Search Results window, right-click the **wn06A_rock_garden** file, and then, from the shortcut menu, click **Open Containing Folder**.

The contents of the My Documents folder display. My Documents is the folder where the wn06A_rock_garden file is stored. After you locate the file you want, you can navigate to the folder in which it is stored. Recall that the currently active folder name displays in the window title bar.

11 Close My Documents, and then close the Search Results window.

Activity 6.2 Using Search Strings and Wildcard Characters

If you are unsure of the name of the file you need, you can search for a partial file name or *search string*. A search string is the sequence of characters, such as a word, phrase, or code, to be matched during a search. You can also include *wildcard characters*—keyboard characters that represent zero or more characters—in a search string. For example, to locate all files that include *garden* in the file name, you can search for this single word. In this activity, you search using the search string *garden* and then refine the search using the search string *gardener*. Finally, you use wildcard characters in the search string.

1 From the **Start** menu, click **Search**, and then maximize the Search Results window.

2 In the Search Companion, click **All files and folders**. In the **All or part of the file name** box, type **garden**

The Search Companion is not case sensitive, which means it will match uppercase or lowercase letters. A list of previous entries that match the characters that you type may display.

3 Click the **Look in arrow**, and then click **My Documents**. In the Search Companion, click **Search**.

The Search Companion displays all nine files that you copied to the My Documents folder in the Search Results window, as shown in Figure 6.5. Although no complete file name matches the search string *garden*, the string is part of the file name of all nine files, including the *wn06A_Gardening_Rhythm1* music file, the *wn06A_Kitchen_Garden_Herbs* document file, and the *wn06A_Jake_Hogardens_dog* picture file. You can refine, or narrow, the search by using a more specific search string.

Figure 6.5

4 In the Search Companion, under **No, refine this search and**, click **Change file name or keywords**.

A **keyword** is a characteristic word, phrase, or code that is used as a search string for conducting a search.

5 In the **What word or words do you remember in the name or contents of the file?** box, over the existing text, type **gardener** Verify that the **Only search file names** option button is selected, and then click **Search**.

This time, only a single file—*wn06A_gardeners_pride*—displays in the Search Results window.

6 In the Search Companion, click **Change file name or keywords**, and then, in the **What word or words do you remember in the name or contents of the file?** box, over the existing text, type **wn06A_garden***

An asterisk (*) is a wildcard that represents zero or more characters. By using this search string, you will be able to locate any file name that begins with *wn06A_garden*, no matter how many additional characters are in the file name.

7 In the Search Companion, click **Search**.

The Search Results list displays five files, as shown in Figure 6.6. You can narrow the search by using a different wildcard character.

File names that match the search string *wn06A_garden**

Figure 6.6

8 In the Search Companion, click **Change file name or keywords**, and then, in the **What word or words do you remember in the name or contents of the file?** box, over the existing text, type **wn06A_gardens?**

In Windows XP, a question mark (?) represents any single character. By using this search string, you will be able to locate any filename that begins *wn06A_gardens* and then has only one additional character in the file name.

9 In the Search Companion, click **Search**.

The Search Results list displays two files: the music file wn06A_ Gardens1, and the video clip file wn06A_gardens2, as shown in Figure 6.7. Recall that Search Companion is not case sensitive.

File names that match the search string *wn06A_gardens?*

Figure 6.7

10 Close the Search Results window.

More Knowledge — Using Wildcards in the Search String

You can also use the asterisk (*) at the beginning of a search string entry to search for any number of unspecified letters, numbers, or other characters. Use multiple question mark (?) wildcards to search for a specific number of unknown characters. For each question mark included in the criterion, any character can be located.

Activity 6.3 Searching by File Type

When you want to refine a search or when you cannot remember a file name you can search for files by type. Recall that file type is the structure of a file that defines the way it is stored on disk and displayed onscreen. For example, you can search for photo files, music files, or document files. In this activity, you create subfolders on the desktop for storing picture, music, video, and text files. Then you will search for files by type and copy them into the appropriate folder.

1 On the desktop, create four new folders named as follows:

6A_Photos

6A_Music

6A_Videos

6A_Text

Recall that to create a new folder on the desktop, right-click a blank area, point to New, and then click Folder. To name the new folder, over the default folder name, type the new name, and then press Enter.

2 From the **Start** menu, display the **Search Companion**, and then maximize the Search Results window.

3 In the Search Companion, click **Pictures, music, or video**.

The Search Companion displays the options for searching specifically for media files. *Media* is a generic term for file types used to communicate information other than text, including sound, video, and graphics.

4 In the Search Companion, click to select the **Pictures and Photos** check box, and then click **Use advanced search options** to reveal the advanced search options.

Use advanced search options displays a check mark, and by clicking this option, the advanced search options are made available for use. Here, you can specify additional criteria, including the storage location, file size, or the date the file was last used. Compare your screen with Figure 6.8.

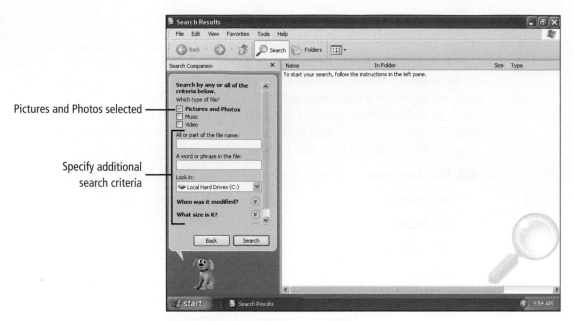

Pictures and Photos selected

Specify additional search criteria

Figure 6.8

5 In the **All or part of the file name** box, type **garden** Click the **Look in arrow**, click **My Documents**, and then click **Search**. Compare your screen with Figure 6.9.

The Search Companion searches through My Documents—and by default its subfolders—to find picture files that have *garden* in the name. It displays the results—four files—in the Search Results window in Thumbnails view.

Four picture files with *garden* in the file name

Figure 6.9

More Knowledge — Finding Multiple Copies of a File

When searching for a file, if you do not specify a folder to search and the file is stored in multiple locations, the Search Companion will locate all copies of the file or all files containing the search string. Each file with the specified search criteria will display in the search results. Be careful about which file you open. The files may have been saved at different times and may not be exactly the same.

6 In the Search Results window, select all **four files**, and then, from the **Edit** menu, click **Move To Folder**. In the **Move Items** dialog box, scroll, click the **6A_Photos** folder on the desktop, and then click **Move** to move the four files into the 6A_Photos folder.

7 In the Search Companion, scroll down if necessary, click **Start a new search**, and then, click **Pictures, music, or video**.

The Search Companion retains the criteria from the previous search.

8 In the Search Companion, click **Use advanced search options**. Click to clear the **Pictures and Photos** check box, and then click to select the **Music** check box. Verify that *garden* displays as the search string and that **My Documents** displays in the Look in box, and then click **Search**.

Two music files display in the Search Results window, as shown in Figure 6.10. The file type icon that displays on your screen may be different from the one shown in the figure. This is controlled by the media software that is associated with music files on your computer.

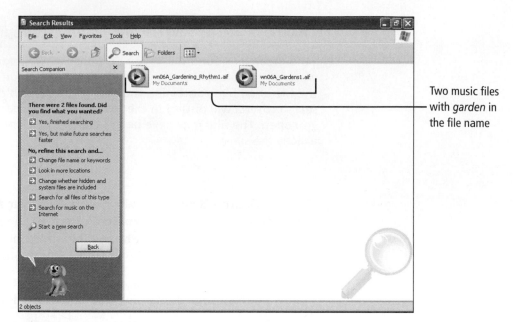

Two music files
with *garden* in
the file name

Figure 6.10

9 In the Search Results window, select the **two music files**, and then, from the **Edit** menu, click **Move To Folder**. In the **Move Items** dialog box, scroll, click **6A_Music**, and then click **Move**.

10 In the Search Companion, click **Start a new search**, click **Pictures, music, or video**, and then click **Use advanced search options**. Click to clear the Music check box, and then click to select the **Video** check box. Verify that *garden* displays as the search string, and that **My Documents** displays in the **Look in** box, and then click **Search**.

One video file displays in the Search Results window.

11 In the Search Results window, select the **video file**, and then use the **Move To Folder** command to move it to the **6A_Videos** folder.

12 In the Search Companion, click **Start a new search**, and then, in the Search Companion, click **Documents (word processing, spreadsheet, etc.)**. Click **Use advanced search options**. In the **All or part of the document name** box, type **garden** From the **Look in** list, click **My Documents**, and then click **Search**.

Two document files match the search criteria.

13 In the Search Results window, select the **two document files**, and then use the **Move To Folder** command to move the files to the **6A_Text** folder.

14 In the Search Companion, click **Yes, finished searching**, and then close the Search Results window.

Activity 6.4 Searching by Other Criteria

If you are searching for a file on your main disk drive, it could take a long time to review all the files. By specifying as many criteria as possible, you reduce the amount of time it takes for the search to be conducted and improve the likelihood that the file you want will be located. Two other criteria that can be used to help locate files are date ranges and file size. In this activity, you search for photo files that were modified in August 2004, and you search for picture files that are no larger than 500 kilobytes in size.

1 From the desktop, double-click the **6A_Photos** folder. On the Standard Buttons toolbar, click the **Search** button [Search] to display the Search Companion. If necessary, maximize the window.

This is an alternative method of displaying the Search Companion. You can also choose Explorer Bar from the View menu and then click Search.

2 In the Search Companion, click **Pictures, music, or video** and then click **Use advanced search options**.

Recall that using advanced search options allows you to specify additional criteria.

3 Under **Which type of file?**, click to select **Pictures and Photos**. In the **All or part of the file name** box, type **garden** In the **Look in** box, verify that **6A_Photos** displays.

By default, the Search Companion enters the current storage location in the Look in box. As you type the search string, a list of previous entries matching the characters you type may display. You can click an item in the list to enter it in the box.

4 To the right of *When was it modified?*, click the expand arrow ⊗.

The list of options that displays can be used to specify a time frame for the search. The default setting is *Don't remember*. Selecting one of these options narrows the search to files that have a time stamp within the specified parameters, such as *Within the last week*. This search parameter is particularly helpful if you cannot remember a file name but know the approximate time frame when it was last used.

5 Click to select the **Specify dates** option.

Here you can choose to look for a file based on the last time it was *modified*—the most recent date the file was edited or changed; the date it was *created*—the date the file was first saved; or the last time the file was *accessed*—opened.

Different Date Format

The example used in this activity assumes that the date format is month/day/year. Many countries use day/month/year, and some use year/month/day. If your computer is set up to use a different date format, you may select the month, day, and year portions of the date as directed, but your screen may not match the figure.

6 Below the *Specify dates* option, verify that **Modified Date** displays in the list box. In the **from** box, click the month to select it, and then type **8** Click the **day** to select it, and then type **1** Click the **year** to select it, and then type **04**. In the **to** box, enter the date **8/31/04** Compare your screen with Figure 6.11.

You have limited the search to files that were modified sometime between August 1, 2004, and August 31, 2004. Depending on the date settings for your computer, the year may display as a four digit number—2004. The beginning and ending dates are included in the search.

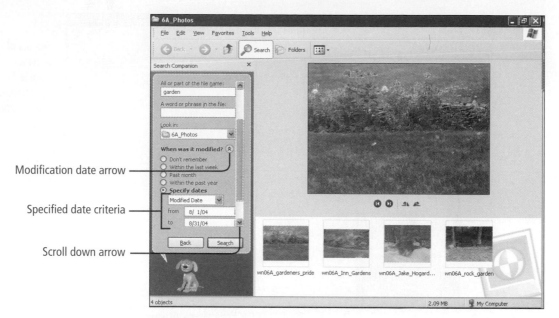

Modification date arrow ——

Specified date criteria ——

Scroll down arrow ——

Figure 6.11

---

7 In the Search Companion, click **Search**. On the Standard Buttons toolbar, click the **Views** button 📑▾, and then click **Details**. If necessary, scroll to the right to see the **Date Modified** column.

The Search Results list displays the two files in the 6A_Photos folder that were modified in August 2004.

8 In the Search Companion, click **Start a new search**, click **Pictures, music, or video**, and then click **Use advanced search options**.

Recall that the Search Companion retains the criteria from the previous search.

9 In the Search Companion, scroll down, and next to *What size is it?*, click the expand arrow ⊗ to display the What size is it options.

Here you can select a range for the file size—*Small (less than 100 KB)*, *Medium (less than 1MB)*, or *Large (more than 1MB)*—or you can specify a size range.

10 Under **What size is it?**, click to select the **Specify size (in KB)** option button. Under **Specify size (in KB)**, click the arrow on the left, and then click **at most**. In the spin box on the right, over the existing value, type **500** Compare your screen with Figure 6.12.

You have specified that you want to find files that are 500 KB or less in size. Recall that KB is the abbreviation for kilobyte, which is approximately 1,000 bytes. A *byte* is a unit of data representing one character.

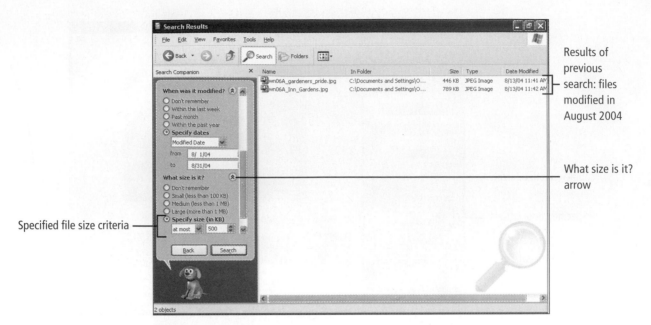

Results of previous search: files modified in August 2004

What size is it? arrow

Specified file size criteria

Figure 6.12

11 In the Search Companion, click **Search**.

Only one file displays in the Search Results list—*wn06A_gardeners_ pride*.

12 If necessary, click the **Views** button 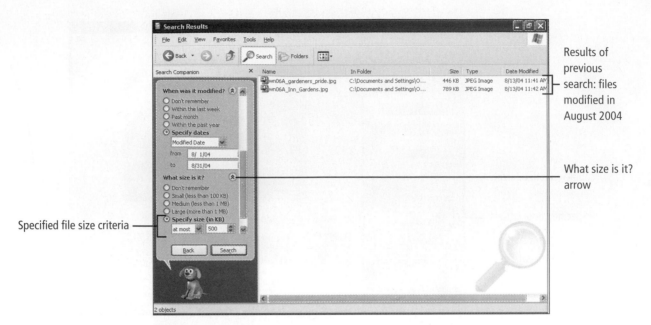, and then click **Thumbnails** so that you can preview the picture. From the Search Results window title bar, click **Restore down** to reduce the size of the window. On your keyboard, press [Alt] + [PrtScr] to copy an image of the window to the Clipboard.

13 Start **WordPad**. On the first line, type **6A Search Firstname Lastname** and then press [Enter] two times. Type **Date:** and then type today's date and press [Enter] two times. Type **I located this garden photo, which is less than 500 KB in size.** Press [Enter] two times, and then, on the Toolbar, click the **Paste** button . Resize the image as necessary so that the entire image will display on one page.

14 Save the **WordPad** file on the desktop with the file name **6A_Search1_Firstname_Lastname**

15 Click the **Print Preview** button , and then, on the Print Preview toolbar, click the **Zoom In** button . Compare your screen with Figure 6.13.

Recall that Print Preview displays the file as it will print on a page and that Zoom In increases the size of the display on the screen.

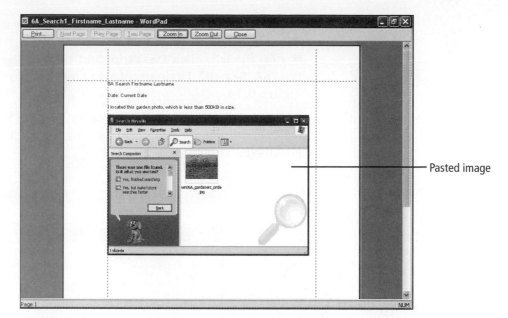

Pasted image

Figure 6.13

16 On the Print Preview toolbar, click **Close**. Save the changes to the WordPad file, and minimize the WordPad window.

You will add more information to the WordPad file later. Leave the Search Results window open for the next activity.

Activity 6.5 Saving a Search

Occasionally, you may be able to use the same search criteria more than once. Windows XP enables you to save search criteria in a search file so that you can conduct the same search without manually reentering the criteria. A ***search file*** is a file in which search criteria are stored. When you open the file, the saved criteria are entered in the Search Companion. After you save the search criteria, you can copy it to a portable storage device, such as a floppy disk, so that you can use the search criteria on another computer. In this activity, you will save the search criteria as a file named *6A_Search2_Firstname_Lastname* on the desktop.

1 Maximize the Search Results window. In the Search Companion, click **Start a new search**, click **Pictures, music, or video**, and then click **Use advanced search options**.

The criteria from the previous search are retained.

2 Verify that the file type is **Pictures and Photos**, that the search string is **garden**, and that **6A_Photos** displays in the **Look in** box. Scroll to verify that the **Modified date** is between **8/1/04** and **8/31/04**, and that the file size is **at most 500 KB**.

3 In the Search Results window, from the **File** menu, click **Save Search**. In the displayed **Save Search** dialog box, in the shortcut bar on the left, click **Desktop**, and then in the **File name** box, type **6A_Search2_Firstname_Lastname** Compare your screen with Figure 6.14.

The Save Search dialog box is similar to the Save As dialog box. You select a storage location and a name for the file. The default file type is *Saved search files*.

Search criteria to save ⎯

Storage location

Search file name

File type is Saved search files.

Figure 6.14

4 In the **Save Search** dialog box, click **Save**. Close the Search Results window.

The search criteria are saved in the file on the desktop. Notice that the icon displays a magnifying glass. You can test the file to be sure it works.

5 From the desktop, double-click the **6A_Search2_Firstname_Lastname** search icon.

The Search Results window displays, with the criteria entered in the Search Companion.

6 Maximize the Search Results window, and then, in the Search Companion, click **Search**.

The wn06A_gardeners_pride file displays in the Search Results window.

7 Close the Search Results window.

Activity 6.6 Searching for Text in a Document

If you need to find a text file but are unsure of the file name, you can search for a notable word or phrase that is within the text of the document. This saves the effort of opening many files trying to locate the one or two files that are relevant. To conduct this type of search, you need to know a unique or unusual word or phrase that is in the document. In this activity, you will create a search based on the content in a text file.

1 From the **Start** menu, click **Search**, and then maximize the Search Results window.

2 In the Search Companion, click **Documents (word processing, spreadsheet, etc.)**.

In this case, *Documents* can include more than simple text files—for example, it could include any file that has text as part of its content. The Search Companion displays the *Last time it was modified* list and a box to enter a portion of the file name.

3 Click **Use advanced search options**. In the **A word or phrase in the document** box, type **petunias** Click the **Look in arrow**, and from the displayed list, click **Desktop**, and then click **Search**.

Windows XP displays one file that meets the search criteria—*wn06A_gardening_todo_list*—as shown in Figure 6.15.

One file meets the search criteria

Figure 6.15

4 Right-click **wn06A_gardening_todo_list**, and from the shortcut menu, point to **Open with**, and then click **WordPad**.

In the open file, notice that the last item in the list is *Deadhead petunias*.

5 Close WordPad, and close the Search Results window.

Objective 2
Search the Internet

Recall that when you know the address of a Web site, you can use Internet Explorer to go directly to that site. If you do not know a Web address, you can use Windows XP to start a search for information on the Internet. The search results display in Internet Explorer as links to Web pages. You can search for a topic, a company, a person, or a map. In fact, you can search for—and find—information about almost anything you can imagine. In Activities 6.7 through 6.11, you search for information to help coordinate an educational trip to a national park.

Activity 6.7 Using a Search Engine Site

To search on the Internet, you use an Internet *search engine*, which is a program that conducts a search for keywords on Web sites and Web pages and then returns a list of the sites and pages where the keywords were found. Internet search engines are available at many Web sites, such as Google and Yahoo, and many Internet Service Providers (ISPs) offer Internet search capabilities as part of their service. In this activity, you will use the Google search engine to locate information about national parks and then print the Web page.

1 From the **Start** menu, click **Internet Explorer**. Alternatively, double-click the Internet Explorer shortcut button on the desktop or click the shortcut button on the taskbar.

Recall that Internet Explorer is the Web browser that comes with Windows XP. The default home page for your browser displays.

2 In the Internet Explorer **Address** bar, type **www.google.com** and then press Enter.

The home page for the Google Internet search engine displays.

3 In the **Google search** box, type **national parks** and then click **Google Search**.

The Google search engine returns a list of links to Web pages that contain the keywords you typed. Below each link, the URL and a brief paragraph of content from the Web page display. Compare your screen with Figure 6.16. Your search results may differ.

Google search text —————

Link to National Park Service —————

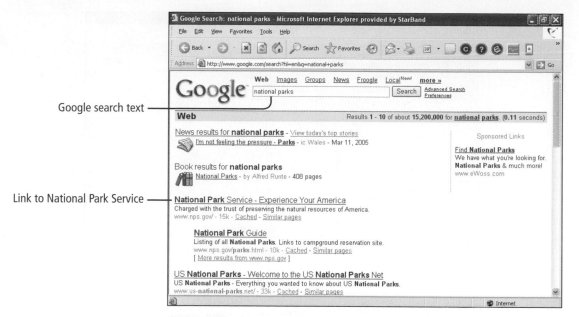

Figure 6.16

4 On the **Google Search Results** page, click the **National Park Service** link.

The home page for the National Park Service from the U.S. Department of the Interior Web site displays. If you are unable to locate the link on the Google Search Results page, in the Address bar, type **http://www.nps.gov** and click Go.

5 On the home page, click **Parks & Recreation**. In the page that displays, to the right of *Search by Topic*, click the **more** link.

Here you can narrow your search to match criteria for your particular interest.

6 Under **Topics/Interests**, scroll if necessary, and then click to select the **Wildflowers** check box. Under the **Activities** column, click **Educational Programs** and **Wildlife Viewing**, and under **Park Type**, click **Seashore/Lakeshore**. Compare your screen with Figure 6.17.

This is similar to using criteria to limit a search for files on your computer. Many Web sites have tools such as this to help you locate the exact information you need.

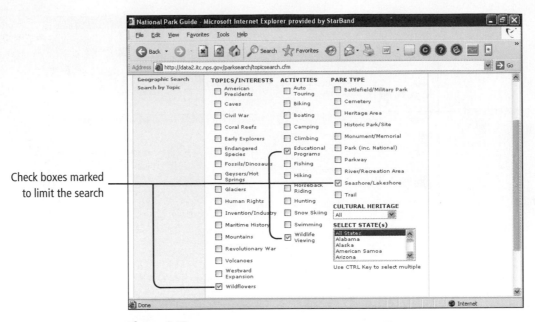

Check boxes marked
to limit the search

Figure 6.17

7 Scroll to the end of the page, if necessary, and then click **Find a Park**.

Five parks match the criteria marked, as shown in Figure 6.18.

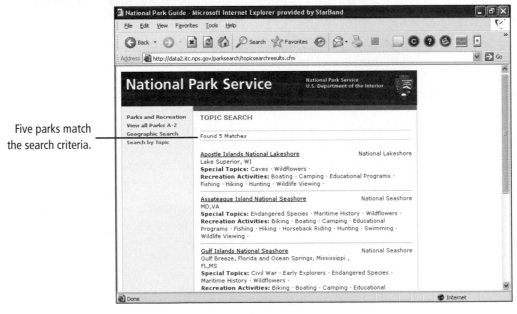

Five parks match
the search criteria.

Figure 6.18

8 From the **File** menu, click **Page Setup**. In the **Header** box, click to the left of the text in the box, and type **6A_Parks_Firstname_Lastname** and then press ⌈Spacebar⌉ to leave a space after your name. If the file name from a previous exercise appears in the header, replace it with the file name for this exercise. Click **OK**.

This adds the project name and your name to the page when it is printed.

9 From the **File** menu, click **Print Preview**. Scroll the window to verify that the information will print on one page and that the project name and your name display at the top.

The Web address displays in the footer area at the bottom of the page.

10 On the Print Preview toolbar, click **Print**, and then, in the **Print** dialog box, click **Print**. Close Internet Explorer. If you have been asked to submit this printout to your instructor, hold it until the end of this project.

More Knowledge — Using Quotation Marks in a Search String

When searching on the Internet, you can help narrow the search results by using more than one key word or a phrase. Enclose the phrase in quotation marks so that the search engine looks for matches to the entire phrase instead of individual words in the phrase. For example, searching for "Alcona County census" will result in fewer and more relevant results than if you were to enter the three words without quotation marks, which would allow matches for the words individually. By using quotation marks, you limit the results to only those Web pages that include those words as a group in the same sequence.

Activity 6.8 Setting Search Preferences

The Search Companion can be customized to suit the way you like to work. For example, you can change the animated character that displays in the Search Companion or disable it completely. You can also change the default search engine that is used to search the Internet. In this activity, you will open and customize the Search Companion to practice changing search preferences.

1 From the **Start** menu, click **Search**. Maximize the Search Results window.

2 In the Search Companion, click **Change preferences**.

Available preferences are listed, as shown in Figure 6.19. ***Preferences*** are choices that enable you to specify how features in a program will act each time you use the program.

Preference options —

Figure 6.19

3 Take a moment to study the table shown in Figure 6.20 that describes the preferences available in the Search Companion.

Search Companion Preferences

Preference	Description
With/Without an animated screen character	Enables or disables the display of an animated character in the Search Companion.
With a different character	Enables you to select from a list of ten animated characters. This option is available only when you select to display the Search Companion with an animated character.
With/Without Indexing Service (for faster local searches)	Enables or disables a file cataloging system that the Search Companion uses to locate files quickly.
Change files and folders search behavior	Choose between the *Standard search*, which prompts you through a basic search process, or the *Advanced search*, which lets you specify your own search criteria.
Change Internet search behavior	Choose whether to use the Search Companion or a *search engine* to conduct a search on the Internet. A search engine is a program used to search for keywords in files and documents on the Internet or World Wide Web.
Show/Don't show balloon tips	Enables or disables pop-up balloons that display tips and suggestions for using the Search Companion.
Turn AutoComplete off/on	Disables or enables the *AutoComplete* feature, which fills in text entries as you type. The text that is entered is based on previous entries you typed.

Figure 6.20

4 In the list of preferences, click **Change Internet search behavior**. In the Search Companion, scroll down to see the list of available search engines.

The one that is currently highlighted is set as the default search engine.

5 Under **How do you want to search the Internet?**, be sure the **With Search Companion** option button is selected. If necessary, in the **Select the default search engine list**, click **MSN**. Compare your screen with Figure 6.21.

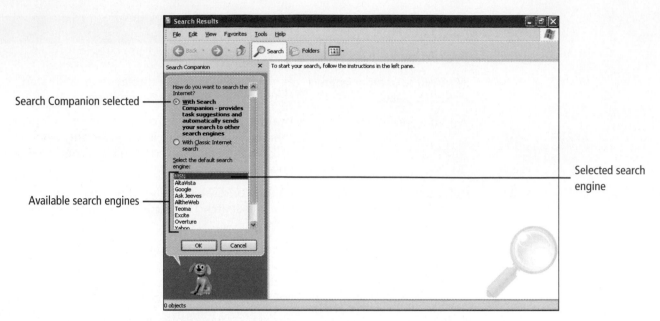

Search Companion selected

Available search engines

Selected search engine

Figure 6.21

6 Click **OK**.

The search engine default is set to use MSN. Leave the Search Results window open for the next activity.

Activity 6.9 Using the Search Companion

You can use the Windows XP Search Companion to start an Internet search. The Search Companion prompts you to enter the information you want to find and then uses the default Internet search engine to display a list of links in Internet Explorer. In this activity, you use the Search Companion to search the Internet for information about camping near Porter, Indiana, where the Indiana Dunes National Lakeshore is located.

1 In the Search Companion, if necessary, click **Other Search Options**. Under **What do you want to search for?** click **Search the Internet**.

The Search Companion displays options for an Internet search.

2 In the Search Companion, in the **What are you looking for?** box, type **lodging in Porter, Indiana** and then click **Search**.

The MSN search results display in Internet Explorer, as shown in Figure 6.22. Your search results may be different. The Search Companion remains displayed so that you can refine your search if necessary.

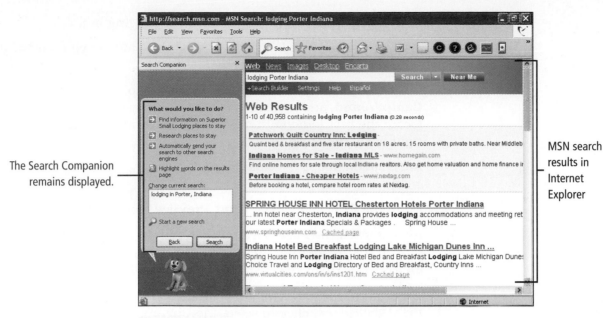

The Search Companion remains displayed.

MSN search results in Internet Explorer

Figure 6.22

3 Next to Search Companion, click the **Close** button ☒ to hide the Search Companion. Alternatively, on the Standard Buttons toolbar, click the Search button to close the Search Companion.

4 On the MSN Search page, scroll down, and then click the **Welcome to the Casual Coast** link. If this link does not display among the first items listed, click **2** at the bottom of the page to view the next grouping of Web sites.

The Porter County Convention and Visitors' Bureau Online! Web site displays, as shown in Figure 6.23.

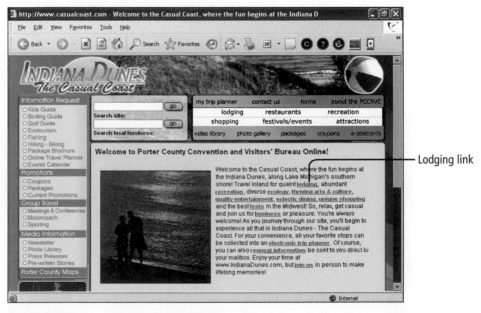

Lodging link

Figure 6.23

5 In the description on the right, click the **lodging** link.

A Web page displays links that can be used to help you narrow your search for the type of lodging you need.

6 Click the **Lodging Type arrow**, from the displayed list click **Campground**, and then click **FIND**. In the resulting list that displays, locate the first *Indiana Dunes State Park* listing, and then, on the right, click the **More Info** link.

Information about the campground at the Indiana Dunes State Park is shown.

7 From the **File** menu, click **Print Preview**. On the Print Preview toolbar, click the **Page Setup** button [icon]. In the displayed dialog box, in the **Header** box, select the previous project name, type **6A_Lodging_Firstname_Lastname** and then click **OK**.

8 On the Print Preview toolbar, click the **Print** button [Print...]. In the **Print** dialog box, click to select the **Current Page** option button, and then click **Print** to print the page. If you have been asked to submit this printout to your instructor, keep it until the end of this project.

Activity 6.10 Searching for Contact Information

Many Web sites are available to help you find contact information for people, businesses, or organizations on the Internet, and the Search Companion includes prompts to help you access these sites. Contact information may include the name and address, and it may also include the phone number. In this activity, you use the Search Companion to look up the address for a boat charter company that is near the Indiana Dunes National Lakeshore. You then copy the information into the WordPad file.

1 On the Internet Explorer toolbar, click the **Search** button [Search] to display the Search Companion.

When you display the Search Companion from Internet Explorer, it defaults to the options for an Internet search.

2 In the Search Companion, in the **What are you looking for?** box, type **find a business address** and then press [Enter].

Pressing [Enter] activates the search. The Search Companion displays prompts for finding contact information, and the MSN results page displays links to Web sites designed for locating people on the Internet.

3 In the Search Companion, under **What would you like to do?** click **Find a company's contact info, financials, or news**.

The Search Companion displays prompts so that you can enter criteria to find a business.

4 In the **What is the company's stock symbol or name?** box, type **Rainmaker Charters** In the **What city?** box, type **Portage** In the **What state?** box, type **IN** as the abbreviation for Indiana. Compare your screen with Figure 6.24.

Criteria for searching for contact information

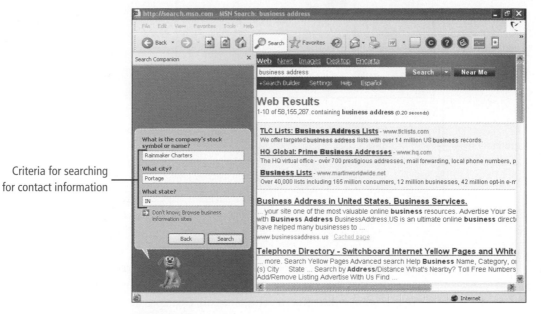

Figure 6.24

5 In the Search Companion, click **Search**.

In Internet Explorer, a Web site designed for locating business contact information displays the search results—in this case, the contact information for Rainmaker Charters.

6 On the **Web page**, drag to select the **four lines** of contact information for Rainmaker Charters.

7 On the **Web page**, right-click the selection, and then click **Copy**. Make the **WordPad** window active, and then press ⌘ + ⌘ to move the insertion point to the end of the document. Press ⌘ two times, type **This is the contact information for the boat charter company:** and then press ⌘ two times.

8 From the **Edit** menu, click **Paste Special**. In the **Paste Special** dialog box, in the **As** box, click **Unformatted Text**, and then click **OK**.

Using the Paste Special command gives you the opportunity to remove the formatting from the Web page. Compare your results with Figure 6.25.

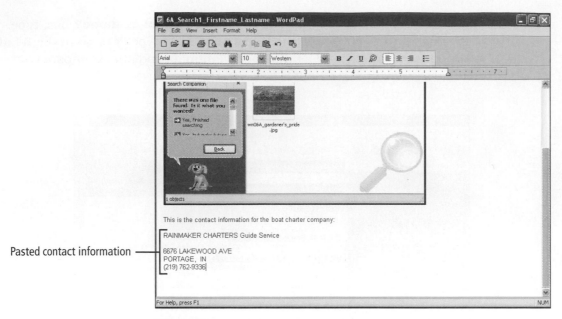

Pasted contact information

Figure 6.25

9 In WordPad, display the document in Print Preview, and then print the document. Save the WordPad file, and then close it. Leave Internet Explorer with the Search Companion open for the next activity.

Activity 6.11 Searching for a Map

You can also use the Search Companion to locate maps on the Internet. Many map Web sites provide driving directions and street maps that you can print. In this activity, you use the Search Companion to look up and print a map of the location of Rainmaker Charters.

1 In the Search Companion, scroll, and then click **Start a new search**. In the **What are you looking for?** box, type **find a map** and then press [Enter].

The Search Companion displays prompts for finding maps, and the MSN results page displays links to Web sites that provide maps.

2 In the Search Companion, under **What would you like to do?**, click **Find place maps**.

The Search Companion displays prompts where you can enter criteria to find a map.

3 In the **What street address?** box, type **6676 Lakewood Ave.** If necessary, in the **What city?** box, type **Portage** and in the **What state?** box, type **IN** Compare your screen with Figure 6.26.

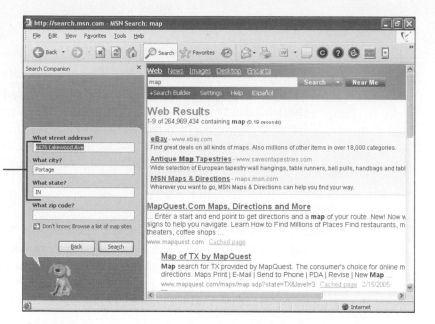

Criteria specified map location ——

Figure 6.26

4 In the Search Companion, click **Search**. On the Internet Explorer toolbar, click the **Search** button [🔍 Search] to hide the Search Companion.

Internet Explorer displays a street map of Portage on a MapQuest Web page. A red star marks the address. MapQuest is a Web site designed for locating maps and driving directions.

Alert!

Search Information Missing

If all the information did not transfer from the Search Companion to the map program, you may see an error message and a form that shows what information transferred and what is missing. Fill in the missing address information, if necessary, and click **Get Map**.

5 In Internet Explorer, on the **Zoom bar** along the right side of the map, click the **Zoom Out** button two times to see the location of the boat charter company in relationship to the Indiana Dunes National Lakeshore. If necessary, scroll to display the entire map on the screen. If necessary, click the **Pan North** arrow at the top of the map to display the shore of Lake Michigan.

The directional arrows around the map are used to *pan* the map, which shifts the display to show a different part of the map.

6 From the **File** menu, click **Print Preview**. Click the **Page Setup** button 🖾, and then, in the **Header** box, replace the project name with **6A_Map_Firstname_Lastname** Click **OK**.

7 Verify that the boat charter location—indicated by the red star—and the Indiana Dunes National Shoreline both appear on the map. If they do not, return to the map, and adjust the map's positioning on the screen. Click the **Print** button, and then, under **Page Range**, select the **Pages** option button and verify that **1** displays in the box. Click **Print**.

8 Close Internet Explorer.

9 From the desktop, move the **6A_Photos**, **6A_Music**, **6A_Videos**, and **6A_Text** folders, the **6A_Search1_Firstname_Lastname** WordPad file, and the **6A_Search2_Firstname_Lastname** search file to the folder where you are storing the solution files for this project. Be sure to remove all these files and folders from the desktop.

10 Check your *Chapter Assignment Sheet* or your *Course Syllabus*, or consult your instructor, to determine whether you are to submit the printed pages that are the results of this project.

End **You have completed Project 6A** ──────────────

Windows XP
6 chapter six

Summary

In this chapter, you practiced searching for files on your computer and for information on the Internet. In Project 6A, you searched for and organized files related to gardening. You started by using the Search Companion to search for a specific picture file by name and storage location. You then searched for files using different search strings and wildcard characters. Next, you searched by file type for picture files, music files, video files, and document files. You organized the files of different types into folders. You searched the picture files for files modified during a specific month and then for files not greater than 500 KB in size. You documented the results of your search in a WordPad file. You also saved the search criteria in a search file named 6A_Search2_Firstname_Lastname. You also practiced searching for a file based on the content within the file. You searched the Internet by using the Google search engine to locate general information about National Parks. You printed a Web page from the National Park Service Web site. Next, you changed the default search engine for the Search Companion to MSN and used the Search Companion to locate information about lodging near the Indiana Dunes National Lakeshore. You printed a Web page about the Indiana Dunes State Campground. You then used the Search Companion to look up contact information for a boat charter company. Finally, you used the Search Companion to locate a map of Portage—specifically, of the location of the boat charter company.

In This Chapter You Practiced How To

- Search for Local Files
- Search the Internet

Concepts Assessments

Matching   Match each term in the second column with its correct definition in the first column. Write the letter of the term on the blank line to the left of the correct definition.

____ **1.** The process of seeking a particular file or specific data.

____ **2.** Terms or conditions that must be met in order to locate the items for which you are looking.

____ **3.** Characters such as a word, phrase, or code to be matched during a search.

____ **4.** Keyboard characters that represent zero or more characters.

____ **5.** A characteristic word, phrase, or code that is used as a search string for conducting a search.

____ **6.** The date a file was most recently edited or changed.

____ **7.** A unit of data representing one character.

____ **8.** A file in which search criteria are stored.

____ **9.** Choices that allow you to specify how features in a program will act each time you use the program.

____ **10.** A general term used for nontext file types.

____ **11.** A program used to search for keywords in files and documents on the Internet or World Wide Web.

____ **12.** A search that enables you to specify your own criteria.

____ **13.** Limiting the search to this location on your computer reduces the amount of time it takes to search for a file when you believe you know where the file is located.

____ **14.** The name of a popular search engine.

____ **15.** To shift a display to show a different part of a map.

A Advanced search

B Byte

C Folder

D Google

E Keyword

F Media

G Modified date

H Pan

I Preferences

J Search

K Search criteria

L Search engine

M Search file

N Search string

O Wildcards

Fill in the Blank Write the correct answer in the space provided.

1. The feature of Windows XP that prompts you to enter search criteria in order to locate the items you are looking for is called the Search _____.

2. The items that match the specified search criteria are called the search _____.

3. In Windows XP, the wildcard character that represents zero or more characters is the _____.

4. In Windows XP, the wildcard character that represents any single character is the _____.

5. If you know when you first saved a file, you can search for it by _____.

6. A search file icon displays a _____.

7. The feature that fills in entries based on previous entries as you type is _____.

8. The search preferences option you should select if you want to change the default search engine for the Search Companion is Change the Internet search _____.

9. To hide the Search Companion in Internet Explorer, click the _____ button.

10. To find a personal address, search for _____ information.

Skill Assessment

Project 6B — Fishing

Objectives: *Search for Local Files and Search the Internet.*

In the following Skill Assessment, you will search your computer for a small picture file from a deep-sea fishing trip. You will capture the image and paste it into a WordPad file, and then you will search the Internet for a definition of *gaff*—a fishing term—that you will copy into the WordPad file. You will name the file *6B_Fishing_Firstname_Lastname* and then print it. The document will look similar to Figure 6.27.

Figure 6.27

1. From the **Start** menu, click **My Computer**. Navigate to the location where the student files for this book are stored. If necessary, from the **View** menu, click **Details**.

(Project 6B–Fishing continues on the next page)

(Project 6B–Fishing continued)

2. In the list of files, locate and select the three files that begin with *wn06B*. In the left pane, under **File and Folder Tasks**, click **Copy the selected items**. In the **Copy Items** dialog box, click **My Documents**, and then click **Copy**. Close the current window.

3. From the **Start** menu, click **Search** to display the Search Companion in the Search Results window. Maximize the window if necessary.

4. In the Search Companion, click **All files and folders**. In the **All or part of the file name** box, type **fish** and then, from the **Look in** list, click **My Documents**. Click **Search**. The Search Results list displays three files. Recall that to conduct a search, you specify search criteria such as the file name or a search string, and the storage location. You may see six files if you stored the original student files in My Documents in another folder.

5. In the Search Companion, click **Start a new search**, and then click **All files or folders**. Under **Search by any or all of the criteria below**, click the arrow to the right of **What size is it?** Recall that you can refine a search by adding criteria, such as file size or modification date.

6. Under **What size is it?** click to select the **Small (less than 100 KB)** option button, and then click **Search**. This time the Search Results list displays only one file—*wn06B_Fish_Success*—which is 76 KB.

7. In the Search Results window, from the **View** menu, click **Thumbnails**. On the title bar, click the **Restore Down** button to restore the window to a smaller size, verify that the thumbnail of the image displays within the window, and then press Alt + PrtScr to capture an image of the window.

8. From the **Start** menu, start **WordPad**. Type **6B_Fishing_Firstname_ Lastname** and then press Enter two times. Type **Date:** and the current date, and then press Enter two times. Type **Subject: Fishing Trip** and then press Enter two times. On the toolbar, click the **Paste** button. Resize the image as necessary to ensure that the entire image will fit on one page.

9. Save the WordPad file on the desktop with the filename **6B_Fishing_Firstname_Lastname** and then minimize the WordPad window.

(Project 6B–Fishing continues on the next page)

(Project 6B–Fishing continued)

10. Close the Search Results window, and then, from the **Start** menu, start **Internet Explorer**. In the **Address** bar, type **http://www.google.com** and press Enter. Recall that Google.com is one of several search engines you can use to locate information on the Internet.

11. In the **Google search** box, type **definition of gaff** and then press Enter. In the list of search results, click the first link—**Web definitions for GAFF**. A page of definitions available on the Web displays.

12. On the **Web page**, locate the text and accompanying link for the second definition. Drag to select the definition and the URL. Right-click the selection, and then click **Copy**.

13. On the taskbar, click the **6B_Fishing_Firstname_Lastname - WordPad** button icon. Press Ctrl + End to move the insertion point to the end of the text. Press Enter two times and then type **Here is a definition of gaff:** Press Enter two times and then, on the Toolbar, click the **Paste** button to paste the definition into the WordPad document.

14. From the WordPad toolbar, click **Print Preview**, and then compare your results with Figure 6.27. On the Print Preview toolbar, click **Print** to display the **Print** dialog box, and then click **Print** to print the document.

15. When printing is complete, close WordPad, saving all changes, and then close Internet Explorer.

16. Move the WordPad file to a removable disk or folder where you are storing the files for this project.

17. From the **Start** menu, click **My Computer**. In **My Documents**, locate the three files that begin with *wn06B* and delete them.

 End **You have completed Project 6B**

Performance Assessment

Project 6C—Location

Objectives: *Search for Local Files and Search the Internet.*

In the following Performance Assessment, you will search the Internet for information about the Virginia sea coast, and you will search locally for a file that contains information about Virginia Beach. You will print a Web page that will look similar to Figure 6.28.

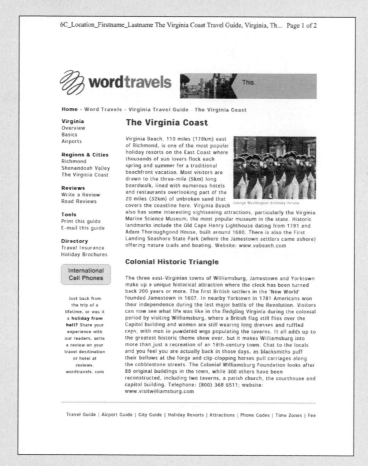

Figure 6.28

(Project 6C–Location continues on the next page)

(Project 6C–Location continued)

1. From the **Start** menu, click **Search**, and then maximize the Search Results window.

2. In the Search Companion, click **Change preferences**, and then click **Change Internet search behavior**. Recall that you can change the default search engine that Search Companion uses to search the Internet.

3. In the Search Companion, under **Select the default search engine**, click **Google**, and then click **OK**. In the Search Companion, if necessary, click **Other Search Options**, and then click **Search the Internet**. Recall that you can use the Search Companion to search for files stored on your computer or to search the Internet.

4. In the **What are you looking for?** box, type **towns on the Virginia coast** and then press [Enter]. Internet Explorer displays the search results in Google.

5. On the search results page, locate and click the link to **The Virginia Coast Travel Guide** at the Web site www.wordtravels.com. The page displays in Internet Explorer.

6. In Internet Explorer, from the **File** menu, click **Print Preview** to display the page as it will print. On the **Print Preview** toolbar, click the **Page Setup** button. In the **Header** box, click to position the insertion point at the beginning of the existing text, and then type **6C_Location_Firstname_Lastname** leaving a space after your last name. Replace a previous exercise file name if necessary. Click **OK** to close the **Page Setup** dialog box. Compare the results with Figure 6.28.

7. On the Print Preview toolbar, click **Print,** and in the **Print** dialog box, select the **Pages** option button, and then verify that the **Pages** box displays **1**. Click **Print** to print the Web page.

8. Display the **Page Setup** dialog box, and from the **Header box**, delete the project number and your name. Click **OK**. Close Internet Explorer.

9. Open My Computer and navigate to the location where the data files for this book are stored. If necessary, change to **Details** view and sort the files by name. Locate and then select the four files that begin with *wn06C*, and then copy them to **My Documents**.

(Project 6C–Location continues on the next page)

(Project 6C–Location continued)

10. From the **Start** menu, click **Search**, and then maximize the window. Click **All files and folders**. In the **All or part of the file name** box, type **coast** and then from the **Look in** list, click **My Documents**. Click **Search**. The list of search results displays all four files—two pictures and two documents—and from the file names you can identify that two are about Massachusetts and two are about Virginia. You can refine the search by adding criteria.

11. In the Search Companion, click **Start a new search**, and then click **Use advanced search options**. In the **A word or phrase in the document** box, type **Virginia** From the **Look in** list, click **My Documents**, and then click **Search**. This time, the Search Results list displays only the document about the Virginia coast.

12. Close the Search Results window.

13. In **My Documents**, locate the four files that begin with *wn06C* and then delete them.

End **You have completed Project 6C**

Project 6D — Golf

Objectives: *Search for Local Files and Search the Internet.*

In the following Mastery Assessment, you will search for a golf picture file. You will also search the Internet for information about golf facilities in the Charlottesville, Virginia, area and print a Web page that you find. The printed Web page will look similar to Figure 6.29.

Figure 6.29

(Project 6D–Golf continues on the next page)

(Project 6D–Golf continued)

1. From **My Computer**, navigate to the location where the data files for this book are stored, and then copy the four files that begin with *wn06D* to the **My Documents** folder.

2. Display the **Search Companion** in the Search Results window. Search for **all files and folders** in **My Documents** that contain the search string **golf** in the file name.

3. Refine the search to locate only the picture file in **My Documents** named *wn06D_Golf3*. Save the search criteria on the desktop in a search file named **6D_Golf_Firstname_Lastname**

4. Start **Internet Explorer**, and go to the **Google** search engine site. Use Google to search for **golf courses in Charlottesville, Virginia** In the search results, scroll down, locate, and and then click the link to the **Birdwood Golf Course at the Boar's Head Inn**.

5. Add the project name and number—**6D Golf**—and your name to the header, and then print the first page only. Compare the printout with Figure 6.29.

6. Close Internet Explorer and any other open windows.

7. Delete the search file from the desktop, or move it to a removable disk or folder where you are storing the files for this project. Remove the project name from the header of the Web page.

End You have completed Project 6D

Problem-Solving Assessment

Project 6E—Hometown

Objectives: *Search for Local Files and Search the Internet.*

In this Problem-Solving Assessment, practice searching for local files and searching the Internet to locate information about your community. Use the Search Companion to locate picture files stored on your computer or to locate music files. Try refining the search using other criteria. For example, search for only small picture files or only large music files. Try searching different locations to find files that you may have stored and then forgotten. Use Internet Explorer to look for information about your hometown—and about yourself. Use a search engine such as Google, Yahoo!, or Ask Jeeves, and search for your hometown. Use the links to find a page that provides general information, and then print it, remembering to add the project number and your name to the header. Search for a map of the area and for contact information for a government official, such as the mayor or town manager. Practice all the skills covered in this chapter so that you are comfortable searching for local files and for information on the Internet.

 End **You have completed Project 6E** ━━━━━━━━━━━━━━━━━━

How to Cite a Source

You should always cite the source of information you use in projects and reports, including quotations, pictures, and other information. There are different rules for citing sources, depending on the type of source—book, magazine, or Web page—and on whether you are citing the source in a caption, bibliography, or footnote. One well-respected source for information about citing sources is the Modern Language Association (MLA). For information about the MLA, go to the organization's Web site: http://www.mla.org. To find out more about the correct format for citations, use a search engine such as Google to search for information about MLA style.

GO! with Help

Learn More About Searching

Use the Windows XP Help and Support Center to learn more about searching for information.

1. From the **Start** menu, click **Help and Support**.

2. On the Help home page toolbar, click the **Index** button to display the alphabetical index. In the **Type in the keyword to find** box, type **Search**.

3. Starting with Search Companion, there are many topics related to searching in the Index list. Click any **topic**, and then click **Display** to display the Help information.

4. When you are finished, close the **Help and Support Center**.

7 chapterseven

Maintaining Windows XP

In this chapter you will: practice these skills.

Objectives

- Set Up a User Account
- Set the Time, Date, and Power Options
- Add Hardware and Software
- Manage Windows Components
- Maintain a Disk

Managing Windows XP

Windows XP works well the moment it is installed. As you use your computer, you may want to add new hardware or software, allow other people to use your computer, or change settings that are controlled by Windows XP. If you have administrator privileges on your computer—most people have these privileges on their home computers—you can customize, fine-tune, and update Windows XP.

In organizations that use Windows XP, one or more individuals will have the responsibility of overseeing systemwide changes—whether there is a single computer, a desktop system, or a network of more than 100 computers. This person, known as a ***computer administrator***, can create, change, and delete user accounts for others, install new programs and hardware, and access all files stored on the computer(s). These tasks can be performed only by someone who has a computer administrator account. Many tasks that a computer administrator can perform are not available to individuals using a limited or guest account.

The skills practiced in this chapter are not meant to be used in a computer lab. Instead, they are meant to be used as references when the need arises to change a feature of Windows XP.

In the activities in this chapter, you will create a user account, and you will set the date, time, and power options. You will add new hardware and software to the computer. You will add and remove Windows XP components, set program access and defaults, and check the Windows Update Web site to be sure your computer is using the most recent version of Windows XP. Finally, you will perform maintenance tasks to ensure the integrity of the hard disk and the data stored on the disk, including checking the drive for errors and *defragmenting* the drive. To defragment means to rearrange data into consecutive sectors on a disk drive. To complete the activities in this chapter, you must have computer administrator privileges on your computer.

Objective 1
Set Up a User Account

Each individual who uses a computer that uses Windows XP has a user account. Recall that there are different types of user accounts, including limited, guest, and computer administrator accounts. An individual who has a limited account has access to his or her files only. A guest account may be used by anyone who does not have an account on the computer. An individual who has a computer administrator account has full access to all files stored on the computer and may make systemwide changes, including creating, changing, and deleting user accounts for others. You must have administrator privileges on the computer to set up user accounts.

Activity 7.1 Setting Up a User Account

To create a user account, enter a name and select the account type. You can modify the account by changing the name, the account type, or the picture associated with the account, or you can delete the account completely. The options for setting up an account are available from the User Accounts category in the Control Panel. Recall that the Control Panel is a folder that provides access to options for customizing system components.

1 On the taskbar, click the **Start** button ![start], and then click **Control Panel**. If a list of Control Panel contents displays in the Contents pane, in the left pane, click Switch to Category View.

The Control Panel Classic View displays a list of all the Control Panel items in the Contents pane and was the only Control Panel display configuration in earlier versions of Windows. As more features were added to the Control Panel, it became necessary to categorize the items. The Category View not only helps you find items, but it also describes the function of the items, which is helpful for those items that have nondescriptive names. In this appendix, all instructions assume that you are using Category View.

2 In the Contents pane, under **Pick a category**, click **User Accounts**. Under **Pick a task**, click **Create a new account**.

The first User Accounts Wizard window opens. Recall that each Control Panel category has a window from which you can pick a specific task or a Control Panel icon.

3 In the **Type a name for the new account** box, type **Lastname**— substituting your last name—as shown in Figure 7.1.

The name that you type is the name that will display on the Welcome screen and the Start menu.

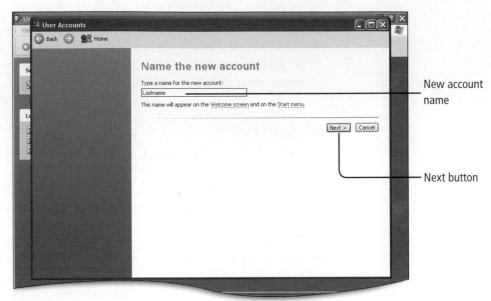

Figure 7.1

4 In the **User Accounts** window, click **Next**.

The second User Accounts Wizard window displays, giving you the option of creating an administrator account or a limited account.

5 Under **Pick an account type**, be sure the **Computer administrator** option button is selected, and then click **Create Account**.

The wizard closes, and the User Accounts window displays, as shown in Figure 7.2. At the bottom of the screen, under the heading *or Pick an account to change*, are pictures that represent each user account on the computer. The new account—*Lastname*—now displays in the list.

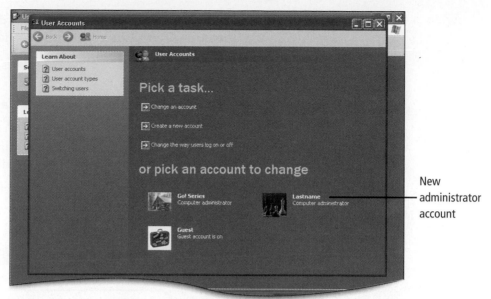

Figure 7.2

New administrator account

6⃞ Under **or pick an account to change**, click **Lastname**.

A User Accounts window displays, listing tasks you can perform on that account.

7⃞ Under the heading **What do you want to change about Lastname's account**, click **Change the name**. In the **Type a new name for Lastname** box, type **Firstname Lastname**—this time substituting your first and last names—and then click **Change Name**.

Windows XP changes the account name immediately, and the new name displays in the User Accounts window as shown in Figure 7.3. All other settings for the account—including the account type and picture—are unchanged.

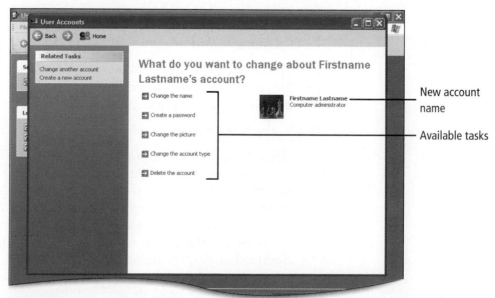

New account name

Available tasks

Figure 7.3

8 In the **User Accounts** window, under **What do you want to change about Firstname Lastname's account?**, click **Change the picture**.

A palette of available pictures displays. The pictures in your palette may differ.

9 Under **Pick a new picture for Firstname Lastname's account**, click the **butterfly**, and then click **Change Picture**.

Windows XP assigns pictures to accounts randomly. If the butterfly is already assigned to the account, select a different picture.

10 Click **Change the account type**, and then click the **Limited** option button. Compare your screen with Figure 7.4.

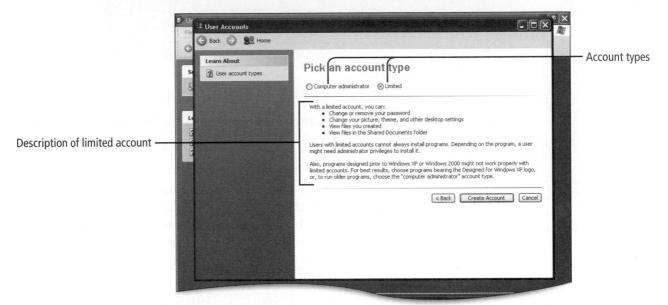

Account types

Description of limited account

Figure 7.4

11 In the **User Accounts** window, click **Change Account Type**. Notice the name, access status, and picture for the Firstname Lastname account.

The owner of this account can now set individualized preferences, store files and folders in a separate My Documents folder, store icons on the desktop, and customize an Outlook Express account.

12 In the **User Accounts** window, click **Delete the account**.

When you delete an account, you delete the files and folders stored in the account owner's My Documents folder and files and folders that the owner stored on the desktop. You also delete the account owner's stored email messages, settings, and preferences—such as items in the Favorites folder—and the display background. Windows XP gives you the option of saving the files and folders from My Documents and the desktop in a new folder. You cannot save the settings, preferences, Favorites, and stored email messages. In this case, you do not need to save anything.

13 In the **User Accounts** window, click **Delete Files**. In the confirmation window, click **Delete Account**.

Windows XP deletes the account and displays the User Accounts window. The account with your name is no longer listed under the heading *or pick an account to change*.

14 From the **User Accounts** window, click the **Close** button ☒ to close the window. Close the **Control Panel** window.

Objective 2
Set the Time, Date, and Power Options

As a computer administrator (even if you are only administering your home computer), you can make systemwide changes that affect all accounts on the computer, including setting the system clock and calendar and setting options for energy conservation. The system clock and calendar determine the date and time that display in the notification area on the taskbar and the format in which they display. In addition, Windows XP uses the time and date settings to mark files with the date and time that they are created or modified.

Activity 7.2 Setting the Date

Computers have an internal clock and calendar that keep track of the current time and date. In this activity, you will use the Date and Time Properties dialog box to verify and change the date and time settings.

1 From the **Start** menu, open the **Control Panel**. Be sure the **Category View** is selected.

2 Under **Pick a category**, click **Date, Time, Language, and Regional Options**. Under **Pick a task**, click **Change the date and time**.

The Date and Time Properties dialog box displays, with the Date & Time tab active.

3 Under **Date**, click the **Month** arrow, and then click **March**. On the **Calendar**, click **10**. Do not change the year.

This selects March 10 as the current date.

Alert!

Problems with Changing the Year Setting

If you change the year setting, even for practice, you can cause software problems. If you have software that is purchased by the year—such as virus definitions—changing the year can cause the program to terminate, and with some programs, changing the year back to its original setting will not reactivate the software. Also, if your computer is running trial versions of software or if you are *beta testing* software—testing software before it is released—changing the date could permanently deactivate the software.

4 Under **Time**, in the box where the current time displays, double-click the **hour**, and then click the **spin box up arrow** to set the **hour** to **6**.

You set each segment of the time—hours, minutes, seconds, and AM or PM—independently. To select a segment, double-click it, or press Tab to move from one segment to the next. Click the spin box up arrow to advance the setting by one; click the spin box down arrow to reduce the setting by one. Alternatively, select the value in the spin box, and type a new setting value.

5 In the box where the current time displays, double-click the **minutes**—alternatively, press Tab—and then click a **spin box arrow** to set the **minutes** to **15**.

6 Double-click the **seconds**, and then click a **spin box arrow** to set the seconds to **47**. Double-click **AM** or **PM**, and then click a **spin box arrow** to toggle to the alternative setting. Click **Apply**.

This sets the current time to 6:15:47 AM—or PM if you are doing this activity in the evening—as the current time and then applies the date and time settings. Compare your dialog box with the one shown in Figure 7.5.

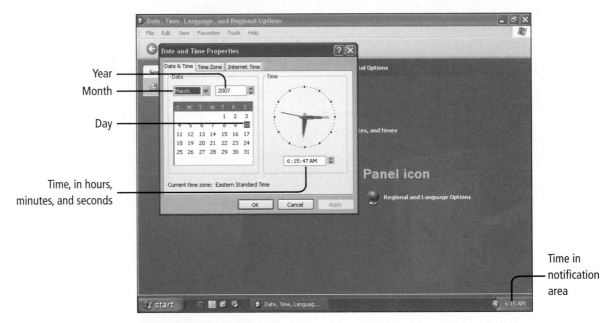

Figure 7.5

7 In the **Date and Time Properties** dialog box, click **OK**. On the taskbar, in the **notification area**, point to the **time** to display the new date in a ScreenTip. Then, double-click the **time**.

This is an alternative method for opening the Date and Time Properties dialog box.

8 In the **Date and Time Properties** dialog box, click the **Time Zone tab**, and then click the **Time Zone** arrow. Scroll and then click **(GMT-08:00) Pacific Time (US & Canada); Tijuana**. If necessary, click to select the *Automatically adjust clock for daylight saving changes*, and then click **Apply**. Compare your screen with Figure 7.6.

This sets the time zone to Pacific time. Notice that if the time zone was not already set to Pacific time, the time on the clock automatically adjusts to the new time zone.

Time zone ——

New time ——

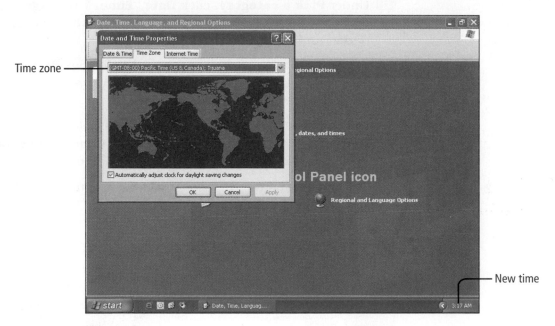

Figure 7.6

9 On the **Time Zone tab**, click the **Time Zone arrow**, and then click the **time zone** in which you are currently located.

10 Click the **Date & Time tab**, and then reset the clock and the calendar to the current date and time.

11 Click **OK**, and then close the **Control Panel** window.

More Knowledge — Synchronizing with a Time Server

Windows XP provides a feature for synchronizing the system clock with a *time server*, which is a computer on a network that maintains an accurate time clock that can be accessed by all computers on the same network. The time server may be on a local network or on the Internet. This is useful because your system clock depends on your computer's internal power supply and so, over time, it may gain or lose time. When you synchronize with a time server, the clock is reset to the correct time. The options for synchronizing with a time server are available on the Internet Time tab in the Date and Time Properties dialog box. If your computer is part of a network that has its own time server, the Internet Time tab is not available.

Activity 7.3 Setting Date and Time Formats

By default, Windows XP displays dates and times—and currency and general numbers—in the standard format for the geographic area in which you live. You can change the way dates and times display by changing the geographic area or by selecting individual formatting options. In this activity, you will change the way the date and time display.

1 From the **Start** menu, open the **Control Panel**. Be sure the **Category View** is selected.

2 Under **Pick a category**, click **Date, Time, Language, and Regional Options**. Under **Pick a task**, click **Change the format of numbers, dates, and times**.

The Regional and Language Options dialog box displays, with the Regional Options tab active. This tab displays samples of the date, time, currency, and number formats for the selected region.

3 Under **Standards and formats**, click the **Select an item to match its preferences, or click Customize to choose your own formats arrow**, scroll, and then click **Spanish (Mexico)**.

The samples change to display standard formats for Mexico, as shown in Figure 7.7.

Selected geographic area ———

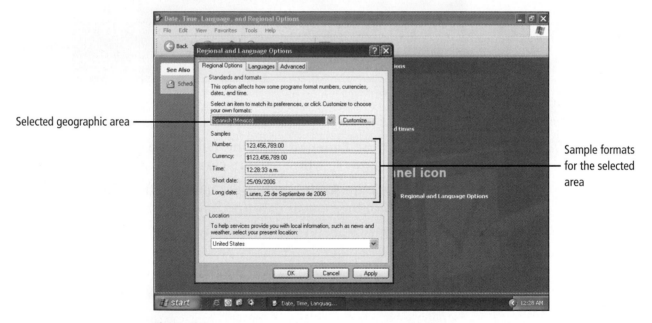

Sample formats for the selected area

Figure 7.7

4 Under **Standards and formats**, click the **Select an item to match its preferences, or click Customize to choose your own formats arrow**, scroll, and then click **English (United States)** to change to the standard formats for the United States, and then click **Customize**. In the **Customize Regional Options** dialog box, click the **Time tab**.

A sample of the current format displays at the top of the tab. You can customize the *time format*—the way hours, minutes, and seconds display. There is only one option for each of the other items—the *time separator*, which is the symbol that displays between the hours and the minutes and between the minutes and the seconds—and the AM and PM symbols. An explanation—or key—for the abbreviations used in the time format notation displays at the bottom of the tab. For example, a single *h* (h) means there will be no *leading zero*—which is a zero in front of the hours between 1 and 9—whereas a double *h* (hh) indicates that there will be a leading zero.

5 Click the **Time format arrow**, and then click **HH:mm:ss** to select a time format that uses a 24-hour clock, a leading zero in front of the hour, and no AM or PM indicator. Compare your screen with Figure 7.8.

Customize the time format ——————

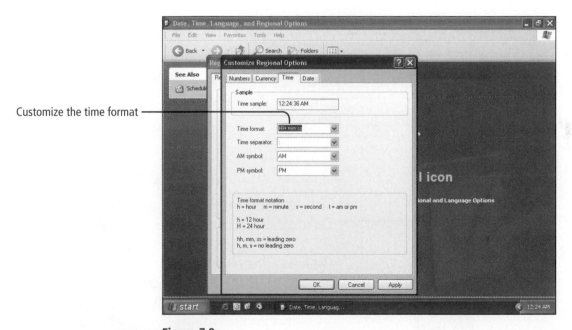

Figure 7.8

6 Click the **Date tab**.

On the Date tab, you can customize formats for the short date, which is the numerical abbreviation of the month, date, and year, and the long date, which includes the day and month spelled out in English, the date, and the year.

7 Under **Short date**, click the **Short date format arrow**, and then click **yy/MM/dd**. Click the **Date separator arrow**, and then click the period (.).

The *date separator* is the symbol that displays between the three parts of the date. By default it is a forward slash (/), but you can select either a hyphen (-) or a period (.). You have set the short date to display as the last two digits of the year, a period, the number of the month, a period, and then the number of the date.

8 Under **Long date**, click the **Long date format arrow**, click **dddd, dd MMMM, yyyy**.

This sets the long date to display as the day spelled out in English, a comma, the number of the date, the month spelled out in English, and all four digits of the year.

9 Click **Apply**. On the taskbar, in the **notification area**, point to the time, as shown in Figure 7.9.

Windows XP displays the date using the new format; the time format does not change until you apply all Regional and Language options.

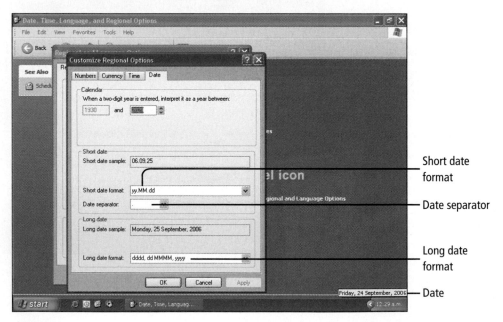

Figure 7.9

10 Under **Short date**, click the **Short date format arrow**, and then click **M/d/yy**. Click the **Date separator arrow**, and then click the **slash**. Under **Long date**, click the **Long date format arrow**, and then click **dddd, MMMM, dd, yyyy**.

11 Click the **Time tab**. Click the **Time format arrow**, and then click **h:mm:ss tt**. Click **OK**. In the **Regional and Language Options** dialog box, click **OK**.

12 Close the **Date, Time, Language, and Regional Options** window.

Activity 7.4 Setting Power Options

Different systems have different energy requirements. For example, a desktop computer that is always connected to an electrical outlet has a constant source of energy, whereas a laptop computer may depend on the life of a battery. In this activity, you will set power options to control the way your computer uses energy.

1 From the **Start** menu, open the **Control Panel**. Be sure the **Category View** is selected. Click **Performance and Maintenance**.

2 From the **Performance and Maintenance** window, under **or pick a Control Panel icon**, click **Power Options**.

The Power Options Properties dialog box displays with the Power Schemes tab active.

More Knowledge — Windows XP Power Options

Windows XP comes with predefined *power schemes* that you can apply to affect the settings of your entire computer system. A power scheme is a collection of power settings that can be applied simultaneously. The settings specify the period of inactivity that you want to elapse before your monitor and hard disks turn off and your system enters *hibernation* or *standby* mode. Hibernation is a state in which your computer saves all data currently in memory to your hard disk and then shuts down. When you bring your computer out of hibernation, all programs and documents that were open are restored to the desktop. Standby is a state in which your computer uses less power when it is idle but remains available for immediate use. Data currently in memory is not saved on your hard disk and will be lost if a power failure occurs.

3 If necessary, click the **Power Schemes arrow**, and then click **Home/Office Desk**.

The settings for the Home/Office Desk computer power scheme display. The available power schemes are designed for different types of systems that have different power requirements, such as a desktop or a laptop, or for a particular amount of energy consumption, such as maximizing the life of a battery. You can change individual settings to customize a power scheme.

4 Under **Settings for Home/Office Desk power scheme**, click the **Turn off monitor arrow**, and then click **After 20 mins**.

5 Under **Settings for Home/Office Desk power scheme**, click the **Turn off hard disks arrow**, and then click **After 30 mins**.

Compare your Power Options Properties dialog box with Figure 7.10.

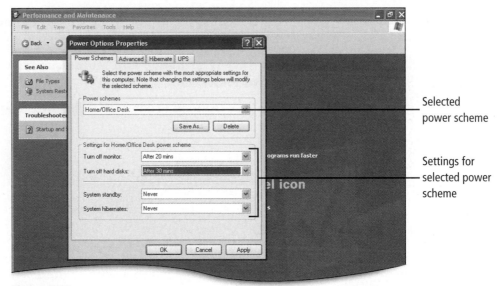

Selected power scheme

Settings for selected power scheme

Figure 7.10

6 Click **OK** to apply the settings and close the dialog box.

7 If you are doing this activity on a lab computer, repeat this procedure to restore the power scheme to its original setting.

8 Close the **Performance and Maintenance** window.

Objective 3
Add Hardware and Software

Windows XP controls the communication between your computer and its hardware devices and between your computer and software programs. When you want to add new hardware or software to your system, use Windows XP to set them up and prepare them for use.

Activity 7.5 Adding New Hardware

A basic computer system usually includes a mouse, keyboard, monitor, and printer. You may want to add other devices, such as a scanner, camera, or microphone. Most devices manufactured since 1995 are ***plug and play***, which means the device will configure itself. In this activity, you will add a plug and play device to your computer. This activity illustrates one of the procedures for setting up new hardware.

1 Plug a **new device** into your computer.

When you connect a plug and play device to your computer, Windows XP detects and sets up the device for use. When Windows XP detects the device, the Found New Hardware icon displays in the notification area. If the ***device driver***, which is the software program that enables Windows XP to communicate with the device, is already ***installed***, the device is ready for use. To install means to copy the program files to the hard disk so that Windows can access them for use.

If the device driver is not already installed, the Found New Hardware Wizard displays on the desktop, as shown in Figure 7.11. Most plug and play devices connect to the USB port, which may be found on the front or back of your computer. Recall that USB stands for Universal Serial Bus, which is a set of connectors used to transfer data between hardware and a computer. A port is an interface through which data is transferred between a computer and a device.

Found New Hardware Wizard

Found New Hardware icon

Figure 7.11

2 In the **Found New Hardware Wizard**, confirm that the **Install the software automatically (Recommended)** option is selected. If the device came with an installation CD, insert it in your **CD drive**. Click **Next**.

Windows XP searches your computer system for the device driver, installs it, and then displays the Completing the Found New Hardware Wizard page. If Windows cannot locate the device driver, it may prompt you to select the location where the device driver is stored. Select the location, and then click OK. If you do not have an installation CD, you may be able to locate and download the device driver from the manufacturer's Web site.

3 In the **Found New Hardware Wizard**, click **Finish**.

The device is now installed and available for use. Some devices require that you restart your computer at this point.

Activity 7.6 Adding New Software

You can use Windows XP to install new software programs for which you have the installation disk. In this activity, you will add the Microsoft Encarta Encyclopedia program to your computer. If you do not have the Encarta CD, use a different program. If you do not have a program, skip this activity.

1 Insert the **Encarta CD** or the program CD you want to install into your **CD drive**.

More Knowledge — Different Ways to Install Software

Software manufacturers use different installation schemes. If you are installing software from a CD, the installation program will often run automatically when you insert the CD in the computer. If this does not happen, open My Computer, open the CD drive, and run the installation program—often called Setup.exe or Install.exe. If you are downloading a program from the Internet, you may have the option to run the program from the Web site or save it to your computer. Some programs, particularly large ones, must be saved to the computer first. When the program is saved on your computer, the installation process begins when you locate and run the saved file.

---

2 If an End User License Agreement (EULA) displays, click Accept to continue. When the Setup—or Installation—Wizard for the new program displays, compare your screen with Figure 7.12. Your screen may differ. If the EULA or the Installation Wizard does not display, open the Control Panel, click Add or Remove Programs, click Add New Programs, click CD or Floppy, and then click Finish.

An **End User License Agreement (EULA)** is a contract between you and the program manufacturer in which you agree to abide by the specified rules and regulations, such as not copying or distributing the program to unlicensed individuals.

The **program CD**, which may be called the **installation** or **setup disk**, is the disk on which the program files are stored.

Figure 7.12

3 In the **Setup Wizard**, click **Next**. Follow the instructions to select options on each page of the wizard.

The options that display in the Setup Wizard depend on the program you are installing. Many programs offer a choice of a *typical installation*, which installs all features using the default settings, or a *custom installation*, which enables you to select specific features and settings to install.

Other options may include in which folder to install the files and whether to display program icons on the desktop or in the notification area. Some programs—such as Encarta—may be installed completely on the hard disk, or you may choose to install only required program files on your hard disk. The second option uses less disk space, but you must insert the CD whenever you use the program.

4 On the **Ready to Install** page of the Setup Wizard, click **Install**.

Windows XP copies files from the CD to your hard disk, performs other installation tasks, and then displays the final page of the wizard.

5 In the **Setup Wizard**, click **Finish** to close the wizard and complete the installation.

Some programs may prompt you to restart your computer before you can use the software.

Activity 7.7 Using System Restore

If a computer problem occurs because of a system change, such as installation of a new program or device, you can restore the system to a point prior to the change. Restoring the system reverts your computer back to an earlier time before the change took place. If you are unhappy with the results of the system restoration—for example, if it does not correct the problem—you can undo the process. Data files stored in My Documents, as well as email messages and personal settings such as Favorites, are not affected by System Restore.

1 From the **Start** menu, point to **All Programs**, point to **Accessories**, point to **System Tools**, and then click **System Restore**.

The first System Restore Wizard window displays, as shown in Figure 7.13. *System Restore* is a Windows XP Accessories program that tracks changes to your computer. System Restore creates an automatic restore point—called a *system checkpoint*—one time each day. It also creates an automatic *installation restore point* each time it detects that a program or device is being installed. You can use System Restore to create a restore point manually at any time and to revert back to any restore point if your system experiences problems because of a change.

Description of System Restore ———

System Restore options

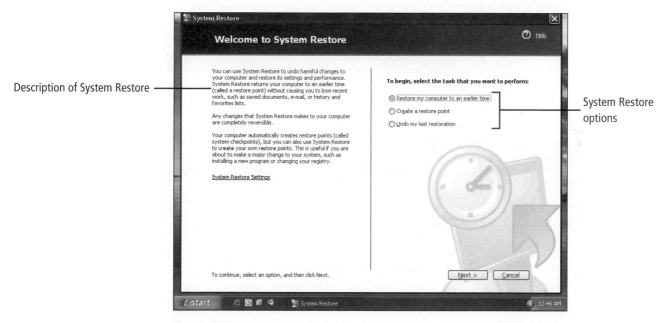

Figure 7.13

2 Under **To begin, select the task that you want to perform**, click to select the **Create a restore point** option button, and then click **Next**. In the **Restore point description** box, type **win10A** and then click **Create**.

Windows XP creates the restore point and displays the information as shown in Figure 7.14 to help you identify the restore point. Your screen will differ.

Time Restore Point was created

Restore Point name

Date Restore Point was created

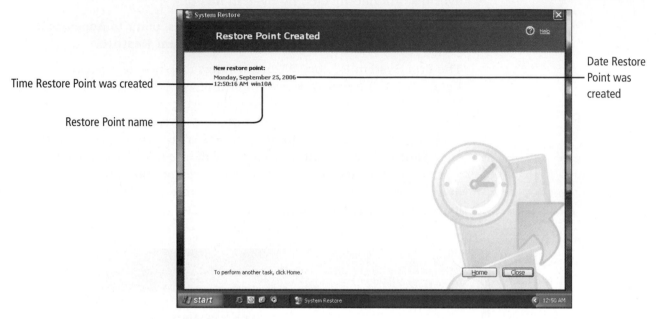

Figure 7.14

3 In **System Restore**, click **Home**. Under **To begin, select the task that you want to perform**, click the **Restore my computer to an earlier time** option button, and then click **Next**.

Windows XP displays a calendar and a list of restore points available for the selected date, as shown in Figure 7.15. Notice that the win10A restore point displays in the list. Other restore points may display also. You can select any date on the calendar and then select any restore point on that date.

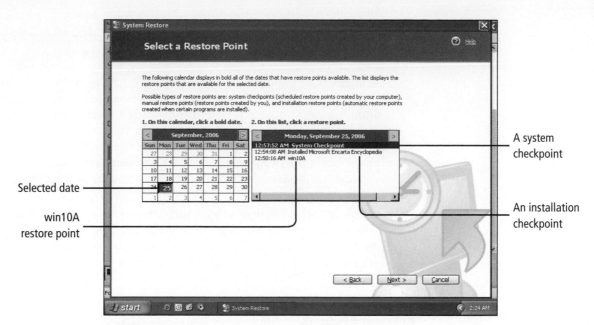

Selected date ⎯⎯⎯⎯

win10A
restore point ⎯⎯⎯⎯

A system
checkpoint

An installation
checkpoint

Figure 7.15

4 On the **calendar**, click the **date one week earlier than today**, or the date you want to return to, to display the list of available restore points for that date. Then, on the **calendar**, click **today's date**.

5 In the **list of available restore points**, click **win10A**, click **Next** to display the Confirm Restore Point Selection window, and then, if you want, click **Next** to start the restoration. Alternatively, click **Cancel** to close the dialog box and exit the process.

The System Restore status displays to provide you with information about the restoration. When the restoration is complete, Windows XP shuts down and then restarts your computer.

6 If necessary, log on to Windows.

The Restoration Complete window opens in System Restore.

7 In **System Restore**, click **OK** to close the program and display the desktop.

More Knowledge — If Your Computer Stops Working and You Are Unable to Get to System Restore

Sometimes your computer will stop working for no apparent reason. This is often caused by a *system failure*, which is the inability of a computer to continue functioning, or a *system error*, which is a software condition that renders the system incapable of continuing to function normally. These errors usually require restarting the system. If the computer *freezes*—stops working—there is a program called the *Windows Task Manager* that can help you overcome the problem by closing programs or shutting down the computer.

To activate Windows Task Manager, hold down Ctrl + Alt, and then press Del. The Windows Task Manager dialog box displays. Click the Applications tab, highlight any open programs, and then click End Task. If this does not correct the problem, from the Shut Down menu, click Turn Off.

Objective 4
Manage Windows Components

You can manage Windows XP components to control access to the programs and features that are installed by default. You can also update your Windows XP program from the Microsoft Web site.

Activity 7.8 Setting Program Access and Defaults

As a computer administrator, you can choose the default programs used for browsing the Web, sending email, playing media, and running Java programs. *Java* is a programming language designed for writing programs that can be safely downloaded to your computer through the Internet. You can also remove access to the Windows XP programs that are installed automatically for these activities so that others on the system cannot use them. In this activity, you will explore the program access and default options available on your computer.

1 From the **Start** menu, open the **Control Panel**. Be sure the **Category View** is selected.

2 Under **Pick a category**, click **Add or Remove Programs**. In the left pane of the **Add or Remove Programs** window, click **Set Program Access and Defaults**.

Windows XP displays the program access and defaults configurations available for your system. A *configuration* is a particular combination of settings—in this case, settings that specify the default programs for each activity and either enable or disable access to specific programs. At least three configurations are available: Microsoft Windows, Non-Microsoft, and Custom. Your computer may have additional configurations.

3 In the **Choose a configuration** list, click to select the **Microsoft Windows** configuration. The option list expands, as shown in Figure 7.16.

The Microsoft Windows configuration sets programs installed with Windows XP as the defaults, as follows:

Web browser: Internet Explorer

E-mail program: Outlook Express

Media player: Windows Media Player

Instant messaging program: Windows Messenger

Virtual machine for Java: Microsoft Virtual Machine

Java allows access to non-Microsoft programs, such as Apple's QuickTime Player or iTunes.

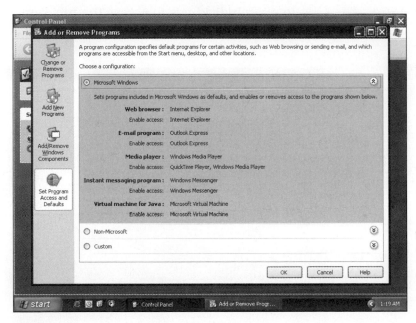

Figure 7.16

4 In the **Choose a configuration** list, click to select the **Non-Microsoft** option button.

This configuration sets any available non-Microsoft programs as the defaults, and it differs, depending on the non-Microsoft programs you have installed. For example, if you have Netscape Navigator installed, it is set as the Web browser, and if you have Apple QuickTime Player installed, it is set as the Media player. Access to all Microsoft programs installed as part of Windows is disabled.

5 In the **Choose a configuration** list, click to select the **Custom** option button, as shown in Figure 7.17.

Use the Custom configuration to select the programs you want to use as the default for each activity and to enable or remove access to programs. The options in the Custom configuration differ, depending on the programs you have installed. Click a program to set it as the default. Click to select an Enable access to this program check box to allow individuals to access the program, or clear the check box if you do not want individuals to access the program.

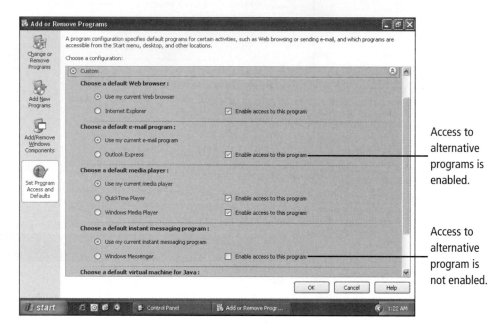

Figure 7.17

6 In the **Add or Remove Programs** window, click **Cancel** to close the window without making any changes.

Activity 7.9 Using Windows Update

Microsoft makes upgrades and improvements available from its Web site so that you can download and install them regularly. In this activity, you will access the Windows Update Web site to review available downloads. To complete this activity, you must have a connection to the Internet.

1 From the **Start** menu, open the **Control Panel**. Be sure the **Category View** is selected.

2 Under **Pick a category**, click **Performance and Maintenance**.

3 Under **or pick a Control Panel icon**, click **System**. In the **System Properties** dialog box, click the **Automatic Updates** tab.

On the Automatic Updates tab, you can choose whether you want Windows to automatically download and install updates from the Windows Update Web site, as shown in Figure 7.18. If you select this option, you may specify the day and time when you want the automatic update to occur. Alternatively, you can select to have Windows automatically download the updates but notify you before installation, notify you if updates are available, or turn off automatic updates completely. If you turn off automatic updates, you can install updates manually at any time.

Option to turn off automatic updates

Link to the Windows Update Web site

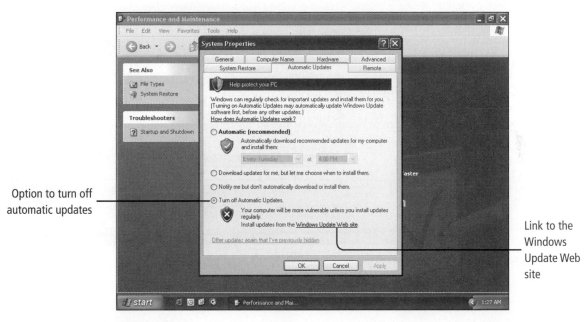

Figure 7.18

4 Near the bottom of the **Automatic Updates** page, click the **Windows Update Web Site** link.

The Windows Update Web site opens in your default browser.

5 On the **Windows Update** Web page, click **Custom Install: High Priority and Optional Updates for your Computer**, and then compare your screen with Figure 7.19.

Windows examines your system to determine the updates that are available. The displayed list is customized for your system. Any *high priority updates*—updates that may affect the security and performance of your computer—display in the main window. The types and number of optional updates that are available display in the left pane. *Optional updates* are not critical to the security or performance of your computer. For example, optional software updates may include new features for Windows XP, and optional hardware updates may include new drivers for devices you have installed.

Click to view optional software updates

Click to view optional hardware updates

High priority updates, if any, display here.

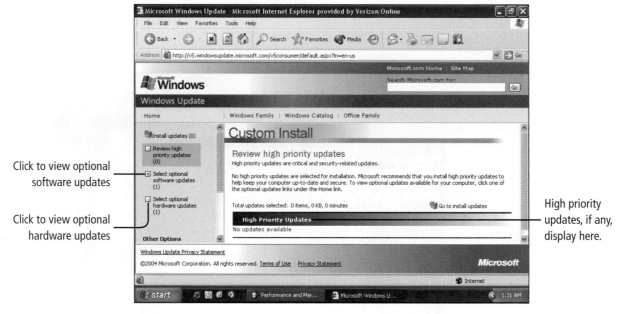

Figure 7.19

6 In the left pane, click **Select optional software updates** to display any available software updates. In the left pane, click **Select optional hardware updates** to display any available hardware updates.

The updates that display differ, depending on your system.

7 Close the browser to close the program without downloading or installing updates. In the **System Properties** dialog box, click **Cancel**. Close the Control Panel.

Objective 5
Maintain a Disk

Disks are mechanical devices that can break or become damaged. If a disk is damaged, Windows may not be able to read from or write to the damaged areas, leaving you with less disk space. Worse, if the disk fails, you may not be able to recover stored data. Windows XP provides ways in which you can prolong the life of your disks and make additional storage space available.

Activity 7.10 Check a Disk for Errors

Errors can occur on a disk as a result of poor handling or because of problems with data. Windows XP comes with a utility program that you can use to check a disk for errors. You may also set Windows to try to repair errors or recover data. In this activity, you will check your hard disk for errors. You can also check floppy disks for errors, but you cannot use Windows XP to check a CD or DVD for errors.

1 From the **Start** menu, open **My Computer**.

2 In the **My Computer** window, right-click the **Local Disk (C:)** icon. From the shortcut menu, click **Properties**.

The Local Disk (C:) Properties dialog box displays with the General tab active. The General tab displays information about the amount of storage space on the drive.

3 In the **Properties** dialog box, click the **Tools** tab. Under **Error-checking**, click **Check Now** to display the **Check Disk Local Disk (C:)** dialog box, as shown in Figure 7.20.

By default, Windows XP checks the disk for *file system errors*, which are errors in the structure in which files are named, stored, and organized. You can select to automatically correct file system errors during the check. If you select this option, the check disk procedure requires that no files be in use; you may have to schedule the check for the next time you start Windows and then log off and restart your computer.

Also, you can choose to check for bad sectors on the disk. *Bad sectors* are areas on the disk that are physically damaged. When checking for bad sectors, Windows will attempt, but may not be able, to recover data stored in the bad sectors. Correcting file system errors and checking for bad sectors significantly increases the time it takes to complete the disk check—possibly to an hour or more—depending on the size of your disk and the amount of data you have stored.

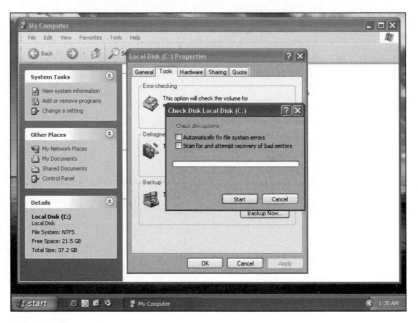

Figure 7.20

4 In the **Check Disk** dialog box, click **Start**.

Windows XP starts checking the disk. Notice that the text in the dialog box title bar changes from *Check Disk* to *Checking Disk*. During the check, a status bar indicates the progress of each phase of the procedure. When the check is complete, Windows displays a message that the disk check is complete. If errors were found, a report may display details.

If a message displays prompting you for the need to restart Windows before the check can start, click Yes, click OK, and then restart Windows. The check will start automatically, and the desktop will display when the check is complete.

5 In the **Disk Check Complete** message box, click **OK**. Leave the **Local Disk (C:) Properties** dialog box open for the next activity.

Activity 7.11 Defragment a Disk

When possible, Windows XP stores files and folders on a disk in consecutive *sectors*. A sector is an area on a disk where data can be written. As disk space is used, Windows may split files and folders into fragments and store them in nonconsecutive sectors. It takes longer for Windows to store and to read fragmented files because it must look for the data in different sectors that may be anywhere on the disk. You can rearrange— or *defragment*—the data into consecutive sectors so that Windows may access data more quickly. In this activity, you will defragment the hard disk on your computer. Defragmenting may take an hour or more.

1 On the **Tools** tab of the **Local Disk (C:) Properties** dialog box, under **Defragmentation**, click **Defragment Now**.

Alternatively, you can start the Disk Defragmenter by opening the Start menu, pointing to All Programs, pointing to Accessories, pointing to System Tools, and then clicking Disk Defragmenter. You can also open the Control Panel, click Performance and Maintenance, and then click *Rearrange items on your hard disk to make programs run faster.*

2 In the **Disk Defragmenter** window, under **Volume**, click drive **(C:)** to select it, and then click **Analyze**.

Windows examines your hard disk to determine how files are currently stored and then displays a message prompting you to defragment the drive if necessary. You can choose to start defragmenting the drive, display a report, or close the box to display the Disk Defragmenter window.

3 In the **Disk Defragmenter** message box, click **Close**.

A color-coded graph displays in the *Estimated disk usage before defragmentation* box, as shown in Figure 7.21. Each colored line in the graph represents a file or part of a file. Red lines represent fragmented files that are stored in nonconsecutive sectors, blue lines represent files in consecutive—or **contiguous**—sectors, green lines represent files that cannot be moved—files that Windows requires for locating data on the disk—and white represents free space on the disk.

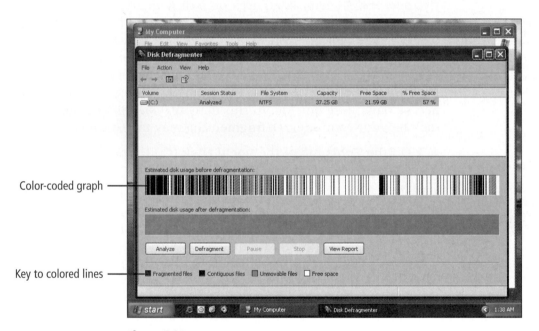

Color-coded graph

Key to colored lines

Figure 7.21

4 In the **Disk Defragmenter** window, click **View Report**.

The Analysis Report dialog box displays detailed information about the disk space on the drive prior to defragmentation, including which files are the most fragmented. You may print the report or save it in text format for future use.

5 In the **Analysis Report** dialog box, click **Close**. In the **Disk Defragmenter** window, click **Defragment** to start defragmenting the drive.

During the defragmentation, Windows changes the graph in the Estimated disk usage after defragmentation box to show how files are rearranged. The time it takes to complete the entire defragmentation depends on the size of your hard disk, the amount of data that is stored, and the number of files that must be defragmented. The defragmentation may take an hour or more. When the process is complete, Windows displays the Defragmentation Complete dialog box.

6 In the **Defragmentation Complete** dialog box, click **View Report**.

The Defragmentation Report dialog box now displays detailed information about the disk space after the defragmentation. You may print the report or save it in text format.

7 In the **Defragmentation Report** dialog box, click **Close**. In the Disk Defragmenter window, compare the graph in the Estimated disk usage before defragmentation box with the graph in the Estimated disk usage after defragmentation box.

You should notice fewer red lines and wider blue lines in the graph after defragmentation, indicating that there are more contiguous files and fewer fragmented files.

8 Close the **Disk Defragmenter**, close the **Properties** dialog box, and then close **My Computer**.

9 **Log off** Windows XP, shut down your computer, and, if necessary, turn off your monitor.

8 chaptereight

Command Line Introduction

When you have completed this chapter, you will be able to explain

Objectives

- What a command prompt is.
- What a DOS command is.
- The purpose of the DATE and TIME commands.
- Why the VER command is used.

DOS Commands

Once you boot your computer and exit any menu system that may have been activated, you will be faced with a command prompt such as C:\>. The command prompt is exactly what its name implies: a request for a command. A command can be either a name of a file containing instructions that tell the computer to perform a certain action (an executable file) or a DOS command that tells DOS to perform some action. In this chapter, you will use three DOS commands: **DATE**, **TIME**, and **VER**. The first two are used to set the system clock and the third is used to find out what version of DOS you are using.

The System Clock

Most computers today have built-in clocks that keep accurate track of the date and time. These clocks are powered by their own independent batteries. If the clock loses track of the date or time or both, you can use the DATE and TIME commands to reset the clock. You can set or change the system date and time by typing DATE or TIME at any DOS command prompt. Two reasons you might need to change the system clock are as follows:

1. The computer's internal clock malfunctioned due to a battery failure or power surge.

2. An incorrect date or time or both was entered earlier.

The proper formats for entering the date and time are the same whether you are doing so during the booting process or whether you issue the DATE or TIME commands. The format for entering the date is mm/dd/yyyy or mm-dd-yyyy. If you prefer, you may enter only the last two digits of the year. You do not need to enter leading zeros for single-digit months or days. For example, for May 3, 1993, you may enter 5/3/93 or 05/03/93.

The proper format for entering the time is hh:mm:ss.hh (the last two h's are for hundredths of a second). You need not enter seconds or hundredths of seconds. Use an A for AM and a P for PM immediately after the minutes. No space is necessary. For example, if the time is 3:30 PM, you should enter 3:30p.

If resetting the clock by this means does not work, your computer may have a setup program that will help you reset the clock. If so, check your computer manual for the appropriate steps.

Checking the Version of DOS

At times you may need to check the version of DOS that you are using to see whether it is appropriate for your intended use. For example, some applications program packages require certain versions of DOS. A program might require DOS 6 and will not work with other versions. Many of the directions in this book are specific to DOS 6, so you should check to make sure your computer is running version 6. To check the DOS version, type VER at any prompt.

9 chapter nine

Command Line Disk Commands

When you have completed this chapter, you will be able to

Objectives

- Find out what files are on a floppy disk (use the DIR command).
- Change the default drive.
- Explain why it is necessary to format a disk.
- List the ways that a volume label can be added to a disk while it is being formatted or changed after formatting is complete.
- Name the two ways to obtain help about DOS commands.

Changing the Default Drive

When you first boot a computer, the prompt is generally C:\>. This means that the C: drive is the active, or default, drive. It is referred to as the default drive because any DOS command you enter will affect the C: drive unless you indicate differently in the command. The default drive is the drive DOS reads first after checking memory for a file or a command. Once you insert a diskette into your floppy drive, you may wish to make the floppy drive the default drive, rather than the hard drive. Changing the default drive simply means making the drive that you designate the active drive. To change the default drive, you simply enter the drive letter followed by a colon and press the Enter key at any command line prompt. For example, when in Drive C:, at the C:\> prompt, type A: and then press the Enter key to make Drive A: the default drive. The command line prompt will change to A:\> indicating that Drive A: is now the default drive.

> ### Note
>
> You cannot make a floppy drive the default unless there is a diskette in it. If you try to make an empty drive active, you will receive an error message.

Finding Out What Files Are On a Disk

When working with floppy disks, you need to be able to determine what files are stored on them. You can display a listing (called a directory) of the files stored on a disk using the **DIR** command.

Using the DIR Command

The DOS command DIR allows you to see the contents of a disk directory. The directory command DIR can be used by itself or with several options. Used by itself, the DIR command lists the filename and extension, the size of the file (in bytes), and the date and time each file on the disk was created or last modified. At the bottom of a directory listing you will find two other important items - the number of files on the disk and—the amount of available space left for use on the disk (in bytes).

To obtain a directory listing with the A: drive active, type

```
A:\>DIR
```

Figure 9.1 shows the directory of a disk loaded in Drive A:.

```
A:\>DIR

   Volume in drive A is EXERCISES
   Volume Serial Number is 15DB-3360
   Directory of A:\

WP       EXE      68656 03-27-92    4:13p
EDITOR   HLP       3048 07-30-90    8:55p
LETTER   TXT        978 05-18-92    8:38p
ROLODEX  EXE     143159 03-27-92    4:18p
FONEDATA DBF      24646 03-28-92   10:41a
FONEDATA DBT       7224 03-28-92   10:41a
MOVIE    LS1        397 01-01-80    1:31a
MOVIE    LS2       1080 01-02-80    1:47a
README   DOC       2068 05-30-92    2:29p
SS       COM      21330 08-26-87    3:59p
CARTER1  TXT         95 05-30-92    2:12p
CARTER2  TXT         91 05-30-92    2:13p
CARTER3  TXT         90 05-30-92    2:13p
CARTER   DBF        103 05-30-92    2:14p
        14 file(s)      272965 bytes
                        447488 bytes free

A:\>
```

Figure 9.1
Displaying a directory of drive A: with the DIR command

Using the DIR/P Command

When there are more files on the disk than can fit on a screen at one time, using the DIR command alone will cause the first files to scroll off the screen faster than they can be read. A way of pausing the screen after one screenful of files appears is to use the option **/P**. Options are also called switches. These terms are interchangeable. For example, to obtain a directory of the A: drive with the pause or "page" option turned on, type

`A:\>DIR /P`

When DIR/P is used, 23 files display and DOS pauses to give the user a chance to look at the files (see Figure 9.2).

```
   Volume in drive A is EXERCISES
   Volume Serial Number is 15DB-3360
   Directory of A:\

WP       EXE      68656 03-27-92    4:13p
EDITOR   HLP       3048 07-30-90    8:55p
LETTER   TXT        978 05-18-92    8:38p
ROLODEX  EXE     143159 03-27-92    4:18p
FONEDATA DBF      24646 03-28-92   10:41a
FONEDATA DBT       7224 03-28-92   10:41a
PHONELST IND       3311 03-28-92   10:41a
PHONESDX IND       1925 03-28-92   10:41a
PHONEFST IND       3311 03-28-92   10:41a
PHONECMP IND       3927 03-28-92   10:41a
ADDRESS  RPT       3534 03-27-92   10:20a
XMAS     RPT       3534 03-27-92   10:20a
VOICLIST RPT       3927 05-28-90    8:35a
FAXLIST  RPT       3927 05-28-90    8:30a
ALLLIST  RPT       6285 07-13-90    9:03p
VOICBILL RPT       3927 05-28-90    8:34a
MOVIE    LS1        397 01-01-80    1:31a
MOVIE    LS2       1080 01-02-80    1:47a
README   DOC       2068 05-30-92    2:29p
Press any key to continue . . .
```

Figure 9.2
Displaying a directory listing using DIR with the /P option

Pressing any key will cause the next screenful of files to appear on the screen. When you are prompted to press any key, press the Spacebar or the Enter key. You can press any of the other keys on the keyboard except Esc. However, the Spacebar and the Enter key are the two largest keys and easiest to find.

Continue pressing any key until you return to the command prompt.

Using the DIR /W Command

If you want to obtain only a list of the filenames and are not concerned with the other information found in a directory, you can use the option **/W** to use the full width of the screen (see Figure 9.3). For example, to obtain a directory of the A: drive with the wide option turned on, type

```
A:\>DIR /W
```

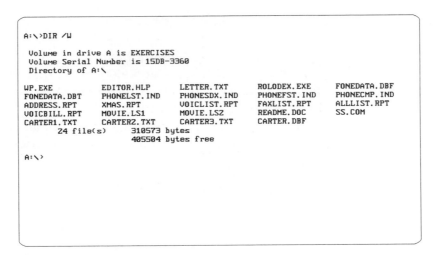

```
A:\>DIR /W

 Volume in drive A is EXERCISES
 Volume Serial Number is 15DB-3360
 Directory of A:\

WP.EXE          EDITOR.HLP      LETTER.TXT      ROLODEX.EXE     FONEDATA.DBF
FONEDATA.DBT    PHONELST.IND    PHONESDX.IND    PHONEFST.IND    PHONECMP.IND
ADDRESS.RPT     XMAS.RPT        VOICLIST.RPT    FAXLIST.RPT     ALLLIST.RPT
VOICBILL.RPT    MOVIE.LS1       MOVIE.LS2       README.DOC      SS.COM
CARTER1.TXT     CARTER2.TXT     CARTER3.TXT     CARTER.DBF
          24 file(s)         310573 bytes
                             405504 bytes free

A:\>
```

Figure 9.3
Displaying a directory listing using DIR with the /W option

Using the DIR /W /P Command

For longer directories, such as those found on hard disks, both the "wide" and the "pause/page" options can be included with the DIR command. The order in which the /W and /P appear does not matter. An example of a directory with both the /W and /P options is shown in Figure 9.4.

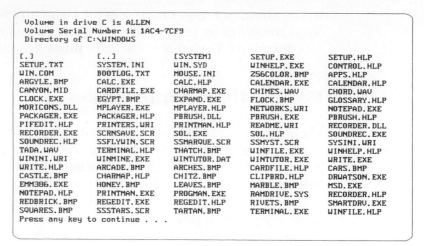

```
Volume in drive C is ALLEN
Volume Serial Number is 1AC4-7CF9
Directory of C:\WINDOWS

[.]              [..]             [SYSTEM]         SETUP.EXE        SETUP.HLP
SETUP.TXT        SYSTEM.INI       WIN.SYD          WINHELP.EXE      CONTROL.HLP
WIN.COM          BOOTLOG.TXT      MOUSE.INI        256COLOR.BMP     APPS.HLP
ARGYLE.BMP       CALC.EXE         CALC.HLP         CALENDAR.EXE     CALENDAR.HLP
CANYON.MID       CARDFILE.EXE     CHARMAP.EXE      CHIMES.WAV       CHORD.WAV
CLOCK.EXE        EGYPT.BMP        EXPAND.EXE       FLOCK.BMP        GLOSSARY.HLP
MORICONS.DLL     MPLAYER.EXE      MPLAYER.HLP      NETWORKS.WRI     NOTEPAD.EXE
PACKAGER.EXE     PACKAGER.HLP     PBRUSH.DLL       PBRUSH.EXE       PBRUSH.HLP
PIFEDIT.HLP      PRINTERS.WRI     PRINTMAN.HLP     README.WRI       RECORDER.DLL
RECORDER.EXE     SCRNSAVE.SCR     SOL.EXE          SOL.HLP          SOUNDREC.EXE
SOUNDREC.HLP     SSFLYWIN.SCR     SSMARQUE.SCR     SSMYST.SCR       SYSINI.WRI
TADA.WAV         TERMINAL.HLP     THATCH.BMP       WINFILE.EXE      WINHELP.HLP
WININI.WRI       WINMINE.EXE      WINTUTOR.DAT     WINTUTOR.EXE     WRITE.EXE
WRITE.HLP        ARCADE.BMP       ARCHES.BMP       CARDFILE.HLP     CARS.BMP
CASTLE.BMP       CHARMAP.HLP      CHITZ.BMP        CLIPBRD.HLP      DRWATSON.EXE
EMM386.EXE       HONEY.BMP        LEAVES.BMP       MARBLE.BMP       MSD.EXE
NOTEPAD.HLP      PRINTMAN.EXE     PROGMAN.EXE      RAMDRIVE.SYS     RECORDER.HLP
REDBRICK.BMP     REGEDIT.EXE      REGEDIT.HLP      RIVETS.BMP       SMARTDRV.EXE
SQUARES.BMP      SSSTARS.SCR      TARTAN.BMP       TERMINAL.EXE     WINFILE.HLP
Press any key to continue . . .
```

Figure 9.4
Displaying a directory listing using DIR with the /W and /P options

In addition to the previously described options, the DIR command has other options to help you obtain a more specific list of the files for which you may be looking.

Displaying the Directory of Another Drive

If you are at a C:\> system prompt, you may wish to view the contents of a floppy disk located in Drive A: or B:. The DIR command by itself simply allows you to view the contents of the default drive. Two ways can be used to list the directory of another drive. The first way is to tell DOS to look in the other drive by placing a drive designator after the DIR command, as follows:

`C:\>DIR A:`

In this command, DOS is currently using Drive C:, but you instruct DOS to display the contents of Drive A:. When you type this command, you must type a space between the command (DIR) and the drive designator (A:). If you do not, you will receive an error message. The "wide" and "pause/page" switches can be used with the DIR command after the disk drive designator.

The second way to list the directory of another drive is to change the default drive from the hard disk (Drive C:) to the floppy disk (Drive A:) and then use the standard DIR command. For example:

`C:\>A:`   You type in A: and press the Enter key.

`A:\>DIR`   DOS responds with the new default drive designator, and you type in the command DIR at the command line prompt.

In the above example, the C:\> is the command line prompt and the A: is what you typed in. Remember that when you reference a disk drive in any command, the letter of the drive **must** be followed by a colon (:).

Formatting Floppy Disks

If you performed a DIR on a brand new disk, you would most likely obtain an error message. The reason is that the disk must first be prepared, or formatted, for use on your particular system. The way that information is stored on disks varies for different families of computers. To cope with this problem, disk manufacturers have standardized disk production. When you purchase a disk, the disk can be used by a variety of microcomputers, using a number of different operating systems. What you are buying is essentially a blank disk that must be customized for use with your particular operating system.

Before you can store information on a disk, DOS must map out the area where information can be stored. DOS must create tracks and sectors that provide addressable areas of the disk where information can be safely stored and located. Creating this structure is called formatting the disk. The command used to create this structure is **FORMAT**. The FORMAT command is most frequently used by itself. For example, to format a disk located in Drive A:, the command is typed

```
C:\>FORMAT A:
```

Warning!

Unless you are formatting your hard disk for the first time or you are reformatting your hard drive on purpose, **do not use the command FORMAT C:**. Always read the messages provided by DOS before continuing with a format.

Once the disk is formatted, the read/write head of a disk drive (see Figure 9.5) can locate or store data using the map that DOS created during the formatting process.

Reformatting a Used Diskette

Sometimes it becomes necessary to reformat a used floppy disk. The most common reasons for doing so are to erase old files or to reformat a disk that has been damaged due to exposure to magnetic fields. The two DOS 6 options that you may use with the FORMAT command when you want to reformat a disk are /Q and /U. These options were added to speed the process of reformatting used diskettes.

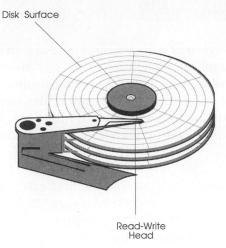

Disk Surface

Read-Write
Head

Figure 9.5
Hard disk drive with read/write head

The option /**Q** tells DOS to perform a quick format of the disk, meaning that DOS only clears the directory listing off the disk but does not change the existing map of tracks and sectors. This option does not check the disk for possible damaged tracks or sectors. To perform a quick format on a disk located in Drive A:, you would use the following command:

```
C:\>FORMAT A: /Q
```

The option /**U** tells DOS to perform an unconditional format of the disk, meaning that DOS will erase all the old format structure and create a totally new format structure. To perform an unconditional format on a disk located in Drive A:, you would use the following command:

```
C:\>FORMAT A: /U
```

Most times, a quick format will provide you with a fast means of reformatting a disk. If a disk has bad tracks or sectors causing data loss, you would need to use the unconditional format instead of a quick format. A disk can also be reformatted by using just the FORMAT command. The standard FORMAT process is slower than using the /U option, because using the standard FORMAT command on a used disk causes DOS to read the disk information first so that you can unformat the disk. If you use the /U option, the disk cannot be unformatted.

Internal versus External DOS Commands

DOS has two types of commands: internal and external. Internal commands are memory-resident because they are stored in memory during a boot and are always available. External commands are disk-resident commands because they are individual files usually stored on the hard disk. DOS must be told where to find the files. Normally, a computer with a hard disk is set up with a PATH command that tells DOS where to look.

The DOS command FORMAT is the first external command you have learned. If you receive an error message "Bad command or file name" when you issue the FORMAT command, you may need to modify the PATH command. If you run into this unlikely situation, your instructor will help you.

Labeling Diskettes

Identifying the diskette you want when you are using a number of floppy disks is important. If you use several diskettes for one purpose, you might wish to identify the order of use or the order of creation. If the diskettes you are using are for different purposes, you might wish to distinguish them with labels.

Placing an external label on a disk is certainly a wise procedure. However, another important habit is to label the disks internally. The DOS FORMAT command provides you an option that can be used to label the disk internally as part of the directory list. The internal label is called a volume label. Prior to DOS 5, the command to add a volume label during a format was

```
C:\>FORMAT A: /V
```

DOS 6 added the following ways to label a disk:

1. DOS 6 will prompt you for a volume label.
2. If you wish to label your disk by using the volume label option, add the option **/V:*label*** to the FORMAT command. Your disk will automatically be labeled when the FORMAT command is completed. For example:

```
C:\>FORMAT A: /V:DATADISK
```

This method provides DOS with the volume label in advance.

The maximum number of characters you can have in a volume label is 11. Use a name that represents the contents of the disk or that provides you with a method of distinguishing one disk from another. Avoid using special characters such as !@#$% &*()+=|\<>?/,.~` when you create volume labels.

Displaying a Disk's Internal Label

Once you have added a volume label to the disk, the volume label will be displayed at the top of the directory list every time you use the DIR command. The specific DOS command designed to display the volume label is **VOL**. To display the volume label of a disk in Drive A:, the VOL command is entered as follows:

```
C:\>VOL A:
```

You can also find the volume label of a diskette in Drive A: by changing to Drive A: and using the VOL command, as follows:

```
C:\>A:       Changes to Drive A:.
A:\>VOL      Displays the volume label of the disk located in Drive A:.
```

Checking a Disk for Damage

If you suspect that a diskette has been damaged or you desire to know more in-depth information about a disk's contents, you can use the DOS command **CHKDSK**.

To use the CHKDSK command, simply type

```
A:\>CHKDSK
```

or

```
C:\>CHKDSK A:
```

DOS will respond with a screen similar to the one shown in Figure 9.6

```
C:\>CHKDSK

Volume ALLEN       created 10-21-1993 8:20p
Volume Serial Number is 1AC4-7CF9
Errors found, F parameter not specified
Corrections will not be written to disk

    8 lost allocation units found in 6 chains.
       32768 bytes disk space would be freed

 212058112 bytes total disk space
  20242432 bytes in 3 hidden files
    532480 bytes in 122 directories
  88539136 bytes in 2899 user files
 102711296 bytes available on disk

      4096 bytes in each allocation unit
     51772 total allocation units on disk
     25076 available allocation units on disk

    655360 total bytes memory
    602960 bytes free

C:\>
```

Figure 9.6
Checking the condition of drive C:

In addition to the information provided during the format process, such as total bytes available and number of bytes in bad sectors, CHKDSK provides you with a few more details, as follows:

1. CHKDSK tells you whether there are any hidden files on the disk and the number of bytes of disk space occupied by them. Creating a systems disk installs two hidden DOS files on the disk (IO.SYS and MSDOS.SYS or IBMBIOS.COM and IBMDOS.COM). A hidden file is a file that does not appear when the directory command is executed.

2. CHKDSK lists the number of bytes used by user files.

3. CHKDSK lists the amount of conventional RAM your system has and the amount of RAM that is available (free). From this information, you can determine how many bytes of RAM are currently being used.

Sometimes DOS can lose track of some disk space when files are deleted or when your computer is turned off with application software still running. If DOS tells you that your disk contains recoverable sectors during the CHKDSK process, you can use the /**F** option with CHKDSK to recover the lost file fragments. DOS will then rename the recovered sectors into files with the extension .**CHK**. For example, if you recovered two sectors, you would find two files named FILE0001.CHK and FILE0002.CHK in the root directory of the disk. You could then delete those files to obtain more disk space.

Creating a Copy of a Disk

Whenever you receive new application program disks, you should make a backup copy of them immediately. To copy a disk, use the DOS command DISKCOPY. The **DISKCOPY** command makes an exact copy of a floppy disk, but it will not work with hard disks. Because DOS tries to make an exact copy, you must use the same type of floppy disk, with the same storage capacity as the original. For example, if the original is a 720K 3½" double-density disk, you must use a 720K double-density disk for the copy. You cannot make a copy from a 5¼" disk to a 3½" disk, nor can you make copies between double-density and high-density disks.

To copy a diskette in Drive A: to another diskette that will also be inserted in Drive A:, type

```
C:\>DISKCOPY A: A:
```

DOS will respond with the message shown in Figure 9.7 asking for the source diskette.

```
C:\>DISKCOPY A: A:

Insert SOURCE diskette in drive A:

Press any key to continue . . .

Copying 80 tracks
9 sectors per track, 2 side(s)

Insert TARGET diskette in drive A:

Press any key to continue . . .
```

Figure 9.7
Copying an entire disk using DISKCOPY

The source disk is the disk from which you are copying. If it is in Drive A:, press any key. After a few seconds, DOS will prompt you for the target diskette, which is the one to which you are copying (see Figure 9.7).

DOS may ask you to swap the source and target diskettes several times before the diskcopy process is complete. The number of times you may have to swap is determined by how much free memory you have and the size of the disk you are copying.

DOS 6 can also format the target disk at the same time it copies the disk's files. However, if the original disk is a double-density disk and the drive you are using is a high-density drive, DOS will try to format the disk as a high-density disk which will be different in size from the original, and the diskcopy process will fail. The best course to follow is to perform CHKDSK on the original and find out what kind of disk it is and format the backup disk as the same size before you begin the diskcopy process.

If you have two identical floppy disk drives, you can perform a diskcopy without having to swap disks by using both disk drives. The command would be as follows:

C:\>DISKCOPY A: B:

or

C:\>DISKCOPY B: A:

Whenever you type a command, you must leave a space between adjoining parts of the command. The different parts are as follows:

1. The command itself (DISKCOPY).

2. Location of the source (A:).

3. Location of the target or destination (B:).

4. Options or switches if required or needed (/P or /W when using the DIR command, and so on).

Clearing the Screen

Some DOS commands, such as DISKCOMP, will leave your screen crowded with information. If at any time you wish to erase your screen, you can type the command **CLS** at the command prompt. DOS will immediately clear your screen except for the new command prompt that appears.

Obtaining Help

You can obtain helpful information about any DOS command by typing HELP followed by the DOS command. For example, the DIR command format and all of its options can be found by typing HELP DIR at any command line prompt (see Figure 9.8).

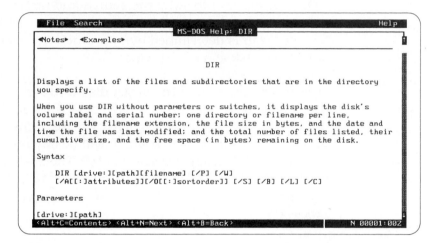

Figure 9.8
Help for the DIR command

10 chapter ten

Command Line File Commands

When you have completed this chapter, you will be able to

Objectives

- Identify valid and invalid filenames.
- Determine the type of file given specific extensions.
- Explain how files are created and displayed.
- Find out whether a file is on a disk without having to list the whole directory.
- Display the contents of a file using the DOS command TYPE.
- Redirect output to a printer or other device.
- Stop a directory list or a file from scrolling off the screen.

Creating Filenames

Part of your ability to manage your disks and find information quickly depends on how successful you are at creating meaningful filenames. This skill normally comes into play when you use an application program. You need to learn how to save the file using an acceptable filename. The rules for naming files are not much help when it comes to making filenames meaningful, but they do place some restrictions on you. The rules are as follows:

1. The filename cannot be longer than eight characters.

2. A three-character extension should be used to further identify files.

3. DOS does not recognize the difference between upper- and lower-case letters. Once entered, DOS will list all filenames in uppercase.

4. Although certain symbols can be used, such as /!@#$%&(){}'', you should avoid using punctuation or symbols in naming files because certain symbols are unacceptable. Some symbols such as *, ?, \, and . have specific meanings in DOS.

5. A period (separator) is used to separate the filename from the extension.

6. Spaces cannot be used in either the filename or the extension.

Any filename longer than eight characters or any extension longer than three characters will not be recognized by DOS. DOS will shorten filenames to the first eight characters and extensions to three characters to conform with proper filename specifications.

When you name files, the computer does not allow you to give the same name to two different files in the same directory. However, it does not stop you from giving names that are meaningless. When you create filenames, keep in mind that you will save time if you use filenames that readily identify the contents of the file. For example, if you were writing the first draft of an essay on President Jimmy Carter, you might name your file CARTER1. The numeral 1 is used to label it as your first draft. The key is to make the filename simple and at the same time make it reflect what the file contains.

In addition to the name of the file, you might want to add an extension or file type designator. Extensions follow the filename and are generally used to classify the type of file. For example, let's say that while writing your essay on Carter, you decided to create a spreadsheet that contains the names and addresses of professors whom you wish to ask for information. To distinguish the file containing the essay prepared using word processing software from the mailing list prepared using a spreadsheet program, you might label your text file CARTER1.TXT and your spreadsheet CARTER1.WK1. In this example, the .TXT extension stands for *text* and .WK1 stands for *worksheet one*. The period (.) is used only as a separator and is found between a filename and an extension.

Certain types of software automatically provide their own extensions, which allow you to distinguish their files from other types of software. For example, Microsoft Word word processing software uses the extension .DOC, and Turbo Pascal uses the extension .PAS. Some software also automatically creates backup files that contain the version of the file before it was revised. These filenames have the extension .BAK (for backup).

File Types

Some file extensions tell you something about the type of file. You should be aware of the following file type extensions:

Extension	Type of File
COM or EXE	*Program files (Command/Executable)*
	An extension of .COM or .EXE means that the contents of the file constitute an executable file or a program. By typing the filename (with or without this extension), the computer will assume you want a command executed. You will find .COM and .EXE files on application program and operating system disks.
SYS	*System files*
	.SYS files control how your computer performs certain actions. One of the system files is CONFIG.SYS, a file used when your computer is started.
BAT	*Batch files*
	.BAT files are files that carry out a series of DOS commands. An example is the AUTOEXEC.BAT file.
BAK	*Backup files*
	.BAK files are the original (or previous) versions of files that were created by DOS or some application software and then altered. A user can also use .BAK as an extension to indicate a backup copy of a file.
DOC or TXT	*Document or text files*
	.DOC or .TXT files are created by using word processing application software.
WKS or WK1	*Worksheet files*
	.WKS files are created when using older versions of Lotus 1-2-3, an applications package for creating spreadsheets. Newer versions of 1-2-3 create files with the extension .WK1. Lotus 1-2-3 for Windows creates files with the .WK3 extension. Other spreadsheet software, such as Excel, create different extensions.
DBF or DTA	*Database files*
	.DBF or .DTA files are created by using database application software.

Extension	Type of File
OVR	*Overlay files*
	.OVR are files found in application software.
BAS	*BASIC files*
	.BAS are files created when using the BASIC programming language.
PAS	*Pascal files*
	.PAS files are created when using the Pascal programming language.

Other extensions can also be used, as long as they follow the rules for creating filenames. See Figures 10.1 and 10.2 for invalid and valid ways of naming files.

Invalid	Why Invalid
MY STORY.TXT	Contains a space.
.TXT	Does not have a filename.
MY,STORY.TXT	Contains a comma.
MYSTORY.TXTE	DOS truncates the extension to 3 characters and saves as MYSTERY.TXT.
PRN.TXT	Contains a device name (PRN).
COPY.TXT	Contains a DOS command (COPY).
MY*STORY.TXT	Contains a wildcard (*).
YOURLETTER.DOC	Contains a filename that is too long. DOS saves as YOURLETT.DOC.

Figure 10.1
Invalid filenames

Valid	Type of File
LETTER.TXT	A text file.
REVENUE.DBF	A database file.
AUTOEXEC.BAT	A DOS batch file.
1234ABCE.333	A filename and an extension.
5551212.XXX	A filename and an extension.
%$#%@812	A filename without an extension designator.
HELLO	A filename without an extension designator.

Figure 10.2
Valid filenames

Note

DOS does not recognize the difference between uppercase and lowercase letters. Once entered, DOS will list all filenames in uppercase. Do not attempt to differentiate files with capitalization.

Tip

When you create a file, you must name the file using a filename that has not already been used, or you will erase the already existing file with the same name. Many application programs will compare the filename you have typed with the other filenames in the directory and notify you prior to allowing you to overwrite an existing file.

The drive letter, filename, and extension are called the filespec. For example, the filespec A:LETTER.DOC includes the drive letter where the file is located (A:), the filename (LETTER), and the extension (.DOC).

Obtaining Partial Directories and Sorted Directories

Once you have created a number of data files, it is often desirable to list specific parts of a directory, rather than listing the whole directory. The DIR command allows you to display a single file, a portion of a directory, or the whole directory sorted in a desired order.

Directory Listing of a Single File

A quick way to know whether you have created a file is to look for it using the DIR command with a filename. This command allows you to determine whether the file exists without listing the entire directory. When you use this command, DOS searches the directory of the active disk for the filename listed and, if found, displays the same information about that file that would appear in a complete directory, but only for the specified filename. For example, to find out whether the disk in Drive A: contains the file LETTER.TXT, you would type

```
A:\>DIR LETTER.TXT
```

or

```
C:\>DIR A:LETTER.TXT
```

If the file exists, DOS will list the file in a directory similar to the one shown in Figure 10.3.

```
A:\>DIR LETTER.TXT

 Volume in drive A is EXERCISES
 Volume Serial Number is 391B-1CDB
 Directory of A:\

LETTER   TXT        978 05-18-92   8:38p
         1 file(s)            978 bytes
                        1140736 bytes free

A:\>
```

Figure 10.3
Displaying information for a single file using DIR

If the file is not found, DOS responds with the message shown in Figure 10.4.

```
A:\>DIR LETTER.DOC

 Volume in drive A is EXERCISES
 Volume Serial Number is 391B-1CDB
 Directory of A:\

File not found

A:\>
```

Figure 10.4
Displaying information for a single file using DIR (cont'd)

Note

DOS will respond with a "not found" message if you incorrectly type any part of the filename or extension. Capitalization, however, is not recognized. Even though DOS lists filenames in all capitals, DIR letter.txt will still list the file LETTER.TXT.

Obtaining Partial Directories with Wildcards

Wildcards accelerate locating specific files when several filenames have similar characters. When you work with long lists of files, you may find it difficult to locate certain files that are in the directory. By using wildcards, you can obtain partial lists of certain types of files. Wildcards are symbols that can be used in place of known or unknown characters in filenames or extensions. The DOS manual refers to them as *global filename characters*. The two wildcard symbols are ? and * (question mark and asterisk). The ? can take the place of one unspecified character. The * can take the place of one or more unspecified characters.

Files that have similar characters in their filenames or extensions can be displayed by using either the * or ? wildcard. Using these wildcards, you could perform such operations as listing all the command files (files with the extension .COM) or all the text files (files with the extension .TXT).

The * Wildcard

Suppose that you have two files named CARTER, one that is a database file and one that is a word processing text file. Although they have the same filename, CARTER, they have different extensions (DBF and TXT). To locate these files on a directory you could use an asterisk in place of the extension, as shown:

```
A:\>DIR CARTER.*
```

This command tells DOS to search for any file with the filename CARTER and any extension.

Another reason for using the * wildcard is for listing all the files with the same extension. For instance, if you wanted to list only the files that had the extension TXT, you would use the command as follows:

```
A:\>DIR *.TXT
```

This command tells DOS to list the directory of any file with the extension TXT.

Using the * wildcard in place of both the filename and the extension would produce the same result as using the DIR command alone, as follows:

```
A:\>DIR *.*
```

This command produces the same effect as A:\>DIR. The first asterisk stands for any filename. The second asterisk stands for any extension.

The ? Wildcard

The ? wildcard can be thought of as replacing any one character. For example, if you want to list a number of files that begin with CARTER but whose filenames include the numbers of the draft, such as CARTER1.TXT, CARTER2.TXT, CARTER3.TXT, CARTER4.TXT, and CARTER5.TXT, you cannot use the DIR command and say DIR CARTER.*. DOS would search the disk for any filename with only the six letters CARTER. The numerals are the seventh character in the filename. Because the last character of each filename differs from file to file, a wildcard can be used in place of that character that is different in each file, as follows:

```
A:\>DIR CARTER?.TXT
```

This command lists all files with names containing CARTER as the first part and any one character following the word CARTER. When using a ? for a character within a filename while using the DIR command, DOS will look for a filename with the characters that surround the question mark and list any files that fit the parameters. See Figure 10.5.

```
A:\>DIR CARTER?.TXT

 Volume in drive A is EXERCISES
 Volume Serial Number is 391B-1CDB
 Directory of A:\

CARTER1   TXT        95 05-30-92   2:12p
CARTER2   TXT        91 05-30-92   2:13p
CARTER3   TXT        90 05-30-92   2:13p
        3 file(s)            276 bytes
                         1140736 bytes free

A:\>
```

Figure 10.5
Using the ? wildcard with DIR

Note that if you have several files, including both CARTER1.TXT and CARTER12.TXT, DOS will only list the file CARTER1.TXT when you use the previous command because you only used one ? following the filename CARTER. CARTER12 has two characters after the common characters CARTER, so the filename does not fit your description. In this example, to list both files, you would need to list two ?s:

A:\>DIR CARTER??.TXT

This command uses two question marks because the maximum number of characters following CARTER would be two.

As you can see, using several ?s could get confusing at times. Rather than A:\>DIR CARTER??.TXT, you might find it easier to use A:\>DIR CARTER*.TXT.

Sorting Directories

In addition to the standard DIR command and the use of wildcards, DOS 6 allows you to use sorting options to obtain directory listings with files listed in a specific order. You can sort directories by filename, by extension, by size, and by date. To sort a DIR list, use the **/O**: option after the DIR command followed by the letter of the sort you want. For example, to obtain an alphabetical list of the files on the EXERCISES disk in Drive A:, you could type

A:\>DIR /O:N

DOS would respond with the screen shown in Figure 10.6.

```
CARTER1  TXT        95  05-30-92   2:12p
CARTER2  TXT        91  05-30-92   2:13p
CARTER3  TXT        90  05-30-92   2:13p
EDITOR   HLP      3048  07-30-90   8:55p
FAXLIST  RPT      3927  05-28-90   8:30a
FONEDATA DBF     24646  03-28-92  10:41a
FONEDATA DBT      7224  03-28-92  10:41a
LETTER   TXT       978  05-18-92   8:38p
MOVIE    LS1       397  01-01-80   1:31a
MOVIE    LS2      1080  01-02-80   1:47a
PHONECMP IND      3927  03-28-92  10:41a
PHONEFST IND      3311  03-28-92  10:41a
PHONELST IND      3311  03-28-92  10:41a
PHONESDX IND      1925  03-28-92  10:41a
README   DOC      2068  05-30-92   2:29p
ROLODEX  EXE    143159  03-27-92   4:18p
SS       COM     21330  08-26-87   3:59p
VOICBILL RPT      3927  05-28-90   8:34a
VOICLIST RPT      3927  05-28-90   8:35a
WP       EXE     68656  03-27-92   4:13p
XMAS     RPT      3534  03-27-92  10:20a
        24 file(s)      310573 bytes
                       1140736 bytes free

A:\>
```

Figure 10.6
Displaying a directory listing sorted by filename using DIR /O:

Only the last 21 files are listed. Earlier files have scrolled off the screen because the /P option was not used.

You can reverse the sort order by placing a minus sign (–) before the letter of the type of sort you want. The following is a list of DIR sort commands and what they do.

Command	Result
`C:\>DIR A: /O:N`	Directory of Drive A:, sorted by filename (a–z).
`C:\>DIR A: /O:-N`	Directory of Drive A:, sorted by filename (z–a).
`C:\>DIR /O:E`	Directory of C:\, sorted by extension (a–z).
`C:\>DIR /O:-E`	Directory of C:\, sorted by extension (z–a).
`C:\>DIR /O:S`	Directory of Drive C:, sorted by size, from smallest to largest.
`C:\>DIR /O:-S`	Directory of Drive C:, sorted by size, from largest to smallest.
`C:\>DIR /O:D`	Directory of Drive C:, sorted by date, oldest to newest.
`C:\>DIR /O:-D`	Directory of Drive C:, sorted by date, newest to oldest.

Displaying the Contents of a File

Normally, when you want to view or print the contents of a file, you will do so from within the application program in which the file was created. There are occasions, however, when you will want to see the file contents without starting the application program. For example, you might be looking for a certain file and want to take a look at the contents of various files to attempt to locate it. A quick method would be to use the DOS command **TYPE** to list the contents of a file on the screen.

For example, the file LETTER.TXT on your EXERCISES disk was created using the word processor contained on the disk. It can be displayed on the screen by typing

```
A:\>TYPE LETTER.TXT
```

DOS will display the file, as shown in Figure 10.7.

```
A:\TYPE LETTER.TXT
Memo 1

To:       Myself
FROM:     The person in the mirror
DATE:     October 25, 1993
SUBJECT:  Giving the grey cells a break

You have to take a break from studying every once in a
while. So lighten up or you are going to burn out.

A:\>
```

Figure 10.7
Listing the contents of a file with TYPE

Certain types of files, such as command (.COM) and executable (.EXE) files, will appear as symbols when displayed in this way. These files have been created using a programming language and converted into machine-readable code that is unreadable for the average user.

Files that you will create using the application programs, however, consist primarily of text. When you use the command TYPE, they will display as text characters, not as unrecognizable symbols. If a file is displayed to the screen in symbols, you should not attempt to alter the symbols in any way or you might damage the file.

Redirecting Output

If you wish to send a copy of the contents of your file to the printer instead of to the screen, DOS allows you to do so. When you use a command to send output to a device other than the screen (This is the default device.), it is called output redirection. The command to redirect information or data away from the screen and to the printer is >**PRN**. PRN is the DOS device name for *printer*.

For example, to send the contents of the LETTER.TXT file on your EXERCISES disk to the printer, you can type

```
A:\>TYPE LETTER.TXT>PRN
```

When this command is executed, only the contents of the file are sent to the printer, not the command.

Stopping Scrolling and Aborting Commands

Two two-key combinations that are useful while using the DIR and TYPE commands are Ctrl-C and Ctrl-S. They can be used to cancel a command or temporarily stop the display. When you type DIR and the contents of the screen begin to scroll, you can stop the scrolling by pressing Ctrl-S. Once the scrolling has stopped, pressing any key will resume the scrolling. On the other hand, if you wish to abort the command, you can type Ctrl-C (or Ctrl-Break), and you will be returned to the command prompt. You can do the same after the TYPE command is issued.

When viewing a directory, Ctrl-S is similar to DIR /P, except that with Ctrl-S you can control the portion of the directory displayed on the screen. After typing in your DIR command but before pressing the Enter key, you may find it helpful to place one finger over the Ctrl key and another finger over the S key. Once you have pressed the Enter key to begin listing the directory, you press the Ctrl-S keys simultaneously to stop the scrolling. If the file you are looking for is on the screen and you have obtained the information you desire, press any key to continue scrolling through the directory. If the file you are looking for is not on the screen when you first stop the directory, be ready to press the Ctrl-S keys again to stop the list after you have pressed the key to begin the scrolling.

Ctrl-S is used in the same way when viewing the contents of a file. The same technique is applied when using the Ctrl-C command to abort a command.

> ### Tip
>
> It is easy to leave the Ctrl key pressed and only worry about pressing the S key to start and stop the scrolling or the C key to abort the command.

Copying Individual Files

Any time you need to transfer a file from one disk to another, you use the **COPY** command. The COPY command allows you to copy a single file or multiple files. In order to use the COPY command, you need to supply DOS with additional information, called parameters. The COPY command requires the name of the drive in which the source file(s) reside(s) (unless the source is in the default drive), the filename of the source, and the destination of the copy (target). The following are examples of how to use the DOS COPY command.

Command	What It Does
`C:\>COPY A:CHAP1.DOC B:`	Copies the file CHAP1.DOC from Drive A: to Drive B:.
`C:\>COPY CHAP1.DOC A:`	Copies the file CHAP1.DOC from Drive C: to Drive A:.
`C:\>COPY A:CHAP1.DOC`	Copies the file CHAP1.DOC from Drive A: to Drive C:.

In the first example, the source file is identified as being on the disk in Drive A: and the target drive—the drive that contains the disk being copied to—as Drive B:.

In the second example, the source file is identified as being on the disk in the default drive (Drive C:) because no other drive is identified. The file-name is CHAP1.DOC. The drive that the file is being copied to (the target drive) is Drive A:.

In the third example, the source file is identified as being on the disk in Drive A: and the target drive as Drive C: (the default) because no other drive is specified.

DOS would not accept the following command for copying a single file:

`C:\>COPY CHAP1.DOC`

If you used this command, you would be trying to copy CHAP1.DOC from the default drive to the default drive. You would, therefore, be trying to copy the file onto itself and would receive an error message telling you that you cannot do this. You need to specify a new location for the copied file.

When you ask for a file to be copied, DOS looks for the file you specified. If you have not given a source drive label, DOS will look in the default drive for the file. If you have given a source drive label, DOS will go to that drive and look for the file. It will load the file into RAM and read the drive name to which the file is to be copied. At this point, DOS will begin to copy the file to the disk. If DOS runs out of space before the file is copied, DOS will give you the following message (see Figure 10.8):

```
C:\>COPY C.COM A:
Insufficient disk space
        0 file(s) copied

C:\>
```

Figure 10.8
Error message from COPY

When the COPY command is issued and there is enough disk space, the light on the source disk illuminates as the file is loaded into RAM. Then the light on the drive that contains the target disk lights up and the file is copied to the target disk. When the process is complete, DOS displays this message:

```
1 File(s) copied
```

You will then be returned to the prompt of your default drive. See Figure 10.9.

```
C:\>COPY COMMAND.COM A:
        1 file(s) copied

C:\>
```

Figure 10.9
Copying a single file with COPY

Tip

Before issuing the COPY command, you should look at the directories of both the source disk (the disk that contains the file or files that you are going to copy) and the target disk (the disk to which the file or files will be copied) to make sure the file exists and the target drive can receive the intended file.

Copying Multiple Files Using Wildcards

If you do not want to use DISKCOPY, which copies all files on a floppy disk, but want to copy several files, copying files using wildcards is much faster than copying individual files.

Filenames or extensions that have one or more similar characters in common can be copied by using either the ? or * wildcard. The ? and * wildcards can be used with COPY in the same way that you used them with DIR.

Some examples of how the wildcards are used with the COPY command are as follows:

`C:\>COPY CARTER?.TXT A:`
This command copies all the files containing the first part of the file-name CARTER, any one character following the word CARTER, and the file extension .TXT from the root directory of the current drive (C:) to Drive A:.

`C:\>COPY CAR*.* A:`
This command copies all files that begin with CAR, regardless of their extensions or the characters that follow CAR in the filename, from the root directory of the current drive (C:) to Drive A:.

`C:\>COPY CARTER.* A:`
This command copies all files named CARTER, regardless of their extensions, from the root directory of the current drive (C:) to Drive A:.

`C:\>COPY *.TXT B:`
This command copies all files with the extension .TXT from the root directory of the current drive (C:) to Drive B:.

`C:\>COPY *.* B:`
This command copies all files located in the root directory of Drive C: to Drive B:.

Summary of the Differences between COPY and DISKCOPY

When the COPY command is used to copy multiple files, the files will copy one by one. Unlike DISKCOPY, when the COPY command is used, DOS packs the files as close together as possible without gaps. DISKCOPY does not rearrange files as it copies them from the source to the target. This distinction between COPY and DISKCOPY is important because when a disk has had numerous files added and deleted over a period of time, some files may become fragmented. A fragmented file is split into two or more sections and stored on different parts of the disk. When files become fragmented, there is an increased chance of losing part of the file as well as loss of disk space. The advantage of COPY over DISKCOPY is that files will be copied without fragmentation. File fragmentation is discussed further in a later chapter.

Unlike DISKCOPY, the use of the COPY command also requires that the target disk be formatted. The COPY command will not write over existing files on the target diskette, but it will write over a file of the same name. Figure 10.10 summarizes the differences between COPY and DISKCOPY.

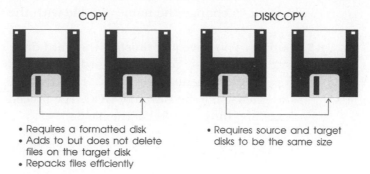

ten

COPY   DISKCOPY

- Requires a formatted disk
- Adds to but does not delete
  files on the target disk
- Repacks files efficiently

- Requires source and target
  disks to be the same size

Figure 10.10
The differences between COPY *.* and DISKCOPY

Renaming Files

DOS provides two ways of renaming files, depending on whether you are copying the file as you rename it.

Using the RENAME Command

The DOS command **RENAME** allows you to change the name of a file without copying the file. Suppose you have just finished working on the chapter of a book that you named CHAP3.DOC, but you discover that this chapter should actually be chapter 4. You can rename it by using the following command:

```
C:\>RENAME A:CHAP3.DOC CHAP4.DOC
```

To use the rename function, type the command, followed by the drive letter (if it is not the default), the filename of the original file, and the new filename. You can change either the filename, the extension, or both. You can also use the abbreviation **REN** instead of the whole command RENAME.

Renaming a File While Copying

If you wish to copy *and* rename a file at the same time, you can do so using the COPY command. To rename a file using COPY, simply add the new filename after the target drive letter. Here are two cases where you might want to change the name of a file with the COPY command:

1. Suppose you have just finished the third draft of the term paper you are writing on Carter. You have named the file CARTER3.DOC. You want to copy the document from Drive C: to Drive A: as a backup, but you want the extension to be BAK, not DOC. The procedure for copying and renaming the extension of the file is:

```
C:\>COPY CARTER3.DOC A:CARTER3.BAK
```

2. Suppose you have been using .NEW as your extension for all your lessons. You wish to rename as .OLD all the chapters in Drive C: that are backups and store them on a disk located in Drive A:. You can rename all the files with the extension .OLD while copying by entering the following:

```
C:\>COPY *.NEW A:*.OLD
```

Erasing or Deleting Files

When using application programs, you will discover that unless you are careful, you can end up with several copies of the same file—even several versions of the same file. The DOS commands **ERASE** and **DEL** allow you to delete unwanted files.

When you delete a file, you may wonder why it seems that a file that took so long to create disappears so quickly. The commands ERASE and DEL (delete) do not really erase a file, they simply replace the first character of the filename so that DOS no longer recognizes the beginning of a file and can reuse the disk space where the old file was stored. ERASE or DEL can be used to delete a single file or a selected group of files. ERASE is used in the following examples; DEL will do exactly the same thing.

`C:\>ERASE REPORT1.TXT`	Erases REPORT1.TXT from Drive C:.
`C:\>ERASE A:REPORT.TXT`	Erases REPORT.TXT from a disk located in Drive A:.
`C:\>ERASE B:REPORT1.BAK`	Erases REPORT1.BAK from a disk located in Drive B:.

`C:\>ERASE B:*.*`	Erases all the files from the disk in Drive B:.
`C:\>ERASE A:*.BAK`	Erases all the files with the extension .BAK from the disk in Drive A:.
`C:\>ERASE A:LET??.TXT`	Erases all the files starting with LET followed by two unknown characters and the extension .TXT from the disk in Drive A:.

Warning!

Do not use C:\>ERASE*.*. If you do, you will erase the contents of your hard disk.

Note

When you use the command DEL*.* or ERASE*.*, DOS asks you "ARE YOU SURE Y/N?" When DOS asks you this question, STOP, and make sure you really want DOS to continue before pressing Y.

Other ways to delete the contents of an entire disk are by reformatting the disk using the FORMAT command or by copying over the disk using DISKCOPY.

Listing and Changing the Attributes of a File

In addition to the file directory that appears when you use the DIR command, other information about each file is also stored. This information includes the location(s) where the file is stored on the disk, whether the file should be hidden from the directory, whether the file should be read-only (protected from deletion), whether the file has been archived (backed up), and whether the file is a system file. You can use the DOS command **ATTRIB** to change or view the attributes of a file.

The Read-Only Attribute

The read-only attribute is used to protect files from accidental deletion. You cannot use DEL or ERASE to delete any file that is marked as read-only, although you can eliminate the file by formatting the disk or by using DISKCOPY.

If you wanted to view the attributes of all the .EXE files on the EXER-CISES disk, you would type the following command:

```
A:\>ATTRIB *.EXE
```

The results appear as shown in Figure 10.11. The "A" to the left of each filename indicates that the "archive" attribute is turned on. This attribute is on by default.

```
A:\>ATTRIB *.EXE
    A            A:\WP.EXE
    A            A:\ROLODEX.EXE

A:\>
```

Figure 10.11
Listing the attributes for .EXE files on drive A:

To turn the read-only attribute for the file WP.EXE located in Drive A: to the "on" position, use the following command:

```
A:\>ATTRIB WP.EXE +r
```

To turn the read-only attribute to the "off" position, use the following command:

```
A:\>ATTRIB WP.EXE -r
```

Some additional attributes that can be changed are the archive, hidden file, and system file attributes. The archive attribute is used to mark each file that has been archived or backed up. When a backup program encounters an archive attribute, it will copy the file to the backup medium (disk or tape drive).

The hidden file attribute (H) is used to prevent a file from being displayed on the directory. Even if a file is hidden, it can be deleted, if you know the name of the file. This attribute is normally associated with DOS system files so they will not appear on the directory.

The system file (S) attribute is used to mark a file as being a DOS system program file. There is no reason for most users to change a system file's attribute or to change a regular file's attribute to make the file a system file.

Obtaining a Directory of Files with Specific Attributes

You can obtain a directory of files with specific attributes by using the **/A** option following the DIR command. You can list read-only files, system files, hidden files, or archive files, as shown in the following chart.

Option	What it Does
DIR /A:A	Lists all files that will be archived during the next backup.
DIR /A:H	Lists all hidden files.
DIR /A:R	Lists all read-only files.
DIR /A:S	Lists all system files.

If you wish to see a directory listing the files that have an attribute that is off, use a minus sign prior to the letter representing the attribute, as follows:

```
DIR /A:-A
DIR /A:-H
DIR /A:-R
DIR /A:-S
```

Using DOSKEY

DOSKEY is a command that stores your past DOS commands in a file so you can list and recall them rather than retype the commands. For example, if you were performing a repetitive copying exercise, you could use DOSKEY to locate the command you were using and edit it for each new COPY instruction. DOSKEY allows you to access approximately the last fifty DOS commands.

To activate the DOSKEY feature, type DOSKEY at any command prompt. After activating DOSKEY, you can step back through your previous commands using the up arrow. When you find the command you wish, press the Enter key to execute the command. In addition, you can list all of your past commands by pressing the F7 key. See Figure 10.12 for a listing of commands recalled by using the F7 key.

```
A:\>
1: cls
2: DIR
3: cls
4: ATTRIB *.EXE
5: cls
A:\>
```

Figure 10.12
Showing the commands stored by DOSKEY

After you find the command you want, press the F9 key and then type the line number of the desired command. Press the Enter key once to place the command into the command prompt and press the Enter key once more to execute the command.

chapter eleven

Command Line Directory Commands

When you have completed this chapter, you will be able to

Objectives

- Explain why hard disks are necessary.
- Describe problems that arise from using one directory.
- Define the term "subdirectory."
- Create, change, and remove a subdirectory.
- Explain the purpose of the TREE command.
- Copy to or from a subdirectory.
- Move a file.
- Rename a subdirectory.
- Copy an entire subdirectory using XCOPY.
- Delete and rename files within a subdirectory.
- Remove a branch of a tree structure.

Organizing Your Files

With the introduction of hard disks, numerous application programs and the files created using them could be placed on one large disk. Although this development eased the problem of having boxes full of floppy disks, the prospect of keeping all the files in one place also posed certain problems.

1. Finding a single file among hundreds of other files can be difficult.

2. Creating new filenames can become a problem because filenames are limited to 11 characters (including the extension).

3. Identifying which data files are associated with a given application program is difficult if the file extension does not identify which application program created the data file.

Fortunately, DOS provides you with the ability to organize your application programs and data files in a hierarchical structure. Rather than using a single directory to store all of your files, you can create additional directories within your main directory known as subdirectories.

What Are Subdirectories?

Subdirectories are directories *you* create to help you organize your application programs and data files. For example, when you install a word processing application program on a hard disk, you normally create a subdirectory where the application program files are stored. Each application program should have its own subdirectory on your hard disk. You may also create other subdirectories for storing the documents you create using those application programs. By organizing the hard disk in this manner, the main directory or your hard disk consists primarily of subdirectories rather than individual files. Floppy disks can also be organized in a similar manner.

Subdirectories can be broken down into further subdirectories. Thus the subdirectory containing an application program can contain its own subdirectories to further organize the data files you create with the application program. For example, the subdirectory containing your word processing program might include one subdirectory for letters to customers and one for interoffice memos. When this type of organization is diagrammed, the result looks like an inverted tree, as shown in Figure 11.1.

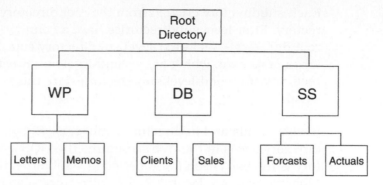

Figure 11.1
Subdirectory structure

Root Directories, Parent Directories, and Child Directories

Although disks are described as having a tree structure, the main directory is referred to as the root directory, not the trunk of the tree. Subdirectories are all descended from the root directory or are within subdirectories of the root directory. For this reason, subdirectories are frequently referred to as child directories, because they are descendants of the root directory. In this context, the hierarchy of directories can be compared to a family tree, with the root directory being the oldest member of the family and each level of subdirectories containing descendants. From the top down, each directory is the parent directory of the subdirectory below. And from the bottom up, each subdirectory is a child of the directory above. See Figure 11.2.

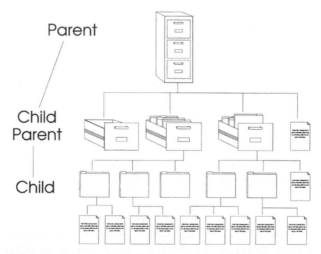

Figure 11.2
Parent-child relationships

Each subdirectory created from the root directory is a first-level subdirectory. First-level subdirectories have a common parent directory (the root directory). Each first-level subdirectory can also have child subdirectories of its own, which are second-level subdirectories. The child subdirectories of second-level subdirectories are third-level subdirectories, and so on.

In commands and in directory listings, DOS uses symbols to indicate directory levels in the tree structure. The DOS symbol for the root directory is the backslash (\). A period (.) symbolizes the current subdirectory. Wherever you are located in a subdirectory system is the current subdirectory. The current subdirectory is also called the default directory because DOS commands will affect the current directory by default. A double period (..) represents the parent directory. You will learn to use these symbols later in this chapter.

Figure 11.3 shows three levels of a tree diagram. The number of levels is limited only by the amount of space you have on your disk.

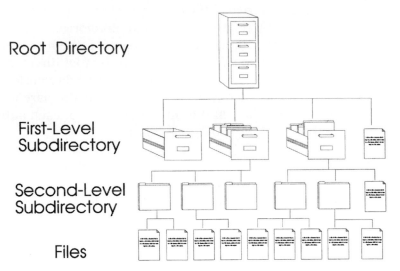

Figure 11.3
Levels of subdirectories

Filenames and Paths

In the previous chapters when you copied a file, you had to know only the filename (including the extension) and the drive in which it was located. When you copy a file that is in a subdirectory, however, you also need to know where the file is located in the subdirectory system. The exact location of a file, including the drive name and directories, is known as the file's path. The complete designation of a file includes both the filename and the path.

Because each subdirectory can keep its files separate from other subdirectories, you can use the same filespec (filename.ext) in different directories. For example, if you were using a word processor and a drawing program that each had its own subdirectory, you could have one text file named KENNEDY.001 and one drawing file named KENNEDY.001 as long as the files were kept in separate subdirectories. This is why you must know both the filename and the path of the file.

Proper Format for Indicating a File and Its Location

When you use subdirectories, you need to understand how to list the location of a file as well as the filename. For example, if you had a file named LETTER1.DOC that was located in the root directory of Drive C:, the complete filespec would be C:\LETTER1.DOC. If the file were located in a first-level subdirectory named WP, the filename would be C:\WP\LETTER1.DOC. If the file were located in a second-level subdirectory named LETTERS, the complete filespec including the path would be:

```
C:\WP\LETTERS\LETTER1.DOC
```

In these examples, the C:\ represents the root directory of Drive C:, WP represents the first-level subdirectory (C:\WP), and LETTERS represents the second-level subdirectory (C:\WP\LETTERS). The backslashes (\) are used to separate the different levels of subdirectories.

Creating Subdirectories and Moving Around in Them

DOS provides commands that allow you to create and remove subdirectories, move from one subdirectory to another, and list the tree structure and its contents. In addition, the DOS commands COPY, RENAME, and DELETE can be used to manage your files in the tree structure.

Making Subdirectories with MD

A subdirectory can be created using the DOS **MKDIR** or **MD** (make directory) command. To make a first-level subdirectory, you must be in the root directory. For example, to create the first-level subdirectory WP, you need to be in the root directory and use the following command:

```
C:\>MD WP
```

Changing the Default Subdirectory with CD

Once subdirectories have been created, you can move to them using the **CHDIR** or **CD** (change directory) command. For example, after making the first-level subdirectory WP, you would move from the root directory to the subdirectory WP with the following command:

`C:\>CD WP`

DOS responds with a command prompt showing the new current drive as follows if you have the PROMPT PG command installed:

`C:\WP>`

Movement within the tree structure can be either away from the root directory or toward the root directory. To move across the tree, you must first move to a common parent and then to the desired child subdirectory.

Viewing Your Directory Structure with TREE

The DOS command **TREE** allows you to view all or part of the subdirectory system. If you use the TREE command while you are in the root directory, DOS will display all the subdirectories contained within the disk, as shown in Figure 11.4.

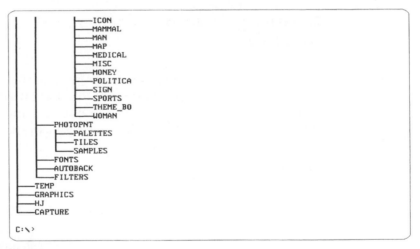

Figure 11.4
Displaying a directory diagram using TREE

Note that if you use the TREE command from within a first-level subdirectory, DOS will list only the subdirectories (second-level, third-level subdirectories, and so on) contained within that subdirectory. See Figure 11.5.

```
C:\WINWORD>TREE
Directory PATH listing for Volume ALLEN
Volume Serial Number is 1AC4-7CF9
C:.
├───WINWORD.CBT
├───CLIPART
└───DOS6

C:\WINWORD>
```

Figure 11.5
Displaying a subdirectory diagram using TREE

The TREE command can also be used to list all of the files within each subdirectory. Just add the /F option. If you need a hard copy, you can also redirect the output to the printer with the following command:

C:\>TREE /F >PRN

Using Your Subdirectories

Once you have created a subdirectory structure using the DOS MD command, you can COPY, RENAME, and DELETE files in subdirectories as you did in the prior chapters using root directories. The only difference is that you need to make sure you have located the correct file and, if you are copying it, that you are sending it to the right place.

Using the COPY Command with Subdirectories

In the previous chapter, you learned the COPY command requires that you specify the source drive followed by the filename you wish to copy, the target drive, and the filename to which the file is copied. In prior chapters, you had to know only the source and target drive designators, such as A: and C:. For example, COPY A:LETTER1.DOC B:. However, when you use subdirectories, you need to provide the path so that DOS knows the exact source file location and target location. For example, if you were to copy the file MEMO1.DOC from the WP subdirectory on the C: drive to the \MEMOS subdirectory on the floppy disk in Drive A:, the command would be as follows:

C:\>COPY C:\WP\MEMO1.DOC A:\MEMOS\MEMO1.DOC

The syntax is simple if you break it down. First, enter the command. Leave a space after the command. Then, specify the source drive, the path of the file, the filename, and the extension. Leave another space. Then list the drive, path, filename, and extension where the file should be copied. If you are not renaming the file, you can leave off the filename from the target location.

To copy the file LETTER.TXT from the root directory of Drive A: to the subdirectory WP on Drive C:, the command is as follows:

```
A:\>COPY LETTER.TXT C:\WP
```

In this example, you do not need to include the path for the source file because the file is located in the default directory.

To copy the same file back to Drive A:, the command is as follows:

```
A:\>COPY C:\WP\LETTER.TXT
```

In this example you do not need to list the target drive or directory because you want DOS to use the default directory, in this case A:\.

Copying an Entire Subdirectory with XCOPY

The COPY command can be used to copy single or multiple files from one subdirectory to another. However, the COPY command cannot copy files from multiple subdirectories at the same time. The command that supports this activity is **XCOPY** (extended copy). XCOPY allows you to transfer a whole subdirectory system from one disk (floppy or hard) to another.

XCOPY has several options that are used to determine what files and what subdirectories are copied during the procedure. A list of these options and their results follows.

Command	Result
XCOPY /A	Copies only files that have had their archive file attribute turned on.
XCOPY /D:mm-dd-yy	Copies only the files with creation dates that are identical to or more recent than the date following the /D.
XCOPY /E	Creates subdirectories on the target disk even if the subdirectories made will be empty.

Command	Result
XCOPY /M	Copies only files that have been modified since the last time the files have been archived.
XCOPY /P	Causes XCOPY to pause before each file is copied and requests confirmation that each file should be copied.
XCOPY /S	Copies all files from the source disk directory and subsequent lower directories to the target disk except for subdirectories that will be empty.
XCOPY /V	Verifies each file as being copied successfully.
XCOPY /W	Waits for the source disk to be placed in the appropriate disk drive.

Using the Move Command with Subdirectories

Whenever you use the COPY command, you create a duplicate of the original file. If you need only to move a file from one location to another without creating a duplicate file, you can use the MOVE command. The MOVE command allows you to move a file from one subdirectory to another and from one disk to another just like the COPY command, except that you move the original file and do not create a duplicate. See Figure 11.6.

```
C:\>MOVE CHAP3.TXT C:\WINDOWS
c:\chap3.txt => c:\windows\chap3.txt [ok]

C:\>
```

Figure 11.6
Moving a file using MOVE

For example, if you were to move the file LETTER1.DOC from the C:\WORD\LETTERS subdirectory to the C:\PERSONAL\LETTERS subdirectory, the command is as follows:

C:\>MOVE C:\WORD\LETTERS\LETTER1.DOC
    C:\PERSONAL\LETTERS\LETTERS1.DOC

If you are already inside the LETTERS subdirectory, you can omit the path of the source directory (C:\WORD\LETTERS\). The destination subdirectory must exist before using the MOVE command, because MOVE will not create a subdirectory.

In addition, the MOVE command allows you to rename subdirectories. To rename a subdirectory with the MOVE command, you need only specify the original subdirectory name and the new name for the subdirectory. For example, if you want to rename the subdirectory C:\PERSONAL\ LETTERS to C:\PERSONAL\MEMOS, the command is as follows:

```
C:\>MOVE PERSONAL\LETTERS C:\PERSONAL\MEMOS
```

> ### Note
>
> You can use the MOVE command to rename a file as you do when you copy a file. However, if you are moving multiple files at the same time, you cannot rename them.

Deleting and Renaming Files within Subdirectories

Files can be erased or renamed within subdirectories in the same way that they are erased and renamed in root directories. The important consideration is that you are in the correct subdirectory, because you can use the same filenames in various subdirectories.

Always make sure you have located the correct file before deleting it. The best way to make sure you are going to delete the correct file is to first move to the subdirectory, view the file, and then delete it. For example, if you wanted to delete the file C:\WP\LETTER.TXT, you should first move to the subdirectory C:\WP, make sure you have the correct file, and then delete the file using the following command:

```
C:\WP>DEL LETTER.TXT
```

Or, bypass two steps and delete the file with the command:

```
C:\DEL C:\WP\LETTER.TXT
```

However, you should make sure you are not going to delete the wrong file. (You might have a file of the same name in another subdirectory.)

Removing a Subdirectory

If you decide to delete all of the files within a certain subdirectory, you will probably want to delete the subdirectory itself as well. To remove a subdirectory, you first need to delete or move all the files contained within that subdirectory and any lower (child) subdirectories and their files. In essence, you must remove everything within a subdirectory before you can remove it.

After removing all files and lower directories, you may remove a subdirectory with the command **RMDIR** or **RD.** For example, to remove a first-level subdirectory, you need to do the following:

1. Delete all files within that subdirectory, including lower directories and their files.

2. Move to the parent directory and use the RD command.

To delete the subdirectory C:\WP, move to the subdirectory with:

`C:\>CD WP`

Delete all of the files contained in the subdirectory with:

`C:\WP>DEL *.*`

You can also delete all files in a subdirectory by typing ERASE SUBDIR and pressing Enter. DOS will tell you that you are about to erase all the files from the SUBDIR and ask you whether you want to continue (Y/N)? For example, if you wanted to erase all the files from the WP subdirectory, you could type

`C:\>ERASE WP`

move to the root directory

`C:\WP>CD \`

and then remove the directory with the command

`C:\>RD WP`

Deleting a Branch of a Tree Structure—DOS 6

You can delete a subdirectory or an entire branch of a subdirectory tree structure by using the **DELTREE** command. This command will delete the specified subdirectory along with any files or subdirectories it may contain.

In the previous section, you learned how to remove a directory by moving into each subdirectory, deleting its contents, and then deleting the subdirectory. Using the DELTREE command, you could complete the entire process with one command as follows:

`C:\>DELTREE WP`

When this command is executed, DOS asks you to confirm the request before proceeding. See Figure 11.7.

```
C:\>DELTREE WP
Delete directory "WP" and all its subdirectories? [yn]
```

Figure 11.7
Deleting a directory and all subdirectories using DELTREE

12 chaptertwelve

Command Line File Editor

When you have completed this chapter, you will be able to

Objectives

- Explain what an editor is.
- Describe the purpose of an editor.
- Describe how EDIT and COPY CON differ.
- Explain the purpose of each menu item in the editor.
- Explain two ways to start the editor.

What Is an Editor?

An editor is a program that allows you to create a file or alter an existing text file. Several types of editors are available:

1. Editors used by programmers who work with such languages as Turbo Pascal®, Turbo C®, or BASIC.

2. More sophisticated editors, known as word processors, such as WordStar®, WordPerfect®, and Microsoft Word®.

3. System software editors, such as the DOS EDIT program.

Some terms used with text editors and their functions are shown in Figure 12.1.

Most text editors and word processors have all of the capabilities listed in Figure 12.1 and more, but each program uses different commands to perform the actions. Some programs like EDIT use pulldown menus. Others require that you select commands by pressing function keys or another combination of keys.

Term	Function
Insert	Places text before or between text that already exists.
Typeover	Erases old text while typing over the top of it with new text (sometimes called overwrite).
Delete	Deletes text.
Block	Specifies a selection (block) of text to manipulate.
Cut	Removes a section of text from a document and places the text into a clipboard (buffer) in the computer's memory.
Paste	Places the text stored in the clipboard into the document where the cursor is located.
Copy	Makes a copy of the selected (blocked) text and places it into the clipboard.
Wordwrap	When you reach the right side of the screen, you can keep typing and the editor will move down to the next line and continue to input text. With wordwrap, you do not need to press Enter at the end of each line.

Figure 12.1
Terminology used with text editors

The DOS Editor: EDIT

The DOS editor (called **EDIT**) is a powerful, yet simple-to-use, text editor. Unlike word processing programs, EDIT does not allow you to use different type styles, different print enhancements (such as italic, bold, and underline), or different type sizes. EDIT cannot perform the complex text manipulations that a word processor does, because it was never intended for that purpose. Rather, EDIT is a program intended to allow all DOS users to create simple text files, such as the batch files you will create in chapter 8. It can also be used to create memos, notes, and other short text files.

Starting EDIT

You can start EDIT either by selecting Editor from the program list area in the DOS Shell or by typing EDIT at any command prompt. You can also type EDIT followed by the filespec of the file you want to create, view, or change.

After you have made your changes, save the file by selecting Save in the File menu, then exit the program using the Exit option in the File menu.

Entering Text with EDIT

When you start EDIT, you simply type to enter text. If you make a mistake you can backspace to erase the incorrect keystroke or position your cursor on a character and delete it using the Del key.

EDIT does not have the popular wordwrap feature that automatically moves you to the next line when you have reached the end of the current line. You need to press Enter at the end of each line as when using a typewriter.

Using EDIT's Menu Commands

EDIT is easy to use because it is menu-driven. Across the top of the screen, you can see a menu bar similar to the menu bar that appears at the top of the DOS Shell screen. The menu items are File, Edit, Search, and Options, as shown in Figure 12.2. When the menus are pulled down the commands shown in Figure 12.3 are revealed.

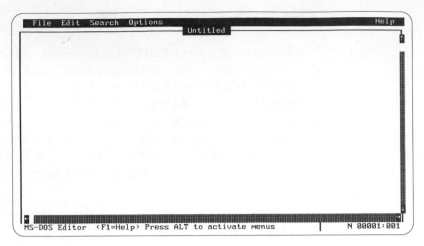

Figure 12.2
The DOS EDIT screen

File	**Edit**	**Search**	**Options**
New	Cut	Find	Display
Open	Copy	Repeat Last Find	Help Path
Save	Paste	Change	
Save As	Clear		
Print			
Exit			

Figure 12.3

To access a menu using a keyboard, you press the Alt key and then press the first letter of the menu item you want. For example, to access the File menu, you would press Alt and F. To access the Edit menu, you would press Alt and E.

To access the menu using a mouse, move the mouse pointer over the menu item you want and click the left button on the mouse to select the menu item.

File. The File menu options allow you to create a new file, open an existing file, save a file, save a file under a new name, print a file, and exit the program.

Edit. The Edit menu options allow you to cut, copy, paste, and clear text. Before you use the edit options, you need to select the text you are going to edit.

To select text with a keyboard, place the cursor at the beginning of the text you wish to select, hold down the Shift key, and use the arrow keys to highlight the text you want. You can then select the Cut or Copy options. This places the text in a special storage location called the clipboard. After you have cut or copied the text, place the cursor where you want the text to be moved or copied. Then use the Paste option in the Edit menu to place the text stored in the clipboard into the new location.

To edit text with a mouse, select the text by placing the mouse cursor at the beginning of the text you wish to select, click and drag the mouse across the desired text, and then release the mouse button. Then select the desired Edit options. The Clear option, in the Edit menu, deletes the highlighted text.

Search. The Search menu options allow you to find a section of text or replace the found text with new text.

Options. The Options menu allows you to change the colors on the screen and to list the location of the EDIT Help file if DOS cannot find it.

COPY CON

Another way to create text files is to use the COPY command followed by the word CON, which stands for console. CON is the device name for the keyboard. This combination tells DOS that you are going to create a file directly from the keyboard.

You can create a file with **COPY CON** at any DOS prompt. You cannot, however, edit a file with COPY CON. If you make a mistake creating a file or want to change a file at a later date using COPY CON, you must recreate the entire file again, thus replacing the old file with the new one. The command to create a file using COPY CON is

```
C:\>COPY CON filename.ext
```

After you press the Enter key to execute the command, you simply type what you want in the file. You should press the Enter key at the end of each line of text. Wordwrap is not available. After you are finished, press the F6 key and then the Enter key to save the file. The F6 key places the Z character (End of File marker) at the end of the file. If you have 8 lines of text and you place the Z marker in line 5, only lines 1–5 will be saved to the file.

twelve

Hands-On Activities
Performance Objectives

After you have completed these activities, you will be able to do the following:

1. Create a text file using EDIT.

2. Edit a text file using EDIT.

3. Create a text file using COPY CON.

How to Start EDIT and Create a Text File

The DOS editor can be started from the Shell by selecting the Edit option from the program list or by typing EDIT at any command prompt. In this exercise, you will start EDIT from the command prompt, view the Help menu, and then create a simple text file named MEMO1.TXT. Use the BACKUP disk in Drive A:, and perform the following steps:

What to Do	What Happens
1 Obtain an A:\> prompt.	Nothing.
2 Type EDIT and press Enter.	See Figure 12.4.

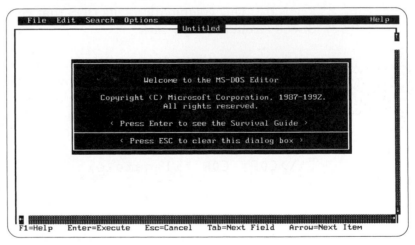

Figure 12.4
The EDIT opening screen

3 Press Enter to see the Survival Guide.	See Figure 12.5.
4 When you are done reading the Survival Guide, press the Esc key to return to the main Edit screen.	The main Edit screen appears.

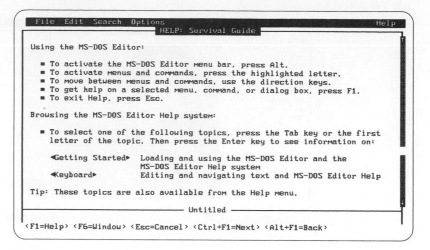

```
 File  Edit  Search  Options                                    Help
                        HELP: Survival Guide
 Using the MS-DOS Editor:

   ▪ To activate the MS-DOS Editor menu bar, press Alt.
   ▪ To activate menus and commands, press the highlighted letter.
   ▪ To move between menus and commands, use the direction keys.
   ▪ To get help on a selected menu, command, or dialog box, press F1.
   ▪ To exit Help, press Esc.

 Browsing the MS-DOS Editor Help system:

   ▪ To select one of the following topics, press the Tab key or the first
     letter of the topic. Then press the Enter key to see information on:

     ◄Getting Started►  Loading and using the MS-DOS Editor and the
                        MS-DOS Editor Help system
     ◄Keyboard►         Editing and navigating text and MS-DOS Editor Help

 Tip: These topics are also available from the Help menu.
                              ─ Untitled ─
 <F1=Help> <F6=Window> <Esc=Cancel> <Ctrl+F1=Next> <Alt+F1=Back>
```

Figure 12.5
The Help screen for Edit

5 Type the text that appears in Figure 12.6. Press the Enter key to end each line of text and to advance to the next line.

The text appears on the screen.

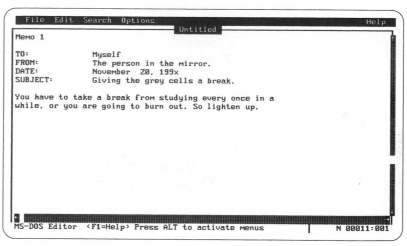

```
 File  Edit  Search  Options                                    Help
                              ─ Untitled ─
 Memo 1

 TO:            Myself
 FROM:          The person in the mirror.
 DATE:          November  20, 199x
 SUBJECT:       Giving the grey cells a break.

 You have to take a break from studying every once in a
 while, or you are going to burn out. So lighten up.




 MS-DOS Editor  <F1=Help> Press ALT to activate menus          N 00011:001
```

Figure 12.6
Creating a memo using EDIT

6 Select the File menu option by either clicking on File with the mouse or by pressing Alt-F.

The File menu appears.

7 Select Save As from the menu list by clicking on it or pressing A.

The Save As dialog box appears. See Figure 12.7.

8 Type MEMO1.TXT in the Filename text box and press Enter.

The file is saved to Drive A: and the Save As dialog box disappears.

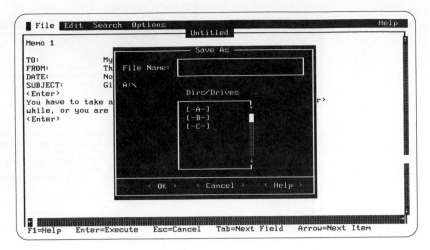

Figure 12.7
The Save As dialog box

---

9 Select Exit from the File menu to exit the EDIT program.

The A:\> prompt returns.

How to Load and Edit an Existing File

Any time you want to edit a file you can select Open from the File menu or type the filespec of the file you want to edit following the EDIT command. In the following exercise, you will load the file you just created (MEMO1.TXT), select a section of text to move, cut it from the document, move the cursor to a new location, and paste the text in its new location. Use the BACKUP disk in Drive A:, and perform the following steps:

What to Do

What Happens

1 At the A:\> prompt, type EDIT MEMO1.TXT and press Enter.

The editor and the file MEMO1.TXT are loaded. You are ready to edit. See Figure 12.8.

2 Use the arrow keys or the mouse to move to the S at the beginning of the sentence "So lighten up."

The cursor is placed at the beginning of the sentence.

3 Press and hold down the Shift key while you use the right arrow key to highlight the sentence, or drag the mouse across the sentence.

The sentence is highlighted. See Figure 12.9.

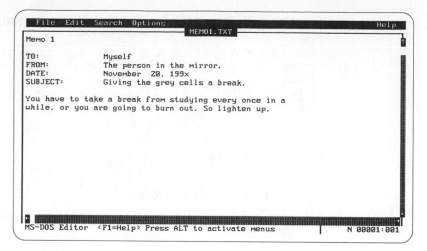

Figure 12.8

Retrieving a file to make changes

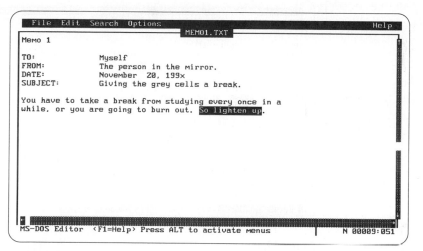

Figure 12.9

Selecting text in Edit

4 Select Cut from the Edit menu.	The text is removed from the document and stored in the program's clipboard. See Figure 12.10.
5 Use the arrow keys or the mouse to move the cursor to the space between the words "while" and "or."	The cursor is on the space between the comma and the o in or.
6 Select Paste from the Edit menu to place the text in the new location.	The text is pasted into the new location. See Figure 12.11.

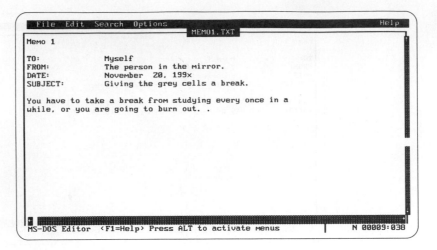

Figure 12.10
Cutting text in Edit

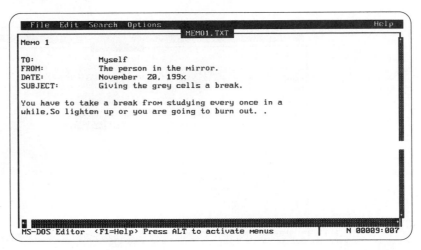

Figure 12.11
Pasting text in Edit

7 Press the Backspace key once and type a period. Then press the Spacebar two times.   See Figure 12.12.

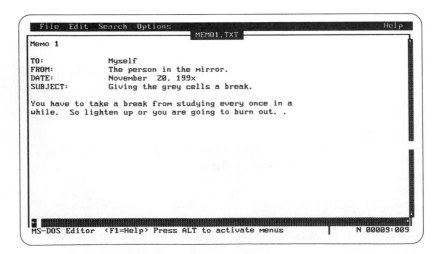

Figure 12.12
Correcting text in Edit

8 Press the End key to move the cursor to the end of the line and press Backspace to remove the extra period.

The period disappears.

9 Select Save from the File menu to save the file.

The file is saved.

10 Select Exit from the File menu to exit EDIT.

The A:\> prompt appears.

Review Exercises

1. Using EDIT, create the file TRIPS.DOC on the BACKUP disk that contains the locations of five places where you would like to vacation.

2. Edit the file so that the places are in alphabetical order.

3. Using EDIT, create the file TODO.DOC on the BACKUP disk that contains a list of chores that you need to do around your house.

How to Create a File with COPY CON

In this exercise, you will create the file MEMO3.TXT using COPY CON. Use the BACKUP disk in Drive A:, and perform the following steps:

What to Do

What Happens

1 At the A:\> prompt, type COPY CON MEMO3.TXT and press Enter.

The cursor moves down one line below the command.

2 Type Personal computers have come a long way since 1981. and press Enter.

The text is displayed to the screen.

3 Type It is hard to imagine that computers less powerful than <Enter> this computer in front of me used to be as large as this whole room. and press Enter.

The text is displayed to the screen.

4 Press the F6 key and then Enter to save the file.

The DOS command Z is placed at the end of the file, the file is saved, and you are returned to the command prompt. See Figure 12.13.

```
A:\>COPY CON MEMO3.TXT
Personal computers have come a long way since 1981.
It is hard to imagine that computers less powerful than
this computer in front of me used to be as large as this whole room.
^Z
        1 file(s) copied

A:\>
```

Figure 12.13
Using COPY CON to create a file

5 Type `TYPE MEMO3.TXT` and press Enter to view the file.

The file is displayed to the screen. See Figure 12.14.

```
A:\>TYPE MEMO3.TXT
Personal computers have come a long way since 1981.
It is hard to imagine that computers less powerful than
this computer in front of me used to be as large as this whole room.

A:\>
```

Figure 12.14
Listing the contents of a file

Review Exercises

1. Create a file using COPY CON called LIST.DOC that contains a list of five items you need to purchase at the grocery store on the way home.

2. Create a file using COPY CON called LIST2.DOC that contains a list of three clothing stores that you frequent.

Summary Points

1. DOS contains its own editor called EDIT.

2. An editor is a program that allows you to create a file or alter an existing file.

3. Three types of editors are (1) editors used by programmers who use programming language software, such as Turbo Pascal® or Turbo C®, (2) more sophisticated editors known as word processors, such as WordStar®, WordPerfect®, and Microsoft Works®, and (3) system software editors, such as the DOS editor, EDIT.

4. EDIT, the menu-driven editor for DOS, is a basic editing program that allows you to perform limited text manipulation.

5. Another way to create text files is to use the COPY command followed by the word CON (console).

6. CON is the device name for the keyboard.

7. You can create a file with COPY CON at any command prompt, but you cannot edit a file with COPY CON. If you wish to change anything in a file using COPY CON, you must start over and recreate the file from scratch.

Application Exercises

1. Using EDIT, create a file on your BACKUP disk called MOVIES.DOC that lists your twelve (12) favorite movies.

2. Using EDIT, move the first five movies in MOVIES.DOC on the BACKUP disk from the top of the list to the bottom.

3. Using EDIT, alphabetize the contents of the file MOVIES.DOC on the BACKUP disk.

4. Using COPY CON, create a file called DOS.TXT that contains a list of five DOS commands that you have learned.

5. Using EDIT, alphabetize the file DOS.TXT.

Comprehension Exercises Answer the following questions.

1. Describe three ways that DOS allows you to create files.

2. How do you move a section of text from one place to another using EDIT?

3. Describe the benefits of using EDIT versus COPY CON.

4. Explain two ways to start EDIT.

5. Can you edit a file using COPY CON? Explain.

Completion Exercises

1. Cut, Copy, Paste, and Clear are options on the _____ menu in Edit.

2. The Help Path is an option on the _____ menu in Edit.

3. Find, Repeat Last Find, and Change are options on the _____ menu in Edit.

4. CON is a device name for _____.

5. COPY CON allows you to _____ a file.

Matching Exercises Choose the correct letter from the righthand column.

___F___ **1.** COPY CON

___A___ **2.** Insert

___C___ **3.** Delete

___E___ **4.** Wordwrap

___D___ **5.** Paste

___B___ **6.** F6

a. Typing mode in which new characters move the old ones to the right.

b. Saves a file when using COPY CON.

c. Deletes text using EDIT.

d. Places text that has been cut from a file using EDIT.

e. Causes text to continue from one line to another.

f. Allows you to create a file directly from the keyboard.

chapter thirteen

Command Line Batch Files

When you have completed this chapter, you will be able to

Objectives

- Explain what a batch file is.
- Explain why batch files are used.
- Explain what batch files contain.
- Describe a number of batch file commands.
- Execute a batch file.
- Explain the purpose of the PATH command.
- Explain the purpose of using a batch file with replaceable parameters.
- Execute a batch file that contains replaceable parameters.

What Is A Batch File?

A batch file is a file containing a series of DOS commands that you use frequently. A batch file is handy and efficient because, once written, it can be started with one command.

For example, if you have a word processing program in the C:\WP subdirectory that you use frequently, you could create a batch file named WP.BAT that contains the following commands:

1. C: makes sure you are using Drive C:.

2. CD\ makes sure that you start from the root directory.

3. CD WP changes to the WP subdirectory.

4. WP starts the word processor.

5. CD \ returns you to the root directory after the word processor is finished.

Once you create a batch file containing these commands, you could type WP and press Enter to perform all of the commands in the file. The purpose of creating batch files is to reduce repetitive typing.

Creating Batch Files

The DOS editor EDIT can be used to create batch files. In this chapter, you will create batch files using EDIT. To create a batch file using EDIT:

1. Type EDIT followed by any filename and the extension .BAT, and then press Enter.

2. List each DOS command on a separate line.

3. Save the file.

Special Commands for Batch Files

Any command that can be given to DOS at a command prompt can be stored in a batch file. These commands include all the usual DOS commands, the filename of any application program, and a number of special commands used for batch files.

A sample of the special DOS batch processing commands, and what each does, is shown in Figure 13.1.

The PATH Command

Batch files can be executed at a DOS prompt by typing the batch filename and pressing Enter. However, because batch files are usually located in the root directory of a disk or within a subdirectory that you create especially for batch files, you should use a command that tells DOS where to look for these files. This command is called the PATH command.

Command	What It Does
ECHO ON	Displays to the screen the commands being executed within the batch file.
ECHO OFF	Prevents the commands that are executed within the batch file from being displayed to the screen.
@ECHO OFF	Prevents the ECHO OFF command from being displayed to the screen, in addition to all subsequent commands.
ECHO (Message)	Displays the message following the ECHO command, regardless of whether the ECHO OFF command has been used before this command.
FOR IN DO	Allows you to carry out a command in a batch file more than once.
GOTO (Label)	Allows you to redirect the batch file to execute commands out of sequence.
IF (Condition)	Allows you to specify a command if a condition is met.
IF NOT (Condition)	Allows you to specify a command if a condition is not met.
SHIFT	Moves the list of parameters you type with a batch command one position to the left. For example, suppose you type three parameters: %1, %2, %3. After a SHIFT command is used, %1 is dropped off, %2 moves into the position of %1, and %3 moves into the position of %2. Parameters are discussed later in this chapter.
PAUSE	Pauses the execution of the batch file until a key is pressed on the keyboard. When PAUSE is used in a batch file, it causes the message "Strike a key when ready" to appear.
REM	Allows you to document your batch files with remarks about their operations. These remarks do not display to the screen if the ECHO is turned off.

Figure 13.1
DOS batch processing commands

A PATH command is included in the AUTOEXEC.BAT file of almost every computer with a hard disk to tell DOS where to find the DOS external files and batch files (For a list of internal and external files, see Appendix C. The AUTOEXEC.BAT file is discussed in the next chapter). For example, the DOS editor EDIT is a program file that is normally kept in the DOS subdirectory with all of the other DOS program files. In order for DOS to be able to find its own program files, you must list the DOS subdirectory in the PATH command. Otherwise, you will be unable to use EDIT, unless you are in the DOS subdirectory or you specify `C:\DOS\EDIT` when you need the program. On the other hand, if the DOS subdirectory is listed in the PATH command, you can use EDIT from any DOS prompt. Listing the DOS subdirectory in your PATH command allows you to access all of the DOS program files without specifically telling DOS where they are. An example of a PATH command is

`C:\>PATH C:\;C:\BATFILES;C:\DOS`

If DOS cannot find a program file or a batch file within the current directory, this PATH command tells DOS to search the root directory, then the subdirectories BATFILES and DOS, as follows:

`C:\`	Tells DOS to search the root directory.
`C:\BATFILES`	Tells DOS to search the subdirectory that was created to contain batch files.
`C:\DOS`	Tells DOS to search the subdirectory that was created to contain the DOS external commands. This subdirectory is listed within the PATH command to enable you to use any external DOS commands from any command prompt.

Note that each directory is separated from the next by a semicolon (;).

Another item to be aware of is the order in which DOS looks for files. If a .COM or .EXE file exists with the same filename as a .BAT file and you only use the filename to execute the program, the .COM or .EXE file will be called up before the batch (.BAT) file. DOS looks for files in the following order: .COM, .EXE, and then .BAT files unless you use filename.ext at the command prompt.

Replaceable Parameters

Replaceable parameters allow you to create generic batch files whose information can be changed when executed. When the file is executed, the information, such as a location or filename, can be indicated with the batch command to execute the batch file. For example, you can create a generic batch file that deletes multiple files when executed. When you execute the file, you type the name of the batch file followed by the parameters that indicate what files are to be deleted and where those files are. This batch file, which we will call DELFILES.BAT, could consist of the following commands:

```
ECHO This batch file is about to erase all of

ECHO the %1 files from the %2 Subdirectory.

.ECHO Press CTRL-C to stop or

PAUSE

CD \

CD %2

DEL %1

CD \
```

When the batch file executes, the "ECHO Press CTRL-C to stop or" will be followed by the PAUSE command that will prompt, "Press any key to continue."

Because it includes the parameters %1 and %2, which you specify each time you use the file, DELFILES is generic and can be tailored to your specific needs. For example, say you want to delete all the .TXT files located in the WP subdirectory. You would execute the batch file using the following command:

```
C:\>DELFILES *.TXT \WP
```

When this command is executed, DOS will *replace* all of the %1s in the batch file with *.TXT and all of the %2s with \WP.DOS will then interpret the batch file as follows:

```
ECHO This batch file is about to erase all of

ECHO the *.TXT files from the \WP Subdirectory.

ECHO Press CTRL-C to stop or

PAUSE

CD \

CD WP

DEL *.TXT

CD \
```

DOS first looks at the batch filename. Then it starts to execute the commands. If DOS finds a % in the file, it looks back to the execution line you typed in and looks for more information. The first extra piece of information after the batch filename is called the %1 parameter. The second is the %2 parameter, and so on. The batch filename and all parameters must be separated by blank spaces.

Hands-On Activities
Performance Objectives

After completing these activities, you will be able to do the following:

1. Create and execute a simple batch file that displays the current directory.

2. Create and execute a batch file that loads an application program.

3. Create a menu system using batch files.

4. Create and execute a batch file with replaceable parameters.

Note

Be sure you have the structure shown in Figure 13.2 completed on the PRACTICE disk before performing the following exercises.

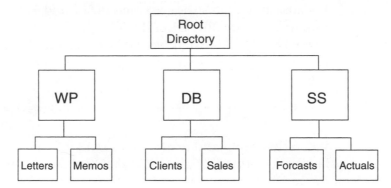

Figure 13.2

How to Create a Simple Batch File

Using EDIT, you will create a simple batch file, named FIRST.BAT, that includes the following commands:

Command	Result
ECHO ON	Displays the commands as FIRST.BAT executes.
CLS	Clears the screen.
PAUSE	Pauses and displays a message.
DIR	Displays the current directory.

In this exercise, the ECHO will remain on. This means that all of the commands will be displayed on the screen, followed by the results. Use the PRACTICE disk in Drive A:, and perform the following steps:

What to Do	What Happens
1 Obtain a A:\> prompt.	Nothing.
2 Type EDIT FIRST.BAT and press Enter.	The EDIT screen appears.
3 At the EDIT screen, type ECHO ON and press Enter.	The text is listed to the screen.
4 At the EDIT screen, type CLS and press Enter.	The text is listed to the screen.
5 Type PAUSE and press Enter.	The text is listed to the screen.
6 Type DIR and press Enter.	Your screen should like Figure 13.3.

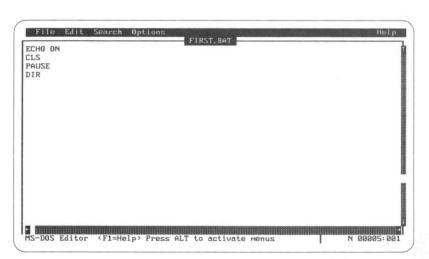

Figure 13.3
Creating a Batch file

7 Select Save from the File menu to save the file.	Your file is saved as FIRST.BAT in the root directory of your PRACTICE disk.
8 Select Exit from the File menu to exit the editor.	The A:\> prompt returns.

How to Execute a Batch File

To execute a batch file, you need type in only the filename for the batch file. However, if you are in a subdirectory other than the one that contains the batch file and the last path command used did not include the subdirectory containing the batch file, you must also list the drive and subdirectory before the batch filename to execute the batch file.

In this exercise, you will execute the batch file FIRST.BAT that you just created. Use the PRACTICE disk in Drive A: and perform the following steps:

What to Do	What Happens
1 At the A:\> prompt, type FIRST and press Enter.	The batch file executes up to the PAUSE command. See Figure 13.4.

```
A:\>PAUSE
Press any key to continue . . .
```

Figure 13.4
Executing FIRST.BAT

2 Press any key to let the batch file continue.	The rest of the batch file executes, and you are returned to the command prompt. See Figure 13.5.

```
A:\>PAUSE
Press any key to continue . . .

A:\>DIR

 Volume in drive A is PRACTICE
 Volume Serial Number is 1C40-1DEZ
 Directory of A:\

WP           <DIR>      11-18-93   10:28p
DB           <DIR>      11-18-93   10:28p
SS           <DIR>      11-18-93   10:39p
FIRST    BAT         28 11-22-93    9:06p
        6 file(s)          1257 bytes
                         891392 bytes free

A:\>
A:\>
```

Figure 13.5
Executing FIRST.BAT (cont'd)

Although this batch file does not do very much, it should give you the feeling for how to create and execute batch files. In the next few examples, you will put the true power of batch files to work for you.

Review Exercises

1. Create a batch file called ALPHA.BAT that uses the DIR command with the Sort option to obtain a sorted directory by filename.

2. Create a batch file called FMTA 144.M byte that performs an unconditional format of a 720K disk located in Drive A:.

How to Use Replaceable Parameters in Batch Files

If you were planning to delete multiple files within a subdirectory, you could create a batch file to perform this activity. In this exercise, you will delete all the .TXT files within the subdirectory WP, using a generic file deletion batch file. Use the PRACTICE disk in Drive A:, and perform the following steps:

What to Do	**What Happens**
1 Obtain a A:\> prompt.	Nothing.
2 Copy all the .TXT files from the root directory of the EXERCISES Subdirectory to the WP directory of the PRACTICE disk.	The files are copied.
3 Use EDIT to create a batch file called DELFILES.BAT with the following commands shown in Figure 13.13:	The EDIT screen appears and the text is displayed as you type it in. See Figure 13.6.

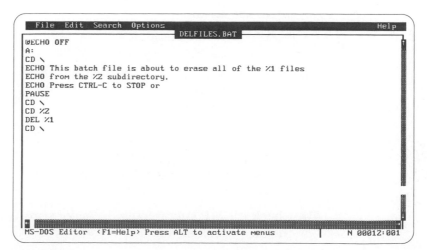

Figure 13.6
Creating DELFILES.BAT

4 Save the file and exit the editor.	The file is saved and you are returned to the A:\> prompt.

5 Type `DIR A:\WP` to make sure the .TXT files are there and then return to the root directory.

The directory is displayed to the screen. See Figure 13.7.

6 Type `DELFILES *.TXT \WP` and press Enter.

See Figure 13.8.

```
A:\>DIR A:\WP

 Volume in drive A is PRACTICE
 Volume Serial Number is 1C40-1DE2
 Directory of A:\WP

.                <DIR>       11-18-93   10:28p
..               <DIR>       11-18-93   10:28p
WP       EXE       68656 03-27-92    4:13p
EDITOR   HLP        3048 07-30-90    8:55p
LETTERS          <DIR>       11-18-93   10:39p
MEMOS            <DIR>       11-18-93   10:39p
LETTER   TXT         978 05-18-92    8:38p
CARTER1  TXT          95 05-30-92    2:12p
CARTER2  TXT          91 05-30-92    2:13p
CARTER3  TXT          90 05-30-92    2:13p
        10 file(s)        72958 bytes
                         884736 bytes free

A:\>
```

Figure 13.7
Displaying a directory listing for A:\WP

```
A:\>DELFILES *.TXT \WP
This batch file is about to erase all of the *.TXT files
from the \WP subdirectory.
Press CTRL-C to STOP or
Press any key to continue . . .
```

Figure 13.8
Executing DELFILES.BAT

7 Look at what the batch file is about to do. Then press any key to delete the files. If you want to stop the batch file, however, press the Ctrl-C key combination.

All the .TXT files in the WP subdirectory are deleted, unless you pressed Ctrl-C.

8 Check the WP subdirectory to make sure the files were deleted.

The directory does not contain any .TXT files. See Figure 13.9.

```
A:\>DELFILES *.TXT \WP
This batch file is about to erase all of the *.TXT files
from the \WP subdirectory.
Press CTRL-C to STOP or
Press any key to continue . . .

A:\>DIR A:\WP

 Volume in drive A is PRACTICE
 Volume Serial Number is 1C40-1DE2
 Directory of A:\WP

.               <DIR>       11-18-93  10:28p
..              <DIR>       11-18-93  10:28p
WP       EXE    68656 03-27-92   4:13p
EDITOR   HLP     3048 07-30-90   8:55p
LETTERS         <DIR>       11-18-93  10:39p
MEMOS           <DIR>       11-18-93  10:39p
        6 file(s)       71704 bytes
                       887296 bytes free

A:\>
```

Figure 13.9
Verifying files were deleted from A:\WP

Review Exercises

1. On the PRACTICE disk, create a batch file called BAKBAT.BAT that copies all the .BAK files from a subdirectory (%1) in Drive C: to the root directory of Drive A:.

2. On the PRACTICE disk, create a batch file called COPYFILE.BAT that copies %1 files from the %2 subdirectory to the root directory of Drive A:.

Summary Points

1. A batch file is a file containing a series of commands that you use frequently.

2. A batch file is handy because, once written, it can be executed using one command.

3. Batch files can be created using the DOS editor EDIT.

4. Any DOS command that can be given to DOS at a command prompt can be used in a batch file.

5. Batch files can be executed at a DOS prompt by typing the batch file-name and pressing Enter.

6. Because batch files are usually located in the root directory of a disk or within a subdirectory that you create especially for batch files, you should use a command that tells DOS where to look for these files. This command is called the PATH command.

7. Each subdirectory within the PATH command is separated from the next by a semicolon.

8. If a .COM or .EXE file exists with the same filename and in the same directory as a .BAT file and you only use the filename to execute the program, DOS will call up the .COM or .EXE file before it calls the batch (.BAT) file. DOS looks for files in the following order: .COM, .EXE, .BAT, then data files.

9. Batch files can be used with replaceable parameters, meaning that when you execute a batch file, you can determine the location and the files to be used when the command is executed.

Application Exercises

1. Using the PRACTICE disk, create a batch file called RSORT.BAT that produces filenames in the root directory of Drive A: sorted in reverse alphabetical order.

2. Using the PRACTICE disk, create a batch file called SIZEDIR.BAT that produces a sorted directory of Drive A: by file size.

3. Using the PRACTICE disk, create a batch file named COPYBAK.BAT that copies all the .BAK files from the root directory of Drive C: to the root directory of Drive A:.

4. Execute the RSORT.BAT file with the EXERCISES disk in Drive A:. How many files were listed?

5. Create the batch file COPYREN.BAT that copies and renames all .TXT files to all .BAK files and that allows you to specify the subdirectory when you execute the file.

✓ Comprehension Exercises

1. Explain the meaning of the command PATH C:\;C:\DOS;C:\UTIL.

2. Explain the purpose of a batch file.

3. Explain what the @ ECHO OFF command in a batch file does.

4. Explain what the PATH command does.

5. Explain what a replaceable parameter is.

6. Explain how to execute a batch file.

7. Describe what can be placed inside a batch file.

8. Explain why you would want to use a PAUSE command in a batch file.

9. Explain why you would want to use a TYPE command in a batch file.

10. Explain where batch files should be stored.

Completion Exercises

Complete the following sentences.

1. A _____ file is a file that contains a series of DOS commands.

2. To execute a batch file, you need to use a filename with the extension _____.

3. %1 and %2 are called _____.

4. The special batch command _____ allows you to carry out a command more than once in a batch file.

5. The command to pause the execution of a batch file is _____.

6. Any command that can be given at _____ can be used in batch files.

Matching Exercises

Choose the correct letter from the right-hand column.

_D_ **1.** PAUSE

_C_ **2.** TYPE

_A_ **3.** PATH C:\;C:\DOS

_B_ **4.** ECHO OFF

_F_ **5.** WP.BAT

_E_ **6.** PATH

a. Tells DOS that if it does not find a file within the current subdirectory, look in the root directory and the subdirectory named DOS.

b. Keeps the DOS commands within a batch file from being displayed onto a monitor as they are being called up.

c. Displays the contents of a file.

d. Prompts the user to press a key when ready.

e. Tells DOS where to look for files.

f. The name of a batch file.